D1601439

Urban Peace-Building
in Divided Societies

Urban Peace-Building in Divided Societies

Belfast and Johannesburg

Scott A. Bollens

Westview Press
A Member of the Perseus Books Group

Copyright © 1999 by Westview Press, A Member of the Perseus Books Group

Published in 1999 in the United States of America by Westview Press, 5500 Central Avenue, Boulder, Colorado 80301-2877, and in the United Kingdom by Westview Press, 12 Hid's Copse Road, Cumnor Hill, Oxford OX2 9JJ

Library of Congress Cataloging-in-Publication Data
Bollens, Scott A.
  Urban peace-building in divided societies : Belfast and
Johannesburg / Scott A. Bollens
    p.   cm.
  Includes bibliographical references and index.
  ISBN 0-8133-3541-8 (hardcover)
  1. Urban policy—Northern Ireland—Belfast.   2. Urban policy—
South Africa—Johannesburg.   3. Conflict management—Northern
Ireland—Belfast.   4. Conflict management—South Africa—
Johannesburg.   I. Title.
HT169.G72B4937   1999
307.76'09416'7—dc21
                                                                            98-29197
                                                                               CIP

The paper used in this publication meets the requirements of the American National Standard for Permanence of Paper for Printed Library Materials Z39.48-1984.

10   9   8   7   6   5   4   3   2   1

To Billy Hutchinson, Joe Austin,
Paul Waanders, and Tshipso Mashinini
Peace, Siochain, Vrede, Uxola

To Claudia
for her enduring love and support

Contents

List of Illustrations   ix
Preface   xi
Acknowledgments   xv

Part 1
Urban Arenas of Nationalistic Conflict

1 Contested Cities   3

  Cities and Intrastate Conflict, 7
  Managing City Conflict, 9
  Notes, 17

2 Prospects and Limits of Urban Peace-Building   19

  Operationalizing Peace, 21
  Building or Impeding Urban Peace, 31
  Notes, 38

3 Belfast and Johannesburg   39

  Research Methods, 41
  Notes, 50

Part 2
Belfast: At the Sharp Edge

4 The Sectarian City   55

  Shifting Demographics, 57
  Political "Direct Rule," 61
  Urban Policymakers, 65
  Territoriality and Community, 69
  Notes, 87

5 British Urban Policy Since 1972   91

  Pursuing Stability Through Neutrality, 91

Neutral Means, Unequal Outcomes, 109
Notes, 119

6 Belfast and Peace   122
Seeking Peace in Belfast, 123
Belfast: Contributor or Burden to Peace? 144
Notes, 149

Part 3
Johannesburg: A Delicate Balancing of Time

7 Urban Policy in Transition   155
Planned Geographies, 156
Political Control, 168
Transformative Urban Policy, 172
Temporality and Urban Policy Choices, 185
Notes, 202

8 Rebuilding Government Legitimacy   207
The Dual Faces of Post-Apartheid Planning, 207
Organizing for Peace-Building, 221
Notes, 237

9 Johannesburg and Peace   240
Key Interventions in Peace-Building, 240
Race, Class, and Sustainability, 254
Notes, 262

Part 4
Conclusions

10 Urban Peace-Building   267
Policy, Polarization, and Peace, 268
Stabilizing and Reconstructing Contested Cities, 281
The Challenge of Urban Peace, 291
Notes, 298

Appendix 1: Research Issues   299
Appendix 2: Interviews Conducted   303
References   309
Index   331

Illustrations

Tables

2.1   Urban policy and governance strategies   24

3.1   Guiding research issues   44
3.2   Classification of interviewees by pertinent characteristics   49

4.1   Percent of 1993 local council seats won   62
4.2   Percent of 1997 local council seats won   63
4.3   Percent of 1998 Northern Ireland Assembly seats won   64
4.4   Belfast peacelines and adjacent neighborhoods   72
4.5   The ten most deprived wards in Belfast   80

5.1   Percentage of Belfast residents benefiting from
       city center employment   118

10.1   Contexts of conflict   271
10.2   Urban peace-building goals, strategies, and techniques   274
10.3   Participants and relationships   279

Figures

2.1   Urban policy and peace-building   22
2.2   Urban ethnic conditions and peace-building   32

4.1   Northern Ireland and Belfast   56
4.2   Religious composition of Belfast city population, 1757–1991   58
4.3   Age distribution of Catholic and Protestant populations
       in Belfast city, 1991   59
4.4   Distribution of Roman Catholics in Belfast urban area   60
4.5   Location of "peacelines" in Belfast, 1994   71

7.1   Johannesburg metropolitan area   156
7.2   Regional context   158
7.3   South Africa and Johannesburg   159
7.4   Group areas in Johannesburg   160
7.5   Grey (mixed) areas in Johannesburg, 1988   161

8.1   Redrawing political boundaries in metropolitan Johannesburg   228

9.1   Decentralization of office employment   256

Photos

4.1   Republican mural in Falls/Clonard neighborhood of west Belfast   54
4.2   Cupar Way peaceline   73
4.3   Sectarian territoriality in north Belfast   75

7.1   Louis Botha Avenue, Johannesburg   154
7.2   Squatter shacks in Alexandra township   164
7.3   Mandelaville squatter camp, Soweto   164

Preface

In this book I explore the role that urban management of ethnic conflict plays in stabilization and reconciliation processes in which strife-torn societies are engaged. The book focuses on the role of policy and planning in contested urban environments and the effects these urban strategies have on moving a society forward from disruptive intergroup instability and hostility toward ethnic accommodation and peace. I explore whether there are lessons for regional and national political negotiations that come from deeply divided cities regarding how to produce more mutually tolerable multiethnic living environments. I examine the hypothesis that urban peace-building, rather than being necessarily derivative of larger political agreements, can be formative of such national settlements.

The research is based primarily on interviews, conducted between January and September of 1995, with seventy-one current and former policymakers, non-governmental organization officials, and academics in the polarized cities of Belfast (Northern Ireland) and Johannesburg (South Africa). By examining two cities embedded within larger peacemaking processes, I seek to identify the lessons—both positive and negative—that city management of ethnic conflict provides for intergroup stability and reconstruction at national and cross-national scales. In beginning a profound redefinition of the parameters of interethnic relationships, Johannesburg and South Africa appear further along the continuum toward genuine peace than do Belfast and Northern Ireland. Whereas Johannesburg policymakers are engaged in urban reconstruction tasks, Belfast officials remain necessarily focused on stabilizing, not transcending, intergroup-group relations. Although both cities have been shaped by deep cultural cleavages, their differing political contexts—Belfast embedded within an uncertain shift from civil war to peace, and Johannesburg engaged in postresolution reconciliation—provide the ability to study the opportunities (and impediments) that urban policymaking contributes to urban and regional peacemaking and peace-building.

An integrative analytic approach combining the perspectives of four disciplines—political science, urban planning, geography, and social psychology—is utilized to study the complex social and ecological aspects of urban ethnic conflict. This study of urban policy connects broader political and ethnic ideologies to urban strategies and their specific territorial outcomes. These urban outcomes, in turn, have significant effects on group identity and well-being and thus ultimately on the extent and manifestations of urban stability and ethnic accommodation. Cities that have been theaters of war and whose physical structure has been created in response to such conflict must shift guiding ideologies from those that are partisan and ethnonationalist in nature to ones that stress civic inclusion and accommodation. Yet, cities are "sticky" and bear spatial, socioeconomic, and bureaucratic legacies that may be major impediments to urban peace-building. The *city* introduces a set of characteristics—proximate ethnic neighborhoods, territoriality, economic interdependency, symbolism, and centrality—that can interfere with the implementation of urban peace-building strategies. Well-intentioned urban policy decisions aimed at conflict amelioration that affect urban land use, housing, economic development, services, and citizen involvement face territorial and psychological hurdles that can obstruct their effectiveness.

Three roles of urban policymaking are evident in efforts to reconstruct or stabilize the two strife-torn cities studied—neutral, equity, and resolver. *Neutral* policymaking by the Northern Ireland government in Belfast seeks abstinence from violence but is insufficient in a city of dysfunctional sectarian territoriality, shifting demographics, and differential needs across Protestant and Catholic communities. In apartheid Johannesburg, the exercise of partisan urban policy highlighted the inherent tensions and difficulties resulting from efforts to compartmentalize the functionally complex and interdependent urban system. In transition and post-apartheid Johannesburg, policymakers have been both *resolvers*, linking city problems to root political empowerment issues, and *equity* planners, seeking to address levels of unmet human need that are distressing. In seeking Johannesburg's reconstruction, however, nonracial processes of market-based "normalization" threaten to reinforce, not transcend, the racial geography of urban regions.

Belfast interviews were conducted between January and March 1995, about five months after the ceasefires announced first by the Provisional Irish Republican Army (IRA) then subsequently by the loyalist paramilitaries. Within the month of my arrival, British Army troops were pulled from the streets of Belfast, no longer backing up Royal Ulster Constabulary police. During my research stay, the British and Irish governments released their Joint Framework Documents, intended to move political discussions toward some mutually agreeable solution. About ten months after my visit, after multiparty negotiations had been consistently delayed over the issue of the decommissioning of Irish Republican Army weapons, the IRA declared the end of their ceasefire with the bombing of a Docklands office building in London.

In May 1998, 70 percent of Northern Ireland voters approved the creation of a new democratic Northern Ireland Assembly with executive and legislative powers and a new ministerial council to encourage Island-side cooperation. In addition, the Republic of Ireland to its south now agrees that Northern Ireland will remain part of the United Kingdom as long as a majority of Northern Ireland voters are in support. Although this historic vote promises to significantly alter those North ern Ireland political arrangements described in this book, the fundamental chal- lenge of how to govern a splintered city remains as problematic today as when my field research was undertaken.

The Johannesburg interviews took place between July and September 1995, approximately fifteen months after the first democratic national and provincial elections in South Africa's history. Nelson Mandela's African National Congress had assumed political control of the country's legislature and a lion's share of provincial legislatures. During my field research, the country was being governed by a power-sharing national government. One month after my interviews, democracy penetrated its last level—that of metropolitan and local govern- ments—when local elections were held in most parts of South Africa, Johannes- burg included.

Despite obstacles faced by urban policy approaches in advancing peace in the two cities, I assert that a reconceptualized urban policymaking can make a con- structive difference not only in improving on-the-ground ethnic relations but also in contributing to the resolution of root political issues in overarching political negotiations at national and international levels. Tangible urban-level efforts and diplomatic national-level negotiations must constitute an inseparable peacemak- ing amalgamation. Urban accommodation without a national peace would leave the city vulnerable and unstable, but a national peace without urban accommoda- tion would be one unrooted in the practical and explosive issues of intergroup and territorial relations. Progressive and ethnically sensitive urban strategies can both contribute to, and operationalize, formal national and local agreements over power, fostering urban ethnic interaction and political compromise.

Scott A. Bollens

Acknowledgments

I extend my gratitude to all the interviewees who graciously provided me access into the sophisticated mind and tortured soul of the polarized city. Reflecting back on these individuals makes me want to both cry over our ability to hurt one another and to celebrate the human soul and its ability to persevere amid the trials of hatred. I now have greater faith in the human spirit and less confidence in elected political leaders. Specific appreciation is extended in Belfast to Brendan Murtagh, Michael Graham, Bill Morrison, Colm Bradley, and Billy Hutchinson; in Johannesburg to Paul Waanders, Tshipso Mashinini, John Muller, Themba Maluleke, and Monty Narsoo.

I acknowledge the hospitality and assistance of Professor Frederick Boal and the School of Geosciences, The Queen's University of Belfast, and Professor Chris Rogerson and the Department of Geography and Environmental Studies, University of the Witwatersrand, Johannesburg. Institutional and foundation support for this project has come from multiple sources, each of which I deeply appreciate: the United States Institute of Peace (especially to Timothy Sisk who has been helpful along the way); the Institute on Global Conflict and Cooperation and the Education Abroad Program, both at the University of California; the Global Peace and Conflict Studies research unit and the School of Social Ecology, both at the University of California, Irvine.

If there is one person whose ideas have been preeminent throughout the project, it is Meron S. Benvenisti, prolific Israeli writer and advocate for peace, whom I initially met in 1987 at a seminar on "divided cities" in Salzburg, Austria. I thank Jonathan Howes, former secretary of the North Carolina Department of Health, Environment, and Natural Resources, for providing me the opportunity to attend that stimulating seminar while I was a PhD student at the University of North Carolina, Chapel Hill. At that seminar, Mustafa Akinci, former mayor of the Turkish Municipality of Nicosia, and Lellos Demetriades, mayor of Greek Municipality of Nicosia, showed me that ethnic relations are between people as well as between peoples. Others have helped me develop research proposals and prepare logistically for field research, including Jay Rothman (Hebrew University and Haverford College), Craig Murphy (Wellesley College), Rachelle Alterman (Technion Institute), Mike McDonald (Williams College), James H. Wolfe (University of Southern Mississippi), Anthony Johnston (University of Ulster at Magee College), and Luis Suarez-Villa (University of California, Irvine). I thank Maura Pringle for castle and church and the Reverend Thabo Makgoba for his interpretation of the role of spirituality in contested societies. I thank Maish and Inez Cohen and Talya Abrahamson for opening up their house and circle of friends, David Goldblatt for a memorable afternoon, Mrs. H. A. Hubbard for support at Wits, and Nelson Zondi for Kwa-Mashu.

Although the thoughts and conclusions reported here are the synthesis of the thinking of many individuals, responsibility for errors lies solely with the author.

S.A.B.

PART ONE

Urban Arenas of
Nationalistic Conflict

1

Contested Cities

This is a study of the prospects for urban peace-building. It explores the role of urban policy as a component of broader strategies to stabilize or reconstruct ethnically polarized societies. It tests the hypothesis that local governmental actions may be necessary correlates of larger regional and national political negotiations, able to bring tangible benefits of peace to the streets and neighborhoods of strife-prone cities. Yet, urban peace-building faces realities and obstacles that are different, and may indeed be more difficult, than faced by broader peacemaking efforts. This study seeks to identify those on-the-ground strategies that are capable of co-contributing to societal reconciliation. How is an urban peace-building strategy operationalized in contested cities having inflammatory ethnic relations and territoriality? In shifting from partisan to peace-building urban strategies, what corresponding changes in the physical, social, political, and economic structuring of a city can, and should, take place? And, what effects do these changes at the urban scale have on the prospects for sustainable peace at regional and national scales?

Cities are frequently divided geographically and politically by income, race, or ethnicity. The focus of this study, however, is on a specific subset of urban areas—those "contested" cities where ethnic and nationalist claims combine and impinge significantly and consistently on distributional questions at the municipal level (Boal and Douglas 1982; Benvenisti 1986). Such cities host alternative and directly opposing cultures (Agnew, Mercer, and Sopher 1984). Conflicts that arise are "ethnonational" wherein one group seeks autonomy or separation (Gurr 1993). Although "particular disputes may be settled or brought under control, the underlying conflicts are not likely to be 'resolved,' but will reappear in other forms and on other issues which require continuous government intervention, thus management" (Esman 1973). A strong minority of the urban population may reject urban and societal institutions, making consensus regarding political power-sharing impossible (Douglas and Boal 1982; Romann and Weingrod 1991).

In most contested cities, ethnic identity[1] and nationalism[2] combine to create pressures for group rights, autonomy, or territorial separation. Such ethnic nationalism is often exclusive and fragmentary, and may constitute a threat to an existing state when an ethnic group aspires to create a nation-state different than currently exists.[3] In ethnically polarized cities, the machinery of government is often controlled by one ethnic group and used to discriminate against competing and threatening groups. In other cases, a third-party mediator may be brought in to govern the urban setting. In either case, the very legitimacy of a city's political structures and its rules of decisionmaking and governance are commonly challenged by ethnic groups who either seek an equal or proportionate share of power (such as blacks in South Africa) or demand group-based autonomy or independence (such as Palestinians in Jerusalem or the Quebecois in Montreal).[4] In the most intense cases, these cities are battlegrounds between "homeland" ethnic groups, each proclaiming the city as their own (Esman 1985).

The severity and intractability of intergroup conflict in these cities can overwhelm the adversary politics between government and opposition common in modern democratic states. Political means are seen as incapable of effectively resolving urban ethnic differences. While doctrines of collective rights, pluralism, or autonomy are invoked by those on the outside, the politically dominant group views resistance by the subordinated group as obstacles to "natural" processes of city-building and assimilation (Gurr 1993; Horowitz 1985). Allocational and housekeeping policies often become politically conflictual, viewed by the subordinate ethnic group as an intrusive imposition of one culture or political claim onto another. The urban arena, and public actions within it, become saturated with ideological, ethnic, and nationalistic meaning.

The governmental paralysis and intergroup antagonisms of these cities set them apart from others which, although divided socioeconomically, have recourse to accepted means of conflict resolution. In most cities, conflicts focus on issues of service delivery (such as housing), land use compatibility, and facility siting (Lineberry 1977; Lake 1987). Yet, these urban conflicts are addressed within an accepted political framework. Questions of what constitutes the public good are debated but largely within a sanctioned framework. For example, African-Americans in the 1960s protested for a greater share of economic benefits, but did so within a political framework they largely accepted. After the 1992 Los Angeles riots, issues of service distribution dominated those of territoriality and sovereignty (Levine and Williams 1992; Baldassare 1994). Gurr (1993) labels these as "ethnoclass" conflicts involving quests for political and economic equality and for cultural rights. Unlike the cities studied here, coalition-building remains possible across ethnic groups and crosscutting cleavages defuse and moderate intergroup conflict (Nordlinger 1972). One of the major roles of urban planning in such circumstances is to ameliorate urban conflict through an acceptable allocation of urban services and benefits across ethnic groups and their neighborhoods. In contrast, policymakers in contested cities manage and regulate not only urban services, but also must cope with ideological and religious expression and other correlates of intergroup tension and hostilities.

Whereas in most cities there is a belief maintained by all groups that the existing system of governance is properly configured and capable of producing fair outcomes, assuming adequate political participation and representation of minority interests,[5] governance in contested cities is often viewed by a not insubstantial segment of the ethnic minority population as artificial, imposed, or illegitimate. In those cases where an ethnic minority acknowledges the authority of city governance, it deeply mistrusts its intrinsic capability to respond to calls for equal, or group-based, treatment. A "combustible mixture" of distributive and political grievances can then combine to turn the attention of subordinated ethnic leaders from urban reform of the existing system to, next, radical restructuring or to, finally, separation and autonomy. The occurrence of intergroup tension and violence in cities divided by ethnic polarization can be qualitatively different than most other cities. Many of these cities are the sites of enduring and consistent interethnic violence laden with political meaning, capable of destabilizing both city life and larger peace processes. The potential for explosiveness in contested cities is more catastrophic and politically salient than the individual criminally based actions of divided cities.[6] In settings where antagonistic sides view each other as threats to their physical, cultural, or social survival, violence can be "rational" in that it is viewed as the only way by an aggrieved ethnic group to change intractable institutions and circumstances (Sisk 1995). Such circumstances, however, can produce "hurting stalemates" where the status quo is mutually damaging and neither side can impose its solution upon the other (Touval and Zartman 1985).

Cities such as Beirut, Sarajevo, Johannesburg, Belfast, Grozny, Nicosia, Montreal, Algiers, New Delhi, Hong Kong, and Brussels are urban arenas susceptible to intense intercommunal conflict and violence reflecting ethnic or nationalist fractures. Until recently, Berlin illustrated the literal tearing apart of an urban area by geopolitical factors. Cities play different roles within larger conflicts, including target for intergroup hostilities, stage for the expression of antagonisms, accommodative arena, and peace-building opportunity. In some cases, a city is the target or focal point of unresolved nationalistic ethnic conflict. For example, Jerusalem is at the spatial epicenter of Israeli-Palestinian conflict which during the five years of the *intifada* cost over 1600 lives (Human Rights Watch 1993). In other cases, the city is a stage for the expression of conflicting sovereignty claims involving areas outside the urban region or for tensions related to foreign immigration. Belfast is the capital city and the most important stage for conflict in contested Northern Ireland, a province which has borne witness to over 3000 Protestant and Catholic deaths over the twenty-five years of civil war. New Delhi is the site of increasing Hindu-Muslim tension and violence as separatist campaigns concerning Kashmir and Khalistan penetrate this center of Indian population and culture. And, urban centers for Germany are platforms for right-wing groups in their displays of hostility toward Mediterranean labor migrants and political refugees. Yet, actions and policies in other cities have shown that they are capable of defusing nationalistic conflict through cooperative communal governance. In Montreal, the enactment of language policy accommodative of the Francophone population has probably obstructed the potential success of territorial autonomy efforts. And, in Brussels, the state and city government structures have provided a legal groundwork for accommodation between Flemish and French speakers.

In other cases, the management of strife-torn cities may play a key peace-building role after cessation of overt hostilities. In the former Yugoslavia, the cities of Sarajevo and Mostar are critical elements in whether enemies can spatially coexist in a workable reconstruction of a war-torn Bosnia that has suffered over 200,000 dead and 1.7 million refugees.[7] Johannesburg is the economic powerhouse and largest urban region in the new democratic South Africa, a country where over 15,000 people have been killed since the mid-1980s in political violence between the former white government and blacks, with thousands more dead from black-on-black hostilities (Human Rights Watch 1993). The physically partitioned city of Nicosia is at the center of the United Nations–managed settlement between Greek and Turkish Cypriots who engaged in a civil war that cost over 10,000 lives in the 1960s and 1970s. In the new Baltic countries of the former Soviet Union, native and Russian populations now coexist uneasily in the urban centers of Estonia, Latvia, and Lithuania. And, the Lebanese political capital and cultural center of Beirut is undergoing physical and social reconstruction after a 15-year civil war that cost over 15,000 Muslim, Christian, and Druze lives.

The intent of this study is not to explain why cities perform different roles amidst ethnic tension, but rather to document actual and potential contributions that city management and policymaking can make toward larger peace efforts. It will do this by examining two cities—Belfast (Northern Ireland) and Johannesburg (South Africa)—embedded within larger peacemaking processes and drawing out the lessons—both positive and negative—that city management of ethnic conflict provides for intergroup stability and reconstruction at regional and national scales. Belfast has been embedded within a problematic British-Irish negotiation process which has recently brought a settlement, and is an urban area of tense sectarianism. Johannesburg is engaged in intergroup reconciliation and reconstruction of its racial geography after resolution of core political problems. Yet, it is faced with massive unmet human needs and gross inequalities. The challenges faced by these two cities—Belfast seeking stabilization of intergroup relations amidst political change; Johannesburg attempting to reconstruct apartheid geography under an accepted governing regime—provide the ability to study the opportunities (and impediments) that urban policymaking contributes to urban and regional peacemaking and peace-building.

Cities and Intrastate Conflict

Urban centers of ethnic diversity are of increasing salience to those studying and seeking to resolve contemporary strife because the scale of world conflict since the 1960s has shifted from international to intrastate. Sixty-nine of the 94 wars recorded between 1945 and 1988 (INCORE 1994) have been intrastate conflicts killing an estimated 17–30 million people and displacing millions from their home countries. Eighty percent of all war deaths since World War II have been internal to national states (Russett and Starr 1989; Brogan 1990). Of the 37 major armed conflicts in the world in 1991, twenty-five of them were intrastate conflicts between ethnic groups or between an ethnic group and a government (Eriksen 1993). Gurr and Harff (1994, 6) document forty-nine "protracted communal conflicts" in the world today that are confrontations between "ethnic groups and governments over fundamental issues of group rights and identity" and "usually involved recurring episodes of intense violence."[8]

Accordingly, military strategists are increasingly focusing on ethnically based animosities that are often intrastate in nature (Gibbs 1989; Schultz 1991; Hoffman 1992).[9] This change in the scale of conflict can be traced, in part, to ethnic groups' feelings of insecurity and threat amidst the disappearance of an overarching internationally based Cold War ideology. The collapse of governing regimes in Africa, the former Soviet Union, and eastern Europe has frequently activated ethnic and national conflict and territorial disintegration (Zartman 1995; Andrusz 1996).[10] Unprecedented levels of global migration and intermixing due to limited economic opportunities or political instability have created countries and cities of volatile ethnic mixes. Only 10 percent of the world's nations remain ethnically or racially homogeneous[11] (Welch 1993; Wright 1993). As many as 100 million individuals now live outside their country of birth or citizenship (United Nations 1993), with guest and other migrating workers eliciting tensions and violence in many places.

As a result of these complex patterns of political and demographic change, the nation-state is decreasingly seen as the territorial answer to the problem of human political, economic, and social organization. The disintegration of many states is compelling international aid organizations, mediators, and political negotiators to increasingly look at substate regions and urban areas as more appropriate scales of involvement. International organizations who have focused peace-building efforts at state levels will need to turn their efforts more toward community peace-building and the establishment of links between international and local organizations (U.S. Institute of Peace 1996). This link would likely build upon post-conflict peace-building activities of the United Nations—most particularly, humanitarian assistance, reintegration of refugees, and rehabilitation of infrastructure—that are already carried out disproportionately in urban areas of unmet needs, displaced residents, and damaged transport, energy, and industrial facilities (United Nations 1996a). The United Nations appears cognizant of the importance of local issues and institutions in the contemporary world. The June 1996 United Nations Conference on Human Settlements (Habitat II) called for adequate shelter for all and sustainable human settlements development in an urbanizing world. The Istanbul Declaration on Human Settlements (United Nations 1996b, c) committed participating states to "a political, economic, environmental, ethical and spiritual vision of human settlements based on the principles of equality, solidarity, partnership, human dignity, respect and co-operation" (Declaration, chapter II: Goals and Principles).

Within ethnically tense and fragmenting states, urban management of ethnic competition has profound consequences for the national, and ultimately, international level. Urban areas and their civilian populations are "soft, high-value" targets for broader conflict (M. Brown 1993). They can become important military and symbolic battlegrounds and flashpoints for violence between warring ethnic groups seeking sovereignty, autonomy, or independence. Cities are fragile and vulnerable organisms subject to economic stagnation, demographic disintegration, cultural suppression, and ideological and political excesses violent in nature. They are significant depositories of material resources and culture vulnerable to penetration or implosion by nationalistic ethnic conflict and violence. Cities are focal points of urban and regional economies dependent on multi-ethnic contacts, social and cultural centers and platforms for political expression, and potential centers of grievance and mobilization. They provide the locus of everyday interaction where ethnicity and identity can be created and re-created (Eriksen 1993). They are suppliers of important religious and cultural symbols, zones of intergroup proximity and intimacy, and arenas where the size and concentration of a subordinate population can present the most direct threat to the state. Much more than at larger geographic scales where segregation of ethnic communities is possible, the proximity of urban living means that contested cities can be located on the faultline between cultures—between modernizing societies and traditional cultures; between individual-based and community-based economies; between democracy and more authoritarian regimes; and/or between old colonial governments and native populations.

Contested cities host antagonistic parties which encounter one another spatially and functionally. In many cases, the proximate and contentious ethnic territoriality found in the residential fabric of a contested city constricts and dichotomizes urban living and circumscribes public policy options. Even when antagonistic groups remain apart spatially in an urban system, however, they will necessarily find themselves in close economic relations with those from across the ethnic divide. Residents live as "intimate enemies," experiencing intensely the contradiction between neighborly relations and the ethnic divide (Benvenisti 1986, 1995). A city is a site where belligerent peoples come together—if not due to intergroup competition over urban space, then to the economic interdependencies inherent to urban living. Nationalistic ethnic conflict intermixes with the day-to-day management of the city in this environment of tight quarters and economic interdependencies between antagonistic groups. In many cases, there may exist a contradiction between nation and city, with nationalist aspirations for separateness and identity conflicting with cities' social, economic, and political interdependencies and diversity.

It is not evident whether a major city that has operated in the midst of nationalistic ethnic conflict will constitute an obstacle or facilitator to larger regional or national peace. A city presents a subordinate ethnic group with the "often-contradictory forces of state assimilation and discrimination" (A. Smith 1993). On the one hand, the economic centrality and/or religious symbolism of a city within a national hierarchy and the close juxtaposition of antagonistic neighborhoods would lead one to anticipate obstruction of a larger peace due to heightened interethnic tension and increased propensity for violent urban actions. Intergroup proximity and interaction characteristic of urban areas may provide sparks to long-simmering ethnic fires. To the extent that a city is a flashpoint, it can act as a major and independent obstruction to the success of larger regional and national peace processes.[12] Yet, the same features of urban closeness and interdependency may lead local political leaders and elites to more readily and quickly engage in workable ethnic compromises and arrangements ahead of larger peace negotiations. Ashkenasi (1988) suggests that the pragmatic needs of communal government will influence city leadership and intergroup relations in a more affirmative fashion than it does national-level ethnic relations. In addition, the realities of urban interdependence may make it more difficult for ethnic groups to live in their own "purified" communities insulated by myths of sameness and communal solidarity (Sennett 1970). Cities may then be buffers against the strong winds of ethnicity and sectarianism. In these cases, the possibility exists that urban-based ethnic arrangements and compromises may facilitate the easing of conflict at larger geographic scales.

Managing City Conflict

This book examines the proposition that cities constitute spatial, economic, and psychological keys to national peacemaking and are necessary anchors to progress in larger political negotiations. Cities and their metropolitan regions appear to comprise an essential analytical scale for studying the contemporary intrastate patterns and processes of ethnic conflict and its effective potential amelioration and resolution. City governing regimes, through their policy effects on ethnic group identity, territorial expression, and objective living conditions, may independently affect—for better or worse—the quality of intergroup accommodation, the propensity for tolerance of the "other," and thus ultimately, the heart and soul of larger political negotiated agreements. Urban policy strategies related to spatial organization, demographic allocation, service delivery and spending, and economic development may have direct links to ethnic groups' feelings of psychological security and fairness in the urban milieu. Urban policies can also influence political mobilization on the part of an aggrieved group, restricting or enabling political opportunities at the city level, or impeding or nurturing the development of local organizing capacity on the part of the out-group (McAdam, McCarthy, and Zald 1996; Tarrow 1994).

One of the greatest challenges facing many world cities today is to facilitate the expression of ethnic and cultural diversity that enriches city life while at the same time working against the physical and psychological barriers, hostility, and violence that can paralyze and impoverish it. Conceptual and practice-based knowledge and models regarding governmental policy amidst ethnic polarization are urgently needed. Applied research in this area will provide to practitioners and officials a better understanding of the complexities of urban policymaking amidst uncertainty and strife.[13] Government practices and public policy are viewed here not as inconsequential to ethnic conflict. This is consistent with cross-national analyses of ethnic conflict which reveal that today's ethnic violence stems as much from actions by political leaders and deliberate government policies as from traditional community antagonisms (M. Brown 1996; Pesic 1996; Lake and Rothchild 1996; Snyder 1993). Concerning the former Yugoslavia, for example, Pesic (1996, 19) concludes that "the principal mechanism for escalating interethnic conflicts in a multinational state begins when political elites in tenuous positions of power successfully portray their ethno-nation as being threatened by another." This evidence that leadership and policy matters means that policymakers at national and local levels operating amid "ancient hatreds" have a constructive role to play, if they so choose, in formulating urban and national policies accommodative of competing nationalisms. In addition, ethnic tension and violence at the urban level provides an important microcosm of intergroup dynamics occurring at more encompassing geographic scales. Applied research involving urban ethnic conflict may thus provide to policy officials at local, national, and cross-national scales a keener awareness of how government authority and its expression affect the dynamics of ethnic nationalism.

Despite the increasing salience of cities to contemporary patterns and processes of intergroup conflict, studies of ethnic conflict management in the disciplines of political science, urban planning, geography, and social psychology have de-emphasized local ethnic policies and their potential relationship to larger processes of conflict or peace. I now discuss each disciplinary strand and its contributions and limitations to the study of city-based nationalistic conflict.

The numerous and analytically rich *political science* models of conflict management focus on political and legal arrangements and mechanisms at the level of the nation-state that might diffuse or moderate conflict. By de-emphasizing applications to city governance and management, these models limit their utility regarding how city officials are to operate in ethnically polarized cities. Micropolitical, or smaller-scale, forms of conflict management in urban areas—such as discrimination and segregation, demographic policies, or community relations—are seen simply as tools of larger macropolitical objectives operating at national and international levels (O'Leary and McGarry 1995). The city is assumed to reflect at a concrete level the playing out of broader imbalances of power. Or, as Rothman (1992) points out, the "low politics" of groups and how they pursue the fulfillment of human needs for their constituents are dismissed as unimportant compared to the "high politics" of states and their promotion and protection of national interests.

Notwithstanding their dismissal of city-based dynamics, political science models of conflict management have important implications for urban management. O'Leary and McGarry (1995) outline two types of methods—those that would eliminate ethnic differences and those that would manage such differences.[14] Methods which seek to eliminate ethnic differences include forced mass population transfers, partition or secession, and integration or assimilation. Ethnic cleansing in Sarajevo (Bosnia-Herzegovina) and apartheid Johannesburg (South Africa) illustrate the application at the urban and regional scale of *forced population transfers*. More commonly, city administrations manipulate demographic proportions and spatially fragment an antagonistic ethnic group in order to achieve the same political objectives as forced relocations. *Political partitioning* of urban space (such as Nicosia, Cold War Berlin, and Jerusalem from 1948 to 1967) can be an important feature of national-level agreements regarding territorial separation. At the same time, urban partitioning introduces practical problems not found at a national scale. Finally, *integration or assimilation* strategies in many ways have greater salience at the smaller-scale urban level than they do at more dispersed national scales. Cities can seek integration through the attempted creation of a civic identity (i.e. Jerusalemite) that would transcend ethnic identity. Assimilation takes this one step further in attempting to create a common cultural identity derived through a melting pot process. Requisite to city-based assimilation would likely be the residential dispersal of ethnic groups throughout the urban setting. This is so because an important means of sustaining urban ethnic identity and preserving a critical cultural mass is through educational and neighborhood segregation.[15]

Methods for managing, rather than eliminating, ethnic differences include hegemonic control, third-party intervention, cantonization or federalization, and consociation or power-sharing. Political stability is achieved by *hegemonic control* at the cost of democracy. One side dominates the state apparatus and channels decisionmaking outcomes toward the favored ethnic group (Lustick 1979; Smooha 1980). Transferring the model of hegemonic control from national to urban scales may not be straightforward. For instance, the proximity and interdependence of urban ethnic populations may necessitate in hegemonically controlled cities greater cooperation or co-optation between political leaders than would be found at national levels. *Third-party intervention* relies on there being an arbiter whose claim of neutrality must be broadly accepted by contending ethnic groups. At the urban scale, this perceived joint neutrality can be difficult because historic imbalances and inequalities are highlighted by a relative deprivation effect induced by physical proximity. Even well-intended policies by a third party can be seen as reinforcing these inequalities, especially if root causes of urban disparities are not addressed.

Cantonization and federalization involve, in the first case, devolution of some government authority to homogeneous ethnonational territories; and, in the second, separate domains of formal authority between levels of government. Urban applications of these concepts include, in the first case, the creation of community or neighborhood-based groups that would advise or decide on local issues. In the second case, there would be the creation of a metropolitan government and subordinate municipal governments. The last model of ethnic management is *consociation or power sharing*. At the national level, this has been the most closely scrutinized option for deeply divided societies. Lijphart's (1968, 1977) "consociational" democracy and Nordlinger's (1972) "conflict-regulating practices" focus on the role of cooperative efforts by political leaders in creating government structures and rules (such as proportional representation and minority veto power) that can overcome and diffuse societal fragmentation. Horowitz (1985) recommends the creation of incentives that would encourage politicians and voters to consider interests beyond their communal segments.[16] Although power-sharing is usually studied exclusively at the national governmental level, it has relevance to the governance of cities split by ethnic nationalism (O'Leary and McGarry 1995).

Another line of political investigation—exemplified by McAdam, McCarthy, and Zald (1996), Gurr and Harff (1994), Tarrow (1994), Gurr (1993), and Weitzer (1990)—explores the cause and dynamics of communal conflict and ethnic group mobilization. Although applied to national settings, its focus on whether relative conditions of deprivation or aspects of an ethnic group's political organization and leadership primarily cause community protest and rebellion has direct salience to urban settings. In the first case, the origins of protest and resistance are found in a sense of injustice and grievance widely shared across out-group members. In the second case, resistance is a function of the actions and skills of ethnic group leaders, organizations, and networks. Targeting relative deprivation as the culprit, city governments could potentially try to ameliorate nationalistic claims and protests by an antagonistic ethnic group through betterment of objective urban conditions. Yet, such a transition from coercive urban control to ethnic accommodation may be associated with an *increase* in violent protest and rebellion by the historically subordinated ethnic group (Gurr 1993). This is so because even though objective living conditions may be improving, long-suppressed political mobilization is energized by the end of coercive rule. In terms of community opposition, urban-based resistance may contrast with the dynamics of national-level opposition. Because cities may be either platform or palliative for community protest, the intensity of urban opposition to potential or actual peace agreements may be different than, and be able to affect, the quality of national-level opposition.

Models and theories of *urban planning* have more directly addressed local governance and administration. However, a major limitation of this literature is that much planning prescription and theory has been dependent upon there being legitimate sources of power and control (Friedmann 1987). Traditional planning practice is rooted in assumptions of the maintenance of a stable state (Morley and Shachar 1986). In contrast, urban planning in ethnically contested cities must act within conditions of instability and uncertainty which call into question the very basis of its traditional practice. Traditional planning is linked to societal guidance, urban reform, and the pursuit of a general "public interest" within the largely consensual policymaking environments characteristic of Western democracies. In contrast, the "public interest" in polarized cities is either fragile or impossible under contested conditions.

Urban planning has tended to focus on technical aspects of land use and development and avoided discussions concerning values and social justice (Thomas 1994; Thomas and Krishnarayan 1994). Equity-based approaches to planning exist that are based on notions of social justice (Davidoff 1965; Krumholz and Clavel 1994). Yet, their emphasis on increasing the representation of disadvantaged groups' interests during decisionmaking does not appear to be generalizable to situations where politics is segmented and antagonistic. In addition, urban planning tends to be ambivalent about how built environments should be structured when ethnic conflict is present. On the one hand, planning and other bureaucratic systems have been criticized for "purifying" and insulating ethnic communities from one another (Sennett 1970). At the same time, Wirth (1931) and his sociological adherents warn that increasing intergroup contact amidst subcultural diversity can intensify friction and undermine the possibility for achieving social consensus.

The role of urban planning amidst ethnic polarization is problematic. Benvenisti (1986) states that planning's use of pragmatic, process-oriented approaches aimed at urban symptoms, not root causes, legitimizes the status quo and institutionalizes the dual, unequal conditions common to urban polarization. Planners' definition of urban problems in universal, civil-libertarian terms can reach a "manageable" solution by a convenient perception of the problem, yet a solution that has little importance when sovereignty and autonomy are the leading issues. The compatibility between dominant forms of power and the exercise of urban planning suggests that the basic paradigm and assumptions of city-building practice may need to be restructured in order for the profession to positively contribute to peace-building. Urban planning in ethnically divided cities can be instrumental in the exercise of state repression and coercion, playing a key role in operationalizing and concretizing partisan ideologies of an empowered ethnic group. In contrast, two models of planning policy described by Friedmann (1987) have potentially more productive roles in the management and reconstruction of polarized cities. A "social learning" model of urban planning allows for the profession to learn from action and practice in ethnically polarized environments, and could be at the forefront in grassroots efforts to accommodate antagonistic ethnicities within the urban milieu. A "social mobilization" or "empowerment" model of urban planning is more radical and seeks emancipation of working people, women, and oppressed ethnic groups (Friedmann 1987, 1992).

Geographic analyses of ethnically polarized environments provide insight into the spatial and territorial aspects and dynamics of such contest. Sack's (1981, 55) definition of territoriality is illuminating: "the attempt to affect, influence, or control actions and interactions (of people, things, and relationships) by asserting and attempting to enforce control over a specific geographical area." A dominant ethnic government in a contested city can seek to contain an antagonistic group's territorial expression (Yiftachel 1995). This can be done through the intentional expansion of dominant group urban space or the constriction of subordinate group space. These efforts seek to prevent the emergence of a powerful, regionally based counterculture which may challenge the ethnic state (Yiftachel 1995). Territorial policies reify power, creating explicit and visible manifestations of power and state authority (Sack 1986). They can displace attention away from the root causes of social conflict to conflicts among territorial spaces themselves (Sack 1986). In the urban setting, this means that international issues of sovereignty and autonomy become reducible to issues over neighborhoods and suburban growth. Urban ethnic territoriality, over time, can also create static and lifeless containers that disrupt and hinder the life-giving dynamics of an urban economic and social system. Urban territoriality becomes worthy of endless defense, no matter its realistic functionality in meeting the defending ethnic group's objective needs. In such a setting, even a well-intentioned urban government's sensitivity toward ethnic territoriality can help sustain and promote ethnic social cleavages (Murphy 1989).

The proximity of urban living introduces problematic features to the effects of territoriality on the part of a dominant ethnic group. To control an antagonistic ethnic population, a dominant ethnic group in many cases will try to penetrate it geographically in order to establish a physical presence and to fragment the opposing group's sense of community. Yet, such penetration forces the protagonist to give up some of the security provided by ethnic separation (Romann 1995).[17] Thus, efforts at territorial control can paradoxically reduce group security. Spatial competition brings antagonistic groups closer together, establishing conditions for further conflict. In other cases, achievement of territorial control at one geographic scale (for instance, that of the city) may expose the dominating group to

demographic and physical threats at the next broader geographic scale (for instance, the urban or metropolitan region). Thus, territoriality may engender further territorial efforts at control in a self-fulfilling cycle (Sack 1986). Yet, it has
been suggested that in contested areas the greater the land area under territorial
control, the less the control over the subordinated population (Akenson 1992;
Williams 1994). As territorial control is expanded, the disempowered population
becomes larger and represents a less tractable opposition. Administrative control
over land and political control over people are not necessarily the same.

Urban geographic treatises identify not only the link between urban space and
subordination, but also point toward ways in which urban space can be shaped in
pursuit of social justice. Harvey (1973) demonstrates how urban spatial form is
instrumental in producing a distributive pattern of income, jobs, housing, property rights, and other urban resources. His territorial distributive justice is a spatial form that fulfills basic needs, contributes to the common good as well as private needs, and allocates extra resources to areas of extreme environmental or
social difficulty. To D. Smith (1994), a socially just geographic is one that reduces
inequality. And, Barry (1989, 146) connects the concept of spatial distributive justice to its institutional basis, highlighting the "institutions that together determine
the access (or chances of access) of the members of a society to resources that are
the means to the satisfaction of a wide variety of desires." This last comment highlights the need in ethnically polarized cities to connect geographic strategies and
outcomes to the motivating ideologies and institutional rationales underlying
them. In other words, we need to connect the spatial to the political. Ethnic
groups commonly endeavor to imprint fundamental ideologies of exclusiveness
or domination onto urban space so as to exert control in an urban environment.
Yet, translation of general moral tenants in an urban system is not straightforward. For example, attempted subjugation of an ethnic minority could imply either spatial integration as a way to dilute their concentration or segregation as a
way to marginalize their urban existence. How political goals are connected to
specific territorial policies, and the effect these territorial outcomes have in turn
on these political goals, is a topic that geographic analyses have de-emphasized.

The *social psychology* of urban intergroup conflict is a final important consideration in a study of how urban policy may facilitate or disrupt political efforts directed at ethnic accommodation and peace. Social-psychological studies of intergroup conflict and urban aggression indicate the immediate sources of ethnic
conflict which must be addressed in efforts at accommodation. Ethnic conflicts of
the type found in polarized cities are only marginally over material interests, but
rather touch deeply on human needs for security, identity and recognition, fair access to political institutions, and economic participation (Cohen 1978; Burton
1990; Kelman 1990; Azar 1991). The proximity of urban living can exacerbate
these felt needs through the effect of relative deprivation and the psychology of im-

balance. The threatened loss of group identity and security amidst conditions of urban conflict—due in particular to urban territorial changes—can be a prime motivator of antagonism and unrest. To a threatened subgroup, psychological needs pertaining to community and cultural viability (measured through the survival, for instance, of ethnic schools or religious institutions in a neighborhood) can be as important as objective needs pertaining to land for housing and economic activities. At the same time, recognition and maintenance of group identity can be an essential building block for peacemaking efforts at urban and national levels.[18]

Psychologists trained in intergroup conflict resolution emphasize that it is not likely to occur through the promotion and preservation of political interests, but rather when the nonnegotiable values of each side associated with human needs and identity needs are met. As Burton (1991, 81) states, "there can be no resolution of a conflict unless it takes into account as political reality the perceptions and values of those who are represented in facilitated discussions." An advantage of conflict problem-solving based on values and needs is that resolution can be achieved through an outcome where both sides gain. In contrast, political negotiations based on interests are often hindered by zero-sum limits. Without addressing core human needs such as identity, security, and economic access, conflicts may be managed for a while by political leaders, but seldom resolved since core human needs are often bypassed by political negotiations. Social-psychological, needs-based approaches to conflict resolution focus on locally based intergroup conflict and thus have salience to urban conflict. However, these techniques are not directly linked to formal policy processes. Indeed, such intergroup deliberations, to be effective, need to be free of the power relations and vested interests of formal politics and policymaking (Kelman and Cohen 1976; Burton 1990; Fisher 1990; Rothman 1992). In cases where conflict management strategies have been applied to urban policymaking, they have been studied where political frameworks are accepted (Susskind and Cruickshank 1987). The current study attempts to highlight the social-psychological effects of urban policy on both historically subordinate and dominant ethnic groups. It seeks to explain the debilitating effects of urban strategies on group perceptions of security, identity, and cohesiveness, and to indicate directions whereby future urban actions can accommodate and respect human needs as part of a larger peace.

Psychologists have also examined the physical ecology (environmental factors) and social ecology (personal characteristics) of aggression. Absent resolution of root causes underlying urban violence, policymakers may seek attenuation of overt hostile acts by either designing physical environments to dissuade aggression or providing opportunities for conflict-reducing intergroup conflict (Goldstein 1994). The former category of environmental design interventions include access control, formal surveillance by security personnel, and the creation of environments that facilitate natural surveillance by residents engaged in day-to-day activities (Wood 1991; Clarke 1992). "Defensible space," for example, is designed so that multiple "eyes on the street" dissuade criminal behavior (Newman 1975). A more hardened approach to environmental crime prevention is described by Davis (1990) in his account of a "militarization of urban space" aimed at protecting against urban aggressors or unwanteds. Social ecological interventions, in contrast, seek to facilitate intergroup contact that will overcome stereotyping and hatred. This assumes that group insularity and prejudice are at the roots of intergroup conflict. Yet, intergroup encounters may actually increase conflict if the groups are not of equal status or do not share some common goals (Allport 1954; Goldstein 1994). This is problematic because in ethnically polarized cities, status—actual or perceived—is not equivalent between groups, but usually of a dominant-subordinate nature. Identity-enhancing and confidence-building community development initiatives on both sides of the urban divide may be necessary for intergroup contact to have any measurable positive effect. Allport's contact hypothesis also explains why psychological approaches to conflict resolution seek to separate intergroup contact from the power imbalances and relations of formal politics.

Each analytical perspective on the management of ethnic conflict—political science, urban planning, geographic, and social-psychological—offers penetrating insights into the dynamics, management, and possible resolution of ethnic conflict. Yet, no single perspective captures fully the complex social and physical aspects of urban strife. This is because they either de-emphasize the local political arena (political science), assume legitimacy of public authority (urban planning), downplay the interrelationship between political motives and spatial practices (geography), or separate intergroup deliberations from formal policy processes (social psychology). This project thus integrates their perspectives in an effort to more fruitfully learn about how governments may stabilize or reconstruct strife-torn societies. Broader peacemaking strategies and techniques must be translated into local on-the-ground tactics having specific territorial outcomes. These, in turn, have significant effects on group identity and deprivation, and thus ultimately on the extent and quality of intergroup tolerance and peace in the city, region, and state.

Notes

1. Ethnic groups are composed of people who share a distinctive and enduring collective identity based on shared experiences or cultural traits (Gurr and Harff 1994). Such group awareness can be crystallized through such factors as shared struggle, territorial identity, "ethnic chosenness," or religion (A. Smith 1993).

2. Nationalism is defined here as in Snyder (1993)—a doctrine wherein nationality is the most important line of cleavage for establishing membership in societal groups, and overrides or subsumes alternative criteria such as social class, economic class, or patronage networks.

3. Nationalism is not necessarily a fragmenting force. Indeed, civic or territorial nationalism can supply an overarching loyalty to pluralistic societies (Lijphart 1977). It is its combination with ethnic identity that "furnishes the spark for the great conflagrations" of today (A.

Smith 1993, 37). Note however that even civic, inclusive nationalism (such as the African National Congress's in South Africa) can be stimulative of conflict in opposing an ethnic regime.

4. In some cities (such as Belfast), both aspirations are present. Republican demands include *both* equal treatment within existing governance structures and nationalistic calls to be reunited with Ireland.

5. Guinier's (1994) provocative argument against the fairness of American democracy takes her close to rejection of existing rules of governance as being inherently incapable of representing minority interests in a majoritarian democracy.

6. Belfast, Northern Ireland—a flashpoint for political violence—has a very low violent crime rate. In contrast, Los Angeles' or Detroit's violent crime rates are overwhelming but politically motivated crimes are minuscule.

7. The Sarajevo urban region consists of a Muslim-majority city next to Serbian eastern suburbs and their Republika Srpska. Mostar is politically shared between Muslims and Croats as part of the new Muslim-Croat federation in Bosnia.

8. Not all nationalistic ethnic conflict is contained within a single state. Ethnic groups can straddle state boundaries and thus require international attention. The Kurdish population resides in four countries—Turkey, Iran, Iraq, and Syria (Gurr and Harff 1994). The Palestinian diaspora resides in the West Bank, Jordan, and Syria.

9. In a report done for the U.S. Army, a global survey of intrastate conflicts identified thirty different present or possible civil war scenarios (Winnefeld et al. 1995).

10. At the time of the end of the USSR (1991), there were 164 identifiable actual and potential ethno-nationalistic conflicts within its borders (Andrusz 1996).

11. Defined as having five percent or less of ethnic minorities.

12. Peace-making and reconstruction at the urban scale can at times be more difficult than at a regional scale. This was illustrated by the need to postpone municipal elections in post-war Bosnia and Herzegovina in August 1996, while national elections—although flawed—were carried out the following month.

13. The urgent need for accommodative policy models was the primary conclusion of a 1987 Salzburg (Austria) Seminar on "divided cities" consisting of over fifty faculty and fellows from twenty countries. The author was rapporteur for that seminar. Countries represented included Germany, Lebanon, Israel, Jordan, the West Bank, Egypt, Northern Ireland, Cyprus, the United States, the former Yugoslavia, Turkey, and Poland.

14. Besides O'Leary and McGarry, inventories of different ethnic management techniques include M. Smith (1969)—modes of collective accommodation; Esman (1973)—regime objectives; Palley (1979)—constitutional devices; and Gladdish (1979).

15. Integration and assimilation may, at the same time, mask the imposition of a core or dominant culture (O'Leary and McGarry 1995).

16. Because these incentives attempt to point politicians and voters inward toward moderation, this approach has been called "centripetalism" by Sisk (1995).

17. Interview with Michael Romann, lecturer in geography, Tel Aviv University, at Jerusalem Institute of Israel Studies, December 16, 1994.

18. Interview with Dr. Nehemia Friedland, professor of psychology, specialist in terrorist negotiations, Tel Aviv University, December 15, 1994.

2

Prospects and Limits
of Urban Peace-Building

Cities are sluggish; they contain physical, economic, and social structures that have crystallized through the years and do not readily change. Analyses of eastern European socialist cities in transition to capitalism, for instance, suggest that socialist urban traits such as under-urbanization, less diversity, and a strongly state-constructed spatial form will not change overnight in capitalist reconstruction (Szelenyi 1996). Instead, many of these cities will evolve gradually as policymakers and emerging markets both reject and adapt socialist urbanization (Harloe 1996). Similar to societies at large, cities in transition from socialism to capitalism will show varied, or "path-dependent," shifts in their physical, social, and economic restructuring (Stark 1990, 1992; Putnam 1993). In political and urban transitions, legacies of past urban policymaking and development constrain and set parameters for contemporary urban reform. French occupation of the city of Algiers led to colonial urban planning which reified French urbanism and control, creating urban forms which solidified the power of the colonizer over the colonized (Celik 1997). In Jerusalem, the twenty years of physical partition from 1948 to 1967 spatially separated Jewish west and Arab east Jerusalem populations, perpetuated city divisions, and led to the neglect of the old city (Bollens 1996). When the rebuilding of war-torn cities is attempted, policy officials engage not with a tabula rasa but with urban forms and activity patterns erected both before and during urban warfare. In the rebuilding of German cities after World War II, radical new styles of German urbanization were not created; instead, the shape of reconstruction was influenced by long-term continuities in city-building practice dating to the early 1900s (Diefendorf 1993). The political and physical postwar reconstruction of the former Yugoslavia faces the terrible legacy of urban "ethnic cleansing" which has created new landscapes of demographic dominance and eradication. And, contemporary efforts to reconstruct debilitated Beirut must somehow accommodate forms of urbanization—such as squatting, refugee camps, and self-sufficient neighborhood networks—which sustained individuals through crises and in the absence of a national government (Yahya 1993).

The sluggishness of city structure implies that although a political transition in a war-torn society may be advancing that proposes stabilization or reconstruction, cities will likely remain rooted to spatial forms and processes created during or prior to urban civil war. In the case of contested cities, transitions in governing regime or strategy which aspire to reconstruct the urban arena face impediments in the city derived from, and given life by, the demands of urban civil war. What provided sustenance and survival during urban strife creates territorial and behavioral limits to city normalization and functionality. This study seeks to identify in two contested cities—Belfast and Johannesburg—the constraints posed by urban geographies created during strife and to ascertain how post-conflict evolution of urban ethnic space can be managed so as to transform these geographic and functional legacies. Peace-building at the city level faces constraints because a strife-torn city exudes an architecture and geography that are daily reminders of the dominance and dysfunctionality of the strife-torn period. At the same time, however, the practice of urban peace-building contains promise because a city's raison d'être—its human interaction and functional independence—may lend itself to ethnic compromise and adaptation.

This chapter develops a conceptual framework to assist in the study of contested cities that are or could be embedded within larger political transitions aimed at stabilizing or reconstructing strife-torn societies. It links the development of a civic, conflict-attenuating governing ideology to specific urban policy strategies intended to operationalize intergroup stability or peace. These policies have distinct effects on ethnic conditions of territoriality, economic well-being, political empowerment, and group identity that can obstruct or promote peace-building at the city and neighborhood levels. Cities are viewed here as constituting important channels through which political moves toward ethnic peace are either enhanced or lessened. Although cities' physical and political structures are not the primary causes behind the success or failure of societal peacemaking efforts, urban arenas are nevertheless viewed as critical links between the broader national and diplomatic intentions of peacemaking and the interpersonal and intergroup dynamics of ethnic peace-building.[1] The urban arena of conflict is worthy of attention because urban policy provides a lever that is generally more accessible to public officials, nongovernmental advocates, and the public-at-large than the higher-level and less tangible political negotiations carried out by government ministers and foreign diplomats. Policies and perceptions at the urban level can more readily reflect changing intentions of government strategies and the public-at-large.

It is posited that city actions can both help *reinforce* and *construct* larger peace settlements. In the first case, qualities of the urban system—intergroup proximity, local community politics, social interaction, and economic interdependency—may assist (or retard) efforts to advance peace after a larger settlement is negotiated. In the second case, urban policymaking may be formative of larger political agreements. Hettne (1983a, 1983b) posits that a society's development does not need to await peace (in the form of disarmament) but rather that properly managed development can create and consolidate peaceful relations. Similarly, I examine whether a city's growth and policymaking can actually facilitate peacemaking at larger levels. In this scenario, change in city policies and well-being do not have to await broader advances of peace, but can create the conditions for such peace through the amelioration of urban intergroup strife. To the extent that broader extra-local political negotiations are stalled or nonproductive, the tangible, on-the-ground strategies at the urban level pertaining to physical structure and empowerment may make the difference between mutual tolerance and armed urban conflict.[2]

Figure 2.1 presents a diagram outlining the relationships between governing ideology, urban policy, urban ethnic conditions, and the advancement of peace at the local level.

Operationalizing Peace

An ideology is a comprehensive political belief system that embraces an inner logic and seeks to guide and justify organized political and social actions (Bilski and Galnoor 1980). In this study, I focus on the ideology of *governments* regarding their desired urban outcomes in a society of conflicting ethnic groups. I emphasize governing ideologies because public authorities operating amidst ethnic unrest must adopt an explicit doctrine that justifies and defends their policies amidst societal fragmentation. The *governing ideology* in a polarized city constitutes an intake or gatekeeper function, either allowing or barring a single ethnic group's claim to penetrate and frame public policy. A state's urban governing ideology can either be ethnonational or civic.[3] In the first case, a single dominating ethnic group controls the government and policymaking apparatus, and morally based doctrines of that ethnonational group regarding sovereignty and cultural identity merge with the state's urban policy. Examples of ethnonationalist urban policy include apartheid Johannesburg and contemporary Jerusalem (Bollens 1998). In contrast, a civic ideology seeks to accommodate or transcend ethnonational ideologies. Examples of civic governing goals include the accommodation of linguistic and cultural differences in Montreal and Brussels. In contested societies and cities that seek the building of peaceful ethnic relations, the guiding ideology behind national and urban management will likely need to shift from ethnonationalist to civic and accommodative in intent.

Despite the benign intent behind civic ideology, its implementation through urban policy in formerly or currently contested cities is not straightforward. Ideology, to be actualized, must be translated into technical prescriptions that seek to move a

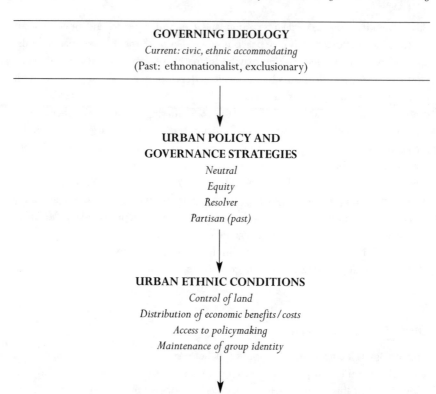

GOVERNING IDEOLOGY
Current: civic, ethnic accommodating
(Past: ethnonationalist, exclusionary)

**URBAN POLICY AND
GOVERNANCE STRATEGIES**
Neutral
Equity
Resolver
Partisan (past)

URBAN ETHNIC CONDITIONS
Control of land
Distribution of economic benefits / costs
Access to policymaking
Maintenance of group identity

PEACE-BUILDING
Impede or Facilitate

FIGURE 2.1   Urban Policy and Peace-Building

society, or in this case a city, toward those final goals or vision. Yet, civic goals pertaining to stabilization, improvement, and reconstruction of cities and their neighborhoods are fraught with ambiguity that may engender multiple interpretations as to which actions are appropriate to achieve chosen ends. The moral and implementation dimensions of ideology have been identified as "fundamental" and "operative," respectively (Seliger 1970). The problem for societies, and political leaders, is that operative ideology does not automatically proceed from the grand visions or moral ends asserted by fundamental ideology. Both liberal economies and communism espouse liberty and equality, yet propose drastically different means as the way to achieve them (Seliger 1970). Or, in other circumstances, equality between ethnic groups may be espoused morally as the best way to resolve polarization, yet how equity may be implemented in societies where there are significant historic imbalances does not proceed automatically from such overall moral agreement.[4]

In this study, I examine in two cities the motivations and intentions behind civic, ethnic-accommodating ideologies seeking to stabilize or reconstruct war-torn urban regions. I will document how these civic visions have been operationalized and carried out in the urban landscape. How is a potential post-conflict evolution of urban ethnic space to be managed so as to effectively transform an urban geography of strife? What urban policies are appropriate for stabilizing or reconstructing strife-torn cities so that urban management contributes to peace-making and peace-building efforts?

Fundamental ideology in an urban system is implemented primarily through urban planning and policy decisions that reify its vision on the ground. City planners and other administrative implementers of ideological goals seek to give concrete meaning to such ambitions as fairness and ethnic accommodation (in the case of civic ideology) or political control and ethnic separation (in the case of ethnonationalist ideology). Formal ideology, however, may not be readily translatable onto the urban landscape. The exercise of urban policy and planning may highlight difficulties in the implementation of a morally based fundamental ideology in a contested society. In particular, the complex interdependencies of an urban arena—economic, social, psychological—can make it exceedingly hard to carry out moral ideologies that seek accommodation or transcendence of ethnic differences. The strict territoriality or community contentiousness emblematic of urban civil war does not necessarily disappear with advances on a larger political front, nor do economic and budgetary forces necessarily lend themselves to the massive redistributive and reconstructive tasks often required to effectively transform a debilitated urban arena. The urban region and its spatial, economic, and social correlates of urban strife may distort and corrupt the efforts of a well-intentioned urban administration.

In this study, I examine the extent of use, and impacts, of three *urban policy and governance strategies*—neutral, equity, and resolver—that could be used to advance urban peace. A fourth strategy—a partisan approach—is discussed in light of its contrariness to peace-building and its past creation in many contested cities of urban obstacles to contemporary peace advancement. These models, derived from public administration and urban planning literatures and identified in Table 2.1, differ in their substantive goals, the extent to which they address root causes or urban symptoms of intergroup conflict, and in the degree to which they incorporate ethnic criteria or not.

A *neutral* urban strategy employs technical criteria in allocating urban resources and services, and distances itself from issues of ethnic identity, power inequalities, and political exclusion. The urban symptoms, not root causes, of sovereignty conflict would be addressed. Residents are treated within local planning processes as individuals rather than members of ethnic groups (M. Smith, 1969). Thus, planning acts as an ethnically neutral, or "color-blind," mode of state intervention responsive

TABLE 2.1   Urban Policy and Governance Strategies

Strategy	Tactics
Neutral	Address urban symptoms of ethnic conflict at *individual level.*
Equity	Address urban symptoms of ethnic conflict at *ethnic group level.*
Resolver	Address root causes/sovereignty issues.
Partisan	Maintain/increase disparities.

SOURCE: Adapted from Benvenisti, M. *Conflicts and Contradictions* (New York: Villard, 1986).

to individual-level needs and differences. Planners and policymakers act in pursuit of benevolent reform (Friedmann 1987). This is the traditional style of urban management and planning rooted in an Anglo-Saxon tradition, and commonly applied in liberal democratic settings (Yiftachel 1995). A government espousing a civic ideology of ethnic accommodation or transcendence may utilize this reform tradition, in full or in part, as a way to bring increased legitimacy to public authority in the reconstructive phase. A neutral urban strategy aimed at benevolent reform would seek to depoliticize territorial issues by framing urban problems as value-free, technical issues solvable through planning procedures and professional norms (Torgovnik 1990; Forester 1989; Nordlinger 1972). It would seek to avoid and prevent urban civil war through professional city-building methods responsive to individual needs on both sides in fair ways. Disagreements and negotiations between ethnic groups would likely be channeled by government toward day-to-day service delivery issues and away from remaining sovereignty considerations (Rothman 1992).

Planning based on the professional tenets of social reform is understood as the application of scientific knowledge to public affairs. To be most fruitful to the state, this function should not be interfered with by politicians or ordinary citizens lacking the expertise of trained planners and public administrators. In particular, the ability to engage in comprehensive and rational problem-solving distinguishes professional public servants from the shorter-term power games of politicians.[5] Frequently, the professional approach to public planning is a top-down, control-oriented one (Tugwell 1935; Simon 1947). Differences within this tradition occur over whether comprehensive, rational decisionmaking is possible (Lindblom 1959, 1977; March and Simon 1958; Etzioni 1968). However, these are more arguments over the best means toward incorporating rationality into public policymaking, not disagreements over the centrality of rationality itself.

Despite its appeal to governing regimes pursuing legitimacy and peace-building, the social conservatism and technical emphasis on land use and development characteristic of the professional strategy tend to limit its utility in addressing issues of race and ethnic relations (Thomas and Krishnarayan 1994; Davidoff 1965). Even in consensual societies, the color-blind approach of much planning has been found to be "insensitive to the systematically different needs and requirements of the population and, in particular, . . . some black and ethnic communities" (Thomas and Krishnarayan 1994). When applied to polarized, collectively segmented cities and societies, professional reform strategies become even more problematic because root causes of ethnic conflict remain unaddressed. In such circumstances, the pursuit of an overall "public interest" through rational analysis and action by the state may accentuate or reactivate preexisting intergroup differences and aggravate conflict because it may be construed as constituting intervention by a public authority deemed "illegitimate" by one ethnic group. Ethnic-neutrality of urban policy, foregoing group-based affirmative or remedial action, may be inadequate to offset historic and current inequalities. More problematic, however, is that treatment by government of socioeconomic and urban-based differences as individual-based, when in fact or perception they are primarily ethnic group–based, sidesteps core conflict issues at potentially great costs to the city and its residents.

A second model, the *equity* strategy, gives primacy to certain ethnic subgroups in the population in order to decrease historic and contemporary intergroup inequalities. The administrator uses equity-based criteria, such as an ethnic group's relative size or need, in allocating urban services and spending (Nordlinger 1972; Esman 1973). An overriding ethic of peace-building may require that preferential treatment be given to those with grievances in order to prevent a re-ignition of armed conflict (United Nations 1996a). Because they seek remediation and compensation for past hurts and wrongs, equity-based criteria will often be significantly different from the functional and technical criteria used by the ethnically neutral professional planner (Davidoff 1965; Krumholz and Forester 1990; Mier 1993; Krumholz and Clavel 1994). An equity planner is much more aware than a professional-technical planner of group-based inequalities and political imbalances in the city, and will recognize the needs for remediation and affirmative action policies based on group identity. Whereas the neutral planner holds close to technical and universalistic criteria, the equity planner will seek the inclusion of the disempowered at the decisionmaking table and a fairer distribution of societal benefits across groups in the city.

In its purest form, the equity urban strategy posits that city planners and administrators should be advocates for those local groups whose interests are traditionally neglected in the formulation and implementation of urban policy (Davidoff 1965). This model is "one infinitely more politicized, committed, and relevant than that offered by the pseudo-professionalism of contemporary practice" (Kiernan 1983, 85). Progressive planning targeted at positive discrimination is employed to lessen urban inequalities in efforts to create a more just city and society. Justice is a broad concept, and I do not attempt here to define its specific qualities. One can say with some assurance, however, that a just city is one that distributes resources in an equitable, fair, and impartial way. D. Smith (1994) states that social justice is manifest in reductions in inequality. Thus, urban policy should move the city closer toward equality of condition across individuals and groups through the disproportionate allocating of urban benefits to those least well-off. Basic human needs—public services, human rights, employment opportunities, food and shelter, and participation in decisionmaking—would be assured by urban development and planning policy.[6] According to D. Harvey (1973), "territorial social justice" is constituted through public spending and income distribution which meets basic human needs, has multiplicative positive impacts throughout the region, and targets extra resources to areas that have special difficulties due to their social or physical environment. He adds that the mechanisms for urban distribution (organizational and economic) should be such that the prospects of the least advantaged territory are as great as they are possible.

Equity planning applied in efforts to stabilize or reconstruct politically polarized cities aims to reduce the urban symptoms of the root conflict, such as intergroup disparities in public services, housing, education, and employment opportunities. This approach assumes that the conditions of ethnic conflict and tension reside, at least partially, in the objective economic disparities of the urban landscape. Ethnicity is thus not avoided as an allocation criterion. Indeed, public policies are designed to improve the urban existence and well-being of an historically subordinate ethnic population (the *out-group*). Such equity or progressive planning may possibly affect the outcome of larger political processes (Yiftachel 1989). This could occur through the incorporation of urban claims dealing with basic needs and fairness into larger negotiations concerning sovereignty and territoriality. Such a connection can be made because, as Friedmann (1992, 66) suggests, "basic needs are essentially political claims for entitlements." Equity planning may also be used by an empowered group in a less accommodating spirit to the extent that it is used in an effort to ameliorate the potential for urban conflict and unrest and thus defer the perceived need to engage in broader sovereignty and political discussions. Special attention to the urban needs of the out-group may be used to legitimize a contested government's control over the city.

There are potential problems inherent in a strategy of conflict attenuation seeking greater urban fairness and service distribution if it is not connected to negotiations over root political issues. In a politically polarized city, it is difficult to disentangle considerations of day-to-day urban issues and needs from the more basic considerations of power imbalance. Human needs in an urban area commonly transcend material conditions to include political and psychosocial elements of mutual respect and coexistence. An urban needs–based allocation of city resources may improve the material conditions of the out-group, but it utilizes a narrowly distributive conception of justice separated from its institutional and political foundations. There also are likely significant political obstacles to an historically empowered ethnic population (the *in-group*) willingly engaging in an equity approach that favors the out-group. In a polarized city, accommodation of the other side's needs may be seen by the in-group as state suicide. Targeting of resources to the out-group may actually mobilize or radicalize the subordinate population, which, in turn, can precipitate opposition from within the in-group to such special considerations (Weitzer 1990).[7] In this sense, urban equity strategies disconnected from political and territorial negotiations may be bounded by the political dynamics of the ethnic communities and may act as a flashpoint for urban unrest and state repression. Equity-based targeting may have to wait until the resolution of core political claims to the city.

The third model—a *resolver* strategy—is the most demanding. It seeks to transcend urban-based symptoms by emphasizing solutions to the root causes of urban polarization—political imbalances, subordination, disempowerment, and threatened group identity. In this way, it seeks to connect urban peace-building to national peacemaking. It is the only strategy of the three that attempts to resolve the conflict, as opposed to manage it. Unlike management of urban symptoms, conflict resolution requires getting to the root of the problem and points to an outcome that may be a permanent solution (Burton 1991). In polarized cities, the traditional paradigm of scientific-based and hierarchical city-building and planning is an important and visible manifestation of territorial and political power by a contested governing regime. Thus, as part of broader efforts to build peace in polarized environments, the resolver urban strategy seeks to reconceptualize the planning of cities and urban communities. The mechanisms and goals of city-building are to be restructured and transformed so that the city facilitates mutual empowerment and peaceful urban coexistence.

Urban policy and planning are positioned as an innovating public policy arena having the potential to empower subordinate urban groups and address root issues of conflict. Policy and planning mechanisms are restructured to facilitate direct collective action from below, not the imposition of scientific-based policies from above. A framework for alternative development may be utilized, geared toward helping the urban poor and disempowered (Friedmann 1992). An urban strategy oriented toward conflict resolution utilizes the concepts and practices of social mobilization, an approach of the far-left that departs substantially from traditional models of policymaking (Friedmann 1987). This model seeks not incremental reform of basic parameters, but rather emancipation and basic structural change that can confront and contradict traditional urban strategies. The model goes beyond the equity-based allocation of urban resources—with its focus on urban symptoms—to pursue urban empowerment for all ethnic groups in the city. A subordinated urban ethnic group makes an important jump from object to subject in moving from the equity approach to the resolver strategy.

In a resolver urban strategy, city issues and policymaking are connected to root political and territorial issues. For example, inadequate community development funding directed to particular ethnic neighborhoods would be linked to the lack of political representation of that group at the decisionmaking table. Urban professionals can play a significant role in documenting and validating each side's territorial and resource needs required for coexistent community vitality and detailing how current ethnonational conflict disrupts the proper functioning of ethnic communities and the city at large. Planning arguments can be brought to bear to outline the basic urban parameters of a sustainable and peaceful settlement, one which meets each side's needs for territorial jurisdiction, control of population movement, and access to resources and to adequate supplies and distribution of labor. Counterplanning (the development of alternative physical plans that refute and challenge government intent), lobbying, and legal challenges at national or international levels are some forms of resistance that can benefit most significantly from urban professional input. Here, urban specialists seek to overcome the systematic and structural distortions of overriding ideologies (Forester 1989), pointing out the unequal outcomes of seemingly "neutral" and "professional" techniques.

Because of their on-the-ground experience in dealing with urban proximity and explosiveness, urban policymakers and planners (both bureaucratic and nongovernmental) may be able to play key participatory roles in broader political negotiations over territory and sovereignty. Based on experimentation, innovation, and adaptation at the local level—what Friedmann (1987) labels "social learning"—urban policymaking may act as an energizer of a larger peace. Negotiation and mediation techniques that link urban policy conflicts to underlying structural conflict over sovereignty, territory, and empowerment can be adapted to larger geographic scales. Urban officials may also assist in efforts to reinterpret policy conflicts in terms other than "zero-sum," a key element of successful negotiation (Susskind and Cruickshank 1987; Kelman 1990). In polarized environments, there is often a territorial formulation needed in addition to urban service and policy agreements (Elazar 1980). In terms of urban governance, accommodation strategies would likely be used that acknowledge as valid both sides of the polarized environment (Lustick 1979). Cooperative or "consociational" design of urban and regional governance can utilize federalist principles that allocate and devolve public authority across different levels or foci of government (Lijphart 1977). For example, there might be the establishment of a degree of self-governance by ethnic groups within a functionally integrated city. Or, a two-tier system of metropolitan and local governance is created that is responsive to each side's territorial ambitions within a physically unpartitioned metropolis.

The resolver urban strategy is essentially confrontational of the status quo in its attempts to link scientific and technical knowledge to processes of system transformation. Such a strategy will not likely come initially from within a bureaucratic state, but would be created through the actions of nongovernmental planners, cross-ethnic political groups, and urban professionals from within the subordinated out-group. If a city regime is willing to engage in an adaptive organizational learning process aimed at conflict resolution, it can create nonhierarchical government structures that facilitate intergroup dialogue and change from below, such as community-based forums that are sources of input and interaction. The resolver strategy demands much change from urban professionals, asking them to transcend the stances—neutral professionalism and urban equalization—of the previous two strategies. The most advanced strategy in terms of its conciliatory potential, it requires that locally based planners engage in constructive intergroup dialogue in circumstances where there are no perceived outsiders. The resolver approach requires a professional role more of "umpire" of an arena of competition rather than a leader of one of the teams (Bailey 1969). Whether urban professionals can be effective umpires acceptable to both sides of the ethnic divide, and whether politically practical means exist by which urban-based issues can be connected to wider extra-local negotiation processes, will determine the success or failure of a conflict-resolution urban strategy.

All three urban policy approaches—neutral, equity, and resolver—represent distinct departures from urban policies utilized in biased pursuit of ethnonationalist goals. A *partisan* urban strategy chooses sides and is a regressive agent of change (Yiftachel 1995). In many cases, urban peace-building will need to confront and counteract the built and psychological legacies of biased city-building. Partisan policymaking furthers an empowered ethnic group's values and authority and rejects claims of the disenfranchised group. The city's governing ideology merges with the empowered group's ethnonationalist ideology. Domination strategies are applied to land use planning and regulation in order to entrench and expand territorial claims or enforce exclusionary control of access (Lustick 1979; Sack 1981). Public policies are endorsed which substantially restrict out-group economic, political, and land-based opportunities. Methods of "institutionalized dominance" provide monopoly or preferential access to the urban policymaking machinery for members of the dominant group (Esman 1973). There are cases where the tools used by partisan urban strategies are explicitly repressive, such as apartheid South Africa. In most cases, however, the important difference between partisan and neutral urban strategies lies not in their visible tools, but more covertly in the goals pursued and their handling of urban ethnicity. In other words, partisan planners may use many of the same tools as neutral strategists and speak a common language of objectivity and rationality. Nonetheless, these tools operationalize a fundamental ideology dominating of the urban landscape. Indeed, many urban planning tools emphasize regulation and control of land use and can thus supply important means to implement partisan goals of territorial control and subjugation. Tools used in public planning for reform and modernization can be expropriated to control an opposing ethnic group (Yiftachel 1995).

Planning provides partisan policymaking with more than the means of implementation, but also a mask of objectivity behind which discriminatory intent can be hidden. For example, seemingly neutral land development and ownership requirements applied by the dominating government can lead to unfair outcomes given contrasting cultural notions of basic urban resources such as land. In this way, technically defensible urban regulations can be used to further the partisan's territorial and political claims. Planning can play an instrumental role in legitimizing the maintenance of existing realities.[8] Planners may well profess to be acting professionally, in the sense of formulating or implementing urban policy in a rational way to improve a citywide public interest. In reality, however, such seemingly objective planning mechanisms may reinforce and reproduce basic societal inequalities because the fundamental ideology shapes what is acceptable on the urban scale.

Partisan planners act foremost as trustees or representatives of the state, and secondarily as urban managers. Planning procedures and tools are used to concretize an ethnonational ideology. At certain times, planning may be needed to address some of the urban contradictions created by ideologically led city-building. Urban planning may then even appear to run at cross-currents with the broader ideology in seeking to preserve certain urban qualities in the face of ideological imperatives. Nevertheless, this is more an issue of how to implement the fundamental ideology with a gentler face than it is an assault on the guiding ideology itself—a disagreement over means, not of partisan goals. Planning is there to further its own side's interests and goals through the imprimatur of professional and scientific expertise. Basic political issues become depoliticized and transformed into technical issues best left to the experts (Forester 1993). However, the "rationality" practiced by such experts is bounded politically by ideological dictates (Forester 1989).

In order for urban policy strategies to play a productive role in intergroup peace-building, partisanship in city-building must be overcome. In many cases, partisan planning has created severely unequal metropolises which now must somehow be normalized in the course of urban and regional peace-building. For partisanship to reign locally while national political negotiations advance would likely create severe drags on a peacemaking process. Neutral, equity, and resolver strategies will be more productive to peace-building, but will likely differ in their potential contributions and difficulty in implementation. Neutral policymaking requires the least of urban professionals because they are to stay removed from urban ethnic issues and consciousness. Equity planning recognizes urban ethnicity and its role in conflict, staying at the level of symptom in remedying the urban patient. The resolver strategy confronts root political issues, but may be asking too much of urban professionals in making the link between the practical and the political. In a sense, neutral policymaking and partisan policymaking represent ends of a continuum, the first being blind to social differentiations such as ethnicity, the second obsessed by them.[9] Yet, in a city and country attempting to overcome con-

flict and inequality, it does not appear that a new governing regime can simply replace partisanship with neutrality. Such a shift would not recognize past group-
based hurts, current disparities in group perceptions and conditions, and the in-
termingling of the seemingly mundane issues of urban governance with the robust
concerns of negotiated peacemaking.

Building or Impeding Urban Peace

Figure 2.2 focuses on the effects of urban policy upon: (1) *urban ethnic conditions*
(social, economic, political, and cultural); and (2) *urban peace-building* (advancement of urban intergroup stability and tolerance). Figure 2.2 is a more detailed
look at the lower half of Figure 2.1.

The first four factors involve *urban ethnic conditions* related to social, cultural, and
economic deprivation and the unfulfillment of basic human needs for identity and
purpose. The relative deprivation theory of ethnic conflict posits such unjust disparities and unmet human needs as a primary motivational force of political action (Gurr
1993; Burton 1990). I now explicate how urban policy may affect each type of urban
ethnic condition—territoriality, economic distribution, policymaking access, and
group identity. Then, I discuss how city policy and governance, and the urban conditions they create, may affect the possibility and sustainability of *urban peace-building*.

Urban policy most concretely affects the ethnic conditions of the urban environment through its significant influence on *control of land and territoriality* (A.
Murphy 1989; Yiftachel 1992; Gurr 1993; Williams 1994). Territorial obstacles to
urban peace-building can be significant, requiring urban policy to confront directly issues of urban territory and land control. Ethnic territoriality can be sustained by community will or through segregatory market forces that relegate certain groups to specific areas. The psychopolitical needs of residents in ethnic
neighborhoods (in the first case) and the imperatives of the free economic market
(in the second case) must be effectively addressed in seeking to restructure the urban system and its stringent ethnic geography.

Commonly, partisan urban territorial policies have been implemented in contested cities to reify power and enforce control over an urban out-group (Sack
1986). Such policies have created urban frameworks that foment ethnic mistrust
and conflict (Yiftachel 1992). Two common techniques of territorial control
amidst ethnic tension aim to: (1) alter the spatial distribution of ethnic groups;
and (2) manipulate jurisdictional boundaries to politically incorporate or exclude
particular ethnic residents (Coakley 1993). Urban policies can significantly manipulate ethnic geographies in cases where an empowered group seeks to dominate a subordinate group through its control over land and the planning machinery. Control over human settlement patterns can be exercised primarily through
two functions of government—regulatory and developmental. In the first case,

---

URBAN ETHNIC CONDITIONS

CONTROL OVER LAND / TERRITORIAL JURISDICTION
Settlement of vacant lands; control of settlement patterns; dispossession from land; control of landownership; determination of planning boundaries; ethnic boundaries and identities.

DISTRIBUTION OF ECONOMIC BENEFITS AND COSTS
Allocation of "externalities"; magnitude and geographic distribution of urban services and spending.

ACCESS TO POLICYMAKING
Formal and informal participation processes; inclusion/exclusion from political process; influence of nongovernmental organizations.

MAINTENANCE OF GROUP IDENTITY AND VIABILITY
Maintenance or threat to collective ethnic rights and identity; education, religious expression, cultural institutions.

URBAN PEACE-BUILDING

FACILITATE OR IMPEDE
Decrease in organized resistance to urban regime; loosening of ethnic territoriality; lessening of interethnic disparities; greater interethnic political inclusion and cooperation; growing respect for collective ethnic rights.

FIGURE 2.2   Urban Ethnic Conditions and Peace-Building

urban governments' designation of land use locations and densities on urban plans, and their granting of building permits, influence the rate and type of growth of opposing ethnic groups, and the extent of ethnic spatial mix. At the same time, existing residents can be internally resettled through such means as demolitions and expropriations done in the name of orderly development or, more generally, the "public interest." Government also has the direct ability to support and facilitate new growth acting in its capacity of developer. In this case, government can expropriate or publicly acquire urban land and then bring to bear several financial tools to subsidize development at locations and levels that it deems desirable or necessary. The combination of a government's regulatory and developmental efforts can significantly affect in a polarized city the demographic ratios between the two sides, change the scale of focus of planning efforts, and reinforce or modify the ethnic identity of specific geographic subareas.

An urban government involved in active territorial policies may seek penetration or dispersal of an opposing ethnic group in order to diminish its group coherence and ability to coalesce politically (Murphy 1989). Penetration and dispersal entail two contrasting projects and illustrate that there is no clear line from the goal of city political control to specific territorial policies. Penetration involves placing members of the dominant ethnicity into areas having an opposing group majority. Such a strategy seeks to fragment or contain the opposition group geographically and to increase the dominant party's surveillance of the out-group. Because it is disruptive of ethnic territoriality, this strategy is potentially conflictual. Nevertheless, it may be deemed necessary by the dominating group because an opposing group's consolidation of ethnic territory in or near a polarized city is viewed by the empowered group as a threat to urban and regional political stability. In contrast, a dispersal territorial strategy uses different means toward the same goal of city political control. Here, the effort is to territorially displace and disconnect the out-group from the urban system. Separation is viewed by the dominant group as both more politically stabilizing and capable of excluding the subordinate group from a city's system of electoral and material benefits. In either territorial strategy—penetration or dispersal—administrative limits on residential migration by the out-group into the city are necessary to solidify urban political control. This usually entails strict city "residency" requirements, tied to historic occupancy or urban employment status.

In addition to its tangible effects on land and territory, urban policy substantially shapes the *distribution of economic benefits and costs* and the allocation of urban service benefits (Yiftachel 1992; Stanovcic 1992; Gurr 1993). Urban land use and growth policies affect such aspects as the accessibility and proximity of residents and communities to employment, retail, and recreation; the distribution of land values; and the economic spin-offs (both positive and negative) of development. The planning and siting of economic activities can significantly influence both the daily urban behavior patterns and residential distributions of ethnic groups. Economic nodes have the ability to either integrate or separate the ethnic landscape. For example, major employment or commercial centers could be placed along ethnic territorial interfaces as a way to turn formerly "no-man's land" into mutually beneficial spaces of intergroup economic and social interactions. In contrast, economic development can be encouraged amidst a subordinate group's territory as a way to solidify or reinforce intergroup separation. At the same time, urban service and capital investment decisions—related to housing, roads, schools, and other community facilities—directly allocate urban advantages (and disadvantages) across ethnic communities. The activity-allocation power of urban government may be used to consolidate intergroup inequalities across a polarized city's ethnic geography by distributing benefits and advantages disproportionately to the ethnic in-group. Alternatively, a benign urban administration seeking urban fairness can allocate activities and spending in order to equalize urban benefits (and costs) across ethnic areas. This will likely mean that urban spending and policy are directed disproportionately in the short term in favor of the subordinate group in an effort to remedy past inequalities.

Urban policy and planning processes can have substantial effects on the distribution of local political power and *access to policymaking* (Yiftachel 1992; Stanovcic 1992; Gurr 1993). Models of conflict regulation commonly applied at national levels (summarized by O'Leary and McGarry 1995) help illuminate different participatory and political options at the city government level. In many contested cities, there may exist a legacy of "hegemonic control" by one ethnic group where the opposing group is fully excluded from the political decisionmaking process. This exclusion can result from direct exclusionary actions of the empowered group or through the out-group's own decision not to cooperate with an authority it does not recognize as legitimate. Even in cases where full, bi-ethnic electoral participation does occur, reliance on majority-minority democratic norms is problematic because cleavages across ethnic groups are rare and cross-community coalition-building is limited. Reliance on majority voting in ethnically segmented cities may thus result in de facto hegemonic control.

In building urban peace, several options are available to replace counterproductive hegemonic control. First, "third-party intervention" removes contentious local government functions such as housing, employment, and services from control by *either* of the warring parties and empowers a third-party overseer to manage the urban region. Sometimes, in the case of Nicosia (Cyprus), the overseer may be the United Nations; in other cases, such as Belfast (Northern Ireland), the urban manager has been a distant yet intentionally benign government—Great Britain. Urban "cantonization" can occur through the devolution of some municipal powers to neighborhood-based community councils or boroughs, which would advise the city government on "own-community" affairs.[10] Urban cantonization is capable of more effectively recognizing the different ethnic communities and needs in a city, and it could moderate some of the adverse effects of an otherwise hegemonic city government. Yet, such devolution may facilitate or disguise continued control by the current governing regime. "Federalization" also implies separate domains of formal public authority and would likely involve the creation of a metropolitan government to manage an urban system of separate ethnic municipalities. "Consociationalism" (Lijphart 1968, Nordlinger 1972) is a fourth political model. It is based on accommodation or agreement between political elites over a governance arrangement capable of managing ethnic differences.[11] Of particular note is the likely utility of local power-sharing arrangements as a local authoritarian or "ethnic" state shifts toward majoritarian democracy, and the usefulness of ethnic proportionality standards in decreasing the bias commonly seen in the urban policing of contested cities.

In circumstances where access to policymaking has been substantially curtailed for one urban ethnic group, pressure for change often is redirected through nongovernmental channels. The web of nongovernmental and voluntary associations that deal with urban issues such as community development, land and housing, cultural identity, social service delivery, and human rights protection constitutes a polarized city's "civil society" (Weitzer 1990; Friedman 1991; Partrick 1994). This organizational web can be an important source of glue holding together a threatened or disempowered minority, providing access to international organizations and their funding, and advocating for change in the urban system through documentation, demonstrations, and protests. Once overt conflict is past and society moves toward accommodation, a city government may affect positively the development and maintenance of such a civil society through the granting of direct funding or technical assistance to community organizations, or negatively through intimidation and restrictions on the receipt of capacity-building international funding for organizations operating within the boundaries of the former contested city.

Maintenance of group identity is critical to interethnic relations in a polarized city. It constitutes in Figure 2.2 the final aspect of urban ethnic conditions affectable by urban policy and planning. Each side in an urban system looks for breathing room in terms of group-based cultural expression and identity. Collective ethnic rights such as education, language, press, cultural institutions, and religious beliefs and customs are connected to potent ideological content. Their exercise of these rights is viewed as a critical barometer by an ethnic group of an urban government's treatment of their rights. In a polarized city, such group identity is reinforced through ethno-nationalist expressions in the urban landscape. These can include symbolic buildings linked to, or hosting, opposition political parties; administrative centers of pseudo-state activity; or murals and other graphic expressions of resistance and territoriality.

Collective identity is connected to relative group worth and is more psychological than the three more material urban conditions previously discussed. For an urban subgroup which feels threatened, these psychological needs pertaining to group viability and cultural identity can be as important as the territorial and objective needs pertaining to land, housing, and economic opportunities. At the same time, the social-psychological content of urban group identity is not immune to concrete government actions. Indeed, it has characteristics that can be enhanced or disrupted through urban policy and planning actions. Urban public policy, for instance, can affect important forms of ethnic expression through its influence on public education (particularly dealing with language) or through its regulatory control over the urban side-effects (such as noise or traffic disruption) of religious observances. Urban service delivery decisions dealing with the location of proposed new religious, educational, and cultural institutions, or the closing down of ones deemed obsolete, can indicate to urban residents the government's projected ethnic trajectories of specific neighborhoods and can substantially threaten ethnic group identity.

The identity, or psychological, needs of an urban ethnic group can be either consolidated or fragmented by where city government places its jurisdictional or planning boundaries. A city can gerrymander its borders to exclude a major share of an out-group's population from the "city"; or, it may enact land use regulations that restrict and spatially fragment urban out-group neighborhoods within the city. Inversely, cities can also redraw boundaries to bring antagonistic sides together under a single city government having a common fiscal base. Here, the effort may be related to attempts to forge a new transcendent cross-group identity as municipal residents. For there to be attenuation of ethnic conflict, a polarized city must be able to manage not only the material, but also the psychological and identity-related, conditions of its antagonistic sides. Even if urban planners and their political leaders are willing to engage in this balancing act, however, they may well be incapable of incorporating nontechnical and subjective aspects of community and group identity into planning processes traditionally biased toward objective and often quantifiable distributive criteria.

These urban ethnic conditions—land control, economic distribution, policy-making access, and group identity—can be important correlates of *urban peace-building* (see Figures 2.1 and 2.2). Movement toward peace in a city can be indicated by increased flexibility or transcendence of ethnic geography, lessening of actual and perceived inequalities across ethnic groups, greater interethnic political inclusion, and growing tolerance for collective ethnic rights. In contrast, signs of urban peace impedance include ethnic territorial hardening, solidification of urban material and political inequalities, and erosion of out-group identity. The magnitude of political mobilization and resistance, affected both by urban grievances and the organizing capacity of energized ethnic groups and leaders (Tilly 1978), is the most visible indication of progress (or retardation) in urban peace-building. Mobilization reflects an ethnic group's capacity—in terms of organization and commitment—to engage in political action and resistance. Such engagement includes nonviolent actions such as verbal opposition, demonstrations, strikes, and rallies; violent protests such as symbolic destruction of property, sabotage, and rioting; and active rebellion in the forms of terrorism, guerrilla activity, and protracted civil war (Gurr 1993).

Whether city policy facilitates or impedes urban peace-building is expected to be dependent upon the policy strategies chosen; the spatial, economic, and psychological conditions and contradictions they generate in the built landscape; and how these affect the organization and mobilization of urban opposition groups. Urban actions are capable of both producing a widely shared sense of deprivation conducive to mass communal resistance and of providing a platform for the purposeful and rational actions of inflammatory ethnic group leaders. In the early stages of organized political resistance, objective urban conditions related to deprivation may be critical. However, once collective political action is under way, these objective conditions can pale in significance to factors related to group organization and leadership (Gurr 1993). In other words, political organization related to ethnicity can reach a point beyond which betterment of objective conditions through urban policy would have only marginal effects on the amelioration of urban ethnic tension. This means that the internal political dynamics and needs of the out-group's political organization, as well as the material needs of its city residents, must be accommodated in urban peace-building efforts. State urban policies can structure the local political system in ways that either restrict or enable out-group political opportunities, and they can frustrate or cultivate the development of out-group organizations and networks that comprise the collective building blocks of political expression (McAdam, McCarthy, and Zald 1996; Tarrow 1994; Tilly 1978). Urban policies can internally fragment the out-group's urban political community through planning regulations that spatially separate out-group neighborhoods or through the preferential channeling of urban benefits to more "moderate" subgroups. Alternatively, urban peace-building policies can provide political opportunities for the former out-group through the redrawing of electoral boundaries, the provision of multiple and decentralized layers of local governance, or by nurturing nongovernmental organizations aligned with the out-group.

Because material grievance and political disenchantment can both contribute to regime resistance, urban peace strategies must restructure both the physical city and the political relationships within it. They must create both material conditions ameliorative of political grievance and a restructured relationship between urban out-group leaders and the new governing regime. Accordingly, I seek in this study to detail the effects of government policies on both the material and psychological states of urban residents, and on the characteristics of the out-group's community organization and the coherency of its political expression and actions.[12]

This chapter has described a process whereby a governing regime's effort to transcend or integrate competing ethnic visions is implemented in a strife-torn urban region. Cities and their constituent parts are sluggish and contain legacies from before and during active conflict. The change from a contested city to a post-conflict city likely does not occur overnight, nor is the transition path leading from one to the other clearly articulated. Transitions must be carefully managed by a governing regime, lest it create new sources of tension or introduce new forms of oppression and abnormality. The urban strategy chosen by the urban governing regime—whether neutral, equity-based, or resolver—plays an instrumental role in attempts to operationalize the vision of a post-conflict city. These urban strategies have independent effects on local conditions—ethnic territoriality, economic fairness, policymaking access, cultural identity, and the city-specific forms and dynamics of political resistance and mobilization—that can facilitate or impede peaceful intergroup coexistence in the city. Urban policy operates at a specific level of analysis and interaction having dynamics, participants, and consequences different than found at regional or national levels. City policymaking may thus be a contributor to the advancement or retardation of peace among antagonistic peoples, and not necessarily subordinate to larger diplomatic maneuvering.

Notes

1. The United Nations (Boutros-Ghali 1992) differentiates between peacemaking (resolving issues that led to the conflict) and peace-building (rebuilding institutions and infrastructures).

2. Unfortunately, this relationship could be reversed. A larger national-level peace process may be held hostage by nonresolution of urban political and territorial issues.

3. I parallel Lijphart's (1977) discussion of nationalism here, in which he differentiates between an "ethnic" or exclusive nationalism and a "civic" or inclusive one.

4. For example, should policy seek equality of opportunity or equality of outcome? Should policy favor removal of discriminatory barriers only, or also take remedial action to compensate for past injustice?

5. Rationality is a key concept of public planning, often denoting the application of verifiable scientific or technical knowledge to the decisionmaking process. It often also implies a style of analysis that is comprehensive and logical (Friedmann 1987).

6. The idea that there should be minimum standards dealing with basic human needs and rights has been endorsed by the United Nations in 1966 in its *Covenant on Economic, Social and Cultural Rights* and *Covenant on Civil and Political Rights*, both of which are legally binding on those countries ratifying them. The International Labour Office (1977) has also proposed and defined a human-needs approach to economic development.

7. This predicted sequence of events is similar to Gurr's (1993) finding that the liberalization of a repressive regime may facilitate mobilization for violent out-group protest which, in turn, can result in the reimposition of coercive rule.

8. This role of planning as legitimating ethnonationalist ideology is parallel to the structuralist or radical critique of urban planning as handmaidens to capitalistic ideology in Western world democracies (Harvey 1973; Piven and Cloward 1971; Saunders 1979).

9. Du Toit (1995) asserts the first would be engaged in by an "autonomous" state; the second by an "ethnic" state.

10. Urban cantonization requires greater devolution of authority than the more common and simpler decentralization of city administrative offices across the ethnic landscape.

11. Elements of urban consociational democracy can be found in Brussels (Belgium) and Montreal (Canada).

12. It is not my intention here to calculate the relative contributions to ethnic conflict of urban conditions, on the one hand, and aspects of an ethnic out-group's political organization and leadership, on the other (see Rule 1988 for an articulation of "relative deprivation" and "political mobilization" theoretical camps). Rather, I am interested in how urban policies may attenuate each of these antecedents of ethnic conflict.

3

Belfast and Johannesburg

I selected Belfast and Johannesburg for study for four reasons. First, each urban region is the most populated within its country and has encapsulated deep-rooted cleavages based on competing nationalisms and arguments over sovereignty or state legitimacy. In Belfast, the stances of pro-British Protestants and pro-Irish Catholics have left little room for political compromise. In Johannesburg, a crushingly exclusionist white Afrikaner nationalism collided with a more inclusive, civic nationalism espoused by the major black political party. Second, each city provides multi-decade accounts of urban planning and management in contested bicommunal environments. In many polarized cities in other countries, the existence of unstable governing regimes prevents analysis of the long-term planning function. Third, since the study relies strongly on face-to-face interviews, the case study cities were chosen to minimize communication difficulties owing to language. Fourth, each city has been engrossed in a transition process tied to movement on a broader political front and thus provides the opportunity to study urban policymaking amid larger efforts at peacemaking.

The Belfast interviews occurred in early 1995, about five months after ceasefires announced first by the Provisional Irish Republican Army (IRA) and then subsequently by loyalist paramilitaries. During my research stay, the British and Irish governments released their Joint Framework Documents, which were intended to move political discussions toward some mutually agreeable solution. This tenuous peace was ended in February 1996 with the reemergence of Republican hostilities, which substantially retarded normalization and improvement of community relations that may have occurred in Belfast during the one and one-half years of ceasefires. After three years of on-again, off-again ceasefires and political negotiations, ideas in the Documents supportive of democratic provincial government and cross-border institutions were eventually incorporated into the April 1998 *Agreement Reached in the Multi-Party Negotiations*. This agreement, approved by Northern Ireland voters in May 1998, is an attempt to restructure Northern Ireland governance in a way mutually agreeable to both Protestants and Catholics. Monumental challenges remain in terms of how to put this agreement into effect and how any provincial or local government in Northern Ireland, no matter how it is constituted, can formulate and implement public policy that accommodates the needs and perceptions of both sides.

The Johannesburg interviews occurred in mid-1995, about fifteen months after the first truly democratic national and provincial elections in South Africa's history. Nelson Mandela's African National Congress had gained political control of the country's legislature and a lion's share of provincial legislatures. The country was by then being run by a power-sharing national government, to be in existence for the first five years of the country's democratic life. During my research stay, a transitional set of appointed local governments was in the process of restructuring urban governance and policy amid preparations for democratic local elections. One month after my in-country research, democracy penetrated its last level—that of metropolitan and local governments—when local elections were held in most parts of South Africa, Johannesburg included. The larger transitions within which the two urban systems exist provide a unique opportunity to not just look backward at the effects of urban policy, but also forward toward possible different urban futures and the role government policy might play in them. I believe strongly that this transitional mood added greatly to the rich and oftentimes self-critical evaluation by those interviewed of the role—past and potential—of government policy amidst ethnic contest.

The two cities share legacies of cultural cleavage, but differ in their political contexts—Belfast entrenched in the uncertain early stages of transition; Johannesburg engaged in post-resolution reconciliation. In beginning a profound redefinition of the parameters of interethnic relationships, South Africa appears to be further along the peacemaking continuum than Northern Ireland. Whereas Johannesburg policymakers are engaged in intergroup reconciliation and urban restructuring, Belfast officials are necessarily focused on stabilizing, not transcending, intergroup relations. During field research, Belfast was seeking to bare-knuckle abstain from conflict absent resolution of core political issues, while Johannesburg was in a recovery stage, having addressed a set of core problem issues sufficiently to jump to another level of awareness. The contrasting political contexts of the two cities provide the ability to study, at different points along a peacemaking continuum, the opportunities (and impediments) that urban policymaking contributes to urban and regional peace.

Belfast and Johannesburg both constitute central stages or arenas for the wider conflict impacting the country or region as a whole because they are both economically dominant centers, and in the case of Belfast, the governmental center. Belfast's size, symbolism, and religious mix make it the most important stage upon which the Northern Ireland conflict is being performed. Larger peace appears improbable without an effective addressing of the differential needs of the two religious and political communities in Belfast. Johannesburg is the most powerful economic metropolis in sub-Saharan Africa, bears key historic markers and memories from the apartheid struggle, and exhibits gross disparities in wealth and human condition. How this urban region is spatially, politically, and economically restructured will likely be a critical influence on the reconciliation challenge facing South Africa in the twenty-first century. Common to both case studies is that the urban systems function as physically unpartitioned wholes while the perceived environments have been one of polarization. No impenetrable physical boundaries are present to separate the conflicting parties.[1]

One delimiting factor in the examination of the cities is the time periods that I chose to study. In the Belfast case, I concentrate on the period from 1972, when Britain assumed direct rule over Northern Ireland. In Johannesburg, I focus on urban policy since de facto urban apartheid started to break down in the mid-1980s. I discuss earlier periods during the twentieth century in each city in terms of the legacies and dilemmas they produce for urban policymakers in the time periods of focus. Thus, for Belfast, the legacy of Unionist-majority Northern Irish governance (1920–1972) is examined. And, in Johannesburg, today's urban policy choices are severely constrained by the legacy of formal apartheid practiced from 1948 to the early 1990s. Although these earlier phases constitute important and essential background, they are not the main stories of this investigation. Rather, the stories here concern how *current regimes* approach and utilize urban policy in the context of historically based ethnic conflict.

It was not possible to address each ethnic or racial conflict in its full richness. To do so would require accounting of Catholic-Protestant relations since the Protestant plantations in Ulster province over 450 years ago and black-white relations in South Africa since the introduction of Europeans over 350 years ago. I suggest that full portrayals of each conflict's complexities would divert attention from my true focus and purpose—urban policy under current regimes during the last three decades. At the same time, I assert that current urban policy circumstances can be studied effectively under their own terms, not those of the historic past, however much those historical antecedents affect what the "city" is today. Indeed, part of the solution to these intractable urban conflicts may require an "intentional forgetfulness," or more majestically stated, a forgiveness, concerning past injustices and harms. Debates over contested cities are so difficult because such deliberations concern not just a city's present and future, but its past as well. A disentangling of the past from current and future urban strategies appears a requisite to successfully negotiating these cities of polarized hostilities.

Research Methods

The case study research method is employed because it is most appropriate for the cross-national study of policy processes (Masser 1986; Cropper 1982). This comparative project will add to the body of knowledge about the differing contexts within which urban policy and planning practice operates cross-nationally. It seeks to escape the assumptions and values of many single-country urban planning studies, bound as they are to a particular context and stage in the development of planning thought (Alterman 1992). I attempt to document the anatomy and effect of ameliorating and exacerbating policy strategies that transcend particular urban and ideological contexts while, at the same time, acknowledging the unique national contexts within which the two cities operate. I suspect that there are aspects of professional planning and policy processes that can be inherently harmful or beneficial to urban intergroup relations in ethnically polarized environments.

Field research consisted of three months of in-country research in each city.[2] The primary information source for this study is the knowledge and experience of key individuals involved in urban policy and administration. The main research tool was the face-to-face interview. Seventy-one interviews are used to construct an ethnographic account of urban policymaking amidst societal reconstruction and political strife, based on close observation of agents' own knowledge and understanding of their actions. I was most assuredly interested in the complex objective realities and influences in these cities. In addition, however, I was curious about how the interviewees made sense of their everyday activities and professional roles. I sought to observe and understand the organizational, cultural, and historical context within which governmental and nongovernmental planners operate. In particular, I observed closely the interplay between the professional norms and values of many policymaking roles and the more emotion-filled ideological imperatives which impinge daily upon the professional's life. The distortions, the omissions, the emphases on some issues and not others, and how urban issues and constituents are defined are all part of the story I wish to tell of urban policymaking amidst contested ethnicities.

The depth of interethnic realities, and the time-consuming nature of interview scheduling and questioning, demanded several intensive months of research in each location. In addition to allowing for face-to-face interviewing, in-country residence facilitated my immersion in the intriguing day-to-day conditions and concerns of "polarized" urban life, as expressed by public officials and people on the street, and through popular media. Collaboration with academic institutions was an essential part of each research stay and deepened the research experience. I used as a work base the Department of Geography at The Queen's University of Belfast; and the Department of Geography and Environmental Studies at University of the Witwatersrand, Johannesburg. Both institutions provided research hospitality, a valuable set of initial community contacts, and an academic base of office support which facilitated my interview scheduling.

My research goals are both descriptive and prescriptive. In each case study, I investigate the influence of ethnic polarization on urban policy and the effects these policies have had on the nature and level of ethnic conflict. I explore this relationship between ethnic nationalism and urban policy in the contemporary periods of the two cities. I examine how urban policymakers acknowledge and treat issues of urban ethnicity amid unstable or transforming political contexts. I seek to develop recommendations, regarding policy goals and implementation means, that would increase the ability of urban policy strategies to build urban peace and lessen deep-rooted ethnic conflict in meaningful and long-term ways. I am curious whether urban-based strategies provide prototypes or lessons for de-escalating ethnic confrontations at extra-urban (i.e., regional and national) levels. Because polarized cities are important microcosms of regional and international conflict, the usefulness of this work is expected to transcend local contexts and extend to regional and national debates over ethnic conflict management.

A set of research issues was compiled prior to field research to provide a framework for interview and secondary research. These issues are outlined in Table 3.1 and described more fully in Appendix 1.

The study investigates the influence of urban ethnicity on the city's institutional context, formulation of development goals, public agenda-setting, decisionmaking, and policy implementation. I concurrently evaluate the changes to city policymaking which are occurring, or may occur, in response to larger peacemaking advances. Throughout, the focus is on how ethnicity has permeated the goals and processes of urban management and control, and how contemporary urban decisions may facilitate or impede opportunities for conflict alleviation at local and regional geographies.

Contextual factors institutionally and legally structure the decisionmaking environment. Legal frameworks and city and neighborhood organizational arrangements may either condone institutional differentiation or seek to integrate or unify ethnic groups within a common public domain. In defining *policy issues and goals* in an ethnically polarized city, urban policymakers and administrators must take a position on ethnicity. Such a position can run the gamut from acknowledging explicitly the presence and effects of ethnic fractures to one that seeks to depoliticize ethnicity by emphasizing universalism and an overarching public interest. Policy goals articulate the city's governing ideology as ethnonationalist or civic. *Urban decisionmaking* is composed initially of public agenda-setting, wherein local policy and planning alternatives to be considered can be restricted by ethnonational and political realities. For those alternatives evaluated, decisionmaking rules—based commonly on technical or equity criteria—are then applied that expose most directly a governing regime's tactics and rationales. The next set of questions—*policy outcomes*—explores the implementation of policy by administrative agents, and constitutes an important lens through which to evaluate the relationship between government goals and their urban operationalization and outcomes. Here, I closely examine on-the-ground outcomes

TABLE 3.1   Guiding Research Issues

Contextual Factors
  Ethnicity and legal frameworks
  Urban institutional differentiation
  Basic values

Policy Issues and Goals
  Urban ethnic issues
  Treatment of ethnic conflict
  The city's interest—policy goals and objectives
  Citizen participation—processes

Urban Decisionmaking
  Agenda-setting
  Decisionmaking rules
  Planning/policymaking roles
  Territorial policies

Policy Outcomes
  Implementation
  Results
  National-local intergovernmental relations

Conflict Outcomes and Mechanisms
  Patterns of conflict amelioration (intensification)
  Formal mechanisms for reducing conflict
  Informal mechanisms for reducing conflict
  Intraethnic effects. Crosscutting cleavage patterns

Community Dynamics and Organization
  Intersection of national and local interests
  Community organization in a controlled environment
  Restructuring community

Change and Evolution
  Changes in urban policy amid transition
  Changes in planning strategies
  Change—underlying factors
  Change—effect on ethnic conflict

NOTE: See Appendix 1 for expanded outline of research questions.

in terms of the distribution across ethnic communities of land use planning restrictions, building permit allowances, housing development, economic activities, transportation, and urban services.

Questions focused on *conflict outcomes and mechanisms* do not evaluate the direct on-the-ground outcomes of urban policy decisions, but how particular policies affect the nature and level of ethnic conflict and tension in the city. Objective and political-psychological outcomes of policy can be significantly different in contested cities because any extension of public authority—even one premised on a criterion of urban fairness—may be deemed as illegitimate and stimulative of resistance and conflict. Accordingly, assessment by government of policy implementation may include ways to contain conflict resulting from it, so as to avoid breakdown of the planning policy. Such mechanisms for coping with ethnic conflict during policy implementation may utilize governmental channels of interethnic mediation or informal contacts between government and minority elites. Also salient within this line of questioning is the fact that public policy cannot only exacerbate friction between ethnic communities, but also internally divide ethnic groups or create communities of interests that cut across the ethnic divide. The next set of issues relates to *community dynamics and organization* and explores survival techniques used by the historically subordinate (or "out-group") population and the forms of community mobilization that resulted. Questions also concern how ethnic community groups can shift from being solely organs of protest and resistance to constructive coparticipants in the creation of alternative urban scenarios. The intersection within each ethnic group of national and local interests is also a salient point of investigation; urban-based interests and initiatives may act either to reinforce or inhibit national political interests and strategies.

The final set of inquiries explores actual or potential *change and evolution* in the relationship between urban policy strategies and ethnicity. I am curious here about the perceived role that urban policymaking should play as part of larger peacemaking and peace-building efforts. Do urban officials view city actions as progressively leading or necessarily lagging changes in basic political parameters? Planning goals and strategies may shift over time due to changes in economic or political conditions; public opinion; or feedback documenting previous policy's damaging effects on the urban intergroup coexistence. Change may be either progressive, moving the urban system closer to political resolution or at least social accommodation, or regressive, tightening further the opportunities for coexistent viability of antagonistic urban communities. I am interested in whether urban policymaking is capable of change in those circumstances where their actions appear to be retarding improvement in interethnic relations. Acting within unstable or shifting political frameworks, it is significant whether urban policymakers and planners adopt a narrow vision of their roles or a position more conducive to change that facilitates problem reframing and social learning.

I utilize urban planning as the main analytical lens in this study because this function of government, through its direct and tangible effects on ethnic geography, can clearly reveal the intent and role of municipal government in a contested city. Plans and decisionmaking procedures are in effect formalizations of often unwritten patterns of power, and thus concretize or reify abstract notions of control

and territoriality. The label "urban planner," in this project, encompasses all officials (government and nongovernmental) involved in the anticipation of a city's or
urban community's future and preparation for it.[3] The category includes, within
government, town and regional planners, urban administrators and policymakers,
and national and regional-level urban policy officials. Outside government includes community spokespeople, project directors, and staff within nongovernmental, community, or voluntary sector organizations; scholars in urban and ethnic studies; and business community participants. The primary urban public
policies examined have direct and tangible influences on ethnic geography and
group identity. They are:

- land use planning
- promotion of real estate development
- economic development
- housing production and allocation
- capital facility planning
- social service delivery
- community participation and empowerment
- municipal government organization[4]

Land use planning by government designates and regulates areas in a city in order
to allocate various types and densities of urban activities, such as residential, commercial, and industrial. It expresses government's intent as to what its future pattern of land uses should be, and identifies the principles and standards that should
be applied in the development or conservation of specific areas. Land use planning
templates overlaid atop the strict territoriality of polarized cities can produce an
uneven and inflammatory pattern of advantage and disadvantage across ethnic communities. *Promotion of real estate development* positions government in the role of
proactive facilitator of development rather than as passive regulator of growth.
Government acts in its capacity as developer by sponsoring, subsidizing, and/or
entering into partnerships with the private sector to build new housing projects,
redevelop deteriorated inner-city areas, or stimulate economic activities. Such
public facilitation of new development in ethnically charged environments may significantly reinforce or modify the ethnic identity of specific geographic subareas.

Economic development policies include government actions that help develop sites
for economic activities, and numerous other public actions that create urban environments attractive to private investment. These include public programs dealing
with the upgrading of transportation links that improve access by economic firms to
resource bases, labor pools, and customer markets; labor force education and training policies; site-specific improvements; the provision of tax breaks and other subsidies; and the maintenance of a general sense of social and economic stability to an-

chor private investment. The location of jobs within a specific ethnic population's territorial space can assure continued population growth for that group. Or, by government promotion of new jobs near out-group locations, economic policies can be used to assure continued separation of one group from another. In terms of *housing*, government becomes involved in delivery and regulation to ensure its quality and affordability and to maintain the quality of neighborhoods. Government can be the full owners and operators of housing (in the case of public housing), can help subsidize the private production of low-cost housing, or otherwise regulate development to assure that housing is delivered at appropriate quantities and prices. Housing policies can have substantial impacts on changing or solidifying basic demographic ratios between groups, citywide and in specific subareas. Housing can become the grounds of great contention as to which ethnic group is benefiting more from government-facilitated housing or is being allocated a greater number of public housing units. Because housing policy is so directly linked to the issue of territoriality in a polarized city, restrictions on housing construction and tenure for an out-group is a common technique used by a partisan governing regime.

Capital facility planning involves decisions dealing with the prioritization, funding, size and location of major public investments such as highways and roads, and water and sewer infrastructure. These facilities are the backbone to urban development, providing accessibility and basic human needs to urban communities. Transportation decisions regarding highway locations and alignments are capable of connecting or fragmenting ethnic communities. At the same time, water and sewer extension decisions can restrict the growth potential of particular ethnic communities by not delivering these vital urban services. The *social service delivery* function of government is instrumental in providing to urban residents services such as education, health, recreation, and cultural facilities. These social services are tied to basic human needs (health) and connected to issues of ethnic group identity (education and cultural facilities). The planned closure of a cultural facility or restrictions placed upon educational curriculum can thus inflame ethnic tensions more immediately than other public policy decisions.

The urban policymaking process commonly articulates government's view of the proper role of *community participation and empowerment*. A city government can delegate or devolve a genuine degree of citizen power through the creation of community councils or neighborhood associations which have some impact on policy formulation or implementation. Alternatively, city governments can pay lip service to citizen participation, engaging in token forms of citizen consultation or outright manipulation of citizen consent through co-optation (Arnstein 1969). Genuine community participation in a polarized city may alleviate some tension in the urban area; however, it may also harden ethnic cleavages and empowerment. Far more clearly, less genuine forms of citizen manipulation and co-optation will likely fan the fires of resentment toward the already contested urban government.

Finally, *municipal government organization* involves both how a city bureaucracy is internally organized and how jurisdictional and electoral boundaries are drawn. The structure of city bureaucracies can influence how government addresses the complex issues of urban ethnicity—either vertically through the lenses of individual line departments; or laterally based on the experiences and viewpoints of multiple departments. Boundary-drawing plays instrumental roles in defining city electoral wards that can politically empower or marginalize ethnic communities, and in defining the "city" itself through municipal border gerrymandering that can include or exclude ethnic neighborhoods. In addition, whether an urban region acts as a set of competing city governments or is coordinated by a metropolitan umbrella government can have significant effects on the degree of interlocal redistribution possible during a post-conflict phase.

Each of these urban policies has substantial potential effects on those urban ethnic conditions, detailed in Figure 2.2, that can facilitate or impede urban peacebuilding. The policies can transcend or solidify ethnic territoriality, they can distribute economic benefits fairly or unfairly, they can provide or discourage access to policymaking and political power, they can enhance or erode collective ethnic rights, and they can incorporate or exclude urban-based political opposition.

The in-person interview was selected over other research techniques because it permits greater depth, enables probing to obtain greater data, and makes it possible to establish rapport with the respondent. Field research entailed 71 interviews (34 in Belfast; 37 in Johannesburg); Appendix 2 lists all interviewees and their institutional affiliations. I used an interview guide that structured and customized the set of topics for each discussant, while at the same time allowing discretion on my part in the ordering and phrasing of questions. Questions were open-ended. This allowed interviewees flexibility and depth in responding and facilitated responses not anticipated by the research design (Mayer and Greenwood 1980). Most frequently, interviews were conducted with individuals currently in policymaking and administrative positions at national, regional, and municipal levels of government. Former government officials were also a rich source of information, providing a longitudinal perspective on current urban issues and problems. I also interviewed representatives (official and unofficial) of the opposition ethnic groups who for various reasons were operating outside of formal governmental channels. Some of these representatives worked for nongovernmental organizations (NGOs) which advocated either a single ethnic group's cause or bridgebuilding between antagonistic ethnicities. Next to current government officials, NGO analysts represented the second largest pool of interviewees. Finally, I talked with several university scholars and a number of individuals with private sector or commercial interests in the contested city.

Core interview lists were developed for each city prior to arrival. They were constructed based on contacts made initially at a 1987 Salzburg Seminar on di-

TABLE 3.2   Classification of Interviewees by Pertinent Characteristics

BELFAST	
Ethnicity	
Protestant	16
Catholic	12
Not reported	6
Affiliation	
Governmental	19
Academic	7
Nongovernmental organization	8
JOHANNESBURG	
Race	
Nonwhite	11
White	26
Affiliation	
Governmental	21
Academic	4
Nongovernmental organization	12

vided cities, from subsequent correspondences with practitioners and scholars, and from research and professional literatures. A vast majority of interviewees were identified after arrival based upon word-of-mouth referrals from initial discussants and academics at my host institution, and through local media, primarily newspapers. Three months of intensive interviewing in each locale allowed me to contact and successfully carry out discussions with over 80 percent of those individuals identified for potential interviews. Of those potential interviewees who were contacted by phone and letter, only one refused to be interviewed. Anticipating that ethnic background and government employment would color respondent perceptions, strong efforts were made to assure there would be a fair distribution of interviewees across ethnic groups and across government and nongovernmental officials. Identification of interviewees by pertinent characteristics is portrayed in Table 3.2. I believe the pool of interviewees in each city represents adequately and broadly the complexities, arguments, and emotions of working and living in a politically contested city. My samples were likely biased toward individuals with moderate, centrist views on urban ethnic conflict and its management. This sample feature is due to my intention to study possibilities in which urban policy can contribute constructively to urban and regional peace. Nonetheless, more extreme attitudes toward conflict management can be found within each interview sample.

All interviews were face-to-face discussions. On average, each lasted about one and one-half hours. Over 90 percent of the interviews were audiotaped[5] and then transcribed. Because of this procedure, misquotations and misinterpretations are felt to be minimal. The audiotaped record also helped to clarify particular sentences where different linguistic habits may have otherwise obfuscated the meaning.[6] Audiotaping did not appear to act as an obstacle to forthcoming and full-bodied responses on the part of discussants. Indeed, it may have brought out livelier and more honest appraisals. Many interviewees were professionally and personally introspective concerning the momentous changes that each society was undergoing and appeared to want their concerns and issues to be "on the record." When interviewees did not want to be quoted directly, I fulfilled this wish in all cases.[7] These "off the record" requests were at a level less than anticipated by the author.

In addition to direct interviews, I investigated published and unpublished city, regional, and national plans and policy documents; implementing regulations; and laws and enabling statutes in terms of how they address urban issues of localized and national ethnic conflict. In cases where material on a particular subject was classified or undocumented, interviews were conducted with policy practitioners and scholars familiar with the policy or project history. In many cases, I was able to obtain copies of such sensitive and provocative material after these interviews. I also derived conclusions from growth, housing, and budgetary spending data, and from a wealth of published analytic reports and academic articles.

Notes

1. Urban polarization can also take the physical form of two-sided partition, wherein opposing sides are physically separated from each other by an impassable physical barrier (examples include pre-1989 Berlin, contemporary Nicosia, and 1948–1967 Jerusalem).

2. Belfast: January–March 1995; Johannesburg: July–September 1995.

3. It is thus far more inclusive than that defined by the city (town) and regional planning profession, specifically.

4. To some readers, urban policing will be noticeably absent from this list. It is a core issue in polarized societies that is outside the scope of this study. I focus on the planning-related and often land-based policies that structure opportunities and costs in contested cities, rather than the maintenance of societal order through police and military force. Policing in polarized societies is commonly systematically biased, politicized, lacking in accountability, and disproportionately representative of one ethnic group (Weitzer 1995). Depending on one's vantage point, policing in polarized cities is viewed either as a source of order or a cause of instability. In Belfast, the local Royal Ulster Constabulary (RUC) is the main police force, supported by the British Army. The RUC continues to be plagued by claims that it is biased against Catholics. As of 1992, only 7.4 percent of the RUC force was Catholic (Livingstone and Morison 1995; Weitzer 1995). Security forces in Northern Ireland have also been targets of political violence, with 287 police officers and 637 soldiers having been killed in 1969–1982 (Livingstone and Morison 1995). In South Africa, the South African Police (SAP) and South African National Defense Force (SANDF) were the main enforcers of discriminatory laws, and were instrumental in the exercise of state

repression and terrorism (Cawthra 1993; Brogden and Shearing 1993). Today, reorganization of South African Police entails increasing the racial representativeness of the force while allaying the fears of white officers; the police force is now 65 percent black (Harber and Ludman 1995).

5. All interviewees were asked at the outset whether audiotaping was acceptable. For seven cases it was not, a low figure unanticipated by the author.

6. All interviews were conducted in English.

7. In the notes to the text, the reader will see in these cases, *Identity of source withheld upon request*.

PART TWO

Belfast: At the Sharp Edge

And schoolboys of another faith and tradition
sit at desks, with solemn faces
And I, expressionless, stare at each,
conscious of the bond and the break between us . . .
And I glance
at each child as I call his name
And their tired faces recall my own childhood
in this same city, but a different childhood.

—John Boyd from "Visit to School"

PHOTO 4.1 Republican Mural in Falls/Clonard Neighborhood of West Belfast. (Photo by Scott A. Bollens)

4

The Sectarian City

Belfast contains inseparable nationalist (Irish/British) and religious (Catholic/Protestant) conflicts. It has been since 1969 a violent city of sectarian warfare.[1] From 1969 through 1994, the "Troubles" in Northern Ireland resulted in 3,169 dead, 38,680 injured, and 10,001 bombings (*The Guardian,* September 1, 1994). Belfast has borne the brunt of this violence. Over 1,000 of the 1810 fatal incidents from 1969 to July 1983 occurred in the city of Belfast (Poole 1990).[2] Forty-one percent of all explosions during the Troubles have occurred in the Belfast Urban Area (BUA), with almost 70 percent of bombings aimed at housing occurring in the BUA (Boal 1995). Attacks on shops, offices, industrial premises, pubs and clubs, and commercial premises have been disproportionately concentrated in Belfast. It is critical to examine Belfast because it is by far the most populated city and the capital of contested Northern Ireland; it thus is an important stage upon which the broader nationalist conflict is performed.

Although religion is a basic component of personal and group loyalty, the conflict is exacerbated by the fact that religious identities coincide strongly with political and national loyalties.[3] The allegiances of Protestant "unionists" and "loyalists" are with Britain, which since 1972 has exercised direct rule over Northern Ireland. Catholic "nationalists" and "republicans," in contrast, consider themselves Irish and commit their personal and political loyalties more to the Republic of Ireland to its south. The border between Northern Ireland and the Republic of Ireland, established in 1920, created a secure unionist majority in the north through the inclusion of six of the nine counties of the historic province of Ulster (see Figure 4.1). Without this border, Protestants would be substantially outnumbered in a unified Ireland.[4] Political boundaries on the island thus create a "double minority syndrome" (Benvenisti 1986); Protestants are an Island-wide minority threatened by possible unification, and Catholics are a minority in Northern Ireland threatened by Protestant and external British rule.

FIGURE 4.1   Northern Ireland and Belfast

Source: Weitzer, R. *Transforming Settler States* (Berkeley: University of Callifornia Press, 1990). Reprinted by permission.

Shifting Demographics

The city of Belfast, like Northern Ireland as a whole, has a majority Protestant population. According to the Northern Ireland Housing Executive (NIHE), the 1991 city population of 279,000 was comprised of an estimated 57 percent Protestant/other and 43 percent Catholic.[5] The Catholic percentage has been increasing over the last few decades due to higher Catholic birthrates and Protestant out-migration to adjoining towns (see Figures 4.2 and 4.3). In 1981, the city of Belfast was about 62 percent Protestant/other and 38 percent Catholic (NIHE figures). In particular parts of the city, Protestant decline and Catholic growth are starkly portrayed by population trends. In north Belfast and Protestant west Belfast together, the Protestant population of 116,000 in 1971 declined to 51,750 in 1991, with expectations of a further drop to 39,000 in 2001 (DOENI 1992a). The religious composition of the subarea was 79–21 percent Protestant-Catholic in 1971; 57–43 percent in 1991; with forecasts for a 48–52 percent Catholic majority in 2001 (DOENI 1992a).[6] The larger region—the Belfast Urban Area (BUA)—is composed of the city of Belfast, plus the surrounding towns of Lisburn, Newtownabbey, Castlereagh, North Down, and Carrickfergus. These suburbs have lesser Catholic populations (on average, about 20 percent) than Belfast city. As such, the 1991 BUA population of 476,000 is approximately 65 percent Protestant/other and 35 percent Catholic (NIHE figures).

Both Belfast city and the larger urban region have faced significant population declines since 1971. Core city declines started before this, with population peaking at 443,000 in 1951. Since then, the core city has decreased in population size by 37 percent. Growth in the urban area but outside the city continued between 1951 and 1971, with development spreading on to the lower slopes of the surrounding hills. Belfast Urban Area population peaked at 582,000 in 1971; since then, urban area population has declined to today's 476,000, a 19 percent decrease. It is only the outer reaches of the Belfast area—a ring of towns within commuting distance of the downtown core—that has shown population growth in the last two decades. The greater Belfast area inclusive of these exurban areas is home to about 727,000 residents, about one-half of the approximately 1.5 million residents of Northern Ireland. The combination of Belfast core city decay, suburban stagnation, and exurban fringe growth has been described by Boal (1994) as a "radical spatial transformation . . . within the urban region that, overall, displays a static population size."

Although the city of Belfast is part of a larger urban region, I focus for most of this analysis on issues pertaining to the city of Belfast proper. I do this because demographic proportions have greater parity, ethnic issues have greater salience, and land use and development problems are more complex and potentially inflammatory in the city than they are elsewhere in the Belfast Urban Area. Regional dynamics in-

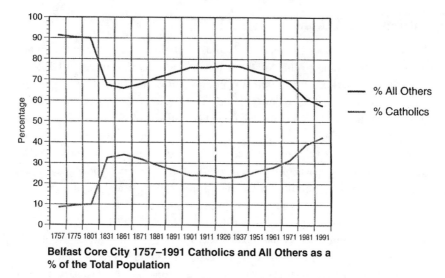

Belfast Core City 1757–1991 Catholics and All Others as a
% of the Total Population

FIGURE 4.2   Religious Composition of Belfast City Population, 1757–1991
Source: Boal, F. *Shaping a City: Belfast in the Late Twentieth Century* (Belfast: Institute of Irish Studies,
Queen's University, 1995), p. 13. Reprinted by permission.

volving growth, migration, and housing can add to or decrease ethnic pressure in the
city. Still, the city proper contains a set of root issues and conflicts which in all likelihood will need to be addressed at the level of the city, not larger, region.

   The city of Belfast's political geography is one of multi-sector segregation that
both reflects and intensifies conflict (Budge and O'Leary 1973; Schmitt 1988)
(see Figure 4.4). There has been a stubborn persistence of Protestant-Catholic
segregation through the decades, with the greatest increases in sectarian separation associated with periods of communal instability (Boal 1996). Throughout this
century, Protestant-Catholic employment segregation has helped create residential patterns of clearly identifiable communities and territoriality (Feldman
1991). Even before interethnic violence ("the Troubles") began in 1969, segregation was widespread, with 64 percent of Belfast households living on segregated
streets that contained less than 10 percent of the other ethnicity (Keane 1990). Intense sectarian hostility and violence, erupting in the summer of 1969, led to
widespread intimidation, sudden and large-scale population movement, and the
burning of whole streets of dwellings. Between 1969 and 1973, in the face of rioting, general disturbances, then terrorist bomb and gun attacks, an estimated
60,000 Belfast residents were forced to leave their homes, moving from vulnerable and destabilizing interface areas to neighborhoods where their ethnic group
was dominant (NIHE 1991; Boal 1982, 1994). This accentuated the degree of
Protestant-Catholic segregation; by 1977, 78 percent of households lived on segregated streets where the minority was less than 10 percent (Keane 1990).[7]

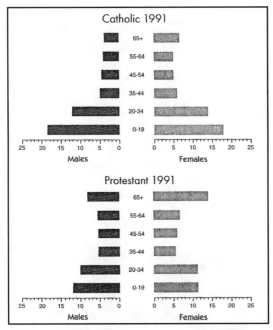

Belfast Core City Population Pyramids (%)

FIGURE 4.3   Age Distribution of Catholic and Protestant Populations in Belfast City, 1991. Note the younger age of the Catholic population and the greater proportion currently in or approaching childbearing ages.
Source: Boal, F. *Shaping a City: Belfast in the Late Twentieth Century* (Belfast: Institute of Irish Studies, Queen's University, 1995), p. 31. Reprinted by permission.

The severity of ethnic segregation is exposed by using a wider geographic scale—the electoral ward. Of Belfast city's 51 wards, 35 contain one religion that dominates 90 percent or more of the population (*The Independent on Sunday,* March 21, 1993). The Catholic neighborhoods of The Falls, Andersonstown, Ardoyne, and Short Strand are easily identifiable; as are the Protestant areas of Shankill, Sandy Row, and New-townards Road (Whyte 1986). The Catholic "heartland" is composed of greater west Belfast, centered on the Falls neighborhood; the primary Protestant "heartland" has traditionally been the Shankill neighborhood. Residential segregation is most intense in the working-class neighborhoods of west and east Belfast and is reinforced through exceedingly low levels of Protestant-Catholic interaction in terms of such activities as movement to bus stop, grocery store, and to visitors or family; and readership of newspaper and football team loyalties (Boal 1969). Catholics make up 55 percent of the city's population west of the Lagan River; compared to only 12 percent east of the River. Thus, the "terms 'East' and 'West' Belfast carry considerably greater symbolic baggage than their directional qualities alone would suggest" (Boal 1994, 147). Economic deprivation is most acute in the predominantly Catholic ghetto of west

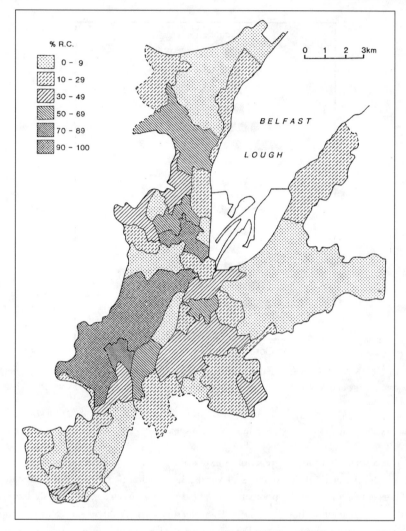

FIGURE 4.4   Distribution of Roman Catholics in Belfast Urban Area
Source: Boal, F. "Belfast: A City on Edge." In Clout, Hugh (ed.). *Europe's Cities in the Late Twentieth Century* (Amsterdam: Royal Dutch Geographical Society, 1994), p. 147. Reprinted by permission.

Belfast, where the unemployment rate among economically active males in 1985 was 47 percent (Gaffikin and Morrissey 1990). South Belfast, more middle-class and with greater owner-occupied housing stock, exhibits greater ethnic mixing than west or east. North Belfast, meanwhile, is in a difficult state of flux of Protestant decline and Catholic growth, with multiple interfaces and isolated pockets of ethnic concentrations (DOENI 1992a). Because of this territorial instability, ethnic violence and terror have been intense. The Duncairn Gardens interface in North

Belfast that separates Catholic New Lodge from Protestant Tiger Bay was described as a "sectarian murder-ground" (B. Morrison, Town and Country Planning Service, Belfast Divisional Office, interview), having been the site of 20 percent of all sectarian violence in the city (K. Sterrett, Town and Country Planning Service, interview).

Political "Direct Rule"

From 1972 to 1998, legislative power for Northern Ireland has been held by the British House of Commons, of which only 17 members come from Northern Ireland.[8] The Unionist-majority Northern Ireland Parliament, the governing body for the province up until 1972 and linked to the formulation of discriminatory and unjust laws, was held to be incapable of fair and capable governance and the British enacted "direct rule" in the midst of sectarian conflict in 1972. Executive power for Northern Ireland under "direct rule" has been possessed by the secretary of state for Northern Ireland, who is chosen from the party ruling at Westminster. The result of direct rule has been "an almost complete absence of representative participation and accountability" (Hadfield 1992). The thinking behind direct rule was that the removal of policy formulation and implementation from the bitter sectarian conflict would make it more efficient and effective (Loughlin 1992). It also means that ministers in charge of Northern Ireland governance take their political cues from Westminster (P. Sweeney, Department of the Environment for Northern Ireland, interview).

The authority of local governance in Belfast and elsewhere in Northern Ireland was significantly eroded by "direct rule." It was at the local level of government that sectarian bias was most evident, especially in the fields of public employment, service delivery, and housing (Loughlin 1992). Thus, the locally elected 51-member Belfast city council has severely constrained policymaking power in planning, urban service delivery, and housing; it is predominantly an advisory body (Hadfield 1992).[9] Instead, most power in these policy areas is located in appointed boards—such as the Northern Ireland Housing Executive—or in central executive agencies—such as the Department of the Environment for Northern Ireland—which are responsible to British ministers rather than to local politicians (Hadfield 1992; Loughlin 1992). Civil servants in Northern Ireland government charged with Belfast urban policy thus see themselves within the political framework determined by Westminster. This centralized policymaking structure is viewed as capable of depoliticizing local planning issues and holding in abeyance the larger community power struggles (Douglas 1982; Blackman 1991). Administrators of urban policies for Belfast view themselves as above local conflicts and often take pride in their technocratic approach (Loughlin 1992).

There are five major political parties in Northern Ireland. Protestant-aligned parties are the Ulster Unionist Party (UUP, also called the Official Unionists) and the Democratic Unionist Party (DUP). While both favor continued links with Great

TABLE 4.1   Percent of 1993 Local Council Seats Won

	Northern Ireland	Belfast City
Ulster Unionist Party	29.0	31.4
Social Democratic and Labor Party	21.9	17.6
Democratic Unionist Party	17.2	17.6
Sinn Fein	12.5	19.6
Alliance Party of Northern Ireland	7.7	9.8
Other	11.7	3.9

SOURCE: Boyle, K. and T. Hadden. *Northern Ireland: The Choice* (London: Penguin), p. 55.

Britain, the UUP is often more moderate than the DUP (Whyte 1990). Catholic-aligned parties are the Social Democratic and Labor Party (SDLP), expressive of moderate constitutional nationalism, and Sinn Fein, the political wing of the provisional Irish Republican Army (IRA), which has advocated physical force as an appropriate means toward separation from the union. The centrist party is the Alliance Party, which favors continued union with Great Britain but advocates the establishment of accommodating structures in Northern Ireland to reduce unionist hegemony.

Whyte (1986) has observed that Protestants in Northern Ireland are socially fragmented in terms of denomination[10] and class but politically unified in support of unionism. In contrast, Catholics are socially cohesive, but face internal political disagreement. Whereas all political parties supported by Protestants favor continued links with Great Britain, Catholics have experienced internal disagreements over how such links might be severed—nationalists of the SDLP favoring constitutional means; republican followers of Sinn Fein advocating physical force—and tend to favor more than Protestants the centrist Alliance Party. There has also been, until recently, greater antagonism between SDLP and Sinn Fein supporters than between UUP and DUP followers (Whyte 1990).

Despite the limitations on the authority of Belfast city council, local elections do illuminate Belfast residents' political allegiances and the direction of future policy with possible devolution of power to local government. Protestant-aligned parties have traditionally controlled the city council. Table 4.1 displays the relative sizes of the major political parties' constituencies in the 1993 local elections, both city-specific and Northern Ireland–wide. Of particular note in the local list is that unionists held close to 50 percent of the Belfast seats (facilitating a working majority on most occasions), compared to 37 percent for Catholic-aligned parties. Also, the republican Sinn Fein showed greater strength in Belfast than provincewide.

In 1997, a significant change occurred when Belfast local elections resulted in the loss of the long-held majority control by Protestant-aligned political parties. Combined, nationalist, republican, and middle-of-the-road Alliance Party representatives now hold 26 of the 51 seats on Belfast city council. This working majority re-

TABLE 4.2 Percent of 1997 Local Council Seats Won

	Northern Ireland	*Belfast City*
Ulster Unionist Party	27.8	25.5
Social Democratic and Labor Party	20.7	13.7
Democratic Unionist Party	15.6	13.7
Sinn Fein	16.9	25.5
Alliance Party of Northern Ireland	7.0	11.8
Other	12.0	9.8

SOURCE: Tonge, Jonathan. 1998. *Northern Ireland: Conflict and Change* (London: Prentice Hall Europe), p. 53; Belfast city council webpage (www.belfastcity.gov.uk).

sulted in the selection of the first nationalist mayor in the city's history. Table 4.2 displays the political configuration of the current Belfast city council, as well as the provincewide distribution. Political support for the republican Sinn Fein increased both locally and nationally since 1993, with its greater support remaining in Belfast.

A significant alteration of Northern Ireland governing institutions and constitutional status is specified in the April 1998 *Agreement Reached in the Multi-Party Negotiations*. This agreement, approved by over 70 percent of Northern Ireland voters in May 1998, transfers day-to-day rule of the province from Britain to a new directly elected Northern Ireland Assembly, in which Protestants and Catholics will have shared power. The accord states that Northern Ireland will remain within the United Kingdom as long as a majority in the province wants to remain there.[11] In response to nationalist desires, the new assembly and the Irish Parliament are to form a North-South Council to coordinate and encourage cross-border cooperation. To reassure unionists, a Council of the Isles will be created to link the governments in Northern Ireland and Ireland with the British government and with new legislative assemblies being set up in Scotland and Wales. All arrangements are scheduled to be in place so that all of these new institutions can assume their functions not later than February 1999.

As specified in the agreement, a 108-member Northern Ireland Assembly was elected in June 1998 based on proportional representation.[12] As Table 4.3 indicates, this polling resulted in an Assembly of dispersed power. The two more moderate parties in the middle—the Protestant-aligned Ulster Unionist Party and the Catholic-aligned Social Democratic and Labor Party—have more seats than the more hardline loyalist Democratic Unionist Party and republican Sinn Fein, although these differences are not great. Splits within the Protestant camp between the pro-agreement UUP and the anti-agreement DUP could jeopardize the workability of the Assembly and other new governing institutions. As in 1997 local elections, the balance of power between Protestant-aligned parties and Catholic-

TABLE 4.3   Percent of 1998 Northern Ireland Assembly Seats Won

	Northern Ireland (108 seats)	From Belfast City Constituencies (24 seats)
Ulster Unionist Party	25.9	25.0
Social Democratic and Labor Party	22.2	20.8
Democratic Unionist Party	18.5	16.7
Sinn Fein	16.7	20.8
Alliance Party of Northern Ireland	5.6	4.2
Other	11.1	12.5

SOURCES: BBC News, Assembly Elections, State of the Parties web page (www.news.bbc.co.uk); *Belfast Telegraph* web page (www.belfasttelegraph.co.uk).

aligned parties showed greater parity from Belfast city constituencies than from throughout Northern Ireland. A 12-member multiparty executive is to be constituted, also on the basis of proportional vote. The Assembly will have authority to pass legislation in devolved areas, which are those currently within the responsibility of the Northern Ireland Departments of Finance and Personnel, Economic Development, Environment (which includes most urban policy functions), Education, Health and Social Services, and Agriculture. No Assembly decision will be approved unless there are parallel majorities in both Protestant and Catholic camps or if it is acceptable to 60 percent of those voting, including at least 40 percent from each camp. The secretary of state for Northern Ireland retains executive responsibility, and the Westminster Parliament legislative authority, for those matters not devolved to the Assembly.

The challenges of governance and policymaking discussed in this book under third-party direct rule remain highly salient under an alternative governance arrangement. This is not to underestimate the extraordinary nature of the negotiated transformation of Northern Ireland's governance. Rather, it is to assert the importance attached to the capacity of any political arrangement, no matter how constituted, to implement programs and produce outcomes that make a meaningful difference in a divided society. Under either direct rule or local rule, some effective policymaking must occur that moves the society toward mutual accommodation and away from rigidity and status quo. Seen in this light, the political negotiations successfully culminated in April 1998 represent a first, but by no means sufficient, step toward normalizing Northern Ireland. The new governing arrangement specified in the 1998 agreement also leaves open the question of urban government and policymaking, the main topic of this inquiry. I discuss ways that urban policy can contribute to reinforcing a possible move toward peace initiated by the April accord and historic May vote. Even with possible advances at regional and international levels, the urban part of the puzzle will remain as problematic under shared local control as it was under British direct rule.

Without effective and progressive policy-making, the new governance of Northern Ireland will produce gridlock. That both sides must concurrently gain from public policy is made clear by two facts. First, the 1998 agreement allows that opposition from either Protestants or Catholics to a policy proposal is sufficient to defeat it. This ability of either ethnic grouping to derail policymaking means that proposals will likely search for common ground. Second, the May 1998 vote itself was not equally supported across sects; one exit poll on election day showed that Protestant support for it barely passed 50 percent while Catholic voter support surpassed 95 percent. The new set of governing institutions in Northern Ireland and the United Kingdom created by the 1998 Agreement will likely blossom or flounder depending upon how well new policies coming from these bodies deliver on both Protestant and Catholic hopes for a different society. "On-the-ground" policies pertaining to housing, economic development, human services, social inclusion, growth, and development[13] will help determine the quality and sustainability of Northern Ireland's new governing institutions.

Urban Policymakers

The public sector—both administrative and security-related—plays a disproportionate role in both Belfast and Northern Ireland. General expenditure per capita in Northern Ireland ($6,800 U.S.) was 35 percent higher in 1992–93 than the United Kingdom average ($5,100 U.S.).[14] Public expenditures for housing in Northern Ireland are more than 50 percent more per capita than in Britain (HM Treasury 1994). Security expenditures per capita are 250 times more than in Britain; industrial and employment expenditures per capita are over 300 times greater. Thus, although government has been removed from local control since 1972, its role is much more significant than in other parts of the UK and Europe. In many ways, the social and physical fabric of Northern Ireland and Belfast has stayed as intact as it has during the ethnic war due to the inordinately large public sector and its provision of services such as housing and employment schemes (P. Sweeney, DOENI, interview).

Under the Northern Ireland Act of 1974, the dominant policymaker concerning urban development and planning is the Department of the Environment for Northern Ireland (hereafter DOENI). It is the intention that the new 1998 Northern Assembly will assume legislative authority in those areas currently within the responsibility of DOENI, in addition to the departments of Finance, Economic Development, Education, Health and Social Services, and Agriculture. How this will affect organizational changes in these executive agencies and substantive changes in policymaking is unknown at this time. The size and reach of the DOENI are such that P. Sweeney (DOENI advisor, interview) labels it the "department of everything" and describes it as a confederation of often disparate services created after direct rule. DOENI goals are set by the secretary of state and are: (1) to strengthen the economy; (2) target social need; and (3) combat terrorism (G. Mulligan, DOENI, interview). Within or connected to the DOENI are five major entities involved in Belfast urban policy.

The Town and Country Planning Service is responsible for creating the framework within which development takes place and for regulating development. Belfast Urban Area plans are statutory (they have the force of law) and establish a broad policy framework for future growth over the next 15 or so years. Physical development policies within an Area Plan seek to clarify the extent and location of future development. In contrast to general plans or zoning schemes in the United States, Belfast Area Plans (like their British counterparts) are more flexible and less specific (G. Worthington, head of Belfast Divisional Office, Planning Service, interview). A second type of plan, local or subject plans, are done for more specific subareas requiring more detailed investigation. They are to be consistent with the broad policy framework of the area plan, although they do not necessarily have the force of law (DOENI 1994c). Recent local plans in Belfast have included those for the Harbor area, the city center (including the major Laganside waterfront project), and the Lagan Valley Regional Park.[15] Most planning and project applications, both private and public, are reviewed by the Planning Service for consistency with the area plan.[16] The Belfast City Council (District Council) is to be consulted during the review process by the Planning Service Divisional Office. In cases where there is a difference of opinion between a District Council and the Divisional Planning Office, the decision is referred to a Planning Service Directorate. In the 1992–93 period, the Directorate decided in favor of the Divisional Planning Service over 85 percent of the time (DOENI 1994b).

Town planning in Northern Ireland has an erratic history. In 1921, upon Northern Ireland's creation, the province broke away from the British system of planning[17] because it was viewed as too complicated, and as addressing problems—such as the spread of suburbs and ribbon development—that were not relevant in Northern Ireland. As J. Hendry (Queen's University, interview) states, the "Irish did not want to be told what to do, especially by the British." After World War II, Northern Ireland copied the British system in a piecemeal fashion. By the time of the first regional plan in Northern Ireland (the *Matthew Plan*), planning was viewed as a way to create a stable context that would stimulate outside investment into the state (J. Hendry, interview). Thus, the Matthew Plan recommended the creation of new towns as a method to stimulate economic growth away from the burgeoning Belfast area, the imposition of a stopline to spatially curtail Belfast growth, and the development of motorways to improve access to hinterlands.[18] Since direct rule in 1972, town planning has been removed entirely from local authorities. Area Plans today are done by the centralized DOENI, and are occurring without a strong regional strategic framework such as proposed by the Matthew Plan (J. Hendry, interview).

The second urban policy unit, the *Belfast Development Office* (BDO), has a more active orientation toward changing and regenerating the urban system. Whereas town planning guides and regulates development, the BDO actively seeks to put things on the ground, promoting and coordinating the physical regeneration of Belfast. It focuses on the physical regeneration of neglected or abused urban areas as a means toward their economic and social revitalization. The BDO is composed of administrators and civil servants, not town planners. Through Comprehensive Development Schemes (CDS), Environmental Improvement Schemes (EIS), and Urban Development Grants (UDG), the BDO seeks to facilitate the rebuilding of Belfast through partnerships between government and private investment. In the 1980s, these three programs expended about 86 million pounds sterling (1991/92 prices) (Cebulla 1994). During the Thatcher years of deregulation, the BDO was instrumental in cutting through red tape in Belfast. Oriented toward single project marketing and development, R. Strang (former assistant director, NIHE, interview) suggests that BDO was a way to short-circuit the statutory planning process in order to more quickly revitalize dying and damaged parts of Belfast.

The BDO has focused primarily on the redevelopment of the city center as a means of regenerating the city at large. In a period of employment decline and population loss, few institutional investors were operating in the central city in the 1970s. Moreover, property development decline was experienced as commercial property became targets of paramilitary bombing campaigns which left the city center deserted and surrounded by a security cordon and manned security gates (S. Brown 1985; Cebulla 1994). The BDO has sought to spatially concentrate public investment incentives to bring both multi-locational retail franchises and office developments into the central core of Belfast, one of the few areas of the city deemed to be "neutral" in terms of sectarian geography. It has heavily subsidized land purchase and assemblage by government through its CDS program, private investment through its UDG program, the improvement of capital infrastructure (such as roads) and the general upgrading of the urban environment through its EIS programs, and entered into agreements with private investors to buy back properties after 50 years (K. Sterrett, DOENI, interview). A prominent central project has been the development of Castle Court, a major retail complex one block from City Hall. In addition, the DOENI created its own development company to develop and leverage private investment for a planned major mixed-use complex—Laganside— along the Lagan River. Outside the city center, the BDO has worked on community regeneration schemes through its decentralized Belfast Action Team (BAT) offices.[19] However, significantly more public expenditures have gone into the city center through CDS, EIS and UDG subsidies than they have into the surrounding neighborhoods through BAT projects. The main benefits from BDO actions are seen as coming from access to new jobs in the "neutral" city center, not from new jobs locating in sectarian neighborhoods (Cebulla 1994; DOENI 1987).

A third major urban policy unit is the *Northern Ireland Housing Executive* (NIHE). It is the comprehensive housing authority for Northern Ireland, charged with the provision of new public housing, the rehabilitation and maintenance of existing units, and the allocation of public housing units to needy households and individuals. It is the largest public housing landlord in the United Kingdom, with direct responsibility for one third of Northern Ireland's housing stock. The NIHE controls about 36,000 properties in Belfast city alone (J. McPeake, NIHE, interview). Housing provision and allocation in Northern Ireland and Belfast have long been contested. Before direct rule, housing policy by Belfast city showed a strong pattern of political influence and sectarian bias (Singleton 1983). The British government identified housing provision as one of the major areas of grievance in the state (Cameron Report 1969). Indeed, one of the "ignition points" for the Troubles was the Caledon Affair, in which an unmarried Protestant girl had been allocated a house in County Tyrone while several large Catholic families remained unhoused (Singleton 1983). In response, the NIHE was created in 1971 to centralize housing policy and insulate it from local political biases. From its first day, NIHE's credibility is closely connected to its use of objective allocation and new-build criteria. Since 1971, the NIHE has built 18,500 public housing units in Belfast city, with another 10,000 in the BUA outside the city (J. McPeake, NIHE, interview). The middle of the 1980s, in particular, was a time of extensive public housing building, about 1500 units per year. The quality of NIHE housing has been praised, with housing and landscaping standards higher here than in Great Britain. R. Strang (interview) explains that "we realized that in order to survive, we had to build to the highest possible standards." By 1991, the level of housing unfitness had been reduced from 24 percent to 8 percent (NIHE 1995). A quasi nongovernmental organization (quango), the NIHE is funded through the DOENI.

Belfast Action Teams (BAT) are one of two means urban policymakers have used to direct regeneration efforts to disadvantaged residential communities. Headed by senior civil servants, these units liaise with local communities through decentralized offices for the purposes of encouraging social and economic regenerative measures. A. Cebulla (interview) claims that while the top level of urban policy emphasizes city center revitalization, BATs (along with Making Belfast Work, discussed below) represent a different track aimed at community deprivation. The BAT program, originally under the auspices of the BDO, established in 1987 and 1988 nine decentralized, community-based government offices charged with connecting community needs to government programs and resources.[20] Each BAT leader was allocated between 700,000 and 1 million British pounds per year to direct to community needs. Although there have been some positive impacts on the ground, no strategic policy drove BAT coordination in the early years. Thus, there were widely disparate BAT approaches and experiences (R. Davison, Shankill BAT leader, interview). In addition, BAT projects at times were inconsistent with the policies and budget priorities of other statutory agencies (V. McKevitt, Ardoyne/Oldpark BAT leader, interview). This independent discretion by BAT leaders led to images of them as "free lance cash dispensers" (R. Davison, interview) and "cowboys with no responsibility who have gone native" (V. McKevitt, interview). Because of these problems, the BAT program was institutionally connected in 1994 to the more strategic Making Belfast Work anti-deprivation program.

Making Belfast Work (MBW) seeks to target resources to the 32 deprived electoral wards in the city. Established in 1988 in the midst of horrendous sectarian tension and violence, it was created as an emergency and tactical response during a time when government authorities thought that they may lose control over Catholic west Belfast (P. Sweeney, interview).[21] MBW established a pot of money that government departments could access if they showed they were redirecting part of their normal budgets into areas of high unemployment and economic deprivation. It was a bidding mechanism that would provide incentives for skewing government expenditures toward deprived areas (Cebulla 1994). It traditionally has funded physical revitalization efforts through the channeling of money to groups (such as churches) not allied with republican and loyalist paramilitaries. A major revision of MBW occurred in 1994 and 1995 that has reoriented the program toward joint community-government partnerships inclusive of all community groups, and toward a broader definition of regeneration beyond solely bricks-and-mortar (DOENI 1994c, 1995).[22]

Territoriality and Community

Sectarian Geographies

> Patrick Corry, aged 61, Catholic civilian. Killed August 2, 1969 by the Royal Ulster Constabulary. Hit on the head with batons during altercation between local people and RUC. Unity Flats off Upper Library Street.
>   **—First death in Belfast attributable to "the Troubles." Sutton (1994)**

> August 31, 1994: IRA announces ceasefire.
> September 11, 1994: Loyalist paramilitaries announce ceasefire.
> February 9, 1996: IRA declares end of ceasefire. Office building in the Docklands (London) bombed.

Sectarian violence and intimidation over the last three decades have created in the city of Belfast rigid sectarian boundaries that have severely fragmented and distorted the urban fabric. During the early years of "the Troubles," many public housing estates quickly self-segregated. In the first eight years of urban civil war, the percentage of households in public housing that resided in streets of complete or near-complete segregation rose from 59 to 89 percent (Boal 1995). The Catholic "heartland" of the Falls areas consolidated. Many Protestants, meanwhile, had a greater ability to out-migrate, due both to higher income status and less sectarian obstacles; and many of them chose this option. In the subsequent decades, Protestant out-migration coupled with higher Catholic birthrates has created a landscape of densely populated and active Catholic neighborhoods, on the one hand, and lower density, socially depleted, and physically deteriorated Protestant communities, on the other.

One is struck in Belfast city with the ever-present sectarian content and symbolism of the built environment.[23] Many areas in the city are easily identifiable as "green" (Catholic) or "orange" (Protestant). Potent and emotion-laden symbols identify whose area one is in—the presence of a Catholic or Protestant church; curbstones painted either green, yellow, and white (Catholic) or red, white, and blue (Protestant); the presence of an Ancient Order of the Hibernians meeting place (Catholic) or "Orange Order" lodge (Protestant); street names and the presence or absence of Irish language translations; and the names of shop proprietors along commercial corridors. The most politically expressive identifiers of sectarian space are the murals painted on the sides of buildings and walls. Republican murals commemorate politically potent historical events such as the Easter Uprising of 1916 or the Hunger Strikes of the early 1980s; celebrate resistance to repressions ("Brits out now"); focus on IRA victories and martyrs; make connections to other international human rights movements (such as in South Africa and Palestine); and commonly portray the Irish Tricolor flag. Loyalist murals, meantime, emphasize historical events such as the lifting of the Siege of Derry in 1689 and King William's successful Battle of the Boyne in 1690 or provide connections to the historic Ulster Volunteer Force; identify contemporary loyalist paramilitaries; and commonly use identifiers such as the "Red Hand of Ulster" and the Union Jack.[24]

The city is one of the physical barriers that symbolically separate proximate Catholic and Protestant residential neighborhoods. Although Belfast is an example of multi-sector segregation rather than two-sided partition,[25] the extent and severity of intercommunity hostilities since the late 1960s has necessitated the building of physical partitions, so-called peacelines, between neighborhoods at sixteen locations (see Figure 4.5 and Table 4.4). These have been constructed in interface areas where rival and proximate communities have engaged in territorial conflict (NIHE 1988; R. O'Connor 1988). Most of the peacelines are located in west and north Belfast, where population shifts following the outbreak of violence in 1969 were greatest. The physical dividers are built of varied materials—ranging from corrugated iron fences and steel palisade structures, to permanent steel or brick walls, to more aesthetically pleasing "environmental" barriers of landscaped railings and multicolored

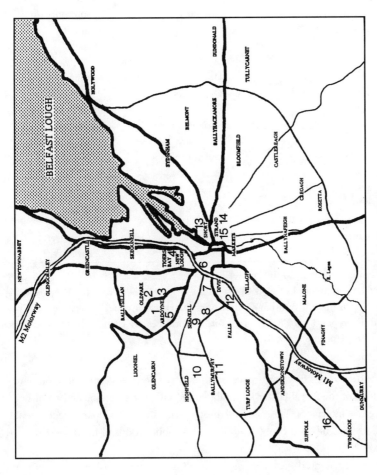

FIGURE 4.5   Location of "Peacelines" in Belfast, 1994

Source: Boal, F. *Shaping a City: Belfast in the Late Twentieth Century* (Belfast: Institute of Irish Studies, Queen's University, 1995), p. 60. Reprinted by permission.

TABLE 4.4   Belfast Peacelines and Adjacent Neighborhoods

	Adjacent Neighborhoods	
Peaceline	Catholic	Protestant
North Belfast		
1. Alliance/Glenbryn	Ardoyne	Alliance
2. Elimgrove Street	Oldpark Avenue	Torrens
3. Manor/Roe Street	Roseleigh	Groomsport Court
4. Duncairn Gardens	New Lodge	Tiger's Bay
5. Crumlin Road	Ardoyne	Shankill
West Belfast		
6. Unity Flats	Unity Flats	Lower Shankill
7. Northumberland/Ardmoulin	Divis Flats	Shankill
8. Cupar Way	Falls	Shankill
9. Ainsworth Avenue	Springfield	Woodvale
10. Springmartin Road	New Barnsley	Springmartin
11. Springhill Avenue	Ballymurphy	Springmartin
12. Roden Street	Falls	Shaftesbury
16. Stewartstown Road	Lenadoon	Suffolk
East Belfast		
13. Lower Newtownards Road	Short Strand	Island
14. Bryson Street	Short Strand	Ballymacarett
15. Cluan Place	Short Strand	Cluan Place

Note: Numbers correspond to Figure 4.5.

SOURCES: Environmental Design Consultants. *Belfast Peacelines Study.* (Prepared for Belfast Development Office in conjunction with Northern Ireland Housing Executive, 1991.) Boal, F. *Shaping a City: Belfast in the Late Twentieth Century* (Belfast: Institute of Irish Studies, Queen's University, 1995).

walls, to "buffer" zones of vacant space or alternative non-residential development. Police stations of the Royal Ulster Constabulary (RUC) are often located on or near these peaceline interfaces. The most infamous peaceline—at Cupar Street—separates the Catholic Falls and Protestant Shankill neighborhoods of inner west Belfast (see Photo 4.2).

The hyper-segregated sectarian and peaceline geography of Belfast has performed vital roles in maintaining community perceptions of security in the context of an urban civil war.[26] B. Murtagh (University of Ulster, Magee College; interview) claims that segregation has been instrumental in furthering ontological security in the face of extremely abnormal living conditions. Peacelines provide a certain psychological security by demarcating a well-defined defensive boundary to a particular community's territory (Murtagh 1994a). In addition, it should be emphasized that such community partitions and peacelines are not the cause of

PHOTO 4.2 Cupar Way Peaceline. Largest of the physical dividers in Belfast, the wall separates the Catholic Falls (left) and the Protestant Shankill neighborhoods. (Photo by Scott A. Bollens)

the problem, per se, but rather reflections of the underlying political and religious conflict (M. Graham, Northern Ireland Housing Executive, interview).

Yet, the physical manifestations of "the Troubles" in Belfast create a set of significant problems both to urban policymakers and the adjacent communities. First, uncompromising ethnic territoriality obstructs efforts to strategically plan for the needs of city residents in terms of housing and community facilities. Second, sectarian interfaces and peacelines create intimidating and inhumane environments debilitative of healthy community functioning.

The problems created by territoriality that affect policymaking are numerous. All cities, by their nature, are dynamic organisms where changing economic and demographic processes occur that involve intricate interrelationships between activities. In the city of Belfast, however, static sectarian boundaries have been overlaid upon these dynamic urban processes so as to create two cities—one Catholic and growing in population; the other Protestant and declining in size. Peacelines and sectarian geography obstruct the natural expansion or evolution of urban space across these boundaries. W. McGivern of NIHE (interview) poignantly states that "Belfast is not a normal city, where neighborhood evolution would be a natural progression . . . where neighborhoods change without revolutions and open warfare developing." The distorting effects of sectarian geography on urban policy are most pronounced in the provision of housing, where "differential demands for housing between Catholics and Protestants interact with static sectarian boundaries" (D. Murphy, Northern Ireland Housing Executive, interview). The conflicting political imperatives impacting upon policymaking are illustrated by these interview comments from two Belfast councilpersons:

> The status quo stands. I'm against anything that alters the status quo because I think it creates fear. Anything that breaks the balance destabilizes and I'm against. (N. Mc-Causland, Ulster Unionist Party)

> I understand, and fully accept, the fears of Protestants concerning an invasion of Catholics into former and current loyalist areas. In the long term, though, Catholic movement to areas that are derelict will occur sooner or later. (J. Austin, Sinn Fein Party)

The Northern Ireland Housing Executive (NIHE) "simply cannot say there is to be a Catholic housing estate in an area that is traditionally Protestant" (J. Hendry, Queen's University of Belfast, interview). Thus, the increasing Catholic needs for housing (due to greater population growth) cannot be met by building new dwelling units in Protestant areas or by locating Catholic residents in existing units there. This is so even though many Protestant areas have experienced depopulation and have vacant land, high vacancy rates, or dilapidated housing (see Photo 4.3). In this way, "peacelines have created a housing demand/supply equation of imbalance" (M. Graham, NIHE, interview). V. Blease, also of NIHE,[27] expresses it this way: "If we didn't have a Catholic-Protestant problem, we wouldn't have a housing problem. The land for housing is there, just not in the right locations." In this ethnically circumscribed world facing housing policymakers, one of two options remain—there is either Catholic overcrowding and the building of Catholic units closer to peacelines than security would otherwise suggest; or urban policymakers must look outside the core city to build new housing instead of using vacant housing stock in core city neighborhoods.[28]

In addition to distorting the *quantity* of available housing, sectarian territoriality obstructs improvements in the *quality* of existing stock. To improve living conditions, planners seek to demolish high-density housing and build lower-density units with more livable open space.[29] But, the high-rise apartment complexes found in some Catholic areas are seen as symbols of territoriality, and the maintenance of these often decrepit high-rise apartments becomes viewed as a way to protect sectarian turf. One famous demolition involved a substantial part of the Divis Flats complex in the Falls neighborhood. Despite being done for solid planning reasons and to improve Catholic quality of life, it was seen by many in the nationalist community as an attempt to dilute Catholic voting power in the city. Efforts to demolish the remaining Divis building and redevelop the Unity Flats

PHOTO 4.3 Sectarian Territoriality in North Belfast. Abandoned Protestant housing in Alliance neighborhood. Although less than 40 percent of the total 1984 housing stock was occupied in 1991, it is "off-limits" to Catholic households. Near the Alliance/Glenbryn peaceline and the Catholic neighborhood of Ardoyne. (Photo by Scott A. Bollens)

high-rise areas in inner north Belfast have similarly faced stern protests and calls to adequately house all Catholics who would be displaced, a hard task given the limited "green" land in Belfast. In this way, attempts to improve housing stock amidst sectarian territoriality may actually exacerbate ethnic conflict.

Sectarian geography also distorts transportation and economic development efforts. One potent example is the construction of Lanark Way in the 1980s, meant to link the Falls and Shankill neighborhoods to a proximate industrial park. In reality, this economic development strategy produced, instead, a connection between the two sectarian heartlands that became an oft-used escape route for terrorists. A gated barrier then had to be created to cut off one of the few intercommunity road connections in west Belfast, leaving a troubling legacy. Ethnic circumscription of Belfast space also disrupts the normal use of community facilities such as parks and leisure centers, social service offices, shopping centers, baby clinics, and community meeting places. In an urban environment where perceived "neutral venues" are few and far between, one ethnic group will often not use the nearest community facility because of the perception that it is trapped in the other group's territory. In a Protestant enclave in west Belfast, for example, only 8 percent of residents used the nearest shopping center because it was per-ceived to be in Catholic territory (Murtagh 1994a).

The most problematic challenge to urban policymakers posed by sectarian territoriality is that it puts them in the political hot-seat when deciding what to do with underutilized Protestant neighborhoods. Referring to the Protestant Donegall Pass area of predominately elderly and dependent residents, R. Strang (formerly with Northern Ireland Housing Executive, interview) speaks of the "drastically depleted and grossly distorted nature of the indigenous population" and asks who is to be planned for there. The government faces a critical choice in responding to this problem of Protestant community decline. In normal cir-cumstances, such areas would experience transformation from one land use to another or from one ethnic group to another. But, in Belfast, the maintenance of community viability is intimately connected to the protection of political ter-ritoriality. To avoid inflammatory territorial changes and incursions, policymak-ers become linked at great public expense with efforts to maintain ethnic terri-tory.

Two examples—Suffolk Estate and Cluan Place—exhibit how government has responded to the political complexities presented by declining Protestant neigh-borhoods. The Suffolk Estate in west Belfast is a small Protestant housing estate surrounded by mainly Catholic housing. Under threat (both physically and sym-bolically) from growing proximate Catholic areas, its population has declined from 1500 to 800 today.[30] Housing stock deteriorated as voids and rent arrears increased in the 1970s and early 1980s. Sectarian conflict has required the build-ing of the Stewartstown Road peaceline separating Protestant units from the busy arterial road. In addition, the NIHE has put over 5 million pounds into the reha-bilitation of residential dwellings in order to maintain community viability for its remaining 800 residents. This huge expense in physical infrastructure and housing rehabilitation achieved some stability; yet, the Protestant population continues to decline in the face of sectarian tension. Meanwhile, pressure for new housing for Catholics in nearby Lenadoon continues to mount. A housing planner (interview)[31] involved with Suffolk presents the dilemma faced by urban policy-makers: "What do you do with Suffolk? Who is to say to Protestants there that there is no future?" The second example, Cluan Place, is in predominately Protes-tant east Belfast but is adjacent to the Catholic enclave of Short Strand and feels under threat from it. Here, similar to Suffolk, per-unit public expenses to main-tain this 20-unit residential subdivision as Protestant have been substantial. A peace wall has been constructed separating the backyards of Cluan Place and Short Strand residences. In addition, infrastructure had to be moved to accommo-date the new partition (R. Strang, interview). Such investment does not make sense from a citywide perspective, but rather is derived from goals pertaining to the maintenance of social-psychological well-being amidst ethnic war.

Besides their adverse impacts on urban policymaking, sectarian interfaces and peacelines create intimidating and inhumane environments that debilitate healthy adjacent community functioning. "Peacelines," asserts D. MacBride (Community Development Center–North Belfast, interview), "tear the heart out of a community." Although they were constructed to provide psychological security, living along a peaceline presents a direct threat, imposes restriction on movement, and creates and reinforces a deteriorated quality of environment. The NIHE admits in a published 1989 report on violence and urban renewal that "the so-called 'peacelines' are in fact a contradiction in terms. They are in many instances characterized not by peace and harmony between neighbors, but by conflict, tension, damage to property and continuing instability." Councilperson J. Austin (Sinn Fein, interview) claims that the "peacelines should never have been put up in the first place" because they reinforce psychological barriers. Communities along the peacelines experience multiple deprivations (Murtagh 1994a, b), including poverty, poor access to services, an image problem, and limited community cohesiveness. The walls have direct adverse effects on adjacent estates, such as deterioration and housing voids (especially on the Protestant side), and cause indirect psychological problems as they present daily reminders of ethnic strife (D. Murphy, NIHE, interview). Peacelines can be important destabilizing influences on communities already suffering from socioeconomic deprivation.

Peacelines are not the causes of ethnic conflict in Belfast, but rather are ugly reflections of the emotion-laden urban geography of fear and territoriality. Physical partitions actually perform a functional role in a conflict environment by providing some sense of community and individual security. In the end, however, they contribute problems of rigidity and citywide dysfunctionality to the Belfast ethnic puzzle that policymakers involved in the land use and spatial development of the city must somehow address. P. Sweeney (interview) sums up the problem— "Belfast will never function as a city with these walls of hate and division."

Deprivation and Inequality

The political and constitutional issues of course are important, but are not overwhelmingly the main frame of reference in which people locate the conflict.
                    —Smith, D.J. (1987), survey of 1672 people in Northern Ireland

Part of the challenge facing any new set of governing institutions in Northern Ireland is an economic one. As many respondents think of the causes of sectarian conflict in terms of social and economic conditions and the rights of citizens (33 percent) as in terms of political/constitutional issues (33 percent) (D. Smith 1987). Catholics as well as Protestants hold this feeling. This makes it important to assess the economic conditions of Belfast and Northern Ireland which existed both before and during the years of interethnic violence and which will pose an obstacle to future peace-building in the city.

Although the city dates to 1603, growth of the textile, shipbuilding, and engineering industries in the late 1800s was what stimulated Belfast's rapid expansion (NIHE 1991). By the late 1800s, Belfast resembled many of Britain's industrial cities—row upon row of "two up two down" kitchen houses in the shadow of textile mills and engineering works. Since 1971, the Belfast region and its economic base have faced significant economic decay and transformation. In 1991, 20.3 percent of the city's economically active residents were unemployed (Northern Ireland Council for Voluntary Action 1993). Over a twenty-year period, over 42,000 jobs were lost to Belfast city residents. Manufacturing employment declined from 30 percent of the city workforce to 15 percent (Boal 1994). The ethnic civil war has contributed to this manufacturing decline, but there were more structural influences too. Whyte (1990) points out the vulnerability of the export-oriented Belfast economy to slumps in the world economy and to sluggish growth in Britain, a major buyer of Belfast exports. Only the service sector has stemmed the tide of economic decay in Belfast since 1971, growing from 23 to 33 percent of the city economy. However, this service growth was not in retail trade, but in government and security-related jobs. Since 1971, these jobs have increased from 6 percent to 16 percent of the local economy. Today, a substantial one out of six city residents are employed in either public administration or security-related expenses. Since the mid-1990s, there has been some economic recovery amidst cessation of hostilities, led by center city retail and office expansion supported by government subsidies. Still, the Belfast city economy remains skewed toward jobs not linked to production of added value, but to the maintenance and stability of a conflicted society.

The size of the public sector reflects both the high levels of need in Belfast as well as the substantial expenditures on law and order. The artificiality of the Northern Ireland economy is linked to the fact that it is substantially subsidized by Britain financially (Gorecki 1995). In 1991–1992, almost 40 percent of total public spending in Northern Ireland came in the form of a direct subsidy, or "subvention,"[32] from the British central government (Livingstone and Morison 1995). In 1992–1993, Boyle and Hadden (1994) report that the subvention was up to 3.5 billion pounds sterling, representing almost 50 percent of total Northern Ireland public expenditure of 7.5 billion pounds. The Belfast economy's shift from manufacturing to public administration and security is traceable in part to the Troubles. Cebulla (1994) observes that the Troubles gave the propensity toward economic de-concentration found in many industrial cities "an added impetus exaggerating the trend." He adds that "total employment in the city may thus not have looked much different in the absence of the Troubles; yet, Belfast's economy has been structurally altered, and its private sector in particular, weakened." Economic activity has also been unequally distributed. Economists F. Gaffikin and M. Morrissey (University of Ulster, Jordanstown, interviews) point out that "long-term economic trends are in many ways global. How-ever, the manifestation of them in relation to particular groups and particular spaces produce complex patterns of disadvantage in Belfast."

An economic gap between Protestants and Catholics sharpens and embitters the sectarian divide. Catholics traditionally have borne the burden of economic disad-vantage in Northern Ireland. Catholic males by 1971 were 2.62 times more likely to be unemployed than Protestant males (Whyte 1990). Ten years later, the Northern Ireland male unemployment rate for Catholics was 30 percent; for Protestants 12 percent (Rowthorn and Wayne 1985). This Catholic-Protestant differential remains today, with the most recent figures in 1991 showing a 28 percent Catholic male un-employment rate and a 12 percent Protestant rate (1991 Census).[33] In a report to the Standing Advisory Commission on Human Rights (D. Smith 1987), factors that could contribute to these Protestant-Catholic differentials—such as class, location, education, and age—were statistically controlled. Yet, there remained a large extent of unemployment differential unexplained. Smith concluded that no adequate ex-planation for this remaining difference has emerged "apart from discrimination and unequal opportunities." In the sectarian geography of Belfast, an additional problem facing residents seeking employment is the "chill factor," with perceived violence a major inhibitor of access of employment (A. Cebulla, Northern Ireland Economic Research Centre, interview). Such inhibition falls more on Belfast Catholics because employment has traditionally been less spatially proximate to them. Eversley (1989) states that a major cause of Catholic economic disadvantage has been "the reluctance of Catholics to take jobs which are located in, or which entail travelling through, what to them are unsafe areas." In a recent Belfast Resident's Survey (Department of the Environment for Northern Ireland 1994b), this effect of sectarian geography is profoundly illustrated. When Catholics in inner west Belfast who were out of work were asked where they would be prepared to work, twice as many indicated "else-where in the European Community (outside Great Britain and the Republic of Ire-land)" than in traditionally Protestant "East Belfast."

Workplaces are commonly segregated environments in Northern Ireland. Employer reports to the Fair Employment Commission (1993) showed in 1992 that more than 70 percent of firms with between 26 and 50 employees, and more than 40 percent of firms with between 51 and 100 employees, had fewer than ten Catholics (or Protestants) in their workforce. Although total employ-ment figures show a religious breakdown (62 percent Protestant; 37 percent Catholic) that is roughly proportionate to the size of each ethnic group's eco-nomically active population, this is masking substantial workplace segrega-tion.[34]

A second method of gauging the differential impacts of economic influences is not on individuals, but across neighborhoods of Belfast. Robson et al. (1994) calculated a "relative deprivation" measure for all electoral wards in Northern Ireland based on a

TABLE 4.5   The Ten Most Deprived Wards in Belfast (highest degree of deprivation listed first)

Ward Name	Religious Composition	
Falls	Catholic	(> 90%)
New Lodge	Catholic	(> 80%)
St. Annes	Protestant	(> 80%)
Clonard	Catholic	(> 90%)
Shaftesbury	Protestant	(> 70%)
Woodvale	Protestant	(> 90%)
The Mount	Protestant	(> 90%)
Island	Protestant	(> 90%)
Shankill	Protestant	(> 90%)
Duncairn	Protestant	(> 90%)

SOURCE: Robson, B., M. Bradford, and I. Deas. *Relative Deprivation in Northern Ireland* (Policy, Planning, and Research Unit. Department of Finance and Personnel. Northern Ireland Office. PPRU Occasional Paper 28; 1994), p. 12.

set of social and economic factors.[35] Nine of the ten most deprived wards in Northern Ireland were in Belfast city. Table 4.5 lists the most deprived wards in the city.

This spatial distribution illuminates several attributes of economic deprivation in Belfast. Catholic disadvantage is apparent in their ward ratings at the top of the Robson deprivation list. If only unemployment rate is examined, six of the seven wards in 1991 were Catholic where the percentage of economically active residents that were unemployed was above 40 percent. However, Table 4.5 indicates that spatial deprivation of Protestant areas is also common, with seven of the ten worst wards in Protestant neighborhoods (using the 14-criteria Robson index). This illustrates the depth of economic and social decay across both communities. Within a traditional and still present circumstance of Catholic-Protestant differentials, both of the antagonistic communities are being hard hit by economic restructuring. A major anti-deprivation program, Making Belfast Work (MBW), has used the Robson index to target 32 wards in the Belfast Urban Area that experience deprivation relative to the Northern Ireland average. In these wards, 49 percent of Catholic males and 37 percent of Protestant males were unemployed (Breen and Miller 1993; DOENI 1995). Such unemployment levels are not only high, but unemployment tends to be long in duration. For both ethnic groups combined, 64 percent of unemployment benefit claimants have been out of work for longer than one year; 36 percent for longer than three years (DOENI 1995).

Urban economic policy must thus address not only Catholic deprivation and lingering Catholic-Protestant disparities, but also Protestant deprivation which is likely contributing to that community's perception of threat and isolation. The level of economic pain felt by the residents and communities of Belfast is severe

and debilitating. What makes the addressing by government of this economic dis-
location more difficult is that it will need to take place in a contested city of traditionally warring communities. As F. Gaffikin and M. Morrissey (interviews) assess, "even normal industrial cities are segmented and polarized through deep
economic and social restructuring over the last 3 decades. In Belfast, this has been
superimposed over sectarian interfaces."

Community Activism Amid Strife

There exist in Belfast complex webs of interaction between community-based,
political party, and governmental interests. In a contested city, political party interests that focus on issues of sovereignty and political control intersect on the
ground with neighborhood interests that focus on issues of urban need such as
employment, housing, and physical conditions. This intersection can be a tangled
web of seeming compatibility but internal friction. The nature and results of this
interplay produce the "public" that seeks to influence urban policy, and which urban policymakers, in turn, must somehow address. Since 1972, communities[36] in
Belfast have had no immediate electoral input into local policy. With this "democratic deficit," Belfast neighborhood activism has often been reactive, obstructive,
and reflective of sectarian division. Extremists and hardliners, often backed by
paramilitaries, have often been able to control community-based processes of involvement with government (D. MacBride, interview; Murtagh 1994a). Such
control can obstruct the amount of independent action exercised by moderate
community leaders and liberals, and can magnify public perceptions of government as biased, uncaring, or even conspiratorial.

   In the midst of horrific violence in the 1970s, there existed an "energetic and
enthusiastic community development 'movement' which did succeed in crossing
the sectarian divide" (Lovett, Gunn, and Robson 1994). In many cases, neighborhood-based opposition to the redevelopment and road-building schemes of government had stimulated interethnic collective action and a sense of solidarity
among working-class communities in the face of a perceived uncaring bureaucracy. For example, Protestant and Catholic community groups united in the
1970s to oppose the proposed Belfast Urban Motorway because of its adverse
cross-ethnic effects on working-class inner-city neighborhoods (Blackman 1991).
Government has also assisted community-based efforts. A Community Relations
Commission, established in 1969, sought "confidence-building" within each ethnic
group—through the stimulation of community development projects and the
nurturing of local organizations—as a means toward betterment of cross-
community relations. Influenced by radical, nondirective approaches to community development, different forms of community organizing sprung up in the
1970s, including neighborhood-based groups, single-issue organizations focused

on such issues as crime, and larger volunteer organizations having full-time staff. Underneath the surface of commonality across community actions, however, was a conflict within the movement about the nature and purpose of community development—was it to support the state or to challenge it (T. Lovett, University of Ulster, Jordanstown, interview)? An additional difficulty was that the devolved power-sharing government of 1974, viewing the community movement as too radical and likely to usurp the function of elected representatives, disbanded the Community Relations Commission.

In the 1980s, community-based activities became increasingly fragmented and co-opted by government through the attachment of strings to the receipt of funding (Lovett, Gunn, and Robson 1994). The Action for Community Employment (ACE) scheme, in particular, has been the subject of much criticism for its "make-work" orientation and its channeling of funds to church-based groups (T. Lovett, interview; C. Bradley, Northern Ireland Council for Voluntary Action, interview). Community groups that were able to buy into ACE schemes "found their concerns narrowed as they had to fit a particular mold set by the funder" (T. Lovett, interview). Similarly, community projects funded by the International Fund for Ireland tended to be top-down, focused on enterprise development rather than community development, and run by clergy and businessmen (T. Lovett, interview). The involvement of Sinn Fein in politics subsequent to the IRA hunger strikes of 1981 had raised fear in government of paramilitary control of community groups in Catholic areas. Government responded to Sinn Fein's emergence in the form of "political vetting,"[37] whereby community groups that "have the effect of improving the standing or furthering the aims of a paramilitary organization, whether directly or indirectly," are excluded from government funding. During this time, the voluntary sector grew and started to fill the void created by the fragmenting and politically vetted community sector.[38] Tension developed between these two sectors, as the voluntary sector at times usurped functions of the neighborhood organizations (T. Lovett, interview). One positive linkage between government and community was established in 1987, with the establishment of Belfast Action Teams as decentralized liaison offices.

In an increasingly difficult environment where broader political and local community issues interacted, cross-community work by neighborhood-based groups decreased in the 1980s. Since the early 1980s, the prevalent pattern has been that community-based activism has reflected or even exacerbated social divisions. For instance, debates concerning urban and housing renewal and new road locations focused on the maintenance of an ethnic group's neighborhood population and thus its territorial defense (NIHE 1988; Blackman 1991). Osborne and Singleton (1982), in a case study of a new west Belfast housing project, viewed the community planning process as a "microcosm of the wider political battle for territory." In other cases, community activism created splits even within ethnic groups, as is evident in the separate Catholic constituencies—church and Sinn Fein—of west Belfast community employment groups (Gaffikin and Morrissey 1990). One exception to this rule of division has been that since 1984, an interethnic coalition of community organizations—Community Technical Aid—has sought to develop cross-community responses to urban plans and projects (R. O'Connor 1988; Blackman 1991).

Efforts to improve Protestant-Catholic community relations in the 1980s and 1990s have been difficult at best. Programs such as holiday schemes were viewed as having temporary effects; "people went back into their communities with no change in attitudes" (B. Hutchinson, community activist, interview). Community relations schemes were viewed by Protestants as "Catholic relations" ploys set up to impress international observers; and by Catholics as counterinsurgency efforts by government (B. Hutchinson, interview). In 1990, a new quasi-governmental body, the Community Relations Council, was established "to increase understanding and co-operation between political, cultural and religious communities in Northern Ireland" (Northern Ireland Community Relations Council 1994a). Its major challenge is to move community relations work beyond crisis management to more proactive and long-term bridge-building between Protestants and Catholics (M. Fitzduff, CRC director, interview). Difficult debates concern the role of government in promoting community welfare, especially the appropriate relationship between community development (CD), a term denoting programs aimed at enhancing life *within* communities, and community relations (CR) programs, aimed at improving life *across* communities.[39] Urban policymakers and community members must find ways to improve and enrich the self-confidence and identity of deprived communities without solidifying ghettoization, community separation, and interethnic competition over government funds.

A potential sea-change in government's treatment of communities is represented by the 1995 Strategy of the anti-deprivation Making Belfast Work program. Community interests are now to be included with those of statutory government agencies and the private sector in "area partnerships," which may undertake an advocacy role, directly undertake local projects, or act as a vehicle to channel public funding to local projects (DOENI 1995, 13). The inclusion of community in policymaking represents an awareness that locally perceived needs may be different than government's, and that community input may improve urban policy. It seeks to address the problem that the priorities of many government bodies which interact with Belfast communities are tied to aggregate measures incapable of tapping into the unique conditions and needs of a particular community (P. Sweeney, interview). However, important issues remain to be addressed in this more inclusive style of government: (1) to what extent will partnerships be *representative* of the nongovernmental and government sectors?; (2) to what extent will they be genuinely *inclusive* of local interests?; and (3) will government be *receptive* to these new sources of community input?

Although intraethnic differences in community dynamics can be at times as great as interethnic ones,[40] Catholic-Protestant differences in the dynamics and coherence of their community organization are nonetheless evident. The out-migration of upwardly mobile Protestants from inner-city neighborhoods has left their former communities fragmented, depleted of professional skills, and commonly absorbed by feelings of threat. In contrast, upwardly mobile residents on the Catholic side for many years could not or did not want to move spatially. Ironically, then, "Catholic communities tend to be more developed organizationally at the same time as they are geographically more constrained" (D. McCoy, Central Community Relations Unit, interview).

We learned that to survive the struggle, we would need an insurance policy around us . . . that insurance policy had to be the community.

— *Joe Austin, Belfast City Councillor, Member, Sinn Fein Party (interview)*

The problem of Catholic church–led community development is that it is not necessarily a very democratic one.

— *Vincent McKevitt, BAT leader, Ardoyne / Oldpark (interview)*

The stereotype of Catholic community organizing in Belfast is that it is confident, articulate, well connected to outside parties, and internally cohesive. There appears to be an element of truth to this stereotype. However, there are important qualifications that should be made to this image of Catholic community dynamics.[41] Primary among them is that significant internal divisions exist between church supporters and moderate nationalists, on the one hand, and republicans, on the other. The introduction of Sinn Fein into politics in 1981 reinforced a growing division between nationalists and republicans. The former group advocates a moderate and constitution-based solution to the Northern Ireland problem and aligns itself politically with the SDLP. It tends to draw from the Catholic middle and professional class, which British-based education, welfare, and fair employment legislation has helped create (W. Glendinning, Community Relations Council, interview). Links between this group and the conservative and middle-class followers of the Catholic church have thus been natural (B. Murphy, interview). Republicans, in contrast, have been more accepting of physical force as an appropriate means toward separation from the United Kingdom and are more likely to align themselves tactically with the Irish Republican Army campaign and politically with Sinn Fein.[42] It tends to draw more from the working class and the dispirited unemployed of the Catholic community. A common feeling is also present among republicans that the Catholic church was too conservative during the Troubles, not supporting them in their time of need and distress (B. Murphy, interview). During the Troubles, Sinn Fein was able to capitalize on this void by articulating the fears of the working-class Catholic community and saying, "we will look after you and protect you in a physical sense" (B. Murphy, interview).

Commonality of opposition to Sinn Fein by the SDLP, Catholic church, and government created partners in practice. Government funding of community regeneration projects was most commonly directed to the "safe hands" of church-based organizations and SDLP-affiliated groups of businesspeople. Community groups with similar social and economic views as Sinn Fein, but not aligned with them, found themselves cut off from government funding. Political vetting made some community-based organizations circumscribe their interests and contacts. Community groups sympathetic to Sinn Fein that have survived under political vetting developed "a certain level of sophistication in using community-based, self-help structures rather than politicians."[43]

It's easy for Protestants to sit back and say "no"; it's harder to say,"this is how we are going to help change events."

—Billy Hutchinson, Springfield Inter-Community Development Project (interview)

While the Protestant population was tapped into government for 50 years, Catholics created their alternative structures and have done it well. Since 1972, we have been left with no structures.

—Nelson McCausland, Belfast City Councillor, Member, Ulster Unionist Party (interview)

Protestant communities are better off, on average, than Catholic communities in terms of social and economic indicators. In many respects, however, it is the Protestants who are "in retreat, having lost so much territorially, culturally, and politically" (J. Redpath, Shankill community leader, interview).[44] Generally, Protestant community organizing has been less developed and active than Catholic, although that gap may be beginning to narrow. The Protestant community feels threatened by change, both at the city level due to demographic and neighborhood decline and at the national level due to a perceived dissolution of constitutional unionism over the last decade. They often have a lack of confidence in their abilities and their elected councillors, and in many areas are unorganized and lack adequate neighborhood-based leaders.[45]

Much of the depletion of Protestant community coherence is traceable to the out-migration of middle-class Protestants from the city of Belfast to adjacent cities. As S. Corbett (Central Community Relations Unit, Northern Ireland Office, interview) explains, "what is valued by Protestant individuals—to be upwardly mobile and move away to better oneself—is damaging from a community development perspective." Often, Protestant leaders today must address a community that has experienced a traumatic and profound sense of loss since the removal in 1972 of the Northern Irish government, a power structure that benefitted and protected Protestants. The "veto" mentality and resistance to change prevalent among Belfast Protestants is not conducive to community organization and development, which is ultimately about bringing forth change. Or, as Redpath states in Wiener (1976) in reflecting upon a Save the Shankill Campaign, "its strength as a veto body is its weakness as an achieving body."

Two smaller political parties on the Unionist side—the Progressive Unionist Party (PUP) and the Ulster Democratic Party (UDP)—have attempted to link political development to local community organizing and development. This represents a source of grassroots actions that contrasts with the prevalent image of traditional Unionist parties—the Ulster Unionist Party and Democratic Unionist Party—as detached from communities. The UDP is linked to the Ulster Defense Association (UDA) paramilitary group. The UDA wrote in 1989 a policy framework, *Common Sense*, which stresses community actions aimed at redevelopment, antipoverty and housing, and points out the working-class bonds and common problems that exist across the sectarian divide. The PUP, with links to the Ulster Volunteer Force (UVF) paramilitary organization, espouses in their manifesto a community development framework as the way forward. One of their leaders is a loyalist ex-prisoner, Billy Hutchinson, who heads the Springfield Inter-Community Development Project (SICDP). This nonprofit organization is seeking to improve life for both Protestants and Catholics along the Shankill/Springfield/Falls interface.

> *"Community relations" in many ways is the antithesis of politics.*
> —*Mari Fitzduff, Director, Northern Ireland Community Relations Council (interview)*

One of the greatest obstacles to effective urban policymaking in Belfast is local city councilors, whose relative lack of power frees them to be extreme in their interactions with government. They often have little to lose from being scaremongers who emphasize division, conflict, and single ethnic identity. Government units become easy targets for local councilors who rant and rave at consultation meetings as a way to show their communities that they care (J. Hendry, interview). Indeed, the confrontational and divisive rhetoric is often key to their being elected. Local politicians increase their "leadership" role most easily by tapping into separate constituencies, not seeking to span them (M. Fitzduff, interview). In their ability to thwart efforts by government to move communities forward, local politicians in Belfast "lead from the back" (D. MacBride, interview).

Local politicians are particular obstacles to the establishment of cross-community bridges. To the extent that better interethnic relations may facilitate demographic shifts with the breakdown of territoriality, community relations are inconsistent with the maintenance of a politician's ethnic constituency. For these reasons, communities are frequently more advanced and imaginative than their politicians on issues such as cross-community relations (M. Fitzduff and K. Sterrett, interviews). At times, community groups are seen as challengers to local councilors; in response, elected officials will curtail distribution of public information to these segments of the community.[46] There are often significant misfits between community beliefs and actions, on the one hand, and a local politician's motivations, belief system, and behavior tied to electoral rewards (M. Fitzduff, interview). In the local politics of contested Belfast, urban issues become subordinated to arguments over nationalism, constitutionalism, and symbolism. One interviewee[47] described the "tragedy of the masquerade" represented by monthly city council meetings that resemble more juveniles on a playground than locally elected officials in a forum.[48] Local issues become lost. For example, the city council provided minimal input into the 1987 Belfast Urban Area Plan as Unionist councilors became preoccupied with the signing of the Anglo-Irish Agreement.[49] The subordination of city welfare is represented by a city council that is "more obsessed with Sinn Fein showing up at a public inquiry than in the development issues of the Shankill" (K. Sterrett, DOENI, interview).

Notes

1. *Sectarian* is commonly used to identify the ethnic conflict in Northern Ireland as that between religious denominations or sects. I will use the "sectarian" and "ethnic" labels interchangeably.

2. More generally, political deaths have been an urban phenomenon, claiming 1.45 lives per 1000 people in urban areas, 0.74 per 1000 in rural areas (Poole 1990).

3. The political meaning behind religious labels is brought out by the fact that the more blatantly sectarian neighborhoods of working-class populations, despite having the lowest rates of church attendance, identify most strongly with Catholic or Protestant labels (F. Boal, interview).

4. The Republic of Ireland is approximately 96 percent Catholic.

5. Northern Ireland Census figures of 1991 show a distribution of 48 percent Protestant/other and 39 percent Catholic in Belfast city. Because more than 13 percent of respondents did not state a religious affiliation (many due to its political sensitivity), these are undercounts. For this same reason, the religious composition for Northern Ireland, overall, must be estimated; in 1981, the Catholic proportion was put at slightly below 40 percent (Compton and Power 1986; Eversley and Herr 1985). In 1991, it was likely greater than 40 percent (Boyle and Hadden 1994).

6. For the city as a whole, the author was not able to obtain through interviews or secondary material government forecasts pertaining to religious distribution. This absence is a good indicator of government's stance toward sectarianism, as I will explore.

7. Keane (1990) found nearly 50 percent of households in 1977 lived on totally segregated streets, where there was no minority presence.

8. Two attempts during this period at "devolving" legislative power to a Northern Ireland Assembly failed. In 1974, a power-sharing Assembly disbanded after 5 months. Between 1982 and 1986, a Northern Ireland Assembly was created but had no power other than the power to debate.

9. In the 1989–1993 term, 11 of 26 city councils across Northern Ireland engaged in power-sharing arrangements between nationalists and unionists, whereby key positions are rotated or committee positions are assigned on the basis of proportionality. Belfast city council has engaged in such practices only minimally (Beirne 1993).

10. The denominations of Belfast Protestants are split between Presbyterian and Church of Ireland, with a lesser percentage Methodist (1991 Census).

11. This provision changing the constitutional claim of the Republic of Ireland upon Northern Ireland was approved by nearly 95 percent of the Republic's voters.

12. The current effort to devolve legislative power to a Northern Ireland Assembly contains certain characteristics which distinguish it from earlier endeavors at devolution. These include approval by the Northern Ireland electorate, linkage with the Irish Republic's relinquishment of its unconditional constitutional claim on Northern Ireland, inclusion of safeguards to protect group rights, greater legislative power, and integration within a larger system of multilayered governance including all of the United Kingdom and Ireland.

13. Not to mention issues such as decommissioning of paramilitary arsenals, release of paramilitary prisoners, and police reform.

14. Source: British government Internet web site—*britain.nyc.ny.us*—1996.

15. A third tier of planning, regional, is done for the all of Northern Ireland. The last one completed was the 1975 Regional Physical Development Strategy.

16. Certain proposed land uses are taken out of mainstream review, such as those affecting the "immediate community" (like police stations). These often require a public inquiry and may be decided by the DOENI minister himself. Oversight of peaceline construction is by the security forces; DOENI does not have authority.

17. The first planning legislation in Britain was in 1909.

18. Northern Ireland is unbalanced in terms of population distribution. The Belfast urban area dominates, with little in the way of second-order or third-order cities. This is why decentralization of economic activities into consolidated new settlements in the 1960s was seen as a means toward overall economic growth.

19. Belfast Action Teams in 1994 were removed from the BDO and linked with the Making Belfast Work unit within DOENI.

20. Belfast Action Teams are built on the model of City Action Teams introduced in Britain in 1985.

21. On March 6, 1988, three IRA members were killed by the British Army in Gibraltar. At the funeral of one of the deceased on March 15 in Milltown cemetery, Belfast, three

Catholics were killed by a loyalist gunman. On March 19, two British Army undercover agents were killed after being abducted at the funeral of one of the March 15 deceased (Sutton 1994).

22. In addition to the urban policy units in the DOENI discussed, the Department of Economic Development (DED) seeks to strengthen and expand the industrial base. Within DED, the Industrial Development Board encourages the international competitiveness of Belfast's economic base, and the Local Enterprise Development Unit stimulates the potential of small businesses, especially their competitiveness for export markets.

23. The author walked and photographed all of the sectarian interface areas in Belfast.

24. See Rolston, Bill. 1992. *Drawing Support: Murals in the North of Ireland.*

25. Two-sided partition, where the two antagonistic parties are hermetically sealed from one another, occurs in modern-day Nicosia, Cyprus; and formerly in Berlin and Jerusalem (between 1948 and 1967).

26. Sectarian interfaces are characterized not solely by physical peacelines, but occur anytime ethnic communities abut each other. They can occur psychologically and behaviorally within streets and blocks, and within so-called mixed areas (W. Glendinning, Northern Ireland Community Relations Council, interview).

27. Comment during question-answer period following author's presentation of field research findings to planning professionals and academics. Queen's University of Belfast, March 22, 1995.

28. In that most suburbs outside the core city are Protestant, attempts to expand Catholic areas outward are also susceptible to sectarian resistance.

29. The "put-back" rate under redevelopment is estimated at about 40 percent (meaning that whereas 100 units would be existing before redevelopment, 40 would be built after clearance). This is due to more livable residential densities, internal space standards, and parking requirements (D. Murphy, NIHE, interview).

30. The Suffolk area has been a source of sectarian conflict since the early 1970s. The future religious complexion of the Lenadoon estate there became the subject of a pitched battle between republican and loyalist paramilitaries and was the stated reason for the ending of the IRA's 1972 ceasefire. Today, Lenadoon is an exclusively Catholic estate (NIHE 1994a).

31. Identity of source withheld upon request.

32. The direct subvention from British central government covers the excess of public expenditures over locally generated taxes in Northern Ireland.

33. Female unemployment rates were also ethnically differentiated in 1991—Catholic 14 percent and Protestant 7 percent.

34. Catholics are underrepresented at senior levels (public sector) and management and administration levels (private sector), although there are positive trends in both cases (British government Internet web site—*britain.nyc.ny.us*—1996).

35. Fourteen criteria were used, including income and job status, health, shelter conditions, physical environment, and education level.

36. Note that the two antagonistic ethnic groups in Belfast are often described as "communities." We are also interested in this section about how political and nationalistic issues penetrate and interact with "community" organization that is often neighborhood based. In this latter use of the term, Belfast has not two, but between 50 and 75 "communities."

37. "Political vetting" is a chiefly British expression meaning "to subject to expert appraisal or correction." It had its origin in a Parliamentary statement on June 27, 1985, by the then secretary of state, Douglas Hurd.

38. The *voluntary sector* consists of large, often provincewide, organizations with professional workers who work on issues like crime, vandalism, drugs, and homelessness. The *community sector* is composed of neighborhood-based groups with unpaid, part-time workers addressing multiple neighborhood issues.

39. An example of CD is place-based physical regeneration, while CR is exemplified by the required "Education for Mutual Understanding" school curriculum (Fitzduff 1993).

40. A difference F. Gaffikin (interview) highlights is that between deprived Shankill Protestants and relatively better-off east Belfast Protestants.

41. This account of Catholic community organizing draws upon accounts of Colm Bradley, who worked for the Falls Community Council during its formative years; and Brian Murphy, who as Springfield BAT leader worked to develop an Upper Springfield Development Trust for Catholic neighborhoods in west Belfast.

42. Electoral strength for the SDLP and Sinn Fein varies across Northern Ireland. Based on 1997 elections, the former has seven members and the latter thirteen members on the 51-seat Belfast city council. Provincewide, SDLP garnered 20.7 percent of local council seats and Sinn Fein 16.9 percent in the 1997 national elections.

43. Identity of interview source withheld upon request.

44. The sense of Protestant loss is illustrated by this not uncommon type of remembrance: "we used to walk down that street as a youth and we were picked up by all the people whose fathers were lecturers at Queen's University and middle-class professionals. Now, the street is 98 percent Catholic" (N. McCausland, interview).

45. This account of Protestant community organizing is based on firsthand accounts and reflections by Jackie Redpath, Greater Shankill Regeneration Strategy; and Billy Hutchinson, former loyalist political prisoner and now director, Springfield Inter-Community Development Project.

46. Identity of source withheld upon request.

47. Identity of source withheld upon request.

48. It is interesting to note that councilors from both sides of the conflict admit that less-publicized committee meetings show much greater Protestant-Catholic cooperation than city council meetings.

49. The Council, with assistance by contracted planning consultants, was preparing in 1996 to engage more constructively with the DOENI regarding the Department's plans regarding transport, housing, and retailing (F. Boal, Queen's University, personal communication, July 29, 1996).

5

British Urban Policy
Since 1972

The test of a policy designed to create public order in the midst of internal war is not whether it conforms to conventional liberal assumptions, but whether it produces order.
—**Richard Rose, Northern Ireland: A Time of Choice**

This chapter examines the approach that Belfast urban policymakers have taken toward the realities and challenges of sectarianism. First, it assesses the general philosophical stance of these policymakers toward the sectarian divide. It examines the specific interaction between policy and sectarianism in four important areas of policymaking: town planning, public housing allocation, public housing construction, and economic development. Second, it examines the effects of this urban policy approach on the: (1) distribution of resources between ethnic groups; (2) perceptions of community residents; (3) distribution of benefits between central city and neighborhoods.

Pursuing Stability Through Neutrality

Urban Policy Principles

Grey—neutrality, autonomy, indecision
Orange—King William III, Ulster, Unionism
Green—shamrock, Ireland, Irish Nationalism
—**A. D. Buckley and R. Paisley, Symbols**

The operative principles for Belfast urban policymakers and administrators have been to: (1) maintain neutrality of government's role and image in Belfast not biased toward either "orange" or "green"; and (2) assure ethnic stability through policy that manages ethnic space in a way that reacts to and reflects residents' wishes.[1] Policymakers face a recurring dilemma in dealing with the inflammatory geography of

Belfast. There is tension within government between proactive strategies aimed at comprehensive urban betterment and reactive, pragmatic responses aimed at urban stability and security. Since these two objectives are often in contradiction—the first assumes a certain urban normality that the second dismisses—policymakers have often had to choose. Commonly, their selection of public actions has been aligned with the second objective of maintenance and stability. Since 1972, policy has been based on rational, objective, and dispassionate measures, often responding to documented need. This policy of "color-blindness" has served organizational goals well, enabling government units to largely overcome the discriminatory legacy of their predecessors. Operating within the most contentious policy arena of housing, the Northern Ireland Housing Executive, in particular, has maintained much integrity as a fair allocator of public housing units through difficult times. W. McGivern, former Belfast regional director of NIHE (interview), states that "the main reason we exist is because we have the credibility." According to the Permanent Secretary of DOENI (R. Spence, interview), "although there are realities out there you cannot ignore, the department seeks in planning and housing to be neutral." The DOENI "is practicing the art of the possible, in a circumstance where they are in a sectarian trap and they know it" (J. Hendry, interview).

Urban policymakers feel the best way to create stability is to respect the needs and desires of communities and residents. G. Mulligan of DOENI (interview), for instance, while acknowledging the inefficiencies of ethnic segmentation, states that "planning does not want to say how the society or economy should change." Instead, government's proper role is to reflect in its policies the needs and demands of residents and neighborhoods. The principle underlying government involvement here has been to "follow the wishes of the people" (D. McCoy, Central Community Relations Unit, Northern Ireland Office, interview) and to "go with the flow" (W. Neill, Queen's University; P. Sweeney, DOENI; interviews). Government policy has accepted that there is a certain inevitability to the conflict, and has "accepted divisions like planners elsewhere assume people prefer cars" (W. Neill, interview). Divisions in society are viewed as based on deep-rooted feelings and reinforced through terror; thus "changes have to come from within people; government cannot change people's minds" (R. Spence, interview). Policymakers and administrators amidst ethnic polarization do not want to be perceived as "social engineers," viewing such a role as producing more harm than good. D. McCoy (interview) states that in Belfast's sectarian complexity "government should not impose a top-down macro view of how the city should work; rather, it should be responsive and sensitive to the needs and abilities of local communities." G. Worthington, Belfast Planning Service (interview) claims that "we must recognize the realities of the situation. If we shifted color (of a neighborhood), the end result would clearly not work. We're not about making social engineering decisions, or ones that would be perceived as such." R. Spence, permanent secretary of DOENI (interview), states that an overall strategy toward managing such a divided city would be extremely difficult to devise and, indeed, would likely be counterproductive in bringing about conflict. Thus, the DOENI accepts peacelines as performing an important security-enhancing function for neighbors (Murtagh 1994a). In a city where "the real border in Northern Ireland is in men's minds," government policy must respect these divides or face adverse consequences (R. Spence, interview). The problem to DOENI, then, becomes not the peacelines per se, but how to strategically meet housing and other community needs given their presence (Murtagh 1994a).

Policymaking in Belfast, even when aimed at mutually beneficial effects across ethnic groups, is not easy. Government sticks close to objective standards and must watch the meanings behind their language in public documents because "words can cause alot of trouble here" (W. McGivern, NIHE, interview). The pressured bureaucratic environment of urban policymaking is described by D. McCoy (interview): "There are too many opportunities for mistakes. We are under the microscope of time. We take no large steps too quickly, lest we close the door behind them and shut out opportunities." Planners and administrators feel that they are in a "no-win" situation in dealing with sectarianism. D. Murphy of NIHE (interview) states that new public housing construction can do little to solve the deep divisions within society, but could have disastrous effects if it infringes upon territorial claims. M. Graham of NIHE (interview) sees his role primarily as "one of damage control in a circumstance where criticism from one or both communities will always be there." He thus finds himself constantly "under the gun and unable to promote the organization proactively." In such circumstances, the proper role of government policy amidst polarization is to pragmatically respond to conflict conditions rather than create a comprehensive approach to dealing with them. The role is that of "societal reflector" rather than as "social engineer." This means that government policy should not be a lever to force change, but should facilitate and help communities in meeting their desires (D. McCoy, interview). In the contentious issue of housing, then, government should facilitate ethnic integration only if and when communities are prepared for it and want it. Until that time, community needs and desires for segregation must be accommodated.

The description of Belfast urban policymaking as "color-blind" is useful in portraying the general philosophical stance of government. Yet, the label goes too far in its implication that officials are unaware of sectarian realities. In actuality, internal policy discussions within government units—usually not for public consumption—clearly recognize the sectarian realities and constraints of Belfast. R. Spence (interview) asserts that "government strives to be impartial, but it is impossible to ignore the sectarianism." Thus, the label "color-blind" is more accurate in describing the intended effects of policy—as not favoring one ethnicity over another—than in characterizing the government's level of awareness of sectarian constraints. B. Morrison, DOENI planner, (interview) suggests that through the mid-1970s, sectarianism was truly a "non-subject" within policy discussions. By the late 1970s, however, the sectarian landscape was more explicitly recognized and acknowledged by government officials—"it was as if we were carrying out a plan for two cities that happened to overlap each other." In dealing with specific projects and policies, "you had to know—orange or green—which area you were dealing with." This is then not color-blind planning in its fullest meaning, but a type of "plural planning" that acknowledges the limiting effects of static territorial claims on dynamic urban processes and interrelationships.

While this plural planning framework is sensitive to sectarian realities, government remains dedicated to *color-blind* (or neutral) impacts so as not to disturb the delicate and volatile territoriality of the city. Government officials do not blind themselves to, or ignore, sectarianism, but rather accept it as a basic characteristic of the urban setting that requires close study in the consideration of policy strategies aimed at improving urban life in Belfast. Indeed, sectarianism must be handled with great caution by paying close attention to the sensitivities of the two communities (W. McGivern, interview). R. Spence (interview) concedes the importance of this color-sensitivity: "Traditionally, we said 'we're blind.' This is an honorable position. However, to carry out our responsibilities further, we must have an understanding of the two sides and their different needs."

I now explore the public stance that government has taken relative to sectarian challenges in specific policy arenas. I first evaluate town planning and its formulation of physical development policies to guide the extent and location of future development, and housing policy dealing with the allocation of public housing units to Belfast residents. These two cases illuminate a consistent neutrality and color-blindness in government's approach toward ethnic divisions.

Planning, Housing Allocation, and Ethnicity

Planning efforts since the 1960s for the Belfast urban area have emphasized physical and spatial concerns, and separated them from issues of localized ethnic conflict (Boal 1990). The *Belfast Regional Survey and Plan of 1962* (Matthew 1964) proposed a development "stop line" around the metropolitan area to spatially limit future growth, and it planned for the development of new towns outside the stop line to absorb spillover population growth. There was no mention whatsoever in the plan of the ethnically divided nature of Belfast. An ensuing detailed plan for the area within the "stop line" took note of ethnic divisions, but asserted that planning cannot be expected to influence them. It stated:

> It would be presumptuous, however, to imagine that the Urban Area Plan could be expected to influence religious . . . factors. Our proposals are designed specifically

to facilitate individual and community choice, so that the social pattern desired by the individual and the community may readily be built up. (Building Design Partnership 1969, p. 5)

In contrast to plans in the 1960s concerned with growth limitation and dispersal, the 1977 regional plan, *Northern Ireland: Regional Physical Development Strategy 1975–1995*, took note of urban and economic decline brought on by demographic, economic, and ethnic factors. First, due to out-migration encouraged by the 1962 Plan, accelerated out-migration due to violent ethnic conflict, and a significant fall in the birthrate, Belfast city had lost 150,000 residents—one-third of its 1961 population—between the early 1960s and middle 1970s. Second, economic shocks in the mid-1970s were leading to lack of economic opportunities and civil unrest. And third, the plan recognized the segregative forces and inter-communal territorial identification within Belfast:

A situation now exists where generally people are prepared to be housed only in what they regard as "their own areas." Whilst every effort will be made to break down these barriers, it will inevitably take many years to remove them completely. In the meantime the position as it now exists must be recognized and taken into account in the development of new housing areas. (DOENI 1977)

Both the 1969 and 1977 plans thus took note of the growing sectarian territoriality and supported a government role that would be accepting and accommodating of such ethnic demarcations. The DOENI's role would be to assure that the physical fabric of Belfast matched as much as possible the ethnic segmentation of its population.

The most recent urban area plan is the 1987 *Belfast Urban Area (BUA) Plan 2001* (DOENI 1990a). Cebulla (1994) gleans from this plan three main policy objectives and priorities: (1) maintain and enhance Belfast's position in the region; (2) improve access to employment for residents from disadvantaged areas in the city center; and (3) enhance the quality of urban living. The BUA plan neglects issues of sectarianism by defining them as outside the scope of planning. DOENI, in its plan adoption statement (1989, 2) "notes the views expressed on wider political, ecological, social or economic matters." However, it states that "it is not the purpose of a strategic land use plan to deal with the social, economic, and other aspects involved." The department had earlier expressed this view at a public inquiry when it stated that the contentious "non-planning" issues of housing and social service delivery are outside the agency's specific domain (DOENI 1988). Not one of the strategic objectives of the plan involves explicitly an ethnic or sectarian issue (DOENI 1990a, 16). G.

Worthington (interview) explains that "we can only take decisions within certain well-defined land use parameters, although our customers don't always appreciate that this is the situation." Echoing earlier plans, the plan largely accepts sectarian divides in stating that "this strategy acknowledges the wishes of residents to continue living within their own areas." Even the bread-and-butter of land use planning work—the forecasting of total and subgroup populations—is excluded from the plan, likely due to its ethnic and political sensitivity. I queried G. Worthington, head of the Belfast Divisional Office of the Town Planning Service, about this compartmentalization of the planning function in Belfast:

Author: What is the appropriate role of town planning relative to sectarian issues?

Worthington: Those issues don't intrude into our considerations. We don't particularly plan for one color or the other—orange or green. We do land use planning, that's it.

Author: Yet, isn't sectarianism rooted in land, and thus land use planning touches very closely?

Worthington: We're aware there are two communities. But in the BUA plan, we are not down to that level of planning. In Belfast, we do not produce land use plans for one territory or the other. We look at the whole area of Belfast in a broad, conceptual, and strategic way. We are not specifically planning for some type of ghetto system.

Author: There is no mention of demographics in the BUA Plan.

Worthington: This was a deliberate policy decision because inquiries into plans tend to get bogged down over demographic projection methods.

Author: Is DOENI assuming there will be a Catholic majority in Belfast city in 15 years?

Worthington: Probably nobody has "overtly" made such an assumption. What difference would that make in land use planning terms in any event? Catholics need all the housing, schools, churches, shops, all the facilities, just like Protestants do.

The last comment illuminates government's public stance. In more consensual cities, town planning of future development and service delivery would likely not be contingent on the forecasted ethnic makeup of the population, as Worthington declares. In Belfast, however, due to the strict territorial borders of sectarian populations—and the lack of Catholic space and underutilization of Protestant space—the relative growth rates of the two populations will have great effects on the size and locations of areas planners designate for housing and other needed land uses. Growth in the Catholic population requires challenging methods such as increasing the density of housing, "fudging" territorial boundaries to allow "green" housing in areas that might be perceived as "orange," or locating housing beyond the city borders of Belfast. Growth in the Protestant population, in contrast, could be met largely through new housing in underutilized and vacant

Protestant areas in the city. As D. Murphy (interview) asserts, "there are more opportunities in the broader planning sphere on the Protestant side than on the Catholic side." In the end, the needs for basic services and facilities may be the same between a Catholic and Protestant individual, as Worthington implies, but the means that government must use to meet those individual needs differ depending upon which side of the sectarian fence those needs appear.

What the BUA plan for 2001 does focus on are land use issues involved in the revitalization of the city center and the commercial development along the city's Lagan River. The Department views this central city emphasis as beneficial to both ethnic communities because it is "neutral territory" (R. O'Connor 1988). This city center emphasis in the midst of sectarian warfare in the neighborhoods has been described as an attempt to "re-image" the city as a nonsectarian center that can be marketed to potential investors internationally (B. Murtagh, interview). In the end, the effort is to "create a city no one can recognize" while the difficult areas and hard issues are largely ignored. J. Hendry (interview) describes it as a "feel good" approach that stresses the city center as normal and good for people and investors. He exclaims that the plan "doesn't mention Catholic or Protestant. It can't. That is the political correctness of the thing."[2]

A second policy arena explored in terms of its relationship to sectarianism involves the allocation of public housing units to households.[3] Since 1969, the official housing policy of the Northern Ireland Housing Executive (NIHE) has been based on (1) fairness and equality of allocations based on need, and (2) impartiality and nonsectarianism. Its 1990 document declares that "the Executive is dedicated to the principle that priority must be given to those in greatest need." The NIHE has sought to create social order and subsequent social assimilation and not to allow for ethnically separate submarkets (Keane 1990). Significantly, at no time in over 25 years has the NIHE been found guilty of political or religious discrimination in its allocation procedures.

The rules followed by the NIHE in allocation are color-blind. The waiting list for public sector housing units is a unitary one containing all individuals or households—both Catholic and Protestant—in need. The list is prioritized so that those in greatest need are highest on the list. For example, those in emergency circumstances (including housing disruption due to civil disturbances or sectarian intimidation) or those with special health and social needs are rated highest. Thereafter, applicants are ranked based on their present housing circumstances, such as degree of overcrowding and lack of amenities or disrepair. There is no identification on the waiting list of the religious affiliation of the applicant, nor does the NIHE classify their estates by religion. Each applicant is required to indicate one or, preferably, two locations at which he or she would be prepared to live, if offered accommodation. An offer of housing considered to be a "reasonable offer" by the

NIHE is one in a "general allocation area" that contains the applicant's selected estate plus those estates nearby that NIHE considers similar (M. Graham, NIHE, interview). After two "reasonable offers" of accommodation are turned down, the applicant is moved down in the priority list.

This seemingly color-blind set of procedures becomes, in practice, a process that: (1) is shaped significantly by ethnic parameters and (2) reproduces Belfast's sectarian geography. First, in the NIHE's geographic delineation of general allocation areas (within which "reasonable offers" can occur), sectarian territoriality is figured in so that an allocation area does not encompass mixed ethnicity (M. Graham, interview). Second, although NIHE does not classify its estates by religion, Belfast's residents and NIHE applicants most assuredly do—individual or household preferences are almost always for estates of like ethnicity. Despite NIHE's color-blind intent, then, public sector households show even higher rates of Catholic-Protestant segregation than private sector households (J. McPeake, interview; Keane 1990). In 1977, 89 percent of public sector households resided on streets that were completely or almost completely segregated, compared to 73 percent of private sector households (Boal 1995). A later 1987 survey indicated that 55 percent of NIHE tenants lived in Protestant estates, 27 percent in Catholic estates, and 18 percent in "mixed" estates (Smith and Chambers 1989).[4] This sorting is due not to deliberately segregative policies on the part of government, but rather to the allocation policy's dependence on self-selection which has reinforced ethnic segregation. Allocation procedures, in their focus on public safety, also overtly accept differential housing markets. Allocation procedures require that displaced public sector households be rehoused in "safe and acceptable" locations, and guidelines note as unreasonable "an offer of accommodation in an area where few of the applicant's religion reside" (Keane 1990). Because of the strict territoriality of housing space in Belfast and NIHE's reliance on individual preference, the intended unitary waiting list becomes, in effect, two waiting lists (J. McPeake, interview; W. McGivern, interview; Singleton 1986). These realities frequently obstruct the Executive's primary goal of housing those in greatest need first (Singleton 1986). Catholics with great housing need, compared to Protestants similarly situated, are more likely to experience the restrictive effect of the city's sectarian geography on the availability of a "reasonable offer."

In summary, principles of urban policy engagement in Belfast have crystallized around government objectives to produce color-neutral impacts on city residents as a means toward stabilizing a volatile city. Government is not unaware of sectarian realities, but does seek policies and programs that do not disproportionately favor one side over the other. In this way, government seeks neutrality, or "greyness," in policy impact in a situation where sectarian color matters. Town planning has largely assigned sectarian issues to policy domains outside its responsibility, leaving the city with no comprehensive or strategic approach to dealing with sectarian divisions. At the same time, housing allocation administrators have rationally designed a color-neutral set of criteria that have made them immune to discrimination claims, yet do not appear to be sufficient to effectively address the complexities presented by ethnic compartmentalization.

The two government activities examined thus far—town planning and housing allocation policy—are similar in that neither directly changes the city landscape in terms of new built structures or urban activities. Town planning sets down a guide for future development, but does not engage in actual development projects. The housing policy discussed deals with the allocation of public housing units to Belfast residents, but applies primarily to units that already exist in the city. In other cases, the allocation scheme is implemented only after the difficult questions of where to construct new units have been answered. Such indirect effects on the urban landscape provide designers of planning and housing allocation policy with the opportunity to seclude themselves behind "neutral" demeanors and procedures. The case is much different, however, when government units are involved in project-based physical changes to the urban system, whether these be new public housing units or new economic activities. In these cases, the direct impacts of government actions on the inflammatory sectarian urban fabric bring the implementing agencies face-to-face with sectarian realities known to but avoided by town planning and housing allocation administrators.

Development Tactics at the Sharp Edge

I now examine the tactics government units employ in dealing with sectarian complexities when involved in project-based changes to the urban landscape. The Northern Ireland Housing Executive new build and redevelopment program has had the most significant physical impact on Belfast neighborhoods, while the Belfast Development Office has utilized physical tools and financing to remake parts of the city's geography. These two units do not have the luxury of distance afforded the Town Planning Service and NIHE allocation managers—their actions have direct, physical, and visible effects on Belfast's inflammatory territoriality.

The NIHE has had to deal with sectarian realities in their redevelopment program, their justification for new public housing construction, the location of housing estates vis-à-vis peacelines and ethnic space, and in how they address integration and segregation of public housing. I now turn to each of these issues.

The construction and redevelopment of public sector housing by the NIHE in Belfast is ultimately linked to sectarian territory—its maintenance, decimation, or enhancement. Upon its creation in 1971, the NIHE had to deal with an appalling housing legacy in Belfast city. The city's Victorian-age housing stock was literally crumbling to the ground by the 1960s. Belfast city council had been both slow and reluctant to provide public housing for renting, partially due to the weighing of local voting power toward business property owners rather than householders (J. Hendry, interview). In 1974, the NIHE revealed that 29,750 units of a total stock of 123,120 dwelling units (24 percent) were unfit for human habitation (NIHE 1991). Large areas of housing were derelict, and in the city's inner areas, 50 percent of city housing was unfit (NIHE 1991). Since 1971, the NIHE has built 18,500 public housing units in the city of Belfast (J. McPeake, NIHE, interview), reducing unfitness levels from 24 to 8 percent during an urban ethnic war.[5] In the peak years of public housing construction in the 1980s, the NIHE was spending about 100 million pounds sterling per year on Belfast housing. Today, the Northern Ireland Housing Executive operates up to 40 separate redevelopment areas of ongoing renewal activity (NIHE 1988). The NIHE construction program, inherited from its predecessor housing agency, was based at first on wholesale redevelopment, involving the large-scale clearing of old row housing and subsequent rebuilding at lower densities. K. Sterrett (DOENI, interview) asserts that many of today's physical manifestations of sectarian problems can be traced not to the troubles themselves, but to the massive clearing and redevelopment of residential areas started in the 1970s. Subsequent programs, encapsulated in the 1982 Belfast Housing Renewal Strategy, have sought to moderate the severe disruption of communities caused by large-scale clearance through the phasing and sequencing of redevelopment, repair, and rehabilitation of existing units for a 30-year life (Housing Action Areas); closer consultation with intended communities; and, more recently, the encouragement of private investment in the renewal of housing areas.

NIHE's construction and rehabilitation program is predicated upon the extent of "urgent need" applicants on the public housing waiting list relative to existing housing opportunities of adequate quality.[6] This is a viable and objective measure to justify new construction. Yet, NIHE's housing programs become intertwined with each side's effort to maintain and solidify their own territory. Housing renewal plans are closely scrutinized by residents and political representatives for their effects on the maintenance of territorial claims. In particular, Protestants advocate new housing construction as a way to revitalize inner-city communities and criticize NIHE for low put-back rates and displacement. Catholics, meanwhile, call for new housing to meet the needs of their growing population and criticize NIHE for not expanding into unused "orange" areas. A complicating factor facing the NIHE here is that the calculation of housing supply and demand becomes convoluted. As earlier noted, the NIHE's waiting list, unitary in intent, becomes a dual waiting list in practice. Accordingly, the NIHE must actually calculate two urgent need measures—one for Catholics; one for Protestants. As M. Graham (interview) states, "NIHE responds to the indirect effect of peacelines in creating differential supply and demand." Similarly, D. Murphy (interview) asserts, "we don't build peacelines; but we do have to deal in our house building with the indirect consequences of them in terms of demography." The fact that "urgent need" applicants are estimated to be about 54 percent Catholic and 46 percent Protestant (W. McGivern, interview), together with the presence of a more constricted public housing supply on the Catholic side, means that a great majority of "new build" over the past 20 years has been in Catholic areas (J. McPeake, interview). Such actions, magnified by the city's territorial constraints on policy,[7] in turn fan the fires of those who claim that the NIHE has been engaged in a program of "de-Protestantization."

In its plans regarding the location of new or rehabilitated housing, the NIHE commonly comes face-to-face with sectarian realities. It acknowledges interfaces and peacelines as "locations where conflict can quite frequently occur and where the Housing Executive is seeking to manage and maintain homes on an impartial basis" (NIHE 1988). The NIHE does not identify a strategic approach to building housing near these areas. Instead, it seeks pragmatic tactics on a case-by-case basis within the limits set by sectarian geographies. In looking where increased Catholic need for housing can be met, W. McGivern (NIHE Belfast Office director, interview) explains that "it is not for us to try to define where a peaceline should be breached, that is a community decision." Similarly, any attempt to turn unused Protestant land into a Catholic transition zone would be tantamount to social engineering (J. McPeake, NIHE, interview). NIHE feels that it is not the proper government entity to push for such sensitive changes to sectarian geography. In proposing redevelopment plans in either community, the Housing Executive feels its role regarding security issues should be limited because "it is not their role to assess risk" (NIHE 1987). Rather, the NIHE is advised by three national agencies on security issues likely to arise from the housing plans. If these agencies, in order to reduce potential intercommunity conflict, require that walls or other physical barriers be constructed, the Executive then builds physical barriers as part of the housing development (NIHE 1987). However, because it is not deemed consistent with housing policy that housing resources be spent on the artifacts of community division, barrier costs are borne by other national agencies. Nevertheless, the Housing Executive admits that "by building barriers between communities, it is unwittingly accentuating the division in local society" (NIHE 1987). Peacelines that separate communities are built for valid short-term stabilization goals and can avert the full-scale evacuation of housing stock under threat. Yet, such government-reinforced segregation goes against nonemergency public objectives. An NIHE (1994a) report recognizes the ill effects of hypersegregation on the housing interests of the Executive. It states that "segregation interferes with the flexibility of the housing market; it requires duplication in terms of the provision of new housing; it creates voids in peace-line and flash-point areas; and it causes otherwise suitable land to become sterile for housing purposes."

The development of the Catholic Poleglass estate in the mid-1970s is a striking example of housing policymakers and planners dealing in a pragmatic way with the city's static sectarian geography. A shortage of land for housing in the west Belfast

Catholic ghetto necessitated one of three responses: (1) breaching of the peacelines in the city amidst an ethnic war to allow Catholic housing on Protestant territory; (2) increased densities and unlivable overcrowding on the Catholic side; or (3) the relaxation of an anti-sprawl regulatory limit to allow Catholic housing on agricultural land beyond the city's borders (and within the administrative boundaries of the unionist city of Lisburn). In deciding on the third response, housing needs and the realities of ethnicity-based territorial constraints on the ghetto's expansion within Belfast city overshadowed the spatial goals of discouraging urban sprawl (R. O'Connor 1988; Blackman 1991; Boal 1990). Still, significant and hostile majority opposition to the expansion of the minority community in west Belfast had to be overcome, from both Belfast and Lisburn local governments. For the Poleglass estate to be acceptable, major commitments were made by ministers and top civil servants to assure that it would be different. B. Morrison (Town Planning Services, interview) recounts a minister's comment to a top civil servant under questioning by the Lisburn council: "This is going to have to be the best bloody housing estate built ever anywhere." Because of a fear that the first houses available would be taken over by the IRA paramilitary, top civil servants, army personnel, and planners facilitated the movement of the first families using a midnight operation. At the same time, housing selection scheme rules were broken in order to accept families on the basis of their community leadership potential. Today, Poleglass is the site of some 2,000 Catholic families—an estate of good-quality medium-density homes with adequate green space and community facilities. It has also avoided much of the violence and troubles (B. Morrison, interview).

The final issue of sectarian salience is how NIHE addresses public housing segregation. The existing policy is that the Executive believes people should have freedom of choice, that NIHE prefers mixed or integrated estates, but that it does not believe in forced integration (NIHE 1994a). In the face of intimidation and violence, people "voted with their feet to move into segregated camps" (W. Glendinning, Northern Ireland Community Relations Council, interview). It became impossible for NIHE to hold some estates as mixed. After 300 homes were burned or severely damaged in the mixed estate of Glenard, for instance, it became impossible to re-create this area in today's Catholic Ardoyne as a mixed estate after rebuilding. Early 1970s violence, similarly, turned the Lenadoon estate from mixed to Catholic. On other occasions, the NIHE had planned the location of new estates in the hope of encouraging integration, but without explicitly promoting the concept (NIHE 1994a).

The NIHE felt that there was little it could do to promote integration or prevent segregation amidst such tensions. Hence, there is no formal policy of promoting integration. In its First Annual Report, NIHE stated that it "does not believe that forced integration is any more desirable than a policy of deliberate segregation." After twenty years' experience, the NIHE (1991, 50) concluded that "the prospect of integrated housing in interface areas is remote. Suspicion and a defensiveness towards existing boundaries and territory remains strong in both communities." Currently, the NIHE is engaged in a tentative discussion about the possibility of ethnic mixing should interethnic hostilities recede. A report by an NIHE advisory group (1994a) discusses the housing costs imposed by territorial segregation and the resulting supply-demand distortions. Significantly, it highlights the larger social costs of segregation, asserting that "integrated estates are likely to be more stable and peaceable than segregated estates" (NIHE 1994a, 10–11). In any evolution of NIHE formal policy on integration, however, government must come to terms with the legacy of Manor Street housing in north Belfast. This area was redeveloped in 1987 and 1988 as mixed housing, resulting in new dwellings occupied by Catholic families at a location that was allegedly Protestant territory. A serious outbreak of violence occurred, with fifteen new dwellings burnt out and vandalized, and subsequently demolished by the Executive. Subsequently, a new peaceline barrier was erected. The government lost its substantial investment virtually overnight and a new physical partition was created. The NIHE today views Manor Street as an "expensive experiment" that failed and whose time is not yet right to try again (M. Graham, NIHE, interview). It represents a partial approach to the problem; an "example of trying to address conflict with housing while not addressing everything else" (D. MacBride, community leader, interview). Indeed, NIHE cannot be expected to promote integration apart from a comprehensive strategy that addresses ethnic compartmentalization on multiple fronts. J. McPeake (NIHE, interview) asserts that "it is hard to generate notions of integration in the housing front when many aspects of life are segregated. There is more to producing integrated housing than producing the bricks and mortar housing product." He points, in particular, to needed changes in employment and education. Absent a multi-faceted approach to sectarian divisions and living with the legacy of integration failure on Manor Street, the NIHE will likely move in a rationally incremental way on the issue of integration. As D. Murphy (NIHE, interview) states, "we are dealing with a considerable amount of public money, so our choices have to be fairly realistic."

Similar to the NIHE, the Belfast Development Office (BDO) seeks physical changes to Belfast's landscape. It is a development facilitation unit that seeks to physically regenerate parts of Belfast and to integrate housing, economic, and planning initiatives (V. Allister, BDO, interview). It controls large sums of urban financial assistance programs—the Urban Development Grants aimed at the stimulation of private investment; Environmental Improvement Schemes aimed at upgrading the urban physical environment; and Comprehensive Development Schemes, which allow for the acquisition and redevelopment of derelict areas. Although most of this funding has been directed at the city center, the development office has also carried out projects amidst the strict territoriality of Belfast's neighborhoods, experiences to which I now turn. I focus on the physical changes that BDO has deemed appropriate when seeking to regenerate an urban fabric laden with sectarianism. Two main physical tactics have been used in non–city center regeneration: creation of neutral land uses between antagonistic sides; and the justification of physical alterations in interface areas based on the forecasted economic benefits of BDO-sponsored projects. Murtagh (1994a) calls these tactics "wedge planning" and "facilitating growth," respectively. Both of these techniques are environmental or physical methods aimed at diffusing sectarian interfaces, and both seek to build mutually beneficial uses along potential lines of conflict. The main difference is in potential effects. Whereas the first method distances opposing sides through neutral infrastructure, the second method seeks economic gains for both sides and could facilitate nontrivial alterations to sectarian territoriality.

Wedge planning introduces a neutral land use as a means of separating rival neighborhoods. For example, redevelopment in east Belfast, using CDS and EIS programs, included the creation of a wide new road—with medians and a major landscaping embankment— that acts as a de facto peaceline. Adding to the separation of antagonistic sides, an elderly housing unit was constructed on the Protestant side. Through these methods, the "physical and psychological distance between the two communities was increased in a needed way" without recourse to the scarring effect of permanent walls (G. Mulligan, interview).[8] J. Hendry (interview) suggests that the use of roads in this way is a likely scenario in the future for underutilized areas in formerly Protestant territory. Yet, road-building itself produces scars and distance, and goes against other city policies endeavoring to de-emphasize car transportation in order to alleviate congestion. In the second type of physical tactic—facilitating growth—there is the introduction not of infrastructure, but a new development project whose cross-community economic benefits are used to justify physical alterations to the interface area. The Northgate development in the Duncairn Gardens area of north Belfast presents an informative illustration of this approach and is now examined. The local problems in this area are multiple and intense. This part of Belfast has been the location for terrible political violence, accounting for 20 percent of all sectarian killings during the troubles (DOENI 1990b). A permanent wall peaceline was constructed dividing Catholic New Lodge from Protestant Tiger's Bay for almost the entire length of the Duncairn Gardens street. There was "galloping dereliction" along the dividing street (B. Morrison, interview)—27 percent of interface frontage had been demolished; and 32 percent of all properties, and 43 percent of commercial properties, were vacant (DOENI 1990b). Catholic housing stock, already unable to meet demand, was endangered further by violence. Much of the Catholic housing fronting the peaceline has front sides grated to prevent damage from petrol bombs, and back doors are used instead for access. Tiger's Bay was fast becoming a ghost town due to Protestant out-migration. Forty percent of Tiger's Bay housing was vacant, and about 1.4 hectares of derelict land lay adjacent to the interface frontage (DOENI 1990b). Psychologically, the remaining Protestant population felt frightened, embattled, and insecure (B. Murtagh, interview).

The BDO and the NIHE coordinated their efforts in Duncairn Gardens to order to "manage the evolution of the area." NIHE had a vested interest in rescuing the area because it contained a large and vulnerable housing stock. Twenty percent of a recently rehabilitated "housing action area" in Tiger's Bay was already vacant, while unmet Catholic housing need intensified. Yet, NIHE was unable or unwilling to lead the effort and turned to the BDO for leadership. The result of this was the Northgate proposal, facilitated by BDO in concert with the NIHE, planning services, and the local BAT. This project will acquire land for an integrated land use scheme, the core of which is to be an economic development district of industrial workshops and enterprises on the Protestant side that aspires to create neutral and mutually beneficial territory between Protestant and Catholic communities. In Protestant Tiger's Bay, 380 houses will be demolished; about 125 will be built anew in different Tiger's Bay locations behind the new industrial activities. Environmental improvements elsewhere in Tiger's Bay will involve "improvements to pedestrian routes, planted areas, and to gardens" in housing estates which have "poor or vulnerable boundaries" (DOENI 1990b). In this way, the plan seeks to consolidate and upgrade Protestant housing stock in an otherwise declining area.

The combination of redevelopment and rehabilitation, and the sequencing of these programs, will likely be able to retain more Protestants in Tiger's Bay than if the whole area was redeveloped at once (D. Murphy, NIHE, interview). Protestants, in effect, would bear witness to the pushing back of the sectarian divide (or at least the thickening of the divide). As one government participant stated,[9] this represented a "novel approach for effectively fudging the peaceline." Yet, in return, Protestants would receive an upgraded and more coherent residential community with access to new employment opportunities. On the Catholic New Lodge side, the thickening of the buffer zone would allow the existing and endangered housing units to be maintained. Catholic residents would also have access to jobs across the street. However, new Catholic housing would still not be able to cross the street, and thus overall supply would not increase. One idea discussed would have rerouted Duncairn Gardens road toward Tiger's Bay, thus opening up opportunities for Catholic housing on formerly Protestant land. Although "we tried to think of a planning reason for doing so" (B. Morrison, Planning Service, interview), this de facto redrawing of the sectarian interface to accommodate Catholic housing needs succumbed due to its potential inflammatory effects. Instead, the NIHE is engaging in the sensitive process of identifying potential new housing areas elsewhere in north Belfast to meet expected Catholic demand.[10] The NIHE seeks to identify these sites based on considerations of land use, access, convenience, territoriality, and the presence of symbols and icons. This assessment asks, "will it be perceived by the other side that you are encroaching on their space?" Such is a risky business.

Actions Without Strategy

Urban policy regarding the built environment of Belfast is engaged in by many government entities, including: NIHE (housing construction); BDO (economic regeneration); Belfast Action Teams (community development); Making Belfast Work (economic and human resource development); and the Planning Service (land use). The first four units are development entities capable of physically altering Belfast's built landscape and thus forced to deal pragmatically with sectarian land issues. Only the last unit—Planning Service—is composed of urban professionals capable of designing a comprehensive, systems-based, and strategic approach to sectarian land issues. Such a strategy would be more proactive and broader than, and thus help guide, the project-based tactics of the development entities. Unfortunately, town planning in Belfast—through its public stand of "color-blindness"—has done little to contribute to meaningful government policy aimed at addressing sectarianism in a productive and sustainable way. Despite the land use and territorially based implications of much of sectarianism, the town planning function, whose professional foundation is land use, has played a minor role in addressing ethnicity. K. Sterrett (DOENI, interview) critically observes, "here and in Britain we seek to contain planning. We teach the rational-comprehensive approach, yet planning all around us is determined by politics." The impact of this is more than simply occupational marginalization. Rather, the lack of an explicit ethnic management strategy sets well-intentioned public actions adrift on the sectarian sea, with awareness only of what can be seen on the horizon, not of its broader sweep or wider dynamics. Lacking a strategic framework aimed at effective management of ethnic space, public actions by government units like NIHE and BDO have primarily been ad-hoc tactics rather than strategic acts; project-based rather than area-based; reactive rather than proactive; and have emphasized vertical rather than lateral government approaches. Planning in the strategic and comprehensive sense has been marginalized.

Town planning is responsible for creating the framework within which development is to take place in Belfast. It could play a central role in providing a reality check and frame of reference that development agencies can use when interacting with contested territoriality. Yet, there has been "no coherent and strategic planning response to the troubles" (K. Sterrett, interview). Town planning has avoided dealing with ethnic conflict directly, leaving it to development agencies to deal with sectarianism on their own terms. Ethnicity becomes perceived not as a "planning" problem. Rather, sectarianism becomes a "security," "housing," or a "community relations" problem separated from a larger strategic perspective (K. Sterrett, interview). Sectarian interface areas received no serious mention in the most recent Belfast Urban Area (BUA) Plan for 2001. When I asked G. Worthington (Head, Belfast Divisional Office, Town Planning Service) about the greatest role that town planning could play in bettering ethnic relations, he claimed that "I'm not sure there is necessarily a role." Belfast town planning "tends to take a 5-mile high view and stands back" from the development process (G. Mulligan, DOENI, interview). Instead of providing a guide for managing sectarian space, Belfast town planning "has entrenched itself in the wall of physical planning, where social, economic and sectarian issues are pushed outside the wall" (J. Hendry, interview). This compartmentalization owes to the 1972 Planning Act of Northern Ireland, which provides town planning with a distinctive identification with land use and excludes issues dealing with the broader interactions between social and physical space (B. Murtagh, interview). It is revealing that the 1972 Act follows its lead from a British town planning system which, itself, has been found to be insensitive to issues of ethnicity. The administration of British town planning has "tended to focus on legal and technical aspects of land use and development and has not involved persistent and wide-ranging debates about the social purposes and goals of planning" (Thomas and Krishnarayan 1994). In addition, British planning practices a "color-blind" approach, in which planning authorities "promote a formal equality which, in practice, is insensitive to the systematically different needs and requirements of the population."[11]

Town planners in Belfast defend their profession's ideology of technical land use competence. Town planner B. Morrison (interview), an otherwise progressive practitioner, views the stance as beneficial. "Planning works quite well behind the scenes," he states; more deterministic actions by government are best left to others. In contested public discussions, "it can be useful for planners to adopt the technical and professional role because it allows them the ability to avoid confrontation" (K. Sterrett, Planning Services, interview). In the sectarian battleground of Belfast, "there is a sense of almost persecution where planners retreat into narrow technical roles" (W. Neill, interview). The town planning process becomes one viewed by planners as properly regulatory, not proactive and intervening. The comments of B. Morrison (interview) are illuminating: "Our regulatory role is our reason for being. To do this cleanly and properly, you would have nothing to do whatsoever with anything proactive. This posture as regulator influences us in terms of what we can outwardly do, or be perceived as doing." Town planning becomes an arbitrator or referee, rather than a player, in the sectarian realities of Belfast. Although town planning provides professional advice and expertise to development agencies, they are constantly aware that they must be viewed as disinterested referees when deciding the fate of project applications.

In maintaining this narrow ground of responsibility, "planners have marginalized themselves, and shut themselves off from urban realities through their shell-like existence" (B. Murtagh, interview). This marginalization and compartmental-ization of town planning have meant that urban policy responsibilities "leak out" in ad-hoc ways into the collection of development agencies like NIHE, BDO, BAT, and MBW. The real cutting edge of public planning in Belfast becomes usurped by those policy professionals in the development agencies willing to work creatively to address sectarianism in ways that town planning has avoided. Yet, tactical ac-tions by government occurring outside an overall strategic framework produce problems. For example, the Duncairn Gardens project led by BDO may be capa-ble over time of solving a localized interface problem. Yet, there is no urban strat-egy that addresses the fact that the general pattern of decreasing Protestant de-mand in the city has produced, and will produce, many more "Duncairn Gardens" in Belfast. Should BDO engage these tactics of interface diffusion at all localized sectarian divides associated with underutilized Protestant land? Or, should there be a concentration of public resources on a targeted set of interface areas? Such a strategy of interface intervention can only be developed based on knowledge of demographic dynamics that extend beyond proximate neighborhoods to include spatial relationships occurring at subarea, citywide, and regional levels. The proj-ect-based orientation of much developmental work cannot get to this level of so-phisticated analysis. In addition, the engagement in tactical actions separated from strategy puts inordinate burdens on development agencies. The NIHE, for in-stance, has a vested interest in the effective management of sectarian space. They oftentimes, then, find themselves out front in government discussions regarding sectarianism and the proper role of government policy. Yet, this extends the NIHE into policy domains outside their housing responsibility. After all, the NIHE is in-volved in only one facet of city-building and should not be expected to design a comprehensive, multi-issue strategy. Rightfully, NIHE "says they want to enable but not to lead" (W. McGivern and R. Spence, interviews).

In the end, developmental interventions by units such as BDO or NIHE into the sectarian complexities of Belfast are not guided by a coherent, citywide strate-gic approach or by a set of guidelines directed at desired physical, social, and eco-nomic outcomes across the city. It is in the design of such integrated principles that town planning could make its most important contribution. No other partic-ipant in Belfast urban policy is capable of such a comprehensive and systematic ap-proach to city-building. Instead, town planning removes itself by emphasizing sta-tic land use allocation and regulatory caution. Tactical actions amidst sectarianism, unsupported by a strategic framework, then run the risk of introducing additional sharp edges to an already barbed city.

The lack of a comprehensive strategy to guide urban decisions in Belfast has also meant that government approaches have been vertical and single-function, rather than lateral and coordinated across functions. There is a lack of coordination be-tween the town planning service and the development office (J. Hendry, interview).

The NIHE looks for another government unit to take the lead in designing the non-housing part of community regeneration (W. McGivern, NIHE, interview). Funding from community-based Belfast Action Teams duplicates and counters other agencies' efforts at times (V. McKevitt, BAT, interview). And, project funding from the Making Belfast Work program becomes absorbed into different government units, rather than connected to a cross-departmental anti-deprivation strategy (B. Murphy, MBW, interview). With a lack of strategic integration across city-building decisions in Belfast, vertical policies and actions are incapable of effectively addressing a sectarian geography that is a complex system of physical and psychological relationships. For example, the closing of a public school by the Department of Education based solely on student population can have symbolic and destabilizing effects on an ethnic community's identity and can exacerbate population declines and housing stock erosion. Thus, single-issue or single-agency approaches will likely be ineffective in enhancing quality of life, and may even intensify ethnic tension. P. Sweeney (DOENI advisor, interview) states that each unit "is technically excellent, but it's the things that fall within the gaps that really make the difference."

In summary, the government's approach to urban policy in Belfast has contained a set of self-limiting features. There is both separation of the town planning function from ethnic management responsibilities and fragmentation of policy along division and department lines. Combined, these factors decrease government's ability to mount an ethnically sensitive strategy that would be both multidimensional (physical, social-psychological, economic, and human development) and interdivisional (integrating planning, housing, and development units). Urban policies have sought orderly changes in the physical development of the city, but actions have been largely reactive to sectarian and societal realities. P. Sweeney, DOENI advisor (interview) reflects upon the deterioration of the Protestant Shankill neighborhood and suggests that it was not government policy that hurt the area, but a combination of major economic shifts and inner-city neighborhood dynamics. Still, policymakers are not off the hook. Rather, "planners could have been alot more progressive in dealing with structural change. All this could have been anticipated. As such, planners stand accused and guilty. They needed to manage the environment rather than simply reacting." He asks a disturbing question: "in a deeply fractured society, is there not a need for government to be more proactive, to be more progressive?"

Neutral Means, Unequal Outcomes

Despite the intended neutrality of government policy in Belfast city, there are uneven outcomes at individual and neighborhood levels. Meanwhile, community perceptions of urban policy can be quite different than the intended color-neutral outputs would suggest. This section examines the effects of urban policy on the: (1)

distribution of resources between ethnic groups; (2) perceptions of community residents; (3) distribution of benefits between central city and neighborhoods.

Housing and Planning Outcomes

In a city with segmented housing and employment markets, a government approach that emphasizes neutrality and equality of opportunity will likely not increase the equity of urban outcomes. Rather, it will tend to neutrally reflect the societal inequalities present. Thus, a neutral policy in an unequal society of dualities and separation will result in unequal opportunities through the replication of those dualities. Where sectarian territoriality constrains much of urban living, neutrality does not necessarily increase equity.

An excellent example of this effect is the NIHE allocation scheme. It epitomizes a neutral, fair, "color-blind" approach to allocating public housing units to those in need. No religious identification is ever part of an applicant's material. And, it is an approach favored by residents battered by sectarianism. An analysis commissioned by the Standing Advisory Commission on Human Rights (STACHR) (Smith and Chambers 1989) found that the executive "has had a striking success in creating confidence in the fairness of the system." This is much to the credit of NIHE. However, this fair system is not producing fair outcomes. The STACHR study of public housing in Northern Ireland found that "in 1987, the public housing system did not succeed in delivering equal opportunities to Protestant and Catholic applicants." This is not due to direct discrimination (of which the study found none), but to the lesser access by Catholics to public housing due to the constraints of sectarian territoriality. The study found clear differences in average time on waiting list (Catholics wait longer compared to Protestants having similar, or even lesser, housing needs). The study found that for 1987, 23 percent of those requesting Catholic estates in Northern Ireland were housed; compared with 42 percent of those requesting Protestant estates.[12] For the Belfast urban area specifically, there is simply less public housing stock in the city available to a Catholic housing applicant. The study classified about 55 percent of NIHE units in Protestant estates and 27 percent in Catholic estates.[13] At the same time, the waiting list in categories classified as urgent need was approximately 54 percent Catholic and 46 percent Protestant in 1995 (W. McGivern, Belfast housing director, NIHE, interview). Thus, Catholics face a disproportionately smaller available housing stock in Belfast at the same time as they experience disproportionately greater housing need. A color-blind policy template premised on applicant choice that is put atop this unequal base of conditions restricts Catholic "choice" to a housing market about one-half the size faced by Protestants.

This combination of neutrality and inequality has led some to argue that NIHE and other government units should monitor more explicitly their impacts across the ethnic divide. D. McCoy of the Central Community Relations Unit of the Central Secretariat (interview) asserts that the "assumption underlying color-blindness is wrong—that an organization that says 'we don't want to know what religion our clients are' cannot discriminate."[14] Rather, religious monitoring of clients and outcomes is needed to see whether a policy is producing unequal outcomes, and to help design corrective policy where inequality is present. J. McPeake (NIHE, interview) similarly suggests that with color-blind policy, there are possible negative by-products of normal operations that you do not know about and thus would not seek to correct. The STACHR report (Smith and Chambers 1989), itself, states the main implication of its findings is that the NIHE "should now move towards explicitly and openly monitoring the results of its policies in light of the need to achieve equal opportunities for the Protestant and Catholic communities."

This policy recommendation has two important parts. First, its call for religious monitoring points Belfast urban policy in a direction away from its reliance on color-blindness and its public nondiscussion of sectarian issues. Second, its aim to achieve equal opportunities directs Belfast policymakers away from their traditional emphasis on impartiality and neutrality. This is so because Smith and Chambers (1989 and 1991) are using a broader definition of equal opportunity that goes beyond the absence of discrimination (as fulfilled by the NIHE) to include a fairer distribution of outcomes. In contrast to a narrow definition of equality of opportunity stressing the absence of obstacles to entry so that all reach the starting blocks, a broader definition calls for the consideration of structural conditions that promote inequality of outcome so that all not only get to the starting blocks, but also can compete fairly in the race. In the NIHE example, all applicants get to the starting blocks, but structural conditions tilt the race toward Protestant applicants. Smith and Chambers (1991) summarize their investigations of housing and employment outcomes in Northern Ireland in this way: "The view that equality of opportunity has been nearly achieved, and that remaining inequality is a reflection of historic discrimination which will gradually disappear, is emphatically contradicted by the weight of the evidence." "Color-blind" equality of treatment by government does not translate directly into equality of opportunity, in the broader sense of this concept. Indeed, neutral government schemes may reflect and reproduce the societal inequalities and dichotomous conditions within Belfast.

The policies and practices of the planning service in Belfast display a similar pattern as NIHE's allocation program—a procedurally neutral program utilized in a structurally unequal sectarian landscape. Procedurally, the planning service engages in a fair and neutral methodology regarding the review of project applications. Indeed, there does not appear to be any bias in project approvals based on the religious composition of the proposed location or the applicant's ethnicity (J. Hendry, interview). Still, the planning service does not address sectarian geography in a strategic way in its area and subject plans. Thus, the inequalities associated with sectarian territoriality will likely remain, and cause the procedurally fair planning approval process to result in unequal outcomes. A lesser number of projects can be proposed to meet Catholic needs because of the lack of land availability in ethnically circumscribed space. At the same time, those projects proposed for "Catholic" areas may face spatial and physical infrastructure constraints that financially jeopardize its success. New-build programs for public housing, in contrast, do seek to decrease Catholic-Protestant disparities by justifying most new construction on the degree of "urgent need" on the waiting list, which is disproportionately Catholic. In the long term, then, this building program, by increasing the number of units available to Catholics, could create a situation where a "neutral" allocation scheme could produce equal outcomes. However, given the current uneven distribution of "Protestant" and "Catholic" estates and the likelihood that territoriality will remain strong in the foreseeable future, it will take decades for this building program to achieve a Catholic housing availability/need ratio similar to that of Protestants today.

A problematic feature of NIHE's new-build program is that it plays an instrumental role in facilitating or perpetuating the ethnic apartheid of the city. Belfast housing planners are faced with a dilemma in the planning of public sector housing. In their allowance for Belfast's polarized geography in allocation and construction decisions, and in their building of peacelines when deemed necessary, housing planners in the short term minimize and contain intergroup conflict or at least introduce no new sources of conflict.[15] NIHE (1991) states, "the prospect of integrated housing in interface areas is remote. Suspicion and a defensiveness towards existing boundaries and territory remains strong in both communities." In the long term, however, publicly condoned intergroup separation can more firmly reinforce and perpetuate divisions (Keane 1990; NIHE 1994a). To the extent that residential mixing is one prerequisite to addressing deep ethnic conflict, politically sensitive housing policy does little to alleviate, and may even intensify, urban polarization. Again, NIHE (1991) concludes, "sadly, while the peacelines provide a physical barrier between both communities, in reality they represent barriers to a permanent solution." The sectarian geography of Belfast was created by the larger problem of ethnic conflict and the intimidation and violence associated with it. However, government policy has facilitated and furthered segregation through its policies. The STACHR report (Smith and Chambers 1989) on housing policy concluded that NIHE actions "may reinforce segregation, although it is unintended." In the midst of urban civil war, this was probably a rational response by public authorities. Yet, B. Morrison (Planning Services, interview) worries that in planning Belfast "we may be in danger of institutionalizing what are artificial boundaries."

Government's condoning of sectarian segregation seeks short-term stability at the expense of longer-term individual and societal costs. There are severe "costs of self-segregation and separation" (M. Fitzduff, Director of Northern Ireland Community Relations Council, interview). NIHE (1994a), for instance, states that segregation perpetuates and exacerbates societal divisions, facilitates control over housing estates by paramilitaries, and fosters a climate that stunts the social development of children. With segregation, learning about the other side comes not through mutual interaction and understanding, but through ugly portrayals and stereotypes. Public authorities will be compelled to deal with these social psychological costs because they can debilitate a city as much as war in its streets. Government's acceptance of sectarian segregation also increases the costs and difficulties of service delivery and urban administration. For instance, the siting of local service delivery offices (social security, for example) based on color-blind, technical methods of activity allocation can produce unequal opportunities if the site is perceived as off-limits to one ethnic group. In this way, a policy may be fair, but the way it is implemented or administered causes inequality (D. McCoy, Central Community Relations Unit, interview). Another example is that a resource center aimed at assisting both communities has to constantly fight against perceptions that it is in one group's territory or the other, and thus not in reality a "neutral venue" (D. MacBride, interview). The incorporation of sectarian realities in siting decisions causes another set of problems that are fiscal in nature. In this case, normal planning methodology for siting facilities based on general population distribution and densities becomes transformed into siting often identical community facilities on both sides of the sectarian interface. This duplication of facilities—parks and leisure centers, social service offices, shopping centers, baby clinics, and community meeting places—taxes public expenditures and consumes land needed for other uses (J. Hendry, interview; B. Murtagh, interview). In the case of public education—segregated into two systems—the underutilization and scattered locations of Protestant schools in north Belfast mean that per-pupil costs there are twice those for Catholic schools.[16]

In a city where territorial changes and incursions can be causes for terrorist violence, policymakers have become linked with efforts to maintain each side's territorial claims. This is especially true for traditional Protestant areas that today are underutilized and which, in a normal city, would have evolved into Catholic areas. Such "Darwinian survival" of neighborhoods is not allowable where maintenance of community viability is closely linked to protection of sectarian territoriality. In an effort to contain civil disorder, government must rescue depleted communities—such as Suffolk and Tiger's Bay—from imminent collapse. Instead of helping these "hospice" neighborhoods through the terminal stage, policy resuscitates these corpses at great public expense. In other cases, policy seeks to sustain a neighborhood "community" that years ago left for peripheral estates. These represent reactive tactics by government that solidify territoriality and promote urban sclerosis, not a strategic approach to addressing the two communities' problems on a citywide basis. R. Strang, formerly with the NIHE (interview), points to the public costs of this approach: "Where is the sustainability of maintaining a sterile territoriality? At some point, we will not be able to afford Belfast."

In the end, the short-term containment and abeyance of conflict have been attempted by Belfast policymakers through color-neutral policies. But, it has been at the expense of long-term social, psychological, and fiscal costs. In this way, the role of policy has been neutral, but its effects have not been benign. B. Neill (Queen's University, interview) questions whether urban policies are "neutral and in the public interest." He suggests that policy has not been neutral in its outcomes, and that it is debatable whether policies that decrease the future social, psychological, and fiscal livelihood of its residents are in the public interest. The long-term consequences resulting from the formalization of ethnic separation through housing, planning, and peaceline policies may paralyze the city for decades after the signing of the 1998 multiparty agreement.

Community Beliefs

Belfast was a city divided along sectarian lines by the planners, not necessarily by the inhabitants.

—*Joe Austin, Belfast City Councillor, Sinn Fein (interview)*

Redevelopment here was like South Africa's policy of clearing out black towns and moving them to the hinterlands. This is what it felt like.

—*Jackie Redpath, Greater Shankill Regeneration Strategy (interview)*

We have been ignored.

—*Nelson McCausland, Belfast City Councillor, Ulster Unionist Party (interview)*

What you do may be "scientific" but it will be viewed through orange or green spectacles.

—*Will Glendinning, N. Ireland Community Relations Council (interview)*

Government policy in the midst of urban civil war is bound to be viewed negatively and with suspicion, and Belfast urban policy does not escape such criticism. Nevertheless, there are aspects of urban policy viewed favorably by community leaders and residents. As mentioned before, the NIHE housing selection scheme has earned the agency high marks for fairness and impartiality. This is a tremendous feat because housing was probably the most contentious issue in Belfast before direct rule in 1972. The NIHE is rightfully proud of their achievements in this aspect of housing policy. Another part of government that has been rated positively is the Belfast Action Teams (BATs), decentralized and community-based liaisons between neighborhoods and government. BATs have had a measurable impact on people's attitudes toward government, helping communities feel they have some role and thus helping overcome feelings of alienation (V. McKevitt, Ardoyne/Oldpark BAT leader, interview). They have also helped improve government's image overall (G. Mulligan, interview). A 1992 survey of 4500 Belfast city residents (DOENI 1994a) assessed the impact of government urban regeneration policy. It found that overall satisfaction with the areas where people live was extraordinarily high (about 80 percent). However, this may be due, says co-author G. Mulligan (DOENI, interview), to a heightened sense of community loyalty in a conflict environment rather than to government policy.

Interviewees and secondary material present a more critical view of public policy. In the least, policy is portrayed as a remote mechanism that avoids the real issues of the city. M. Fitzduff, executive director of Northern Ireland Community Relations Council (interview), takes the NIHE to task for construction decisions that "facilitate apartheid." D. MacBride, who works for a north Belfast community resource center (interview), characterizes government agencies as ignoring the difficulties and having their heads in the sand. She asserts that public entities are unaware of how their rigidly designed programs and definitions adversely impact Belfast's neighborhoods. Under direct rule, government is remote and distant, information is hard to get, and it is difficult for nongovernmental organizations (NGOs) like MacBride's to identify the key personnel in government. G. Worthington, DOENI planner (interview), is aware of these perceptions: "Planners have a poor image in Northern Ireland. That's probably our fault. On the other hand, we can't be right all the time."

More than this characterization of government as aloof, there is the underlying current that urban policy has intentionally harmed one ethnic group or the other. G. Worthington (interview) knows that there is "certainly a perception out there that there is a hidden agenda; always the perception that 'everything is done on the other side of the peaceline.'" D. MacBride (interview) feels there is a sense that government "plays the 'sectarian card,' playing one community off against the other." And, J. Austin (Belfast councillor, Sinn Fein, interview) asserts that political events have made it expedient for town planners to divide the city along sectarian lines. Urban policymakers experience strong criticism from both ethnic communities, usually for different reasons (M. Graham, NIHE, interview). Catholic criticism targets government's inability to expand housing to meet their growing needs. Linked to the Catholic perceptions is the larger political issue of sovereignty. J. Austin (interview) summarizes the nationalists' view as having been abandoned and punished by the Northern Ireland state. In terms of livelihood, Austin says, there is a "case-hardened acceptance that nationalists don't get employment unless they are cheaper or low-skill; that employment has been the unionist reward for supporting the state." Protestant perceptions center on public actions' effects on community displacement and the feeling that policy is biased toward Catholics. N. McCausland (Belfast councillor, Ulster Unionist Party, interview) asserts that "DOENI bureaucratic bungling has destroyed Protestant neigh-borhoods in North Belfast" by replacing demolished housing too slowly to retain his constituencies there. He also states that the "government approach has been too reactive to the political shouting," pumping money into moderate nationalist enterprises in efforts to counter Sinn Fein's extremism. Many Protestants feel that the government is moving too quickly and closely to what they perceive as nation-alist initiatives (S. Corbett, Central Community Relations Unit, interview).

A common claim among Unionists has been that policy has had the intent of "de-Protestantizing" certain parts of Belfast city. Central to this perception is the history of the Protestant Shankill neighborhood. The Shankill area has severely de-clined, from 76,000 population in the 1960s to 26,000 today. According to a local resident survey, the most important factor contributing to this decline was not the sectarian troubles or economic decline, but government housing redevelopment programs.[17] J. Redpath (Shankill community leader, interview) describes the community as being "mugged by redevelopment and then left lying there."[18] A statement in the local newspaper (*Shankill People*, February 1995) sums up resi-dent attitudes toward past housing policy: "Redevelopment has torn the commu-nity of the Old Shankill apart and has never put it together again. The planner built flats and soul-less housing estates; they moved thousands of people to out-side Belfast; they bulldozed the shops and wrecked the Road." The reality of 1970s urban redevelopment in areas like the Shankill is that both sides—government and community—are partially correct. First, government was acting in response to an existing and forecasted decline in the Shankill population (an area seriously eroded through economic shifts). As such, the community is wrong, in part, to view redevelopment programs as a cause of population change, rather than a reac-tion to change. On the other hand, the way government proceeded with redevel-opment—large-scale clearing that outpaced rebuilding—was devastating to the community, both in terms of physical stock and community coherency and lead-ership. The pace of clearing dispersed the population from Shankill Road to pe-ripheral estates, left behind a depleted population, and took apart the community as an organic whole.

In its most extreme "conspiratorial" form, public perceptions exist which claim that security and military reasons underlie planning policy. These claims fall into three categories (Murtagh 1993). First, there is the claim that the Northern Ire-land Office engineers population movements in a way that leads to more homoge-neous and thus policeable ethnic space. Second, there is the perception that the police and British Army are involved in the design and layout of housing develop-ments to secure them more effectively (Hillyard 1983; Cowan 1982). Third, there is the accusation that key planning decisions—such as housing demolitions and the building of the Catholic suburban Poleglass development—are dictated by wider political considerations. Murtagh (1993) and this author find no conclusive evidence of these conspiracies, political agendas, or the presence of "hidden planners."[19] Rather, what appears to be happening is that conspiracy perceptions are a consequence of government not having an explicit planning framework for dealing with the realities of ethnic space. W. McGivern of NIHE (interview) proposes that the downside of government's neutral approach is that people fill in this void with conspiracy stories. And, W. Glendinning (Community Relations Council, interview) forecasts that the "avoidance by government of the real schisms in the city will continue to fuel fears and distrust." The negative public perceptions of government as uncaring, biased, or conspiratorial confirm that intended policy neutrality is a difficult task in a contested environment. Government must calculate in the future whether such negative perceptions are outweighed by real achievements on the ground. A government approach that is more open and strategic about sectarian realities may provide significant benefits to future Belfast governance.

Neighborhood Distress

The neutral stance of urban policymaking in Belfast has also tended to sidestep ethnic neighborhoods in important ways, favoring safer and less sectarian geographic areas of focus. Much attention of urban policy and financial assistance has been directed at the city center, and these efforts have stimulated a renewal of the city core. Yet, social and economic deprivation in the city's neighborhoods remains sadly intense and there is little improvement. There is a nagging impression that city center benefits are not reaching the downtrodden in the neighborhoods, and may even be gained at their expense. City center revitalization, supported through financial tools, has improved the position of the service sector there and has enhanced the city's position in the region (A. Cebulla, interview). The benefits of this attention were expected to be increased job opportunities for the residents of Belfast's ethnic neighborhoods. This would be consistent with one of the goals of the BUA plan 2001: "to improve access to employment by concentrating investment in areas which can be safely entered by both communities in the city" (Cebulla 1994, 15). The city center would provide a "neutral venue" for ethnic workplace mixing, combating the inhibition of labor mobility by real and perceived violence that had been documented as early as 1977. And, the city center job emphasis could help break the segregative effects of neighborhood-based employment.

Survey results of employed Belfast residents (Cebulla 1994) displayed in Table 5.1 indicate that city center revitalization is not providing meaningful work benefits to Belfast residents. It appears that residents outside Belfast city have been the major beneficiaries of new city center jobs. To the degree that they have more disposable income than city residents, they would also disproportionately benefit

TABLE 5.1   Percentage of Belfast Residents Benefiting from City Center Employment

	% of Service Jobs Citywide	% Belfast Residents Working Retail Jobs
City center	21.8	4.9
Wider city center	44.1	7.9

SOURCE: Cebulla, A. *Urban Policy in Belfast: An Evaluation of Department of Environment's Physical Regeneration Initiatives* (Belfast: DOENI, Central Statistics and Research Branch, 1994), p. 92.

from new shopping opportunities. Within the city, the survey showed that residents in Protestant east Belfast were most likely to access the city center job market (Cebulla 1994, 93). The study concludes that for city residents, the position of the city center as an employment focal point was marginal (Cebulla 1994, 92). As A. Cebulla (interview) states, "the working class residents have a hard time fitting into the 'image' of the city center as plush and for middle-class consumption."

In one sense, this constitutes unfair criticism of DOENI's city center policies since policymakers do not have control over the recruitment and employment policies of new retailers. In addition, low access to center jobs is probably due to low skill and education attainment levels, again outside DOENI's domain (R. Spence, permanent secretary of DOENI, interview). In this spirit, A. Cebulla (interview) states that it can be said that the DOENI has done their job, but that these programs are not going to solve the city's problems. Yet, since employment access to the city center was a key aspect of DOENI's BUA plan, some way must be found to link the city center strategy in a proactive way to the improvement of conditions in the city's disadvantaged communities. Absent this, socioeconomic deprivation will persist in city neighborhoods and community leaders will feel abandoned by policy. A recent public report (Sweeney and Gaffikin 1995, 9) presented the view of many in the nongovernmental sector that the city center development orientation has been "at the expense" of neighborhood renewal. Thus, not only is the city center focus not substantially helping the job prospects of neighborhood residents, but at least perceptually, it is interfering with them.[20]

There are few signs of change in the level or pattern of social and economic disadvantage in Belfast's neighborhoods over the last 25 years (Northern Ireland Council for Voluntary Action [NICVA] 1993; Cebulla 1994; J. Harrison, MBW, interview). The main anti-deprivation program, MBW, spent 120 million pounds sterling in its first six years in efforts to stem economic disadvantage. Still, according to economic researchers F. Gaffikin and M. Morrissey (interview), all indicators of deprivation indicate insignificant changes. In a study of area deprivation from 1971 to 1991, NICVA (1993, 12) found that "unemployment levels have progressively and disproportionately increased in the wards ranked highest in each analysis." Although the citywide unemployment rate stayed constant from 1981 to 1991, there is "a greater inequality in the distribution of unemployment now than in the 1980s" (NICVA 1993, 11). In fifteen of the city's 51 wards, the percentage of the economically active who were unemployed in 1991 was 30 percent or higher (citywide figure was 20.3 percent). The MBW claims that 3,000 new jobs have been created directly or indirectly through MBW spending in its first six years (DOENI 1994c, 7). However, program output measures are not linked to ward residents (J. Harrison, interview; Gaffikin and Morrissey, interview). Without this data, and in light of little improvement in area deprivation levels, it must be concluded that MBW was not reaching its intended goals of stemming economic disadvantage in Belfast's deprived neighborhoods.[21]

In terms of Belfast urban policy outcomes, this evaluation finds that neutral policies often reflect social and economic inequalities and are incapable of addressing two communities having different objective and perceived needs. In this way, neutrality is a means toward an end, not an end in itself that guarantees certain outcomes. In addition, government in contested Belfast, despite some hard-earned praise in certain policy areas, is seen as uncaring, biased, or conspiratorial. Both Protestants and Catholics feel their community needs are not being addressed in an effective and responsive manner. Most dispiriting of policy outcomes, however, is its insignificant effect on lifting residents and their neighborhoods above levels of social and economic deprivation. Urban policy has provided to neighborhoods physical benefits through improved public housing and amenities rather than personal upliftment through job opportunities and human development programs. With this imbalance, the NIHE will increasingly play the role of landlord of a robust housing stock for the long-term unemployed (R. Strang, interview).

Notes

1. These conclusions are based on interviews with government officials in DOENI central office, DOENI Town and Country Planning Service (Belfast Division), NIHE Belfast Regional Office; the Central Community Relations Unit–Northern Ireland Office, Central Secretariat; and with academics who have been involved in Belfast urban policy formulation and evaluation.

2. There is a total absence of the words "Catholic" and "Protestant" from the BUA Plan 2001 (DOENI 1990a).

3. I focus here on allocation of public housing units. Urban policy dealing with the redevelopment and construction of public housing units presents a different set of issues and is treated in the next section.

4. "Mixed" estates are where the minority comprises 5–30 percent of the population (NIHE 1994a).

5. In reality, the troubles may have stimulated redevelopment. Singleton (1986) states that "housing reform and comparatively large injections of public money have been used in an attempt to achieve wider objectives related to the acceptance of the Northern Ireland State by 'disaffected' citizens." Money for Northern Ireland public housing stayed high even through the Thatcher years of fiscal restraint and retrenchment.

6. "Urgent," or priority, need applicants include those who are homeless, or facing threat of homelessness, due to natural emergencies, familial breakdown, or civil disturbances; those suffering from special health and social conditions; those living in an unfit house to be closed or demolished; and "key workers" (NIHE 1990a).

7. Without sectarian territorial imperatives, the extent of new housing for Catholics would be attenuated because vacant existing units in today's "orange" areas could be used to meet some of the need.

8. The West-Link motorway elsewhere conveniently separates Catholic west Belfast from Protestant inner south Belfast. Still, a peaceline had to be built that fronts onto the expressway.

9. Identity withheld upon request.

10. This is existing unmet demand plus need created by future New Lodge redevelopment that will rebuild at lower densities.

11. The narrow definition of town planning in Britain may be further channeled in Northern Ireland. W. Neill, planning academic (interview), hypothesizes that civil servants brought with them during the introduction of direct rule a certain ethos that they should address urban problems directly. Planning-related decisions were thus appropriated by civil servants working in development agencies separate from town planning.

12. The religion of the applicant was not recorded, while the ethnic composition of the estate was classified in the STACHR report. The assumption used was that only Catholics request "Catholic" estates; Protestants "Protestant" estates. Household type and need differences between ethnic groups were not behind the percentage disparity; indeed, when these were controlled statistically, the disparity increased rather than lessened.

13. Eighteen percent of units were classified as in a "mixed" estate. Although this supplies some additional housing for Catholic applicants, it does little to narrow the gap between Protestant and Catholic access to the public housing market.

14. Another interviewee (name withheld) asserts that color-blindness is a falsehood anyway in NIHE allocation because "one can often find out the religion of a client through various devious ways."

15. This assumes that mixed estates may increase the potential for violence. Incidents at Farrington Gardens (now Catholic Ardoyne), Lenadoon, and Manor/Roe support this assumption. Yet, the relationship between residential patterns and potential for violence is not that clear (J. McPeake, NIHE, interview). For instance, segregated estates, more vulnerable to control by paramilitaries, may be more stimulative of urban civil war.

16. The Belfast Education and Library Board is responsible for state (Protestant) schools; the Catholic Church controls Catholic education. The integrated school sector is small.

17. As reported in Report Back Evening, February 6, 1995. Greater Shankill Community Planning Weekend.

18. The most emotive expression is the "Rape and Plunder of the Shankill" from Wiener, R. (1976).

19. Murtagh and this author would agree with Dawson (1984) that redevelopment has been used in certain areas in efforts to minimize intercommunity contact along the interfaces. This is qualitatively different than the fuller-bodied conspiracies discussed here.

20. A 1994 assessment of urban policy in Britain concludes that property-led renewal often occurs at the expense of community development, and argues that there should be more community-targeted assistance (Robson et al. 1994).

21. Starting in 1995, monitoring was to link MBW project data with area and resident outcomes.

6

Belfast and Peace

Cities, by definition, are about conflict and contested space. It's how you manage conflict that is the issue.

—**Paul Sweeney, Advisor, Department of the Environment (interview)**

Nobody is neutral in such circumstances. Everyone is partial. The key is to make positive use of this partiality.

—**Mari Fitzduff, Director, Northern Ireland Community Relations Council (interview)**

The reactive and neutral posture of urban policy in Belfast has sought containment and abeyance of conflict. Yet, the intended neutrality and community-reflective nature of urban policy appears insufficient to effectively address the complexities presented by ethnic compartmentalization. The ability to restructure the city in a normative and positive sense is foreclosed as government works only within the territorial blinders of its communities.[1] Belfast's urban policy approach has relied on single-dimensional responses by individual government units to complex urban phenomena having physical, social, and psychological aspects. A strategy to coordinate public interventions has been sacrificed to often ad-hoc project-based tactics by different government units at different times. This has decreased government's ability to mount an ethnically sensitive strategy that can constructively advance the welfare of the city's neighborhoods and residents. The policy-neutral posture suffers from unequal outcomes, poor public acceptance, and ineffectiveness in addressing deprivation in Belfast's ethnic neighborhoods.

This chapter examines the elements of an alternative approach to Belfast's urban policy—one more progressive, proactive, and openly cognizant of the city's potent ethnicity. Such a policy approach will be criticized by some as being too risky to implement in the early stages of Northern Ireland's political restructuring. I argue, however, that it is essential to consider these policy options so that more constructive urban actions could be taken as part of, and contribute to, larger peacemaking efforts in the future. Urban actions may help anchor and re-inforce advances in larger political negotiations, bringing tangible benefits of peacemaking to city, neighborhood, and resident. Such a different urban policy approach will challenge policymakers to move beyond the feeling that any ap-proach by government other than passive reflection amounts to intrusive and po-tentially damaging "social engineering." In the housing field, for example, alter-natives to a color-neutral approach were commonly equated by interviewees with an integrationist agenda that might force ethnic groups to live side by side despite their preferences for segregation. Despite these concerns, many of those polled recognized the need for some movement by government toward more progressive and proactive management of ethnic problems and issues. B. Murtagh (interview) states, for example, "planning and policy should go beyond the passive reflection of urban needs and demands and take on the social respon-sibility to effect change." This chapter seeks to outline, through the use of emerg-ing, more progressive strands of urban policy, a proactive role for future North-ern Ireland governments in dealing with ethnic issues that would lie between passive reflection of need, on the one hand, and social engineering, on the other.

Seeking Peace in Belfast

Progressive Ethnic Engagement

Who in this room can say that sectarianism has had no role to play in where we live, work, go to school, have as partners? If this is false, why is there no mention of sectarianism in govern-ment plans and documents?
—**Will Glendinning, Development Staff, NI Community Relations Council (interview)**

We're not ignoring sectarianism, but addressing it in a subtle way.
—**Housing Planner,[2] NIHE–Belfast Division (interview)**

A progressive ethnic strategy would acknowledge that single issue–based inter-ventions into city-building (whether it be land use planning, economic develop-ment, or housing) ignore the complex reality of sectarian geographies. Its goal would not be the integration of antagonistic groups per se, but the coexistent via-bility of those sides within the urban system, whatever spatial forms and living patterns that might entail.[3] Murtagh (1994a) states that such coexistent viability will not come through color-neutral procedures, but through a more explicit ac-counting of ethnic factors in planning and development decisions. For example, he suggests that government engage in ethnic audits or impact statements that would forecast the impacts of proposed actions on community identity and stabil-ity. Qualitative, perceptual analysis would complement traditional projection tools of land use planning, and community relations objectives—aimed at the improvement of interethnic tolerance and understanding—would be a central part of area plans and strategies. An ethnic management strategy would seek to bring sectarian considerations and issues more publicly into the planning and policy process. W. Glendinning (interview) recommends that planning and service delivery agencies consider locational, social-psychological, community identification and maintenance factors in their plans and actions. He equates civil servants under the current approach with the family of an alcoholic. Like such a family confronting the disease, Belfast urban policymakers often have dealt with sectarian issues out of shock and in emergency situations. He suggests that there is power in more openly talking about sectarianism and policy before the shock comes. In the end, government officials come to terms with sectarianism in one way or another—either on a proactive and engaged level or a reactive and disjointed one.

The challenge to government officials is to talk honestly among themselves and with their citizenry about something which they have denied they do. In some ways, such as ethnic audits or impact statements, these new planning roles would only make more explicit what happens in government anyway (B. Neill, interview).[4] We saw earlier that the "color-blind" label more accurately describes the intended effects of policy—as not favoring one ethnicity over another—than in characterizing the government's level of awareness of sectarian realities. J. Hendry (interview) points to the high awareness by the Planning Service of the sectarian implications of proposed projects that come through their offices, and the author often found within the walls of government a sophisticated appreciation of the complexities of sectarianism. Nevertheless, this call for explicitness asks much of government officials—to come to terms with their own fears and feelings along the path of a more candid incorporation of sectarian issues into public policy processes (M. Fitzduff, interview). "By asking people to discuss these things," states W. Glendinning (interview), "you're asking them to expose their roles, to get beyond their professional demeanor." What would change under a more explicit strategy is that policy discussions of ethnic content would be shared with other government units and with community groups. Gained from more explicit accounting of sectarian realities would be an enhanced ability to design a multidimensional urban strategy, and the feeling by communities and citizens that they have some ownership of the public programs and a stake in assuring their successful outcomes. This would decrease suspicion of government and the propensity of residents to attribute ill and conspiratorial motives to government. As C. Bradley (NICVA, interview) asserts, "if government had been more explicit and honest up front with its explanations, conspiracies would not have filled the void in the past."[5]

An ethnic management strategy would challenge public officials to redefine the town planning function beyond its traditional role in Northern Ireland as land use arbitrator. The town planning profession, with its training in urban comprehensiveness and interrelatedness, is best qualified to prepare a multidimensional approach to ethnic management. To do this, however, town planning must be forced to break out of its entrenchment behind the wall of technical issues of land use allocation. Murtagh (interview) asserts, "cultural specificity is a legitimate planning concern; instead, planning's goal is to be a technical and rational process." Similarly, B. Neill (interview) suggests that, since town planning's forte is land use and territoriality, the "symbolic appropriation of urban space—through murals and other territorial claims—is very much a planning issue." Because sectarian conflict has many urban dimensions—one of which is spatial—the planning of sectarian Belfast should broaden in both its substantive reach—to encompass social-psychological and community identity issues—and its professional skills—to include community relations and conflict negotiation. Town planning would move from its current technical and land use orientation to incorporate consideration of the social, economic, and psychological dynamics and requisites for the coexistent viability of Protestants and Catholics.

A progressive ethnic strategy would not view the two ethnic groups only in terms of their spatial and population requirements; or in terms of only objective need. Instead, it would analyze ethnic communities as complex urban subsystems that contain interrelationships, dynamics affiliated with either viability or decay, and different lines of feedback (W. Glendinning, Community Relations Council, interview). This represents a more holistic view of ethnic community functioning that includes social-psychological issues of community identity. Interventions into these urban subsystems based only on land use considerations are naive and potentially dangerous (R. Strang, interview). Based solely on the criteria of population density and range, for example, planners would argue for the closing of a local State (Protestant) primary school in a declining area. Yet, the closure can send emotional and practical signs to the Protestant community and increase their feeling of threat. Murtagh (1994b) suggests that the social-psychological effects on the viability and sustainability of ethnic neighborhoods be injected as a decision criterion in the investment programs and capital and revenue decisions of public sector organizations. The key to assure the coexistent stability of competing spatial groupings is to maintain or develop differential local institutions such as community centers, health centers, youth clubs, schools, and churches.[6]

A progressive ethnic strategy would by necessity also have to engage multiple government units laterally, rather than the current circumstance of nonintegrated vertical responses. "For too long," says D. Murphy (NIHE, interview), "different departments have gone their own way, resulting in no comprehensive housing-social-economic approach to renewal." V. Blease, chief executive of the NIHE, suggests that explicitness of sectarianism is occurring in individual government units, but not across unit boundaries.[7] These vertical governmental responses and actions are incapable of addressing urban ethnic subsystems in a holistic way. The coordination of interdepartmental activities that has occurred has been the result more of innovative, lateral thinking individuals within government, rather than a normal and structured practice (P. Sweeney, DOENI, interview). A report (DOENI 1993a) written by planners within the NIHE and Planning Service argued for the routinization of such coordination through the development of an integrated regeneration strategy composed of housing, social, economic, and environmental/physical components. It appears most important that the developmental and regulatory functions of government, currently separated institutionally, be brought closer together.[8] Town planning can provide an urban system–based frame of reference and strategy able to guide developmental agencies in their interventions into contested territoriality. At the same time, the project-based experiences of development agencies such as the NIHE and BDO can provide models that town planners can use in the development of a citywide strategy of ethnic management. In addition, the report asserted that government actions be set within the wider demographic and economic changes of the region, and that they not address urban issues on a neighborhood-by-neighborhood basis.

The possible move toward a progressive ethnic strategy by government is on the minds of people both within and outside government. Whether it is a local politician stating that "it is difficult to see change coming and participate in it" (N. McCausland, interview), or a civil servant claiming that "we have learned and will continue to learn" (V. Allister, BDO, interview), the perception is that there is something better than the existing model of urban policy. More innovative, lateral thinkers are now in high positions within the DOENI. For example, the former director of the Northern Ireland Voluntary Trust was special advisor to the permanent secretary of DOENI, bringing with him a progressive community perspective. The permanent secretary himself was the designer of a community relations unit within the Central Secretariat, described below, and a principal architect of the cross-community Education for Mutual Understanding (EMU) compulsory component of all Protestant and Catholic public school curricula. In addition, institutional reorganization has placed the major social/economic policy, Making Belfast Work, within the heretofore physically oriented DOENI, thus increasing opportunities for needed policy integration. And, importantly, the 1989 Fair Employment Act provides the Northern Ireland government with a valuable precedent in modifying government policy amidst political controversy to more fully acknowledge ethnicity and more strongly pursue fair outcomes.[9]

Peace-building in Northern Ireland aimed at energizing and reinforcing the 1998 multiparty agreement will demand that the traditional protective approach by urban policymakers developed in the midst of urban civil war be reevaluated. It is incumbent upon urban policy professionals to help guide Belfast urban residents and neighborhoods away from their comfortable blinders. P. Sweeney (DOENI advisor, interview) asserts that "DOENI must be part of the overall change process in Northern Ireland. We have the responsibility to push back barriers, to open up, and to ask fundamental questions." B. Murtagh (interview) states that "planners cannot change the broader societal context, but they can affect people's quality of urban life and ease tension. Peace will only hold if there is accommodation of differences; and planners can help here."

Emerging but isolated examples of new urban policy approaches exist in the city that consider sectarian realities more progressively. I turn to four notable examples in the next two sections—Northgate, Springvale, the Central Community Relations Unit, and Making Belfast Work. These experiences inform policy officials about both the rigorous requirements and fresh opportunities of an ethnic strategy premised on coexistent viability of competing ethnicities.

Signs of Change

Acknowledging Ethnic Community Dynamics. The Northgate development in the Duncairn Gardens area of north Belfast was discussed previously in terms of how it seeks to physically restructure the sectarian divide in order to diffuse the interface. It seeks to create a more consolidated, coherent Protestant residential area, through demolition and subsequent partial rebuilding, that would be buffeted from the old interface by an industrial/economic project. Meanwhile, the effective moving back of the interface will allow breathing room for Catholic housing units previously susceptible to destabilization. I focus now on two additional important aspects of this project: (1) the interagency cooperation used; and (2) the incorporation into the replanning of the area of a sophisticated analysis of the multiple facets of sectarian geographies. In 1990, the Under-Secretary (Planning and Urban Affairs) in the DOENI created a working group chaired by the head of the Belfast Development Office that included personnel from the Planning Service and the local Belfast Action Teams. The NIHE, at the same time, was a key stakeholder in the area, with about 30 million pounds sterling invested in the community area since 1976 (DOENI 1990b), and had lobbied for public sector attention to the stabilization of the Duncairn area. There were three objectives of the interdivisional work group (DOENI 1990b).[10] The first was to propose environmental ways of diffusing the interface, which had led to downturns in commercial activity, increased security barriers, and a declining and retreating Protestant community in Tiger's Bay. A second objective was to deal with housing problems "where contrasting features of the two communities combine with territorial and land constraints to produce a major housing problem." And, thirdly, the group sought ways to improve economic opportunity in the area (1991 unemployment rates were 48 percent in Catholic New Lodge and 30 percent in Protestant Tiger's Bay). The interface problem was deemed central and determining; and proposals sought to achieve long-term stability for the area.

The Northgate concept is not based on color-blind and banal discussions of land use allocation, but employs a finely tuned sensitivity to sectarianism and its social, spatial, and psychological correlates. Sectarian geography is mapped in detail. For example, the study reports (DOENI 1990b) that "Catholic territory continues to extend north along the Antrim Road and westwards along the Cliftonville Road. This trend represents an erosion of formerly 'mixed' areas." Elsewhere, it states that "there is a collective perception in the Protestant Tiger's Bay community of being gradually outflanked by Catholic territory." Most revealing of government's awareness is the section examining the possible community responses—from local residents, local politicians, local church authorities, and local commercial interests—to DOENI's economic and housing actions. The area is characterized as one of mutual fear and suspicion, home to strong paramilitary organizations on both sides, and where Protestants are afraid of the Catholic spread across Duncairn Gardens street into Tiger's Bay. The report continues that "the lack of NIHE activity in Tiger's Bay is interpreted as part of a government plan to allow the housing stock there to deteriorate to the stage where most of the Protestant population will leave." This Protestant fear is described by the working group as "extremely deep-rooted." In the Catholic New Lodge, meanwhile, there is resentment over being "fenced in"; and there is a fear of loyalist paramilitary strikes.

Because of the feeling of threat by the Protestant population in Tiger's Bay, the report anticipates possible adverse reaction to the development of an industrial/commercial project in what used to be Protestant residential fabric. The report candidly states that "there is a real possibility of adverse reaction if the support of the community cannot be engineered by careful preparation of the ground." A net increase in residential units is considered as a means of trying to reestablish the Protestant neighborhood; however, the NIHE view "is that present demand does not justify the building of any new homes in the area." At the same time, NIHE might react favorably to a plan that would demolish most of its vacant rehabilitated housing and create a new physical barrier that would improve the security of remaining and rebuilt NIHE housing investments. NIHE would obtain a solution to the housing decline in the area and a more secure environment for its investment. The fact that the plan would demolish about twice as many Protestant houses as would be rebuilt "could become something of a political or sectarian issue." Thus, it will be important that new houses are seen to be under construction before demolition of the older housing begins, to reassure residents that there is a commitment to the area.[11] Still, however, local political reaction is expected to be negative, especially from Unionist councilors who perceive that the proposals "could lead to a further reduction in their votes." Such negative political reactions—"local councilors have the potential to stir up local opinion against the proposals"—are viewed as jeopardizing the investment potential of the industrial/

commercial district and its ability to play a central role in the diffusing of the ethnic interface. A further complicating factor is that redevelopment would require the demolition of an under-used Church of Ireland (Protestant). The report anticipates "vociferous protest from the congregation." The demolition of 21 commercial establishments is also expected to generate some negative reaction from traders, although this would be mitigated by their successful relocation.

The major problem, cites the DOENI report, is that the project "might be opposed on sectarian grounds, as taking away too much of the former Tiger's Bay area." While local residents should be delighted with the proposals, "the only potential difficulty therefore is that local politicians, or some local residents with very strong views, might swing opinion against the proposals." The working group worries that "major irrational opposition could create significant obstacles; and that many of the local residents could be easily persuaded by individual politicians or others claiming to represent the community." To diffuse such possible negative reaction, the government task team suggests that an existing Tiger's Bay community group with views sympathetic to the project's overall goals be nurtured and supported. In this way, local politicians and extremist residents could be outflanked. The current work of the community group "might usefully be built on, and the study proposals could even be presented as a response to the view of local residents." In this way, "the community is prepared, and indeed should come forward with some of the ideas itself." It is expected that the community group's views "can be influenced towards ideas closer to the study proposal and local support obtained before any of the proposals are made public."

The Northgate development strategy illustrates how government might pursue multiple objectives amidst a complex territoriality. It does this by using an interdivisional approach to policy development, utilizing land use planning, economic development, and housing expertise along with input from the ground by decentralized BAT liaison offices. BDO brings to bear its expertise and financial tools regarding economic and commercial regeneration. The NIHE has knowledge of local housing markets and the practicality of rebuilding the residential stock. The planning office analyzes the various links between the proposed land uses and activities in the study zone. And, BAT participants are able to tap into community and sectarian perspectives on proposed governmental actions. Through such integration, planning problems arising from sectarianism are addressed in a sophisticated and comprehensive way. Northgate shows that government is capable of analyzing the potential social, spatial, political, and psychological impacts of their actions on ethnic community identity. Government analysis takes stock of each of the major participant groups in the urban subsystem, how negative public reaction may be mitigated, and endeavors to work with moderate community representatives. However, its approach toward community participation resembles more manipulation than consultation and runs the risk of antagonizing needed allies. In the end, the Northgate proposal is to be commended more for its innovative conceptualization than for its methods of community consultation.

Bridging the Ethnic Divide. The Springvale development scheme is an economic regeneration initiative begun in April 1990 by the Belfast Development Office. Its innovativeness lies in how the proposed development project and major public investments have been configured to geographically and functionally span sectarian communities. The study area covers almost 700 acres of a two-mile river valley in west Belfast that bridges both Protestant and Catholic territories. The area is characterized by high unemployment, housing pressures on the Catholic side, a poor physical environment, and inadequate service facilities (DOENI 1992). The regeneration opportunity presented itself when a long-established engineering company downsized and relocated, leaving a prime vacant area perceived to be in Catholic territory next to the arterial Springfield Road. DOENI subsequently purchased the abandoned site and other land which transcended the Springfield Road, a known demarcation between Catholic and Protestant areas. In addition, the BDO extended the regeneration area beyond these purchased sites to include most of the river valley stretching north and west. This further brought the Protestant community into the planning area and connected the two ethnic communities conceptually. The development opportunity thus links the two sectarian territories and is an abrupt change from DOENI's commonly used tactics emphasizing compartmentalization and segregation of ethnicities.

The Springvale project undertook a creative and genuine process of community consultation that can act as a model for future government-community partnerships. A community steering group of about a dozen residents representing both sides of the sectarian divide was formed after a conceptual plan for the area was put forth by the BDO. The involvement of this community group worked successfully to change the flavor of the project to better fit with community-felt needs. The representation of both Protestants and Catholics on the community steering group stayed intact and productive through the adoption of the development scheme in late 1992. Whereas the community steering group saw advantages to joint Protestant-Catholic planning, they perceived the need to create separate ethnically based organizations to participate in the implementation of the development scheme. As such, the group persuaded the DOENI to fund two separate organizations to carry out the implementation—the Foundry Regeneration Trust on the Catholic side; and the Forthriver Regeneration Trust on the Protestant. The model suggested here of joint planning–separate implementation suggests that separate communities may come together to work productively on issues of mutual interest and benefit. At the same time, collaboration does not have to occur throughout the development process but appears most critical in the setting of basic guidelines regarding types and allocations of activities.

The plan, adopted in October 1992, includes to the south of Springfield Road (in perceived Catholic territory) new housing to meet Catholic demand, a job training center, an Industrial Development Board advanced factory, and a new Springvale Business Park. Road access to and from the business park was a matter of much public discussion because of the territoriality of the area. In the end, a second access road was incorporated into the site design to assure Catholics of their personal security (V. Allister, Springvale Development Team, BDO, interview). Internally, roads will have security barriers and gates and be clearly identified as private roads because of "the fear that gunmen wold run up and down the road" (V. Allister, interview). In Protestant areas north of Springfield Road, there are to be major improvements and expansions of public recreation facilities, a new children's park, and a new industrial park. The Springvale initiative thus attempts to address both the differential and common needs of the two ethnic groups within its project area. It aims to address the housing needs of Catholics at the same time as remedying the underprovision of outdoor recreational facilities proximate to Protestant areas. Meanwhile, the project responds to the cross-community need for jobs by creating economic activities in the southern portion that are physically and psychologically accessible to both communities. Although private investment has not been forthcoming into the development area in the first three years, there was by early 1995 a significant amount of public infrastructure and investment in place that could act as a catalyst in the future.

The potential for bridging the ethnic divide increased when the University of Ulster expressed interest in the possibility of having a campus in west Belfast. DOENI, in its preliminary evaluation of the Springvale area for the campus (DOENI 1993b), states, "in selecting the site for the proposed campus, it was felt desirable to span the Springfield Road to counter pressures of territorial identity which might be expected to mount in relation to an institutional proposal sited firmly on one side of the road or the other." Of critical importance in the evaluation was the question of access and the "front door" to the proposed campus (DOENI 1993b). Although the campus would be primarily within Protestant territory, the access to the campus would be much easier from Catholic territory via Springfield Road than from the Protestant Shankill area. But, this would further the belief by Protestants that the campus would be a University of West Belfast for Catholics (B. Morrison, Planning Services, interview). Accordingly, the DOENI (1993b) evaluation of a Springvale campus draws attention to the need to link the campus by an accessway to either a major motorway or to ethnically mixed south Belfast. Through these means, the proposed campus would have ease of access to and from the rest of the urban region and province, and would not be seen as captured within the Catholic confines of west Belfast. As DOENI (1993b) states, "the perception which potential students and their parents have of the area is therefore of vital importance. Investment, and for many this may include investment in children's higher education, favors areas which are perceived to be safe and readily accessed."

A potential campus in Springvale challenges development planners to move away from their traditional approach of ethnic compartmentalization and segregation. If Springfield Road remains as the main accessway, the route could be "sanitized" through widening and the creation of security walls; or, new traffic caused by the campus could be integrated within the existing street fabric. V. Allister (interview) suggests that the latter approach is desirable, because a sanitized route "doesn't send the right message to a community such as this one." In addition, the police force, the Royal Ulster Constabulary (RUC), advised in a 1994 feasibility study by Touche Ross that the access road and the site itself be walled. This resembles traditional urban policy in Belfast and would likely create a prison for students and staff designed to keep the locals at bay (*The Guardian*, February 28, 1995). V. Allister (interview) again takes this approach to task—"if the university is to be a success, it's only because it doesn't have walls around it and it has programs in place that link it to the communities." In total, the Springvale initiative represents the potential for establishing links and bridges within a contested environment, rather than the building of breaks and walls. Physical decisions such as those regarding a potential campus will send emotive symbols to future generations about either what Belfast aspires to in hope or accepts in resignation.

Pursuing Fair Treatment by Government.   The Central Community Relations Unit (CCRU) was established in 1987 within the Central Secretariat to advise the Secretary of State for Northern Ireland on all aspects of the relationship between ethnic communities. The Unit has three broad roles—to help formulate new ideas and strategies to improve interethnic relations; to challenge policymakers throughout government to take into account the effects of proposed policies on interethnic relations; and to review periodically policies and programs as to their effects on community relations. Government community relations policy is based on three prime objectives (CCRU 1995): (1) to ensure that everyone enjoys full equality of opportunity and equity of treatment; (2) to increase the level of cross-community contact and cooperation; and (3) to encourage greater mutual understanding and respect for different cultures and traditions. One of the creators of the CCRU, Ronnie Spence (interview), asserts that social and economic divisions will always be associated with instability, whether there is "peace" or not. As he points out, "it is a destabilizing influence if you feel worse off than someone else." Thus, it is critical that government be acutely aware and tackle the divisions created by differentials of social and economic justice and in parity of esteem. In other words, it is not enough for government to stand back in a neutral stance and leave unaddressed these destabilizing inequalities.

The CCRU represents an important point of change within government. With its review and challenge role, there is the formalization at a high level of authority of ethnic impact analysis within the policy process. P. Sweeney, DOENI advisor (interview), claims that it is the "most important move in government in the last 20 years." Policy Appraisal and Fair Treatment (PAFT) requirements mandate that government units turn in annual reports to CCRU describing the projected impacts on intergroup relations of their policies. The presence of CCRU will undoubtedly advance the extent of ethnic impact analysis within government. Critical to its future role, however, will be its breadth of review and challenge powers, its ability to effect meaningful policy change, and whether its definition of equality of opportunity and fair treatment is construed narrowly to mean removal of barriers or more broadly to require active remedying of inequalities.

Northgate, Springvale, and the CCRU are cases of innovative urban policy that consider more progressively and holistically the sectarian realities of Belfast. They are, however, policy strands which have not been knitted together into a strategic urban program. Still needed is a citywide strategy to inform policymakers as to when and where to invest public money for the purposes of rebuilding city neighborhoods and normalizing Belfast's urban fabric. In other words, when should the Northgate or Springvale approaches be repeated and in what locations? Are there areas where progressive approaches are not appropriate and may even be harmful? Significant issues are now examined pertinent to the formulation of a comprehensive ethnic strategy that would be directed at the coexistent viability of competing ethnicities.

Targeting Local Need

In targeting public resources, how are we to address Catholic objective needs and Protestant grievances related to alienation?
                              —Paul Sweeney, DOENI advisor (interview)

One cannot in some neat abstract academic way disaggregate the interplay of political forces from the cooler abstract understandings of need.
                              —Mike Morrissey, University of Ulster, Jordanstown (interview)

Protestants will always lose the argument about deprivation.
    —Billy Hutchinson, Springfield Inter-Community Development Project (interview)

What if 6 Sinn Fein projects get turned down and the "hard men" of Ardoyne feel excluded?
                              —Frank Gaffikin, University of Ulster (interview)

An urban strategy aimed at coexistent community viability would call for government to target—spatially focus—resources in those areas in need where investment can make the most meaningful contributions to Protestant and Catholic community prosperity. The main experience that Belfast has had with spatial targeting of neighborhoods has been the Making Belfast Work (MBW) program initiated in 1988. The difficulties and evolution of this program thus inform a consideration of government's capacity for channeling investment in a strategic way. First, although intended as a need-based program in its first years, MBW became in practice more a politically determined program. This illustrates the dangers of not having an investment strategy. Second, the reframing of the MBW program in 1995 to link it to a community regeneration strategy gives government an important first lesson in formulating a citywide framework of investment.

Making Belfast Work is a spatial targeting program begun in 1988; today it is the government's main method of "targeting social need" (TSN) in Belfast. TSN is one of three main priorities that guide government spending in Northern Ireland (D. McCoy, CCRU, interview; NICVA 1994; F. Gaffikin, interview).[12] It is a government initiative and set of spending principles announced in 1991 which address areas of social and economic differences by targeting government policies and programs. The thinking behind TSN is that community differentials contribute to divisions in the population by sustaining feelings of disadvantage and discrimination which in turn influence sectarian attitudes to broader political and security issues (Knox and Hughes 1994). Targeting to overcome disadvantage in a polarized city is problematic. In that disadvantage disproportionately affects Catholics, a TSN-based program by implication would have to positively discriminate (M. Morrissey, interview). One of the most detailed government statements on TSN speaks delicately about this issue:

> I must stress that the programme is about targeting resources and policies to address disadvantage and is not about positive discrimination which would be unlawful under existing law. However, since the Catholic section of the community generally suffers more extensively from the effects of social and economic disadvantage, the targeting of need will have the effect of reducing existing differentials. (Secretary of State to Standing Advisory Committee on Human Rights, March 10, 1992)

There is controversy over the means deemed appropriate for addressing differentials, owing to the difference between narrow and broad interpretations of the concept of *equality of opportunity* (Smith and Chambers 1991). In the first case, obstacles and discrimination are lifted so that all can play on a level playing field. In the second case, in addition to removal of barriers, affirmative action is utilized to compensate for inequalities and the legacies of past discrimination so that all have an equivalent chance on that level playing field. Such a difference is highlighted by the contrast between the Fair Employment (NI) Act of 1976, which relied on narrow removal of discriminatory barriers and voluntary compliance, and the 1989 Fair Employment Act, which requires the use of broader affirmative action goals and timetables to remedy underrepresentation of Catholics in the workforce (Department of Economic Development 1989; Knox and Hughes 1994).

For many years, Belfast urban policy was devoid of any spatial targeting of community deprivation. This was not due to lack of knowledge. As early as 1977, a Belfast Areas of Special Social Needs (BAN) report documented two major need syndromes in the city's neighborhoods—one characterized by unemployment and low incomes; the other by poor physical and shelter environments.[13] Nevertheless, the three main public investment tools (UDG, EIS, and CDS) were directed into the city center. Urban development grants (UDGs) were seen as incapable of stimulating private investment in neighborhoods and, indeed, efforts to increase the UDG subsidy amount in deprived neighborhoods had shown limited effect (Cebulla 1994). Thus, in its efforts to balance economic opportunity in the city center and the addressing of social needs in the wider city, the MBW program was introduced as one of the means to address neighborhood-based disadvantage.

The MBW program directs spending to 26 of the 51 wards in the city deemed most deprived based on a 14-criteria measure of social, economic, and physical factors. These "core" wards take in one-third of the city's population.[14] The total religious composition of MBW wards is about 55 percent Catholic and 45 percent Protestant (J. Harrison, Research Officer, MBW, interview). This propensity for disadvantage to be a Catholic phenomenon gained the program in its early years the label of "targeting Catholic need." In actuality, the number of eligible wards currently is roughly equal for each community (DOENI 1994c; DOENI 1995). MBW is a program that spatially and indirectly targets neighborhoods rather than directly targeting individuals (Gaffikin and Morrissey 1990; Birrell and Wilson 1993). The expectation is that the benefits of job creation, physical improvements, and job training to deprived neighborhoods will flow to the people who live there. MBW was initially housed at the top of the governmental hierarchy in the Central Secretariat and was provided with about 20 million pounds sterling per year to spend. The intent of MBW was that resources would be distributed based on need to community groups in order to address the lack of economic opportunities and poor quality of life. Another important role that MBW was to play, through its Belfast Special Action Group (BSAG) of top civil servants, was to challenge and encourage mainstream departments, through MBW funding incentives, to redirect budgetary priorities toward addressing disadvantage.

The experience of MBW from 1988 through 1994 did not meet expectations (DOENI 1994c; Sweeney and Gaffikin 1995). Although intended as a need-based program, there is a "messy negotiation with the real world when you try to intervene in an abstract level on the basis of need" (F. Gaffikin, interview). The program sacrificed its program goals to political expediency, both in terms of who received funding and the types of projects funded. On the Catholic side, money would be channeled to the "safe hands" of church-based organizations and those related to the moderate nationalist SDLP party, bypassing groups associated with Sinn Fein (interviews: C. Bradley; J. Austin; V. McKevitt; R. Davison). In terms of projects, hardware in the form of new capital investment and enterprise centers became favorite symbols to MBW officials because of their visible political payoffs in legitimizing the program. In its first six years, MBW tried to walk a tightrope between responding to objective need (its intent) and political demands and imperatives. This resulted in an ad-hoc allocation of resources, a lack of transparency in funding decisions, and, ultimately, a program driven by clientalism. MBW funding responded in tactical and piecemeal ways to the short-term demands of different forces rather than seeking strategically to balance them within a long-term framework (F. Gaffikin and M. Morrissey, interviews).

In 1994–1995, MBW engaged in a major revision endeavoring to address these sources of ineffectiveness. Its spending was now to "address need and not merely respond to demand" (DOENI 1994c), meaning that a strategic approach would now anchor the program from the strong political winds. The "need" driving program funding will in part be defined by "area partnerships" which are to be representative and inclusive of community, public, and private sectors. In this way, need is not to be statistically measured by government bureaucrats, but defined in a consensual fashion by government-community entities.[15] MBW funding will also likely direct its attention more than in the past to long-term capacity-building through education and training, especially of youth. In this approach, there is a shift toward empowering people to look for and access jobs rather than focusing solely on job creation and new capital investment (J. Harrison, MBW, interview). People, as well as physical areas, are to be regenerated through education, and training in community organization and leadership (P. Sweeney, interview).

This reorientation of MBW toward a more rationalistic approach based on need presents both opportunities and potential new problems. The process of self-evaluation it undertook showed innovative leadership and a government unit open and willing to learn.[16] In many ways, MBW is a test-bed for government in redefining its role amidst the complex sectarianism of Belfast. The MBW shift is a move away from a culture of responding to those political demands that are articulated most clearly toward a partnership approach emphasizing agreement on the needs of an area (B. Murphy, MBW deputy director, interview). An important observation here is that MBW is not seeking to move all the way from political demands to objective need, but to some consensual development by public, private, and community sectors about what "need" entails and requires in each specific neighborhood. Indeed, community-defined need can differ significantly from objective need in the political terrain of Belfast. The new reliance on community partnerships was, in fact, predicated on the fact that "what people on the ground want and what government's perception of the needs of an area are don't necessarily match" (J. Harrison, interview). Inclusive community involvement is a positive step forward. The main difference between old and new MBW might be that a more inclusive community organization may now be making demands on government rather than politically biased ones. The formulation of community-defined needs is also important for government in its efforts to sensitively respond to the qualitatively and quantitatively different needs of its Catholic and Protestant communities. This is something government has a hard time doing when it applies its own universal criteria of allocation.

Nevertheless, without a sufficient anchoring in citywide strategy, the newly designed program may be blown around by the winds of community-defined need. This would be to the detriment of cost-effective targeting and would reinforce an entrenched and sclerotic territoriality. Needed is a strategy of community investment that can be used to review whether bottom-up, community-expressed "needs" are compatible with citywide objectives. In this way, community needs are matched up against a strategic framework that provides an important reality check. Such a community investment strategy could have a well-defined neighborhood prioritization scheme to assure that MBW public investment does not simply respond to the "area partnership" board that can shout the loudest politically, is best organized, or has the greatest capacity to develop successful MBW proposals.

Sectarian segmentation and competition make it extremely difficult to target government resources on deprived areas and individuals in Belfast. In particular, disaggregating political needs from socioeconomic needs is problematic. Nevertheless, targeting is absolutely essential in a historically unequal society where inequality contributes to political division. The MBW experience points out the dangers of a government targeting policy that acts outside a strategic framework. Although eligibility for MBW funding is successfully premised on need, actual allocation to groups and projects through 1994 has been ad hoc and driven by political demands within the defined wards of deprivation. Under its revised format, MBW seeks to respond to the qualitatively different needs of its Catholic and Protestant population through community-inclusive partnerships. The move toward consensus-based definitions of need through area partnerships, however, necessitates that government formulate a citywide strategy of investment that can guide its responses to community-perceived needs and desires.

Coexistent Community Viability

> Unless you deal in the setting of policy with the fact that these two communities are moving in different directions, you're in trouble. You don't want to hold Catholics back, but you must move Protestants ahead.
>
> —Jackie Redpath, Greater Shankill Regeneration Strategy (interview)

Many strands of Belfast urban policy are driven by need criteria that are quantifiable. The foremost examples are the justification of new public housing construction on the basis of "urgent need" on the waiting list; the linking of public housing redevelopment to the magnitude of housing "unfitness" as defined in provincial statute; and the eligibility for MBW funding premised on a statistically sophisticated measure of deprivation. The use of these objective and often quantifiable need criteria increases the defensibility of government actions amidst contested terrain. Such criteria help buffet government from the strong political and sectarian winds. The allocation of MBW funding shows the strength of these winds and how political imperatives and clientalism can overshadow efforts to target public resources effectively.

The concept of "need," however, takes on added complexity in a city of social-psychological territoriality. Catholic objective needs of housing and associated urban amenities contrast commonly with Protestant needs for community maintenance and identity which are less tangible and harder to quantify. Objective need-driven "neutral" policy, although rational from a government view, is not sensitive to these differential needs of Belfast's ethnic communities. From a purely quantifiable need viewpoint, many Protestant neighborhoods, due to out-migration and thus lack of demand for new housing, are not viable for government investment in housing and social services. To put money there would be inefficient and ineffective and in normal cities it would not occur. Yet, in Belfast's sectarian landscape, such areas cannot always be avoided by policymakers because territory is equated with political claims. For these reasons, some Belfast urban programs are making initial and tentative steps toward criteria other than quantifiable need. DOENI now "recognizes the community needs of an area that might require us to go beyond the strict standards of the Housing Executive that might say we shouldn't do it" (R. Spence, permanent secretary, interview). And, two of DOENI's member units—MBW and NIHE—display shifts. The need criteria which guide the revised MBW are not necessarily quantifiable need as defined by government but need as defined by community-government partnerships. And, the NIHE has taken initial steps away from strictly need-driven housing construction in its 1995 *Belfast Housing Strategy Review:* "The Executive remains open to the evaluation of new building in areas of low demand taking account of community views, financial risks, and future viability where wider regeneration goals are being pursued."

The NIHE, at times, has adroitly bent its need-based rules to achieve wider community regeneration goals. In areas where the NIHE is incapable of declaring a redevelopment program because the housing is not statutorily unfit (but nonetheless facing substantial vacancies and in poor shape) or housing demand is not present, the NIHE has had the DOENI take the lead through its declaration of the area as a Comprehensive Development Scheme (CDS). A CDS allows the clearing of substantial areas that can include housing, and an alteration in subsequent land uses. The NIHE contributes housing as part of the picture (often at levels much lower than that cleared), but there is also commonly commercial, industrial, or environmental improvements as part of the scheme. The NIHE in this way is able to consolidate and improve their housing stock for those people who want to stay. W. McGivern (NIHE, interview) contends that "we have effectively created housing need by taking out significant numbers of housing units." Without the CDS process, it would have been more difficult for the NIHE to justify their expenditures in an area of high vacancies and low demand. Still however, as W. Mc-Givern (interview) asserts, "housing alone does not solve the problems faced by the Protestant community. With only new houses built, there will be simple leapfrogging and voiding of other houses in the city." What is needed, then, are fuller regeneration efforts that do not simply move Protestants around, but attract some back into Belfast's neighborhoods. Thus, the hope is that the nonresidential part of community regeneration efforts will, over time, lead to increased housing demand and an upward spiral toward fuller community viability and functionality. One housing planner[17] stated, "housing can not be in a vacuum. At the end of the day, we are only landlords. You generate a community and we'll house them."

Besides the Duncairn/Northgate example already discussed, an illustration of how community viability can be factored into policy decisions took place regarding the Alliance neighborhood of north Belfast. This Protestant neighborhood is on a peaceline and suffers from terrible physical dilapidation and low housing demand. On need criteria only, this would be an unlikely place for public investment. An NIHE (1990b) report states that the area "appears to have entered into terminal decline." Of the 445 houses in Alliance in 1984, 127 had been demolished and a further 147 were vacant by 1991. The 171 occupied houses in 1991 represented 37 percent of the total 1984 housing stock (DOENI 1992a). Household and population figures were forecasted to decline further; the waiting list for housing there was not significant. The NIHE concluded (1990b, 4) that "expenditure to bring dwellings up to required standards is simply not value for money even if the Executive had such funds available." Need-based policy would allow this neighborhood to die. However, if you tell Protestants that there is no need in Alliance, "people will laugh" (D. MacBride, interview). Local residents and their politicians argued that if investment into Alliance was not forthcoming, the whole neighborhood would deteriorate, with decay spreading subsequently to the neighboring Glencairn community. At that point, stated the argument, pressure would mount for the peaceline separating Protestant Alliance from Catholic Ardoyne to be moved into Protestant territory to accommodate new Catholic housing on heretofore Protestant land. Escalation of tension and violence would accompany such territorial incursions. Failure of the NIHE to respond to calls to regenerate Alliance would be viewed as conspiracy (DOENI 1992a). The NIHE, as part of a DOENI comprehensive development scheme that will clear substantial areas and build workshop places, approved a plan where it will rebuild more houses than objective need may dictate but at a level less than full put-back. Of the 400 houses originally in Alliance, 100 houses will be rebuilt after clearing, in phases of 25 to test whether demand may justify it. The Alliance neighborhood will not be physically re-created as it was, nor will it be left to die due to its sectarian importance. The hope is that a rebuilt Alliance, although smaller in housing units, will be more vital.

Notwithstanding their positive impacts on community viability, these and any further shifts in government policy away from quantifiable need-based policy in order to address areas of demographic decline and physical decay are, and will be, problematic. First, this shift toward a broader definition of "need" would severely stress the urban development budget and lessen the ability of policy to target objective need. At some point, policymakers would not be able to afford the continued maintenance of Belfast's neighborhoods. Second, it is doubtful that the strategy would be effective in achieving its goals if money is spread around the multiple Protestant neighborhoods of decline. R. Strang (interview) claims that "further injections of capital hardware (housing, buildings and cosmetic environmental works) are essentially empty gestures if in 'Protestant' locations the socioeconomic structure is so malformed and damaged as to preclude any realistic prospect of natural community regeneration." He lambastes the "scenario that by building houses in declining areas, busloads of cherry-cheeked children will fill out all the houses." He argues that public housing and investment in areas where need exists more in a political than an objective sense will likely exacerbate the problem of nonviability. This is so because investment where objective need is not present will produce a supply of housing that the community cannot support. The result will be housing voids, disuse, and dilapidation that will over time erode even the more stable parts of the neighborhood.[18] Thus, an investment program aimed at sustaining Protestant community viability must be targeted at certain areas to avoid a wholesale maintenance of ethnic territories which is self-defeating and corrosive. A third problem related to moving away from a strictly need-based urban policy is that it exposes government to the strong sectarian winds of Belfast. As W. McGivern (NIHE, interview) says, "criterion other than the statutory 'unfitness' definition may be appropriate. But, we are then moving out of the comfort zone." Catholics would make a legitimate argument that any lessening of the government's commitment to addressing objective need would be a retreat from social justice and responsible governance.

We are left with two inadequate policy choices. The current need-based formulae are not sufficiently sensitive to the differential types of need across the ethnic divide. On the other hand, a broadening of the definition of need to include community viability would address the "Protestant" problem in Belfast but, in the end, would probably do more harm than good to Catholics and Protestants alike. Urban policy does require greater proactive management of the ethnic map than under current need-driven criteria, able to pursue viability of antagonistic communities. At the same time, if policymakers try on too wide a scale to assure Protestant community viability, they will spend a significant amount of money in a holding pattern directed at maintaining Belfast's sterile mosaic of ethnic territories. R. Strang (interview) exclaims, "government can stick their fingers in dikes and holes all over the place, but it may not make sense."

What is needed is a citywide strategy that identifies and prioritizes community need so that wider regeneration initiatives (like in Duncairn Gardens and Alliance) can be appropriately targeted to areas capable of recovery. At the same time, areas not worthy of investment should be abandoned, with residents encouraged to relocate, through transfers, to areas targeted for public investment. This strategy would utilize criteria supplemental to objective need, but they would be sufficiently defensible to anchor the strategy against strong political winds. It would be necessary to its success that multiple government participants play roles in the formulation and implementation of the citywide investment strategy. A broadened and imaginative town planning profession could contribute meaningfully by assessing the developmental, spatial, and socioeconomic aspects of neighborhoods and prioritizing their potential for community viability. It is only town planning that is capable of having a citywide view of the relationships between and within Belfast's sectarian neighborhoods. Making Belfast Work, already designed as a targeting program, would likely constitute the primary vehicle for skewing spending toward those neighborhoods most worthy of public investment. The number of MBW-eligible wards might be reduced or prioritized to achieve citywide objectives more effectively. Belfast Action Teams "are an ideal mechanism for taking the temperature out there on the ground" (J. Harrison, interview); as such, they would be key mediators between community-articulated needs and citywide strategic objectives. The host DOENI would be instrumental in integrating its units' activities related to community investment, continuing to shift from its historic emphasis on physical and land use development to include the social and economic dimensions of community-based regeneration.

Strategic Investments.   A citywide strategy of community investment needs to meet the differential needs of Protestant and Catholic communities on an equitable basis. Since needs are different, however, equity does not imply replication of policy for the two groups, nor even numerical balance in government outputs. Rather, equity means that policy should be sensitive to the unique needs of each community while keeping in mind the overall good of the city. Decline in the Protestant population must be managed, not neglected, in order to produce a vital but geographically consolidated Protestant population. Investment in Protestant areas could be based on a triage model.[19] This means that investment should be targeted to certain areas with the best chances for community viability. These areas should be close to employment opportunities (actual and potential), be capable of building upon growth's economies of scale, and have the potential for active community participation.[20] They would be the focus of government support, in terms of housing (including speculative housing not tied to documented need), social services such as education, environmental improvements, and job training. But this is only one-half the picture for the Protestant community. In other areas characterized by poor living conditions, voids and blight, there should be transfers of public housing tenants to targeted areas of community investment and subsequent clearance of these decayed communities. This is the hard part of the strategy politically. As one housing planner states (interview),[21] "This model pre-supposes non-viability in certain situations. How do we get to that stage and who develops the message? Who is to say there is no future for Protestants in Suffolk?"

Despite inevitable Protestant outcry and political resistance, this policy and message is not only socially responsible, but absolutely essential for effective governance and the betterment of Protestant living conditions citywide. The current government strategy of color-neutrality, in fact, does more harm than good to the Protestant community and to the public fisc. Consolidation under a triage planning model, in contrast, has a better chance at truly regenerating the Protestant communities of Belfast. This strategy would not simply be a reallocation of local population across Protestant neighborhoods. Rather, consolidation of government efforts and interagency community regeneration would provide the chance to expand the Protestant population base in the city through renewal of targeted neighborhoods. For Protestants, the choice is between a Belfast of marginal estates and neighborhoods that perpetuate a static territoriality and a Belfast that enhances viability and identity for a set of "heartland" Protestant neighborhoods. For government, the choice is between public expenditures that protect a geographic holding pattern derived from urban civil war and spending that creates more focused and vital parts of Protestant Belfast. Opposition to this shift in government policy would come not only from Protestants, but from the Catholic community too. According to D. MacBride (interview), "there is more awareness by Protestants of Catholic housing needs than recognition by Catholics of Protestant needs for community maintenance." Catholics would have to accept that housing policy, in addition to building houses in response to need, has a legitimate role in maintaining and enhancing viability of selected Protestant areas. Under a new government approach, Catholics would gain from a more viable Protestant community that would be less burdened by the sense of threat and able to develop confidence in itself. Such a Protestant population could be able to engage as more willing and productive partners with Catholics in seeking urban reconciliation.

A citywide strategy of coexistent community viability must also be capable of meeting the objective needs of the Catholic community. In the circumstances of rigid territoriality sustained by current policy and with a threatened Protestant population, these needs are hard to meet. To the extent that a community viability strategy is able to spawn greater Protestant urban confidence amidst a continued peace, the sectarian territorial limits on Catholic expansion may be attenuated in certain places. Such loosening of Belfast's ethnic geography through engaged Protestant-Catholic negotiation would benefit Catholics. A strategy of coexistent viability could also open up opportunities for community relations not now possible under government's color-neutral approach. B. Murtagh (interview) suggests that place-based negotiations in the forms of covenants or contracts could be possible between specific Catholic and Protestant neighborhoods. For example, an agreement could stipulate that some Catholic housing could be built in Protestant territory in return for a guarantee of increased community facilities or speculative housing for Protestants. These agreements would move perceptions away from a win-lose situation and formalize interethnic cooperation.

Any loosening of territoriality due to a shift in government policy toward coexistent viability may open up opportunities for integrated housing. Yet, government strategy must be sufficiently sensitive to the fact that neighborhood interfaces present different challenges across the city in terms of the potential for community tension. Urban policy should not force integration upon city residents, but facilitate it in more stable areas for households who are motivated. In cases of volatile and threatening neighborhood instability, on the other hand, urban strategy's enhancement of the coexistent viability of communities may well entail the continuance of spatially segregated neighborhoods for decades to come.

Integrated housing would disproportionately benefit Catholics because such housing, by necessity, would be built in orange areas heretofore foreclosed to Catholics. If peace were to advance in Northern Ireland, the NIHE (1994a) indicates that the development of integrated housing in a few trial areas may be desirable. An interesting characteristic of such an integrated housing strategy is that the NIHE, in actuality, would have to allocate to Protestant households a greater share of the estate than their need figures would otherwise elicit (J. McPeake, NIHE, interview). Otherwise, Catholics would tend to overwhelm the intended mixed estate due to their disproportionate magnitude on housing waiting lists.[22] For Catholics, it is a tradeoff but a beneficial one. They may not get as many placements in the estate as objective need would dictate, but they would have greater housing availability overall because such integrated estates would open up "Protestant" land. From a public interest view, integrated housing is also important because it directly counters the hypersegregation of the city's neighborhoods.[23]

These are the components of a Belfast urban strategy that is not color-neutral, but sensitive to the differential needs of its two communities. It responds to both the social and psychological needs of the Protestant community for community viability and identity, and the objective needs of the Catholic population for housing and room to grow. The strategy is based on "color where color matters." This shift in government approach will place the public sector in the middle of the overall change process in Northern Ireland and Belfast, not relegate it to the color-neutral sidelines. The public investment strategy responds to the fact that change and difficult decisions must be part of urban policy if it is to play a role in advancing peace in Belfast and Northern Ireland. It will not be easy for government to depart from objective need criteria that have been moderately successful in legitimating its authority over a contested city.

In a new Belfast, government must be more explicit with its communities about the goals and objectives that it is pursuing. Development agencies such as NIHE and BDO must be more up front and provide the reasons behind proposed actions. As we have seen, there are some steps being taken by government toward a more imaginative and holistic approach toward community need. However, doubts remain as to its desired publicity. One planner comments, "if we go explicit with some of the things we are doing, we could inflame the situation." In the end, however, as one housing planner asserts, "we must come up front and stop hiding behind the euphemisms." A case in point illustrates the pitfalls of euphemisms and opaque steps. In consultations with communities regarding the Belfast Housing Strategic Review, the NIHE language concerning the possibility of building units in areas of "low demand" is most assuredly code for Protestant community regeneration.[24] Sinn Fein representatives saw clearly through this code and severely criticized the movement away from objective need criteria. On the other hand, Protestant politicians were not strongly supportive because the wording was buried in bureaucratic language and did not illuminate an overall strategy toward bettering Belfast's Protestant communities. The step toward a new approach then faltered. Instead, the NIHE and other government units should pursue fuller and more explicit strategies and enunciate the advantages to both Protestants and Catholics from an urban strategy of coexistent viability.

Belfast: Contributor or Burden to Peace?

The resolution of the broader Northern Ireland conflict will depend on whether Alliance and Ardoyne or Tiger's Bay and New Lodge can get along.
            —**Brenden Murtagh, University of Ulster–Magee College (interview)**

We need to create a notion of how, without violence, things can move forward.
            —**Billy Hutchinson, community leader (interview)**

On the eve of potentially momentous political change, Belfast looks to the unentangled outsider as if it is a war zone with both sides losers. It is a place of physical dereliction and windy rain; of sadness and introspection. In many ways, the change that was upon the city during the mid-1990s period of on-again, off-again ceasefires and negotiations resembled an alcoholic who had stopped drinking, but was doing little to change those habits linked to drinking. Peace was at hand, but it was a tenuous one lacking progress toward a political settlement that would solidify it. Indeed, the condition approximated more the absence of war than the presence of peace. The reemergence of Republican hostilities in February 1996 substantially retarded any normalization and improvement in community relations that may have occurred in Belfast during the preceding one and one-half years of ceasefires. Although elections in Northern Ireland in June 1998 to create a 108-member Northern Ireland Assembly could be a catalyst for peace, the hard issues of arms decommissioning, prisoner release, and policing remain after generations of ethnic bloodshed. It is not hard to be downcast about Belfast's future.

Belfast is the most important stage upon which this seemingly intractable political conflict is being performed, and is thus connected intimately to any larger peace. In Belfast, urban circumstances dealing with jobs, housing, social services, and community identity can modify—for better or worse—the influence of political tensions on city residents. In a future in which new governing institutions in Northern Ireland face monumental changes, it may be urban-based, on-the-ground strategies that make the difference in Belfast between peaceful coexistence and the reemergence of armed urban conflict. Whether Belfast urban policy is able to effectively address the differential needs of its two communities may determine the future quality of life in this city more than the institutional and constitutional changes enacted in 1998.

In the least, it seems that urban policy should do all that is necessary not to create obstacles to peace-building. More than that, however, those involved in the formulation and implementation of urban policy have a responsibility to more proactively facilitate and enable the coexistent viability of both urban communities in Belfast. Amidst the uncertainty of political change, urban strategies of inter-group accommodation may offer one of the few potential authentic sources of ethnic centripetalism and tolerance. They can contribute to larger peace-building efforts practical principles which foster the coexistent viability of antagonistic sides in terms of territorial control, urban resources, and preservation of ethnic identity. Peace-building efforts at the level of daily urban interaction between ethnic groups and between individuals are indispensable not only to urban stability, but because they can provide breathing spaces of hope amidst the daunting challenges of political changes.

We have seen in Belfast how urban policy and planning have attempted to neutrally address the sectarianism that has fundamentally shaped the city's social geography. The policymakers of Belfast attempt to deal pragmatically on a neutral basis with the day-to-day, local-level symptoms of sovereignty conflict. This neutrality on the part of town planning in Belfast, however, is a retreat from its potential to contribute to ethnic management. Despite the land use and territorially based implications of much of sectarianism, the town planning function has played a minor role in addressing ethnicity. Centralization of the planning function to an extralocal level has removed territorial questions from the local level in an effort to depoliticize planning. Generally, attempts by Belfast policymakers to separate development goals from ethnic realities may be politically expedient, but they appear to be neither realistic nor effectual. This centralized technocratic approach, according to Douglas (1982), might hold temporarily in abeyance community power struggles, but it will contribute little toward solving them. There is also a difference in Belfast planning between a national perspective focusing on specific interventions and a local perspective more encompassing of, and sensitive to, daily urban living (Blackman 1991). Because it emphasizes piecemeal rather than comprehensive planning, the centralization of local policymaking in Northern Ireland has produced fracturing of urban policymaking among numerous extralocal bodies, and the substantive separation of spatial planning concerns from the broader social concerns of housing, social services, and ethnic relations.

We have witnessed how policies regarding land use planning and housing allocation that are neutral in intent can reinforce sectarian disparities. The exclusion of distributional issues from metropolitan plans and the use of neutral public housing allotment formulas likely reproduce rather than moderate ethnic segregative patterns. Although this approach contains intergroup conflict in the short term, it likely hardens territorial identities and further discourages a climate for intergroup negotiations in the long term. In an unequal society of dualities and separation, color-neutral policies will result in unequal opportunities through the replication of those dualities. Where sectarian territoriality constrains much of urban living, neutrality does not increase equity. There have been public actions by government units that, out of necessity, address sectarianism on the sharp edge. The direct impacts of these government actions on changing the sectarian fabric bring the implementing agencies face-to-face with the sectarian realities known to, but avoided by, town planning and housing allocation administrators. New building and redevelopment of public housing become intimately connected to issues of territorial maintenance, while economic development schemes by BDO such as in Northgate can disturb existing sectarian dynamics. Yet, those urban policies which address sectarianism do so without the aid of a strategic framework aimed at effective management of ethnic space. Thus, government actions have primarily been ad-hoc tactics rather than strategic acts; have been project-based rather than area-based; have been reactive rather than proactive; and have emphasized vertical rather than lateral government approaches.

The urban policy framework used for the past 25 years aimed at neutrality, maintenance, and stability may no longer be appropriate in Belfast. Its reactive protection of the status quo defends a rigid and sterile territoriality, and rein-forces the physical and psychological correlates of urban civil war. As Belfast and Northern Ireland shift uneasily along the continuum from civil war to peace, ur-ban policymakers confront the question of whether, and when, urban policy should shift direction so it is a progressive part of the peace-building process and not a burden to it. For urban policy to meaningfully contribute to peace-building, the process and practice of city-building in Belfast would need to be reconceptual-ized. Urban policy requires greater proactive management of the ethnic map than under current color-neutral criteria. Such progressive ethnic management by government would be more strategic than its past "societal reflection" role, but less remote and mechanistic than a "social engineer" role. In transcending color-neutrality, there is a need for the following qualities in government: (1) proactive; (2) ethnically aware (and explicitly so); (3) able to strategically address the differ-ent needs of Catholic and Protestant communities; (4) integrated across govern-ment functions; and (5) conducive to diverse community input. Acknowledge-ment of the different needs in a divided city presents government with significant obstacles. The end that government should strive for in such a circumstance is the *viability* of the two communities. It is community viability and identity that are keys to peaceful urban living amidst political contest. The goal of progressive eth-nic management would be the coexistent viability of antagonistic groups within the urban system, whatever spatial forms and living patterns that might entail.

A citywide strategy of community investment would need to be developed to meet the differential primary needs of Protestant and Catholic communities on an equitable basis. Since needs are different, however, equity does not imply replica-tion of policy for the two groups nor even numerical balance in government out-puts. Rather, equity means that policy should be sensitive to the unique primary needs of each community while keeping in mind the overall good of the city. Both Protestant and Catholic communities have significant objective and psychological needs related to social and economic deprivation and group identity. Yet, primary needs contrast across ethnic groups—objective ones in the case of the Catholic population for new housing and community services versus social-psychological needs of the Protestant population for community viability and identity. Effective governance should address both these community needs because, in a deeply di-vided city, one community's needs are not more important than the other's.

A key consideration in future policymaking will be how government addresses the less tangible social-psychological needs of Belfast Protestants. We have seen that a blanket approach to maintaining Protestant territory will likely fail, leading actually to worsened conditions of currently fit housing stock. In this sense, unan-chored tactics aimed at maintaining all Protestant neighborhoods would be worse than government taking a hands-off approach entirely. As an alternative, decline in the city's Protestant population should be more strategically managed in order to produce a vital but geographically consolidated Protestant population. The goal here is not maintenance of Protestant territory, but viability of Protestant community. All participants—Protestants, Catholics, government—would likely agree that it is the vitality of people and community that is important, not the protection of a lifeless and dysfunctional geography of hate. Community viability would thus be developed as a criterion that supplements, not replaces, objective need-based measures for allocating public resources and activities in Belfast. Significantly, both the rationales and operational forms of new supplemental criteria would need to be clear and defensible. If not, public policy, heretofore supported primarily on need-based foundations, will find itself blown by the strong sectarian pressures of Northern Ireland.

Viability objectives connote not the diffusion, but the concentration and targeting, of public resources across Protestant Belfast. A citywide strategy could be developed that identifies and prioritizes Protestant neighborhoods in terms of their potential for regeneration. Public initiatives such as Duncairn Gardens and Alliance could then be appropriately targeted to those areas most able to recover; for instance, those with potential private sector interest and where communities can be rebuilt around existing and new community facilities and infrastructure. At the same time, this strategy requires that difficult decisions be made concerning which neighborhoods be cut off from publicly funded life support. Similar to a medical doctor utilizing a triage approach to an emergency, public resources would be concentrated on those ill neighborhoods that would most benefit from treatment. A consolidated, more viable Belfast Protestant community would over time feel less threat, and could assume a greater willingness to allow some normalization of Belfast's geography to meet a portion of Catholic objective needs.

Multiple government and community participants would play roles in the formulation and implementation of an integrative vision and policy for community regeneration that addresses effectively the differential needs of Belfast's ethnic communities. These include town planning, Making Belfast Work, Belfast Action Teams, the Department of the Environment generally, and community-based "area partnerships." Town planning has a moral and professional responsibility to shift out of its technical and land use blinders to incorporate consideration of the social, economic, and psychological dynamics and requisites for coexistent viability of Protestant and Catholic groups. Training and education of professional planners through professional organizations, like the Royal Town Planning Institute, and local universities, such as Queen's University of Belfast, should prepare planners to deal with the complex issues of planning amidst ethnic difference. This calls for studio-based workshops that involve students in the multidimensional analysis and planning of ethnic neighborhoods. Students and practitioners should be exposed to the rudiments of ethnic impact analysis, qualitative surveying, conflict resolution, and community relations techniques. In the end, ethnic content in courses will inculcate in students the ability to empathize with "the other." After all, planners must come to terms with their own views of ethnicity and race before they can be expected to plan for peaceful coexistence.

Participants other than town planning will also play key roles in a new Belfast urban strategy. The anti-deprivation Making Belfast Work program, already designed as a targeting program, would be a primary vehicle for skewing spending toward those neighborhoods most worthy of public investment. Belfast Action Teams would be key mediators between community-articulated needs and city-wide strategic objectives. And, the host DOENI would be instrumental in integrating its units' activities related to community investment and planning. One of the more important roles of a new urban strategy would be that it would guide government in its increased interactions with communities. Community involvement through proposed "area partnerships" must not occur in a strategy vacuum but rather needs to be anchored by a public strategy of community viability and investment. To maintain connections to community groups and leaders, the new urban strategy within government should not be structured hierarchically. Rather, it should penetrate multiple units and agencies and provide numerous points of access for community input. In this way, numerous government units are capable of social learning and adaptation within a guiding framework of community viability. Collaborative structures within government would also help institutionalize those innovative city-building approaches which currently depend upon the support of lateral-thinking individuals in key governmental positions.

This would be a Belfast urban strategy not color-neutral but sensitive to the differential needs of its two communities. It responds to both the psychological needs of the Protestant community for community viability and identity, and the objective needs of the Catholic population for housing and room to grow. The strategy is based on color where color matters. This shift in government approach would create an urban policy able to contribute to, and reinforce, larger peace-making efforts. Peace will demand this type of responsible governance.

Notes

1. Livingstone and Morison (1995) make a parallel argument in evaluating the broader state of democracy in Northern Ireland. Where political initiatives will not be pursued unless they have the support of both communities, the capacity of democratic politics to restructure society is largely forsworn.

2. Name withheld due to confidentiality.

3. The alternative to current urban policy "isn't that people will have to live in integrated estates, but that they can have that choice" (W. Glendinning, N. Ireland Community Relations Council, interview.)

4. For example, the NIHE seeks advice from the local BAT leader about whether house-building for Catholics along a transitional zone may be perceived as intruding on

Protestant territory. The BAT leader monitors neighborhood icons and symbols, and the ethnic affiliation of nonresidential activities.

5. Bradley recounts that when government started a Targeting Social Need program, it issued no explicit guidance. Local politicians filled this void with rhetoric ("targeting Catholic need"). With subsequent greater community involvement, program objectives have been clarified and both communities now feel ownership of it.

6. Because greater ethnic sensitivity would likely result in service duplication and decrease efficiencies of public investment, a beneficial supplement to such a policy approach would be a citywide strategy that prioritizes neighborhoods on the basis of potential increase in viability per investment unit.

7. Comment made in question/answer period subsequent to author's presentation of research findings. March 22, 1995, Queen's University.

8. Planning Services and the Belfast Development Office, for example, report to different undersecretaries within the DOENI.

9. The 1989 Act significantly strengthened the 1976 Act, which had relied on voluntary action by employers not to discriminate. The 1989 Act requires all concerns with more than ten employees to take "affirmative action" (including the setting of goals and timetables) if fair participation across religious groups is not being provided. Absent formal quotas, the Act has been able to apply considerable pressure on employers to take action to secure a reasonable balance between Protestants and Catholics (Boyle and Hadden 1994).

10. This report by DOENI, *Northgate Enterprise Park: Interim Report*, was never published. Only 30 copies were printed for internal circulation only. This confidentiality is indicative of the perceived sensitivity of dealing with sectarianism in a candid way.

11. In a publicly disseminated glossy brochure on the project, the DOENI is disingenuous in stating that "the development of the Northgate Enterprise Park creates the opportunity to develop a number of sites for new housing."

12. The other two are combatting terrorism and regenerating the economy.

13. The precursor to this report was Boal, Frederick W., P. Doherty, and D. G. Pringle. 1974. *The Spatial Distribution of Some Social Problems in the Belfast Area*. Belfast: Northern Ireland Community Relations Commission.

14. Robson et. al (1994) developed the deprivation measure. Six additional "core" wards lie outside Belfast city. MBW also identifies additional wards that have pockets of deprivation or specific problems of disadvantage. These may be eligible for MBW funding, upon meeting certain requirements.

15. The "need" described here is that which will guide specific government funding and project decisions. Objectively measured need (by the Robson index) determines ward eligibility for MBW funds.

16. Indicative of its openness to change, several former critics and community spokespeople were brought into the process of evaluation and redesign of MBW.

17. Anonymity requested.

18. As R. Strang (interview) colorfully comments, "areas that are blocked up, have broken windows and dirt areas provide a great adventure playground for kids on bikes, but it is not rational housing policy."

19. R. Strang (interview; and DOENI 1992a) refers to this as a "clearance/heartland" strategy.

20. The Shankill area appears to be a logical target of community investment under this triage model.

21. Identity withheld upon request.

22. The Standing Advisory Commission on Human Rights (1990) anticipates this circumstance in stating "NIHE should be exempt from strict applications of anti-discrimination law in cases where the goal is maintaining integration" (CM 1107 para 4.53–54 and 6.19).

23. The increased selling of NIHE housing units to eligible tenants and the emergence of a stronger private housing market may also facilitate integration, or at least the breakdown of ethnic boundaries. New owner-occupied housing construction was up to 85 percent of all new build in Northern Ireland in 1994, reversing the trend toward greater concentration of NIHE housing. The downside of such private housing growth to city planners is that it occurs primarily outside Belfast city borders.

24. This is a firsthand account of a housing planner who participated in the consultation exercise. Identity withheld upon request.

PART THREE

Johannesburg:
A Delicate Balancing of Time

We spent the night drumming and dancing
Singing songs of courage
Was it not the last
We would be together?
When the ripening period comes
We catapult
Into the waiting world
Like the seed of dry pods.

I'm a Man, *Mzi Mahola (1994)*

PHOTO 7.1 Louis Botha Avenue, Johannesburg. (Photo by Claudia L. Shambaugh)

7

Urban Policy in Transition

Johannesburg anchors a geographically disfigured urban region of enormous and gross economic and social contrasts. The urban region presents dual faces: one healthy, functional, and white; the other stressed, dysfunctional, and black. The most luxurious suburbs on the African continent and downtown skyscrapers of iridescent modernity coexist with townships and shantytowns of intentionally degraded living environments, poor infrastructure, and social facilities. The physical consequences are stark and constant reminders that the past is not yet past. As Wills (1988) states, "the shadow of apartheid planning will be evident in the geography of the city for years to come." With the establishment of the multiparty Government of National Unity, and the national democratic elections in April 1994, hope and opportunities for urban change coexist with the emerging awareness by policymakers of the now-uncovered, stark, and raw conditions of black Africans. Johannesburg is in many respects experiencing the benefits from its national peace settlement process more than Belfast. Such peace and reconciliation provide opportunities for shifts in urban policy goals and ideology. Accordingly, this account of Johannesburg focuses on how the city's geography of separation might be normalized and democratized, although much aware that apartheid geography may be reinforced and perpetuated through even seemingly benign forces.

Can urban policy strategies in the Johannesburg urban region play a significant role in transforming the racial geography and legacy of the urban system? Interviews and research focused on the intent and potential impacts of land use development, housing, community empowerment, economic, and governmental reorganization policies that are emerging, or could emerge, in post-apartheid Johannesburg. I evaluate the institutional and programmatic alternatives for addressing the difficult challenges posed by Johannesburg's racial geography. Johannesburg's is an unfolding story of transformation from one society to an uncertain new one. A possible future of political peace is upon South African policymakers, entailing both tremendous opportunities and challenges.

Planned Geographies

The Johannesburg (central Witwatersrand) metropolitan region contains at least 2 million people (1991 Census). The borders of this metropolitan region are coterminous with the jurisdiction of the Greater Johannesburg Transitional Metropolitan Council (GJTMC) created in December 1994. The region, outlined in Figure 7.1, consists of Johannesburg central city (1991 Census population: 615,500); Alexandra township, Sandton, and Randburg to the north (over 300,000 population combined); greater Soweto (1991 Census population: 890,800) to the west; and the areas of Eldorado Park, Ennerdale, and Lenasia to the southwest (about 180,000 population). These official populations are all likely undercounts.[1] The Central Witwatersrand Metropolitan Chamber in 1993 (reported in I. Turok

FIGURE 7.1   Johannesburg Metropolitan Area
Source: Turok, I. "Urban Planning in the Transition from Apartheid, Part I: The Legacy of Social Control." *Town Planning Review* (65, 3: 1994), p. 248. Reprinted by permission.

[1994a]) estimated a regional population closer to 3.5 million, with Greater Soweto at about 1.8 million, and Johannesburg city just under 1 million. Black residents are in the majority in the Johannesburg metropolitan region, making up at least 60 percent of the population compared to 31 percent white, at the most (Mabin and Hunter 1993; Rogerson and Rogerson 1995).[2]

The Johannesburg urban region is functionally connected to the larger Pretoria-Witwatersrand-Vereeniging (PWV) metropolitan complex. The core of the metropolitan complex, and Johannesburg's raison d'être, is the older east-west growth axis associated with gold mining, coal mining, and manufacturing that stretches about 25 miles to the west and 30 miles to the east. This axis along what was once the world's richest gold-bearing reef is known as the Witwatersrand ("white water's ridge"), referring to the gold-producing geological formation. The Witwatersrand region is functionally linked to two urban cores—Pretoria about 35 miles north; and Vereeniging about 35 miles south. Altogether, as shown in Figure 7.2, these areas compose the larger PWV complex, which in 1991 was home to an estimated 8 million people (Urban Foundation 1990a). The PWV complex contains approximately 20 percent of South Africa's population. It dominates the first tier of the South African urban hierarchy, followed by the second-tier urban regions of Cape Town and Durban (see Figure 7.3). It also dominates demographically and spatially the Gauteng Province, one of nine demarcated under the new 1994 dispensation.

The Witwatersrand part of the PWV is the most important economic center and the most populous and prosperous urban agglomeration on the subcontinent (Parnell and Pirie 1991). The metropolitan region of Johannesburg has long played the leading financial and commercial role in South Africa as the locus of major corporate activities, although within the region office functions are decentralizing from the central city to the northern suburban areas of Sandton, Rosebank, and Midrand (Rogerson 1996). The industrial base, meanwhile, is experiencing formal de-industrialization and restructuring, with an increasing informal employment compensating for reductions in formal manufacturing employment. Mining in the "city of gold" now plays a minor role in the economy due to resource depletion, falling world price levels, and growing capital intensity of gold production (Central Witwatersrand Metropolitan Chamber 1993; Rogerson and Rogerson 1995).

The urban landscape of the Central Witwatersrand is characterized by racially segregated townships, cities, and informal settlements/shantytowns created in response, directly or indirectly, to Group Areas apartheid legislation. The hypersegregated nature of Johannesburg is due to the unique, comprehensive, and retroactive state powers brought to bear in the active implementation of apartheid policy from 1948 to 1990. Urban apartheid's cornerstone was the 1950 *Group Areas Act*.[3]

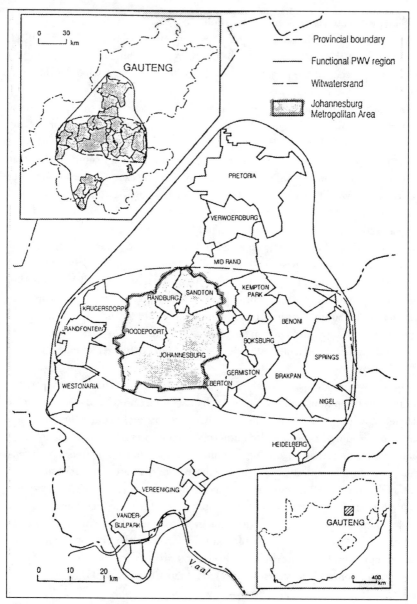

FIGURE 7.2   Regional Context

The Johannesburg metropolitan area anchors the Witwatersrand region, which itself is part of the larger Pretoria-Witwatersrand-Vereeniging urban functional area. Gauteng is one of the nine provinces of post-apartheid South Africa.

Source: Beavon, K. S. "Johannesburg: Getting to Grips with Globalization from an Abnormal Base." (Paper presented at the Pre-Habitat II Conference on The World Cities and the Urban Future. Tokyo. August 1995), p. 4. Reprinted by permission.

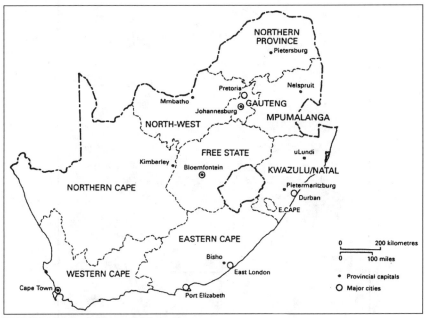

FIGURE 7.3   South Africa and Johannesburg
Source: Cawthra, Gavin. *Securing South Africa's Democracy: Defence, Development, and Security in Transition* (Hampshire: Macmillan and New York: St. Martin's, 1997), p. xiii. Reprinted by permission of Macmillan Ltd. and St. Martin's Press.

Towns and cities were divided into group areas for exclusive occupation by single racial groups[4] (see Figure 7.4). Sharp teeth to the Group Areas legislation were subsequently supplied by the 1954 *Natives Resettlement Act* and 1955 *Group Areas Development Act*, which gave the government the ability to expropriate land and force removals in order to fit the races into the newly drawn group areas. This retroactive ability makes apartheid unique among segregative schemes in the world, and created tremendous hardships on nonwhites. Platzky and Walker (1985) estimate that 730,000 blacks had been resettled (displaced) in South Africa's urban areas between 1960 and 1983. In Johannesburg specifically, clearance and forced removals of black western ghettoes and freehold areas in the 1950s and 1960s,[5] most notably Sophiatown, occurred amidst much vocal outcry. In accordance with Group Areas delineations, receiving zones for blacks displaced from nonblack group areas were commonly remote, isolated, and peripheral. In Johannesburg, this was an area approximately twelve miles southwest of, and spatially disconnected from, the white city. Two pre–World War II black "locations" (Orlando and Pimville) existed there where some housing for blacks had already been built. With the emergence of apartheid, however, this area, increasingly identified as the South Western Townships, or Soweto, became a major dumping group for blacks displaced from "white" Johannesburg.

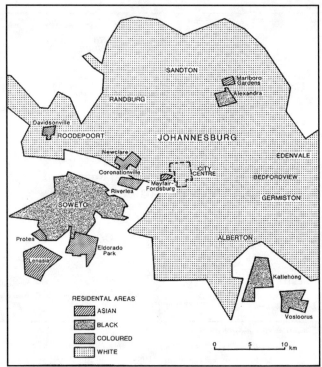

FIGURE 7.4   Group Areas in Johannesburg
Source: Parnell, S. M. and G. H. Pirie, "Johannesburg." In Lemon, A. (ed.).
Homes Apart: South Africa's Segregated Cities (London: Paul Chapman, 1991),
p. 135. Reprinted by permission.

For the first three decades of their existence, Soweto's townships bore little or
no resemblance to normal functioning cities (Beavon 1982). The landscape was
one of monotonous rows of hundreds of small houses with bare landscaping and
minimal community facilities. Retailing and commerce had long been restricted
in Soweto as inappropriate to a dormitory area for black labor working in white
Johannesburg. Socially, continuity and stability of black families and communities
had been stymied by restrictive and distorting land use regulations. In the late
stages of apartheid, some advances had occurred, such as the signing of 99-year
leasehold arrangements (Parnell and Pirie 1991). Nevertheless, the larger legacy
of the subordination and fragmentation of Soweto's communities and residents is
pervasive and debilitating.

Urban apartheid policies in South Africa through the early 1980s were remark-
ably effective in achieving their residential segregation goals. Even as late as 1991,
only 8.6 percent of the urban population in South Africa lived outside their designated group areas (Christopher 1994). In the Johannesburg urban region, the pragmatic segregationism of the pre-apartheid era had been rigidly formalized, bru-

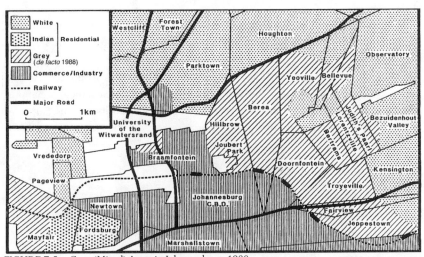

FIGURE 7.5   Grey (Mixed) Areas in Johannesburg, 1988
Source: Rule, S. "The Emergence of a Racially Mixed Residential Suburb in Johannesburg: The Demise of the Apartheid City?" *Geographical Journal* (155, 1989), p. 198. Reprinted by permission.

tally enforced, and extended in Kafka-esque directions by apartheid policymakers and planners. In the end, the apartheid regime created "an urban system fundamentally at odds with the majority of people using it" (Central Witwatersrand Metropolitan Chamber 1993). The two worlds of Johannesburg had been torn apart, creating mental maps of race and space that will long outlast the formal end of the apartheid regime.

The 1980s and early 1990s exhibited an incremental unraveling of urban apartheid in Johannesburg both remarkable and inevitable. De facto desegregation across group area boundaries occurred during this time due to the "inexorable conflict between a functionally integrated urban economy and legally enforced social, economic and residential separation" (Urban Foundation 1990d). Although apartheid development policy sought to constrain it, black urbanization in the region has been, and will continue to be, the dominant demographic trend in the future, increasingly transcending the artificial divisions of apartheid urban geography (Urban Foundation 1990a and 1990c). The functional and economic connections of blacks to Johannesburg's urban economy eroded not only state-level apartheid goals but also helped dismantle de facto the urban apartheid goals of residential segregation. Johannesburg in the late stages of apartheid exhibited a "diverse spatial re-ordering bearing little resemblance to the apartheid city" (Saff 1991). Residential mixing (or "greying") occurred in both high-rise rental areas and middle-class neighborhoods of detached owner-occupied homes (see Figure 7.5).

In apartheid's unraveling, social and economic interdependencies in the urban system both reflected and precipitated its unworkability. The exercise of urban policy and planning in operationalizing apartheid ideology highlighted the inevitable tensions and difficulties resulting from efforts to segment functionally complex and interdependent components of the urban system. At first, arguments at this operative level of ideology led to modifications in certain planning instruments (such as "free settlement area" exceptions to the Group Area Act) to address urban realities while maintaining the larger edifice of apartheid racial policy. Eventually, the operationalization of apartheid exposed its serious faultlines and facilitated its seemingly abrupt transmutation.

Human Welfare and Needs

In 1988, Mshenguville (Soweto) consisted of 31,254 jam-packed tin dwellings. Calculated at an average of five persons to a shack, the population would then have stood at 156,270. The tin shacks lean virtually one against the other, with a mere passage between them. The settlement lacks streets and roads; 198 chemical latrines, two ablution blocks and numerous water taps had been provided. Garbage piles up in every nook and cranny; a smell of poverty permeates the shantytown. It is overcrowded, squalid and ugly, yet it is also vibrant and irrepressible in its own sordid way.

—**Harry Mashabela (1990),**
Mekhukhu: Urban South African Cities of the Future

Income distribution is grossly skewed in South Africa. White people earn nine times as much as blacks, blacks constitute 94 percent of the country's impoverished population, and 80 percent of the country's wealth is owned by 5 percent of people (African National Congress 1994; B. Turok 1993). In Johannesburg region, black Africans inhabit several "geographies of poverty" (Central Witwatersrand Metropolitan Chamber [CWMC] 1993). Concentrated poverty is found in *formal housing in township areas*. The two primary areas in the Central Witwatersrand are Alexandra and Soweto, the latter an amalgamation of 29 townships over ten miles southwest of, and spatially disconnected from, Johannesburg. Soweto is the largest black residential area in South Africa, encompassing almost 20,000 acres. Alexandra, in contrast, encompasses less than 1,000 acres, hemmed in by white residential areas, and is proximate to high-income Sandton and white suburbs to the north. It has been estimated that 178,000 formal bricks-and-mortar dwellings exist in Soweto and "Alex" (*South African Township Annual* 1993). The location of the built environment in the Soweto townships, however, imposes heavy costs in terms of commuting to work and stores. *Hostels* have been built to shelter workers in industrial and mining activities nearby, and face significant tension politically, ethnically, and physically. There are at least 51 hostel complexes in the Central Witwatersrand urban region (Gauteng Provincial Government 1995c). In the larger PWV urban complex, it was estimated in 1990 that there were over 300,000 hostel beds, many used by more than one occupant sleeping in shifts. This concentration of hostels around Johannesburg represented 67 percent of the national total (South African Institute of Race Relations 1994).

A common location of poverty is the *backyard shacks in townships and free-standing shacks on vacant land in townships* (see Photos 7.2 and 7.3). These are characterized by near-inhuman conditions of living, lack of secure tenure, inadequate standards of shelter and sanitation, and lack of social facilities and services. It has been estimated that there are about 140,000 informal shacks in Alexandra and Greater Soweto townships (*South African Township Annual* 1993).[6] In addition, there are *informal shack settlements outside townships*, located beyond the urban fringe or in peri-urban locations. Spatially disconnected from even the rudimentary services of townships, these settlements are often erected in areas of geotechnical or political susceptibility (T. Mashinini, Urbanization Department, Metropolitan Johannesburg, interview). The growing number of informal settlements that are on the urban periphery blur the distinction between city and country and strain the extension of infrastructure to these areas (D. M. Smith 1992; Horn, Hattingh, and Vermaak 1992).

In *inner-city zones*, black urbanization is producing an evolving residential fabric in the city of Johannesburg. In the past five to ten years, both before and after the abolition of Group Areas segregatory law in 1991, the significant "greying" that has occurred is associated with overcrowding of formal housing, illegal occupation of commercial buildings and office blocks, backyard shacks, and rooftop accommodation. Finally, there are *domestic workers and their families who live in quarters in the backyards of affluent suburban homes*. Their domicile is often overcrowded and terribly inadequate compared to the host house, although their level of shelter and services is generally better than the five options above. The affluent part of the white population of the Johannesburg urban region lives disproportionately in the northern suburbs of Sandton and Randburg, and along the northern arterial roads of Johannesburg city. These areas, not coincidentally, are locations of booming office, commercial, and specialty retail outlets. Lower- and lower-middle-class whites, meanwhile, are housed in the less prestigious south Johannesburg area, which is closer to the mines and exposed to fragile geologic conditions.

An enormous proportion of very basic needs is presently unmet in South Africa—both urban and rural. Urban basic needs include income; jobs; housing; land tenure; the basic services of water, sanitation, electricity, and circulation; and personal security. In Gauteng Province, 45 percent of the adult population has *annual* incomes less than R3000 (=$833/year); approximately two-thirds earned less than the bare subsistence level of about R10,000 a year (=$2,778/year) (Development Bank of Southern Africa [DBSA] 1995a).[7] Such poverty is a black phenomenon. In South Africa in 1992, the percentage of black households having incomes less than R8,400 a year was 54 percent, compared to 25, 8, and 3 percent for "coloured," "Indian," and "white" households, respectively (South African Institute

PHOTO 7.2 Squatter Shacks in Alexandra Township. (Photo by Scott A. Bollens)

PHOTO 7.3 Mandelaville Squatter Camp, Soweto. (Photo by Claudia L. Shambaugh)

of Race Relations [SAIRR] 1994). The official unemployment rate for the province in 1994 was 28.7 percent of the economically active population (DBSA 1995b), with the rate significantly higher for black Africans.[8] This is likely an underestimate of the true level of joblessness in that the official rate excludes demoralized workers not seeking employment. It is also noted that a not insubstantial percentage of those defined as "employed" are active in the informal sector of unregistered businesses. In 1991, the formal economy in the province was employing only about 50 percent of the labor force (DBSA 1995a).

For most of the last eight decades, the possibility of land and home ownership had been denied to black Africans.[9] Nationally, 87 percent of the land is owned by the minority white population. In terms of formal (bricks and mortar) housing, it is estimated that a 500,000 housing unit backlog currently exists in the province (M. Narsoo, Director of Housing, Gauteng Provincial Government, interview). In addition to the estimated 5,000 new family formations each year, this means more than 100,000 new housing units must be produced *in the province* each year for the next 5 years. As M. Narsoo (interview) notes, "if you are not delivering housing at this level, you are actually exacerbating the backlog." For sake of comparison, the number of formal housing units built *in all of South Africa* in 1991 and 1992 was 32,000 and 27,000, respectively (Building Industries Federation of South Africa data reported in SAIRR 1994).[10] It is just not the quantity but the affordability of new formal housing units that is critical (Tomlinson 1990). It is estimated that 50 percent or more of the black population in the Johannesburg urban region cannot afford the lowest priced formal housing unit of 40,000 Rand,[11] even with a 15,000 Rand subsidy going toward land purchase and shelter (J. McCrystal, Johannesburg city planning department, interview). In a study of nationwide trends, of the 580,000 households looking for alternative housing arrangements, only about 100,000 could afford a 45,000 Rand housing unit, given a 15,000 government subsidy and current bank practices (L. Schlemmer, business consultant, interview). At different times over the past two decades, blacks have been able to purchase their homes under either 99-year or 30-year leasehold schemes. Mashabela (1988) estimates that 34 percent of formal houses in Soweto had been purchased by the end of 1987. This still means, however, that when informal housing is included, only about 15–20 percent of householders in Soweto own the shelter they live in.[12]

Due to the shortage of formal housing opportunities (in terms of both supply and cost), much black urbanization in the Johannesburg region has come in the form of informal settlements. "Informal" dwellings include backyard shacks and outbuildings within townships, and free-standing shacks within and outside designated townships. The PWV metropolitan complex was estimated to contain in 1989 an astounding 2.5 million people living in 635,000 informal dwellings (Urban Foundation 1990a).[13] Over 400,000 shacks are backyard shelters within townships, over 150,000 are occupied outbuildings within townships, and about 50,000 are "free-standing" shacks on vacant land (either within or outside formal townships). If accurate, this would mean that the black population in the larger PWV complex living in informal conditions had surpassed the number living in formal housing in black townships (Urban Foundation 1990a). Growth in the "free-standing" types of informal settlements has mushroomed over the last five years. Within only the Central Witwatersrand region, it was estimated that by 1995 there were between 60,000 and 100,000 "free-standing" informal dwellings in 78 identified shack settlement communities that sheltered between 340,000 and 500,000 people (interviews: T. Mashinini and E. Ebdon, Urbanization Department, Greater Johannesburg Transitional Metropolitan Council). This "free-standing" informal population is of greater concern to policymakers than the two more prevalent types of informal settlement—backyard shacks and outbuildings—because free-standing settlements tend to be most disconnected to rudimentary services and facilities and are often erected in areas of geotechnical or political susceptibility (T. Mashinini, interview).

In addition to access to formal income, housing, and landownership, basic urban services to black Africans are often lacking. In South Africa, about 15 percent (4 million people) of the urban population has access only to untreated, unreticulated drinking water (Ministry in the Office of the President 1995).[14] About 30 percent of the urban population has access only to minimal sanitation (shared toilets and unimproved pit latrines). In terms of electricity, over one-half of South Africa's urban population lacks access. In the PWV, 18 of the 48 black townships in the metropolitan area were 50 percent or less electrified (SAIRR 1994). In the Soweto area townships, electricity services were more adequate than elsewhere in urban South Africa. Still, Mashabela (1988) reported that only 30 percent of the houses in Soweto had running water, while the rest used lavatories and taps which were supplied from substandard mains. Waterborne sewerage was available, but maintenance was inadequate with blockages and overflows widespread. Many informal settlements in Soweto had no access to rudimentary services such as waterborne sewerage.

The remote location of most black townships relative to work puts inordinate pressures on the regional transport system and imposes substantial costs on black commuters in terms of money, personal safety, and time.[15] Calculation of morning-hour traffic patterns shows huge flows of commuters from black areas—Soweto, Alexandra, and Tokoza in southeastern Johannesburg—to employment in white areas—Johannesburg central business district, Roodeport, Sandton, and Germiston (JOMET 1992). Commuting costs for black Africans typically consume around 10 percent of an urban family's household income (Tomlinson 1994). Residents in most black townships face a lack of continuity in, and capacity of, arterial roads, a legacy of operational difficulties in public transport, and problems in connecting from one transport mode to another efficiently. Faced with these problems of the public transport system, many black Africans use the burgeoning system of "kombi" taxis or minibuses, which now supply forty percent of the commuter trips in the region (JOMET 1994). The system is geared toward travel to and from black townships and the Johannesburg Central Business District, the dominant destination point in the morning. The kombi system offers greater point-to-point convenience than other public transport modes, but has suffered from significant violence between minibus-taxi associations (JOMET 1994). Since the kombi industry is not subsidized by the government, fares bite into the low income levels of black working-class commuters.

A final and important basic need not being met for both black and white residents of the Johannesburg region today is personal safety. Violence, in a politically motivated form part of the Johannesburg landscape for three decades, has taken on a distinctly different contemporary form. Today, Johannesburg is coping with criminally motivated violence levels among the highest in the world. Politically motivated violence has been a fact of life in South Africa since the early 1960s. Four main cycles of violence can be identified—1960–1963 after the Sharpeville massacre at an anti-pass rally; 1976–1977 set off by Soweto school boycotts over the introduction of the Afrikaans language; 1984–1987 subsequent to the establishment of a new constitution giving limited political rights to Indians and coloureds, but not to blacks; and 1992–1994 violence in the East Rand (Johannesburg) and Natal areas involving black-on-black violence and involvement by South African security forces. From 1984 through 1993, almost 19,000 people were killed in political violence, including 3700 in 1993 alone (South African Institute of Race Relations 1994). The 1992 and 1993 violence leading up to the national elections in April 1994 was particularly deadly, costing about 3,500 deaths in each of the two years (SAIRR 1994).[16] Violence has fallen into two main forms: terrorism by small organized groups and rioting by less organized crowds. Far more lives were lost in riots than from terrorism in each period, and the most deadly rioting involved black-on-black violence. Hewitt (1993) asserts that during the first three periods, "violence posed little threat to whites and to the South African security forces." The 1992 and 1993 period of political violence, however, was characterized by greater loss of life and injury to policemen and soldiers.

During and after the transition away from apartheid to democratic governance, criminal violence has been widespread. The end of apartheid may be the immediate cause, raising black expectations and highlighting the "intensely felt deprivation" that is associated with violence (Gurr 1968, 1970).[17] During and after the transition, the country experienced a spectacular decline in political crimes. At the same time, general crime has soared out of control. In 1994, over 60 people per 100,000 population in the Witwatersrand region were murdered, including 88 policemen in the first 10 months of that year. Vehicle hijacking rose 50 percent nationwide over the first eight months of 1994, with the total value of cars stolen over a 12-month pe-riod in Gauteng Province estimated at 95 million Rand (Harber and Ludman 1995). Nationwide, in the first seven months of 1994, armed robberies were up 17.7 per-cent over the previous year (Smit 1995). Official police statistics for 1995 paint a continuing gloomy picture, as reported crime levels nationally increased a further 5.8 percent over 1994 (Rodney 1996). The crime rate regarding serious crime in-creased by 346 cases per 100,000 population between 1994 and 1995.

Unlike political violence before 1994, contemporary crime and violence have penetrated into formerly "white" Johannesburg, spawning high perimeter walls around northern suburb residences, omnipresent 24-hour "armed response" pri-vate services, and a general sense of paranoia among Johannesburg whites. In black areas, the breakdown of authority in any form during the years of apartheid has created a significant criminal element (called *tsotsis*), whose actions are often more criminally related than politically related (Hewitt 1993). Such violence is a major question mark concerning Johannesburg's reconstruction efforts and ap-pears, as President Mandela stated, to be related to "the culture of non-compli-ance with the status quo, rooted in the period of illegitimate government" (*The Star*, August 4, 1995). Such noncompliance extends widely in the new South Africa, encompassing white-collar crime such as money laundering and tax eva-sion that costs the country billions of rands (L. Schlemmer, interview).

Political Control

We have a rambling, shambling democracy now in South Africa that will get its act together sometime down the line.
              —Monty Narsoo, Director of Housing, Gauteng Provincial Government

From 1948 to the early 1990s, the Afrikaner-based National Party developed and implemented the policies of apartheid or separate development. One is tempted to draw parallels between the Johannesburg (South Africa) case and the Belfast case of bicommunal conflict and argue that Johannesburg too has been a battle-ground between mutually exclusive nationalisms—one white/Afrikaner; one black. Indeed, such parallels have been made (Giliomee and Schlemmer 1989). White Afrikaner nationalism most assuredly fits within this scenario in its crush-ingly exclusionist ideology and methods. However, Sparks (1988), in his authori-tative account, portrays the mainstream black African nationalism in South Africa as inclusivist and not exclusionary of whites.[18] Support to this thesis is provided by the African National Congress's primary policy declaration, the Freedom Charter, which states that "South Africa belongs to all its people, black and white alike." As such, the South Africa case of which Johannesburg is part appears to rep-resent a less intractable clash of nationalisms than seen in Northern Ireland.

Since February 2, 1990, South Africa has experienced the wondrous and tumultuous steps along a road of irrevocable change away from the apartheid regime of the Afrikaner-based National Party. Sparks (1994) notes that the speech by F.W. DeKlerk on that February date, declaring the unbanning of all black liberation groups and his readiness to enter into multiparty negotiations to work out a new constitution, "was to race relations everywhere what the collapse of the Berlin Wall was to communism." Subsequent on-again, off-again multiparty national negotiations from 1991 to 1993[19] reached agreement on a transitional constitution and executive council, and on the procedures for the country's first democratic elections—for national and provincial legislatures—in 1994. National negotiations also were successful in establishing the makeup of a multiparty power-sharing executive cabinet to be configured based on election results, and the process by which the final constitution would be created by the national legislature. With the election on April 26–29, 1994, a five-year "government of national unity" formally replaced the old apartheid regime. The African National Congress (ANC) and Nelson Mandela captured 63 percent of the national vote (giving them 252 of the 400 National Assembly seats). At the provincial level, the ANC took control of 6 of the nine provincial legislatures, including Johannesburg's Gauteng Province.[20] In that province specifically, the ANC garnered 58 percent of the vote, compared to 24 percent for the National Party. This distribution of political power at province level is important because under the new governance arrangements provinces are likely to be given responsibilities independent of both national and local levels.

In terms of local and metropolitan restructuring of governance, in many ways this transformation occurred in negotiation paths independent of the above national processes. It was evident local governance had to be transformed to overcome the virtual coincidence of race, residential area, and local government in South Africa. The geographic distance between races created by apartheid urban policy worked in parallel with administrative separation and subordination. Since 1973, black townships like Soweto had been politically and financially detached from white areas (Beavon 1992). This administrative decoupling undermined the fiscal base of Soweto, making self-government after apartheid fiscally unviable (T. Hart, interview).

At the national level, as early as 1991 an Interim Measures for Local Government Act had encouraged neighboring black and white local councils to cooperate in service provision or, if possible, seek larger consolidation of political boundaries. Real progress on reforming local governance did not occur, however, until early 1993, when a national Local Government Negotiating Forum (LGNF), composed of equal numbers of representatives of the then-existing provincial and local authorities ("statutory") and of the nongovernment sector excluded under apartheid ("non-statutory"), was established.[21] This Forum's recommendations were incorporated into the 1993 Local Government Transition Act (LGTA). This act articulated a multiple-step approach to reforming local governance rather than creating a completely new system of local government at one time (D. Ewing 1995). In the first phase, local negotiating forums based on joint statutory-non-statutory representation would nominate members of new transitional forms of local and metropolitan governance. These appointed councilors would then run local government until elections were to be held. These local elections would occur sometime after national elections and would be based on newly demarcated local and ward boundaries that would politically integrate white and black areas.

In the Johannesburg urban region, discussions regarding local and metropolitan governance reorganization were further along in the process, and more advanced in substance, than the national-level negotiations regarding local government. The pioneering metropolitan discussions here acted as a model for discussions elsewhere in urban South Africa. The impetus for the early consideration of local government reform in the Witwatersrand was the crisis brought on by the boycotting of the payment of rent and service charges in Greater Soweto (I. Turok 1994b; Shaw 1994). The boycott, initiated in 1986, called attention to the illegitimate form of local governance in Soweto, the racial compartmentalization of local government financing, and the resulting inadequate levels of urban services. Crisis and paralysis of governance resulted. Negotiations to end the boycott began in 1989 and in 1990 agreement was reached in the form of the Greater Soweto Accord. The signatories included the Councils of Greater Soweto, the Soweto People's Delegation (a civic organization), and the provincial administration.[22] The Accord sought resolution of the boycott issue, but also put the Johannesburg region on a path of metropolitan governance reform from which it never stepped off. Most pertinent here was agreement to establish a Central Witwatersrand Metropolitan Chamber (CWMC) that would be a negotiating forum to investigate and formulate non-racial and democratic structures for local and metropolitan government.

Established in early 1991, the Chamber initially included 14 local government bodies and 8 community-based "civic" organizations (Shaw 1994). This membership list expanded over time and, in 1993, political organizations were invited to participate. The most significant participants to the Chamber were the Johannesburg City Council and the Civic Associations of Johannesburg, which included the Soweto Civic Association. The goals of the Chamber were twofold: one set related to responding to crises, in particular the nonpayment issue; the second set dealt with broader government transformation issues and longer-term policy development. In terms of government transformation, among the ideas the Chamber discussed was the civic associations'—and later the ANC's—call for a "single city–single tax base" encompassing the whole of the urban region. More immediately, the Chamber investigated various forms of transitional government structures that could be created, pending elections, that would fill the political vacuum created by the rejection of the authority of many local governments associated with the old regime. As Shaw (1994) observes, "appointed councils were to be seen not as an end in themselves but as a step towards the goal of legitimate and democratic local government." Pursuant to the national Local Government Transition Bill signed in early 1994, the Chamber was reconfigured into a Metropolitan Negotiating Forum containing 50 percent nonstatutory representatives (those excluded under apartheid) and 50 percent from statutory groups. This Forum then appointed members to an interim council—named the Transitional Metropolitan Council ("TMC")—which would manage urban affairs until local and metropolitan elections.

Metropolitan negotiators were charged not only with the complex and delicate task of determining who would sit on the 100-member TMC, but also confronted questions such as how to politically redemarcate the metropolitan region into local governments and what powers a metropolitan government would hold relative to them. In December 1994, the TMC was established as the interim caretaker and policymaker for the urban region, pending elections to occur in late 1995. The African National Congress held a plurality, although not majority, of the nonstatutory seats, while the Johannesburg city and National Party held primacy on the statutory side (Shaw 1994). The demarcation and allocation debates, meanwhile, extended well beyond that time, involving basic disagreements about the boundaries and roles of new local governments (called Metropolitan Sub-Structures, or MSSs) in post-apartheid Johannesburg.

An initial ANC proposal for local government restructuring sought the "stitching of townships to cities" so that they would no longer be marginalized, and a strong metropolitan authority. Statutory representatives, meanwhile, proposed eight MSSs that would politically carve up Greater Soweto and politically separate some black areas from white ones.[23] After significant contention, a Special Electoral Court in August 1995 approved a 4-MSS model, stating that it most effectively eliminated the racial political geography of old group areas. In each of the four MSSs, there was an existing and functioning administration—Johannesburg, Sandton, Randburg, and Roodepoort. At the same time, each of these administrations would have responsibility for managing black townships within its MSS borders: much of Greater Soweto in Johannesburg; Alexandra in Sandton; Diepkloof, Orlando East, and Pimville in Randburg; and Dobsonville and Meadowlands West in Roodepoort. It was this 4-MSS configuration that would provide the framework for 1995 local and metropolitan elections. Important intergovernmental allocation decisions remained to be decided until after local elections, dealing with the distribution of power between metropolitan and local governments, the levying of rates and taxes, redistribution across MSSs, setting of urban service levels, and land use and development authority.

Local elections in the Johannesburg urban region occurred in November 1995.[24] Electoral rules specified that 60 percent of the seats in each MSS were to be ward-based; the other 40 percent based on proportional representation (PR) rules. For the metropolitan council, 60 percent of the councilors are to be appointed by the MSSs while 40 percent are directly elected by PR. In a compromise with white authorities primarily in the Johannesburg region, the national local government law specified that at least one-half of electoral wards had to come from pre-existing white (including Indian and Coloured) authority areas. This basically locked in a 30 percent (one-half of 60 percent) representation in each jurisdiction from nonblack areas.[25] This was agreed upon by the multiparty negotiators to ensure minority representation (Ewing 1995).

The results of the complex and difficult negotiations concerning local government reorganization were, by contrast, relatively straightforward: the voting in on November 1, 1995, of absolute ANC majorities in all four MSSs, and a resulting inevitable absolute majority on the metropolitan council. From a high 74 percent majority in the Central Business District/Soweto local authority to a low 53 percent majority in the Sandton/Alexandra MSS, the ANC moved from excluded status to being in control of all local and regional governments in South Africa's largest and most powerful urban agglomeration.[26] It is within this political context that urban policymakers are faced with a series of difficult choices regarding the future of post-apartheid Johannesburg.

Transformative Urban Policy

Apartheid's main monument is the way we structured our cities.
    —*Herman Pienaar, Former Planner, Johannesburg City Planning Department*
                                                                          (interview)

There are layered imperatives during the change from one administrative structure to another. Where does one place one's priorities?
                                        —*Tim Hart, SRK Engineers, Johannesburg (interview)*

Since the early 1990s, consideration and initial formulation of alternative, non-apartheid urban policies for a democratic Johannesburg have been occurring. These discussions have taken place concurrent with the tremendous political and structural transformations at local, metropolitan, provincial, and national levels discussed earlier. In essence, the governance system for Johannesburg has been required to cope with dual fundamental pressures. Not only were urban leaders being asked to deliberately change the basic parameters of political participation, organization, and governing philosophy, but they had to consider and design alternative development policies to address urban needs and repair the damage of apartheid policy. In the first case, urban leaders had to engage in a self-transformative and democratizing process; in the second, a policy development role aimed at repairing and reconstructing Johannesburg's torn fabric and addressing the vast black-white disparities inherited from apartheid South Africa. This section

explores the dynamics, substantive contributions, and difficulties of these transition-period urban policy processes. In the first part, I describe the process-
oriented aspects of formulating new urban development policies. In the second
part, I explore the substantive outputs of these planning and policy processes.

Urban Policy in Transition

Tshipso Mashinini. Raised in Jabava, Soweto. Involvement with Civic Associations of Johannesburg. Member, Planning Framework Task Team, Central Witwatersrand Metropolitan Chamber. Current position: Deputy Director, Urbanization Department, Johannesburg Administration, Greater Johannesburg Transitional
Metropolitan Council.

The roles of Johannesburg's urban policymakers during the transition period from
1991 (start of CWMC) to the end of 1995 (the local and metropolitan elections)
were multiple and frequently overwhelming. Policymakers had to both resolve basic political issues of transformation and formulate new government priorities to
pursue post-apartheid visions. On the one hand, the Chamber was charged with
negotiating the restructuring of metropolitan governance in terms of institutional
structure and process, the inclusion of diverse personal histories heretofore marginalized, the goals of such governance and its reach, and, indeed, the very definition of urban governance itself. They also prepared for the formal electoral participation of all the urban region's residents and the establishment of new citizen
consultation procedures to meet the pent-up demands of city residents for inclusion. On the other hand, and in the midst of these time-consuming and taxing
processes of self-transformation and democratization, urban officials had to also
formulate new urban policies that would begin to reconstruct Johannesburg's dysfunctional physical and human geography and to implement urban equity policies
to lessen the huge disparities in urban opportunities and outcomes across race.

New democratic urban policy had to be formulated during an incremental,
phased, and frequently disjointed process of local and metropolitan government
transformation. There were at least four different manifestations of local and metropolitan governance from 1991 to 1995, with disjunctions occurring between each
phase, and within specific phases, due to the evolving and broadening inclusion of
stakeholder groups.[27] It was a complex and fluctuating system of governance that
had to respond to both the intense unmet basic needs of Johannesburg's urban majority and the heightened expectations associated with the emergence of a post-
apartheid regime. Together, these combined to generate passionate and powerful demands for the articulation and implementation of alternative urban programs and
policies to replace the illegitimate apartheid system. Transition-period policymakers
could no more easily turn their backs on the unmet urban needs of Johannesburg's

majority then they could try to reverse the transformative and democratizing processes that were changing the central parameters of Johannesburg governance.

In the negotiated self-transformative process, Johannesburg officials engaged as resolvers of basic political issues, recognizing that black political empowerment and restructuring of urban governance were critical prerequisites to effective equity policymaking. Discussions transcended sole emphases on the urban symptoms of racial polarization and targeted the need to radically transform and restructure apartheid-based urban governance. Only after basic issues of political transformation were satisfactorily addressed could policymakers focus on equity policies aimed at the urban symptoms of past racial conflict—gross disparities in urban opportunities and outcomes across race. Policymakers could then work to restructure urban policy toward explicit goals of social justice and away from the technocratic and partisan norms that had heretofore supported it.

A key aspect of government's role in promoting urban equity after apartheid is its articulation of a vision for future growth and development. Town planning, through its effects on the spatial and physical elements of a metropolitan region, is capable of creating an urban form that acts as a basic structuring device for other objects of urban policy—be they jobs, housing, transport, or bulk service provision. In the transformation from apartheid to urban democracy, it becomes the main role, and challenge, of town planning to change an intentionally dysfunctional urban form to one that connects the majority to urban goods and resources. Planners themselves recognized in an early policy document their central role in reconstructing Johannesburg, stating in CWMC (1992a) that "any attempt to restructure the apartheid city will have to commence with the restructuring of urban form in order to provide a context for the more complex and longer term process of restructuring the functional relationships between housing, jobs, and movement." In other words, attempting to deal with the symptoms of apartheid without reconstructing its basic structuring device—urban form—would be futile.

In the early years of the transition period (1991–1995)[28] of Johannesburg urban policy, planners were operating in a statutory planning context that itself seemed to be unraveling. Even as late as 1995, "there was no plan to guide the growth of the Johannesburg city or region" (Jan Erasmus, Metropolitan Planning Department, Johannesburg, interview). A Draft Guide Plan for the Central Witwatersrand had been developed in 1986, but never approved so it provided no statutory guidance. There was no land use plan for all of Johannesburg; rather, development plans were in place only for specific geographic areas. Citywide planning suffered as these development plan "parts did not make a whole" (M. Gilbert, Johannesburg city planning department, interview). Johannesburg did have a 1979 town planning scheme which zoned specific parcels by land use, but there was no larger policy plan to guide this zoning. The planning scheme underwent 22 amendments between 1980 and 1993, often without support from a larger guide or structure plan. And, quite consistent with apartheid ideology, these town planning schemes were not done in the traditional black areas.

Within this disorganized planning statutory context, local and regional governments in Johannesburg first began to explore the possibilities of post-apartheid city-building principles prior to larger political agreements or transformations. In 1992, the Johannesburg metropolitan transportation authority assumed in their modelling calculations that the Group Areas Act would be removed from the statute books by 1995 (JOMET 1992). It also sought for the purpose of creating a more efficient transportation system the "containment and compacting of the urban form," an early refutation of the basic apartheid tenants of dispersed and compartmentalized urban form (JOMET 1992).[29] The city planning department of the city of Johannesburg also showed an awareness of the need for change in basic urban planning policy. During 1991 and 1992, the department engaged in an analysis of strategic issues and embraced heretofore unacceptable planning strategies such as integration, city normalization, and policies addressing the inequalities of the apartheid city (M. Gilbert, Johannesburg city planning department, interview). These discussions within pre-transformation structures of local and regional governance, however reformist they were in intent, ultimately became shackled by the growing illegitimacy of their authority structures. Plans and actions proposed were preempted by the broader processes of political transformation.

The task of constructing post-apartheid principles of city building in Johannesburg was undertaken by the transition governance structure of the CWMC out of a sense that apartheid urbanization would continue absent any new direction. In November 1991, the Chamber first enunciated the need for new planning policy in the face of a proposal by an apartheid governing unit to build a new black town some twenty miles south of Johannesburg. The plan for a new town of some one-half million blacks would have reinforced the fragmented and dispersed apartheid spatial form. The Chamber postponed the proposal and instead commissioned a study of land availability closer to existing settlement, job opportunities, and infrastructure; and agreed that an overall strategy plan be done for the region to articulate a vision of a post-apartheid Johannesburg region.

Lawrence Boya. Advocate for the Civic Associations of Johannesburg (CAJ) during the transition. According to one observer, he "carried CAJ interests single-handedly for several months on the CWMC." Member—Planning Framework Task Team of the Chamber. Current position: Chief Director, Development Planning. Gauteng Provincial Government.

Such a strategy plan, called the Interim Strategic Framework (ISF), was conceptualized and formulated during the work of the Central Witwatersrand Metropolitan Chamber. The ISF was developed by two Chamber subgroups—the Planning Framework Task Team and a smaller ISF Working Group subcommittee of the Task Team. The fifteen-member ISF Working Group was composed of representatives from the Civic Associations of Johannesburg, a nongovernmental technical assistance provider (Planact), Metropolitan Planning Department of Johannesburg, City Planning Department of Johannesburg, a business-sponsored think tank and advocacy group (Urban Foundation), a government-sponsored funding entity (Development Bank of Southern Africa), the South African Property Owners' Association, Rand Mines Properties, and the architecture and urban design firm under contract (GAPS). The larger Task Team included similar representation, plus members representing Soweto and white Roodepoort, Randburg, and Sandton City Councils. The ISF—a physical and spatial plan—was to guide land use, infrastructure, and transportation planning and decisions in the urban region in terms of both short-term crises and longer-term urban restructuring processes (CWMC 1992a). First, *policy guidelines* would be developed to document existing problems and identify common principles to shape future policy. Second, *policy approaches* would articulate methods whereby problems could be addressed in principled ways. Finally, the *implementation strategy* would outline roles and responsibilities of engaged participants in carrying out chosen policies (CWMC 1992a; CWMC 1993).

   Interim Strategic Framework I: Policy Guidelines (ISF 1) was prepared for the Chamber in November 1992. The document states that future ISF policies and programs must address the immediate and severe problems of homelessness, displacement of the poor on the periphery, and inadequate bulk service provision and transportation infrastructure through actions that are guided by a longer-term vision of urban and metropolitan viability. It also explicates a set of eleven principles to guide future policymaking, including those of community participation and empowerment, transparency, inclusivity, choice, integration, and sustainability (CWMC 1992a). ISF 1 also identified eight "strategic areas" discussed below. Those involved in this early phase of ISF development reflect on its consensual output despite serious political agendas and on the ability of those heretofore excluded from governance to hold their own in the process. H. Pienaar (then with Johannesburg City Planning Department, interview) describes ISF 1 as a political, not planning, process whereby political parameters were articulated that would guide future city design. Despite hidden agendas, ISF 1 work resulted in important mutual trust between the government and "non-statutories" (civic organizations, in particular). Cross-fertilization of government and civic ideas occurred. For example, some of the earlier work on strategic issues by the City Planning Department dovetailed with the post-apartheid ideas of the civic organizations (M. Gilbert, Johannesburg City Planning Department, interview). Informal links also developed between the Metropolitan Planning Department and Planact, a nonprofit service organization representing the civics on technical issues (L. Royston, Johannesburg metropolitan planning department, interview). For their part, the civic organizations in the early part of the ISF process did not have the technical capacities, and thus had to rely initially on nongovernmental groups like Planact (L. Boya, Chief Director: Development Planning, Gauteng Province, interview). Nonetheless, the civics' advocacy ability played an instrumental role in keeping the process going (Graeme Reid, general manager, Planact, interview). Such was their impact that the ISF in the early stages was viewed as more closely aligned with nonstatutory than governmental interests (L. Royston, interview).

Based on the policy guidelines, *ISF 2: Policy Approaches* was completed in June 1993. The document articulates spatially and physically a set of principles aimed at addressing short-term needs and longer-term urban restructuring. It seeks to develop an "inherent and compelling urban logic" that could guide post-apartheid decisionmakers (CWMC 1993, 2). Spatial restructuring was positioned at the core of addressing the full set of urban apartheid wounds related to housing, service delivery, and access to urban opportunities. To some government planners, the process of articulating a new urban logic was a liberating experience in terms of their planning thinking, which heretofore had been based on a control-oriented British-type system. After a while, says H. Pienaar (then with Johannesburg City Planning, interview), "I was able to speak my own mind" not aligned with a strict political mandate. Pienaar continues about the role of the ISF process in harnessing and tempering his ideas about alternative planning, "I grew up in the (ISF) process. It was like an open window. Hearing the non-statutory side made me realize we had to liberate ourselves much more about the way we think about planning and densities." Although the work was dealing with planning issues of spatiality, urban services, and land use, the arguments behind ISF 2 remained political. Through working group activities and consensus building, "all views moved to the center, which is a fairly grey area" (H. Pienaar, interview). To the civic organizations and their partners, participation in the ISF process represented a shift from being outside activists and antagonists to being inside the policymaking process. Several nonstatutory members of the Planning Framework Task Team are now employees of metropolitan or provincial government in the new democratic regime.[30] The experience gained through Chamber negotiations provided many of these heretofore excluded individuals with a first entrée into the world of governance and policymaking.

The second stage of the ISF represented an essential process of social learning and negotiation. Prepared during a time of organizational uncertainty and anxiety, the working group saw the "processes through which the ISF is derived . . . as important as its outputs" (CWMC 1993, 4). Substantively, the policy guidelines and approaches in the ISF 2 regarding urban compaction, densification, empowerment, and equity represented a significant move forward and a radical departure in think-

ing about city-building. In the end, "ISF changed quite fundamentally the way people think about planning and the role cities play" (G. Reid, Planact, interview). H.
Pienaar (interview) echoes this sentiment: "ISF 2 is a benchmark of an entire paradigm shift about how we think about the urban system; it is one of the most significant documents in the planning history of this country." Civic organizations gained
a major victory in the process in their ability to open up the debate regarding the
anatomy of the post-apartheid city (L. Royston, Metropolitan Planning Department, interview). The consensual group process used in articulating new urban
policies for Johannesburg appeared successful in the framing and definition of
problems, negotiation between competing interests, and the formulation of new
policy directions.[31] However, in the next proposed stage—policy implementation—the group process ground to a halt, representing a major failure of the ISF.
The third stage of implementation strategy was to connect policy development
with specific actions by government that would address the intense immediate
needs—in terms of housing, services, and urban opportunities—of the urban system's majority. The ISF 2 document was distributed to the general public, relevant
organizations, and parties for comments. A great deal of debate was generated
from the document ranging from praise to strong criticism (Johannesburg Metropolitan Planning Department 1995). Attempts to finalize the ISF 2 document were
made, but concerns about underlying issues made a final consensus document impossible, leaving ISF 2 without legal or binding authority. The needed link between
policymaking and implementation was disrupted as consensus broke down.

The ISF process within the Metropolitan Chamber was the most significant exercise in reconceptualizing city-building in Johannesburg during the 1991–1995
transition period. At the same time, two national-level policy processes—the negotiated formulation of housing policy and the development of a national urban
strategy—were ongoing which likely would have profound impacts on Johannesburg's residents and physical space.

The formulation of a new housing policy to address the severe shelter crisis was
the task of the National Housing Forum (NHF). The Forum, created in August
1992, was one of several created during negotiations over new governance
arrangements. Each was comprised of interest groups and shareholders from civil
society as well as government representatives and was to discuss key issues and formulate new policy frameworks within specific substantive areas.[32] The NHF
included an intentionally broad array of interests, including civic organizations,
construction and materials supply companies, banks, pension fund companies, insurance and finance houses, mass-based political groups, employers, trade unions,
and development organizations. After two years of negotiation and discussion with
the then-national Ministry of Housing, a National Housing Plan was approved by all
parties, the main part of which was government-sponsored housing subsidies to
low-income people. At the same time, however, the NHF did not reach consensus

on the relative roles that the private sector and government should play in housing provision. The fact that the statutory housing bodies created after the 1994 election—the National Housing Board and nine Provincial Housing Boards—were also structured to include as wide an array of interests as possible meant that such unanimity would be unlikely, a point that would complicate housing delivery by the new democratic government (M. Narsoo, Gauteng Department of Local Government and Housing, interview).

The development of a national urban policy was addressed by the Reconstruction and Development Programme (RDP) unit in the Office of the President. The RDP, proposed originally by the African National Congress, is the effort by the new government to create an integrated, coherent socioeconomic policy framework. The program is aimed both at addressing the deep wounds and inequalities of apartheid and creating long-term sustainability. As part of the RDP, an interdepartmental task team on urban development was established as an integrating mechanism for the formulation and coordination of urban policy. Its objective, according to C. Olver (director, RDP Development Planning, Ministry of the Office of the President, interview), is to mobilize the resources of different urban stakeholders and sectors, and to build unity, around the city development process. Work groups of the urban development task team worked on the specific parameters of new national urban policy, and issues pertaining to public investment in infrastructure, government loans, reconstruction of violence-torn areas, and the problem of low rent and service payments by township residents (C. Olver, interview). The drafting process entailed months of consultation with national, provincial, and local governments, plus experts and other urban interests. It recommended, as discussed later, reform of the planning system and the creation of a major investment program for urban infrastructure and services. Left unanswered, however, was whether national urban policies could be implemented effectively by subnational governments, or whether a more centralized RDP urban policy framework would be required.

The transition period of 1991 to 1995 required that there be the negotiated formulation of new urban policies and forms of governance. As the Central Witwatersrand Metropolitan Chamber had to negotiate itself through the phased development of new local and metropolitan governance structures, it also was conceptualizing and formulating a physical and spatial plan—the Interim Strategic Framework—that elucidated post-apartheid city-building approaches. Meanwhile, negotiations over housing, planning, and investment policies at national and provincial levels—by the National Housing Forum and its subsequent statutory bodies, and by the RDP urban development task team—faced the challenge of creating new policies and programs while lacking internal consensus over how such policies would be implemented. Each negotiation process examined faced the difficult challenge of undertaking both the self-transformation of public authority and the formulation of new policy. Accordingly, imperatives for broad inclusiveness in negotiations would often conflict with the needs to advance specific new post-apartheid policies.

Untying Apartheid's Knots:
What Should a Post-Apartheid City Look Like?

Patrick Flusk. 31 years old. Born and raised in the "coloured" township of Riverlea, Johannesburg. Involved in political activities since 14 years of age: students' movement and school boycotts, ANC, civic organizations. Appointed councillor, Greater Johannesburg Transitional Metropolitan Council, by ANC, December 1994.

The "new orthodoxy" of post-apartheid urban planning, asserts Mabin (1995), is the paradigm of the compact city. The elements of this model include densification and infilling of underutilized areas, spatial and functional integration, and a spatial form that facilitates a complexity of diverse activities and urban opportunities. Whereas apartheid policy dispersed the Johannesburg urban region, the Interim Strategic Framework for metropolitan Johannesburg seeks to condense it. Whereas urban apartheid divided the urban system through the intentional creation of urban discontinuities and gaps, the ISF aspires to stitch together and integrate the torn parts and peoples of Johannesburg. Whereas apartheid separated and isolated peoples and urban activities through mono-zoning, the ISF seeks to create complexity in the urban system through mixed-use, nonracial land use regulations. And, whereas apartheid policy gave spatial form to racism and minority authoritarian rule and constrained urban opportunities to nonwhites, the ISF seeks to create a physical realm in which democracy finds meaning and form through the equal access to urban resources and goods across races.

The *Policy Approaches* document of the Interim Strategic Framework (ISF 2) indicts the planning profession for its emphasis on regulatory control and monofunctional zoning that seeks order, compartmentalization, and uniformity. The ISF associates such simplistic zoning with the creation of a spatial context that heightens tension and conflict. Taken to its most extreme form—the Group Areas Act—mono-zoning creates islands of privilege, vested interest, and ownership that residents defend vehemently from perceived "invasions" from outsiders (CWMC 1993, 6). ISF 2 points to the tension present at the fringes of such mono-zones and states that "it is this conflict and tension within the urban system that most eloquently highlights the failure of present approaches to planning" (CWMC 1993, 6). As an alternative, the ISF asserts that a spatial form that encourages urban diversity makes levels of tension unsustainable because it becomes difficult to define territories over which ownership can be claimed. Accordingly (CWMC 1993, 11), "the ISF must thus seek to engender the patterns of urban complexity that undermine the strength of exclusionary areas (and hence conflict) and actively seek the blurring of zone boundaries and the integration of hitherto isolated areas into the mainstream of the urban system."

Equity-based, post-apartheid city-building principles aspire to stitch together apartheid's urban discontinuities and integrate the torn parts and peoples of Johannesburg. Key facets of this city-building articulated in the ISF are the densification and infilling of the existing urban system and the upgrading and renewal of those parts of the urban system under stress.

The densification approach is at the heart of the compact city strategy. It seeks to encourage growth inward around already developed areas that are close to employment opportunities, have access to high levels of services and facilities, or fill in urban discontinuities intentionally created by apartheid planners. It seeks to direct growth to formerly white areas that benefitted in the past from low population density and access to high levels of urban services. Spatially, growth is to be targeted to the inner city, to mixed-use activity nodes of intense, spatially clustered development, and to activity corridors of linear mixed-use development. Densification of the existing urban system would facilitate residential development closer to urban employment and shopping opportunities. In this way, urban spatial form is related to increased access by blacks and low-income households to urban opportunities and human betterment. Indeed, densification would be a primary means to increase opportunities for blacks to enter the residential fabric of the "white" city (Tim Hart, SRK Engineers, interview).[33]

Vacant land is to be assimilated into the urban system. The development of vacant land far beyond the urban fringe was a common practice of apartheid planners, isolating individuals and communities far from urban opportunities. The ISF calls for vacant land to be targeted for development that is proximate to employment opportunities, has access to urban services and infrastructure, or fills in the spatial gaps created by apartheid policy (such as the buffer zone that separates Johannesburg city from Soweto townships). The legacy of apartheid's special treatment of white Johannesburg increases the chances that desirable urban vacant land exists today. As J. van de Merwe (interview) points out, "one of the ironies of apartheid is that we have service capacity in areas close to employment." The ISF concedes that a certain amount of vacant land on the periphery will be developed to meet the demands of the urban poor. At the same time, government should prioritize for development vacant land that is closer and more connected to the existing urban system. A land availability study found in their broad analysis of the metropolitan area a "substantial amount of available land"[34] (CWMC 1992b). Overall, 9,330 hectares not constrained by geological conditions were rated as high priority for low-income residential development.[35] Such lands could accommodate between 180,000 and 450,000 low-income housing units.[36] This is to be compared with estimates of between 350,000 and 450,000 new dwelling units needed by 2000 to accommodate existing backlog and expected black population growth in the Johannesburg urban region (CWMC 1992b, 9).[37] Based solely on the physical attributes of vacant land and planning criteria dealing with proximity to existing urban services and opportunities, it appears that a sufficient land supply is available to meet urban need.

Concurrent with densification is to be the upgrading of those areas under stress due to inadequate housing, poor or nonexistent services, and inadequate social facilities. Whereas the first approach implies the relocation of poor blacks to areas of greater opportunity, upgrading targets those areas where the poor currently live. Formal communities and informal settlements in areas such as Soweto, Lenasia, and Riverlea to the southwest, and Orange Farm and Sebokeng to the far south, are in need of substantial upgrading. ISF planners are cognizant, however, that such upgrading must be done in a way that integrates these areas into the larger urban system rather than relegating them to being dormitory areas in perpetuity. Thus, upgrading and renewal of peripheral areas must seek to extend the urban system's economic and infrastructural networks to these marginalized communities. This tension between in-place upgrading, on the one hand, and the normalization of metropolitan land use and settlement patterns, on the other, is a central one in post-apartheid planning and one to which I return later.

The ISF 2 plan elucidating these principles of post-apartheid city-building was praised for its ideas. L. Bremner (TMC councillor, interview) lauds the objectives of compactness and integration. Planners who worked on the ISF (M. Gilbert and H. Pienaar, Johannesburg City Planning, interviews) express strong support for ISF principles that relate spatial form to maximizing urban opportunities and creating a sustainable environment. The plan poses a bottom line to urban policymakers—"how can everyone access the opportunities of the urban system equally?" (M. Gilbert, interview). A. Motsa, planner for the nonprofit Planact organization (interview), feels ISF's main contribution is helping policymakers think about growth regionally, not just in terms of projects, and to use the nexus between urban activities and the transport network as a defining framework. In many respects, the ISF 2 plan represents a paradigm shift in Johannesburg planning, "fundamentally shifting the way local government bureaucrats, heretofore used to doing a particular way of planning, viewed their role" (L. Royston, Johannesburg Metropolitan Planning, interview). Such a conceptual shift may have been due as much to the timing of the ISF as its substance. J. Muller (University of the Witwatersrand, interview) points out that the city-building concepts of ISF were common-sense and had been discussed by Johannesburg and Soweto "during the height of the Nationalist Party era." Thus, it may have been not the uniqueness of these ideas, but the timing of their articulation relative to the political transformation process, that increased their impact on how Johannesburg urban policymakers view urban form and function.

However influential the Interim Strategic Framework has been in changing the mind-sets of city-builders, it was not readily translated into specific implementation steps. The resulting disconnection between policy development and implementation actions puts the ISF in danger of being relegated to the bookshelf. In Johannesburg's case, implementation strategies would be absolutely essential in transforming the urban system's racial geography. For example, the targeting and identification of available vacant land in the ISF 2 represents only a first step in the development of low-income residential units. Without an implementation strategy that would detail community consultation procedures, efforts to assimilate the poor into the urban complex can fail due to intense "not-in-my-backyard" conflicts over land and housing. Or, the goal of residential densification may be unfulfilled if, as in some inner-city neighborhoods (like Jeppestown and Troyeville), the private sector is not showing interest amidst concern over effective black demand. Here, without an implementation strategy detailing the potential role of government in facilitating private sector involvement, the densification concept may not be translated onto the ground.

Some policy officials interviewed felt that the ISF's overly technical language inhibited translation into implementation. "At the political level, we have been dreadfully frustrated," states L. Bremner (TMC councillor, interview), adding that because of the lack of an ISF implementation strategy, it has been overtaken by other legislation in effecting change. J. Erasmus (Johannesburg Metropolitan Planning, interview), a supporter of the strategic principles in ISF 2, nonetheless concedes that core ISF terms such as "urban complexity" were not clearly operationalized. Similarly, L. Royston (interview) criticizes the inaccessibility of some of the ISF 2 language, viewing it as a spatial and physical approach disconnected from management and institutional implementation. The ISF process stopped short of its aspirations of directly effecting change in Johannesburg's urban system. Nonetheless, "in some senses it is a dead document; in other ways it is not" (L. Royston, interview). It was a consistent view of interviewees that whereas the specific ISF process was terminated, the principles put forth by ISF appear to have had a vital life of their own subsequently. P. Flusk (interview) states that "although we have moved on, the debates since ISF 2 do not contradict it." Indeed, the ideas associated with the compact city model—integration, densification, vacant land infill, accessibility to urban opportunities, upgrading—are part of many ongoing policy discussions, project proposals, and urban strategies by local, provincial, and national levels of government. In many respects, the ISF urban designers and policymakers lost the battle, but won the war. Or, as L. Royston (interview) explains, "the debate has been won on another level."

At the project level, two prototype developments—aimed at inner-city densification (*Jeppestown Oval*) and spatial integration (*Baralink*)—are closely linked to compact city principles. The Jeppestown-Oval 230-unit housing development would be the first large affordable housing scheme in the inner city of Johannesburg in twenty years. It will be a major test of the ISF's densification goal and whether inner-city homeownership opportunities can be provided that will accommodate black income levels (J. McCrystal, Johannesburg City Planning, interview). The Baralink project[38] is a planned mixed-use residential-commercial-industrial project on 1500 hectares that would spatially and functionally connect Soweto townships with Johannesburg. It seeks "to correct the distorted spatial pattern of the apartheid city" and to develop "urban form that is more democratic in that it empowers people to access the city and its facilities, rather than being separated from these" (Thorne 1995). In addition, local planning efforts appear aligned with ISF principles in spirit, if not in name. For instance, a medium-term working group of the Transitional Metropolitan Council is identifying "potential development areas" based on their accessibility to employment opportunities and their filling in of urban discontinuities, and local development frameworks being formulated emphasize integration and accessibility as guiding principles (interviews: J. van de Merwe and M. Gilbert).

Compact city building principles have also been carried forward into many emerging urban strategies at provincial and national government levels, promising possibly greater impact than local efforts. A new planning system created by the 1995 Development Facilitation Act (and discussed later) puts forth principles for land development that include integration, proximity of residence and employment opportunities, compactness of growth, correction of historically distorted spatial patterns of settlement, and optimum use of existing infrastructure in excess of current needs. New guidelines for housing proposed in the White Paper on Housing (South Africa 1995) assert that government should assure that well-located land, near to transport and work opportunities, be used for housing. It is also significant that compact city principles are explicitly incorporated into the new government's guiding policy framework—the Reconstruction and Development Programme (ANC 1994; South Africa 1994). In section 4.3 of the RDP, urban development objectives state that "housing, transport, electrification and other infrastructure and service programmes should promote access to employment opportunities and urban resources, and the consequent densification and unification of the urban fabric." In addition, "new low-income housing should be situated near employment opportunities wherever possible."[39] Finally, the draft National Urban Strategy published in 1995 by the Ministry in the Office of the President estimated costs of a proposed national infrastructure investment program based on five urban spatial patterns consistent with compactness, accessibility, and integration goals.[40]

The parallel and consistent thrusts of the different policy debates and initiatives indicate that there is adequate consensus over what a post-apartheid Johannesburg urban region should look like. Local, metropolitan, and national policy frameworks each propose a similar set of city-building principles to guide Johannesburg away from the scars of its past. Nevertheless, the organizational flux associated with the process of local governmental self-transformation created difficulties in translating such vision into action. In addition, there are urban realities—the sheer size and urgency of unmet urban needs, land and housing market forces, and socio-spatial conflict—that create deterrents to the realization of this vision of a compact and spatially integrated city. Specific choices by urban policymakers concerning the prioritization of urban needs, and about the timing and sequencing of urban policy initiatives responsive to these needs, will have significant effects on whether urban policy transforms or reinforces the racial geography of its past. It is these issues—each related to temporality and urban policy choices—to which I now turn.

Temporality and Urban Policy Choices

Many retrospective accounts of apartheid's demise suggest that its downfall was inevitable—that it was only a matter of time—due to economic interdependencies and the strains of maintaining it. When investigating the dynamics of public policy in post-apartheid Johannesburg and South Africa, one is struck by the fact that temporality—the matter of time—remains a critical attribute of public policymaking. The phasing and sequencing of reconstruction efforts are evident by such words as transition, interim, pre-interim, transformation, and disjunction, as are time scales targeted by policy—the short-term or longer-term futures. In contrast to the backward assessment of apartheid's demise, I use temporality in a forward sense to emphasize: (1) the influence of temporal disjunctions on policymaking, and (2) the fact that many dilemmas faced by post-apartheid policy planners involve making choices about proper time scales and sequencing of policy. Both in the self-destruction of apartheid and now in the conscious design of post-apartheid policies, it has been, and remains for policy officials, a matter of time.

For post-apartheid public policymaking to operate effectively, it must engage in a delicate balancing of time in two respects. First, the phased reconstituting of basic structures of local and metropolitan governance creates disjunctions that disrupt and delay coherent policymaking. Policies must be developed that can withstand, and evolve during, changing stakeholder membership and shifting governance structures. In this case, temporality influences policymaking. Second, policy choices must be prioritized and sequenced relative to two different temporal imperatives—one dealing with short-term, crisis-related needs; the second with the development of a longer-term framework conducive to metropolitan sustainability. In this case, policy attempts to navigate society effectively amidst temporality. In the next sections, I focus on the temporal qualities and demands of urban policymaking amidst political transition. First, I examine the influence of transitional organizational disjunctions on the coherency and outcomes of policymaking. Second, I explore strategic policy choice amidst uncertainty and the conflicting imperatives of short-term and long-term development needs. Third, I focus on the tensions faced by policymaking in attempting to achieve both temporal and spatial objectives.

Transitional Disjunctions

> One underestimates the kind of black hole created by the collapse of an empire.
>
> **—Monty Narsoo, Director of Housing,**
> **Gauteng Provincial Government (interview)**

> We have been stuck in the transition.
>
> **—Tshipso Mashinini, Urbanization Department,**
> **Metropolitan Johannesburg (interview)**

There were four manifestations of local and metropolitan governance in Johannesburg during the 1991–1995 period within which urban policymaking was developed. There were transitional disjunctions between each phase, and within specific phases, due to the evolving and broadening inclusion of stakeholder groups. This organizational flux of metropolitan governance created a shifting terrain for policymaking which disrupted a continuity needed to turn post-apartheid urban principles into reality. The self-transformative function of local governance to a certain extent debilitated its ability to engage effectively in its policy development role. Frequently, discourse over post-apartheid urban policymaking seemed to await, and need, a broader process of democratization to give it potency and validity.

The local government restructuring process started with the creation in early 1991 of the Central Witwatersrand Metropolitan Chamber as a forum bringing together local government bodies and civic organizations. The Chamber's membership evolved and broadened over the next three years, eventually bringing in political organizations in 1993. In early 1994, pursuant to the national Local Government Transition Act (LGTA), the Chamber was reconstituted as a Metropolitan Government Negotiating Forum. This forum of joint statutory-nonstatutory membership appointed an interim Transitional Metropolitan Council (TMC) for the greater Johannesburg region, which began deliberations in late 1994. Finally, local and metropolitan government elections occurred in November 1995, resulting in a democratically elected greater Johannesburg Metropolitan Council and metropolitan substructures. Engagement in urban policy formulation amidst such substantial institutional transition is problematic. Urban policy amidst self-transformation requires, in the least, that urban choices be made amidst significant uncertainty and, at a more demanding level, a critical self-evaluation of the paradigms and basic assumptions of urban policy practice and administration. Both these processes—choice amidst uncertainty (examined here) and critical self-evaluation (discussed in Chapter 8)—are part of the contemporary landscape of Johannesburg urban policymaking.

Johannesburg urban policy formulation and implementation inevitably suffered due to institutional flux and complexity. L. Bremner (Johannesburg TMC member, interview) reflects that "it was very difficult to sustain service delivery and meet expectations of the people raised prior to the national election while trying at the same time to negotiate a transition." Since early 1994 alone, the national law concerning local government transition created a phased transition period containing many hurdles that had to be overcome through negotiations. Such negotiated settlements concerning basic structural and organizational changes in local governance would often, by necessity, take prominence over governmental efforts to meet the severe needs of Johannesburg's majority and to otherwise normalize the disfigured geography of the urban region. In the end, L. Bremner (interview) worries that the victim during this process may have been local government itself.

Temporal and organizational disjunctions were created as political party representatives were incorporated into the Chamber, first in June 1993, and again in early 1994 pursuant to the national act on local government transformation. This reconstituting of membership in metropolitan negotiating forums created discontinuities in the policy development process. As L. Bremner (interview) observes, "some of the victims of the transition were people who had been in the Chamber for a long time." In particular, representatives of civic organizations who had been involved for years with the Metropolitan Chamber were replaced by members of political groups who were new to the process and had established independent political party structures in places like Greater Soweto. Accordingly, civic representatives were marginalized and not brought into the new appointed local governance structures of, first, the negotiating forum, and then the Transitional Metropolitan Council.

The broadening of membership responded to genuine needs for inclusion; in many ways, the new ANC players had a greater political legitimacy than civic representatives. At the same time, however, this necessary self-transformative process disrupted the development of Johannesburg urban policy and is illustrative of *self-transformative* imperatives subordinating *policy development* objectives. The organizational shifts of the political transformation period contributed significantly to the implementation difficulties of the Interim Strategic Framework (P. Flusk, TMC councillor; L. Bremner, TMC councillor; Jan Erasmus, Metropolitan Planning; L. Royston, then with the nonprofit Planact; interviews). The ISF 2 plan had been published prior to the reconfiguration and broadening of membership on the larger metropolitan forum and the smaller working groups, including the one working on the ISF plan. "When political parties then entered the metropolitan negotiations, the dynamics shifted fundamentally," says L. Royston (Planact, interview). The change in stakeholder membership created a loss of institutional memory regarding the process and rationale behind ISF development. As Jan Erasmus (interview) observes, "The minute you get a new role player on board, you immediately have to take them through all the arguments."[41] Vision-building for the urban region became problematic in such an unstable institutional context. Members of interim government structures did not feel they had the authority or job security to project, and make commitments, into the future (T. Mashinini, interview).[42] In addition, documents like the ISF from the superseded Metropolitan Chamber were viewed with great skepticism by the new political players (L. Bremner, interview); and were viewed as products linked to the apartheid regime (Ben van der Walt, Gauteng Provincial Government, interview).

In the end, changing stakeholder membership within transition governance structures combined with the nonoperationalization of ISF concepts within the planning documents to erode consensus required to turn ISF urban policy concepts into reality. Even in a stable organizational environment, the interim strategic framework would likely have faced difficulties in implementation due to the disconnection within the ISF between concepts and suggested concrete steps. What ultimately disabled the ISF process, however, was not the technical process, but the organizational and membership shifts that constituted the essential self-transformation process. Yet, the true test of urban policy principles (such as densification, integration, and compactness) during structural transformation may not be their short-term translation into concrete actions but their simple ability to survive as guiding concepts in a post-transformation future. On this survival test, ISF principles are scoring higher marks. First, we have seen that these concepts have permeated policymaking at other governmental levels—provincial and national—further along in their self-transformation, and are guiding locally initiated projects and programs in the Johannesburg area. Second, ISF authors may have appropriately geared their ISF 2 document toward this goal of principle survivability. The ISF 2 document did not seek to develop a common physical vision or blueprint of Johannesburg's future. Rather, it sought to "present an inherent, compelling logic that invites future decision-makers to persist with these initiatives in a way that a consensus vision may quickly be put in place" (CWMC 1993, 2). In other words, the message of the ISF authors was not intended solely for the audience of current policymakers and was not dependent on short-term consensus. Thus, although consensus over the ISF did break down, ISF principles may still be able to act as vehicles for consensus in the longer term. Those urban policy principles able to withstand, and even be strengthened by, the shifting terrain of self-transforming local governance would have passed a rigorous test of time.

In summary, organizational changes were a necessary part of the move away from the apartheid regime and consisted of the phased reconstruction of metro-politan and local structures of governance and bureaucracy carried over from the old regime. Despite their essential nature, the self-transformative aspects of local governance to a certain extent debilitated its ability to engage effectively in devel-opment of post-apartheid urban policy. They produced significant organizational disjunctions that decreased the coherency and dampened the outcomes of policy-making during the transition period. Yet, the disruption and delay of policy for-mulation and implementation during the transition period may not be the sole story. If formulated policy principles are sound, they may penetrate or leak out to other levels of government—provincial or national—or act as de facto guidance for specific projects and programs. In the end, the true test of policy formation amidst institutional disjunctions may not be their short-term translation into con-crete actions but their simple ability to survive as guiding concepts in a post-trans-formation future.

The ISF experience shows how temporal disjunctions and uncertainties of change can significantly intrude upon the development of new urban policy. Yet, urban policymakers have the capacity to act as independent influences in guiding society amidst temporal uncertainty, a possibility to which I now turn.

Public Policy and Competing Time Scales

Ish Mkhabela. BA degree in biblical studies and geography. 15 years of commu-nity organizing experience associated with South African Consulate of Churches. Part of the Black Consciousness movement. Founding member of the Azanian Peo-ple's Organization (AZAPO). Currently, director of the Interfaith Community De-velopment Association, and Chairman of the National Housing Board.

This essay investigates the role of urban policy in effecting change amidst uncer-tainty, and how policymakers attempt to address the different and, at times com-peting, time scales of urban needs. In a circumstance of extreme urban social needs, it is tempting to design short-range policies and programs to address crisis situations. Focus by policy officials on the short term becomes even more accept-able in a society where long-term plans have historically been racist and restric-tive blueprints, and where they today may build up expectations and fan the fires of entitlement in the new South Africa (J. Muller, interview). Still, however, there is the need to have some longer-term framework that can guide and increase the impact of short-term actions. This need is illuminated most clearly in a dilemma facing policy officials today—that short-term actions detached from a more comprehensive vision of city-building may unwittingly reinforce the racial geography and inefficiencies of the apartheid city. I highlight this issue of competing time scales by exploring the uneasy relationship within interim metropolitan development strategies between policies aimed at crisis control and those that would pursue metropolitan sustainability.

> *Our responses to crises and needs have to be governed by a certain vision. This is the real tension, the real crux of the problem.*
>
> **—Tshipso Mashinini, Urbanization Department,**
> **Metropolitan Johannesburg (interview)**

> *There may be a case for subsidies to Soweto on reconstruction grounds, but there is not a case for it in terms of economic growth.*[43]

The Interim Strategic Framework 2 (Policy Approaches) outlines a fundamental choice facing policymakers in its subtitle—*Dealing with Crisis Issues in the Immediate Term and Restructuring the Metropolitan Urban System into a Sustainable Future.* On the one hand, urban policy must respond to dire needs felt by the urban majority concerning housing, services, employment, and other urban opportunities. At the same time, though, ISF short-term actions should in the aggregate lead to the construction of a post-apartheid city that is compact, integrated, complex, diverse, and sustainable. These two imperatives—one short term, the other long term—can at times run at cross purposes. For instance, solely responding to the housing shortage through rapid delivery of shelter and services may alleviate crisis conditions. However, due to lower land values and less community opposition on the urban fringe, such housing and services would likely be on the periphery. These housing actions without the support of a comprehensive spatial framework would thus fortify, not transform, the racial apartheid geography of separation and isolation. The ISF (CWMC 1993, 3) is aware of this tension between temporal imperatives, stating that a preoccupation with rudimentary housing provision increases the "prospect of reinforcing existing urban patterns that are unsustainable and lead ultimately not only to an inefficient system, but an ineffective one."

In moving toward a post-apartheid Johannesburg, urban policy must assuredly seek to repair the urban wounds and redress the tremendous urban inequities of the past. Yet, while engaging in such remedial actions, "the longer term view of reshaping the urban system into an effective, sustainable model must also be borne in mind" (CWMC 1993, 3). To some, this call for a longer-range vision and plan might seem an unnecessary obstacle to addressing long-neglected needs (and in some cases it will act that way). However, unguided short-term actions can harm the very people they are trying to help if the immediate benefits they provide are disconnected from the more diverse opportunities of the larger urban system. This represents a fundamental dilemma of the ISF and most post-apartheid urban policy. CWMC (1993, 3) states: "The ISF must thus strike a delicate balance in delivering in areas where disparity is now most acutely felt, yet set in place the basic tenets of an urban order that systematically addresses disparity through a logic that is fundamentally geared towards the needs of a viable urban system."

During the ISF process, there was vacillation between these two policy demands. As first proposed, the ISF was to concentrate on the spatial and physical elements of the urban system in the short term (CWMC 1992a, 4). It was expected that the ISF would help facilitate decisionmaking related to crisis demands for land for residential and employment purposes, while serving as a point of departure for a separate longer-time metropolitan development plan that would come later.[44] Since the ISF's "intent originally was to be a quick and dirty method of addressing immediate problems, it failed in this sense" (Jan Erasmus, Metropolitan Planning, interview). As the process lengthened in time and its scheduled third phase of implementation fell victim to a breakdown in consensus, it became apparent that the ISF was not providing needed guidance for short-term actions (L. Royston, Metropolitan Planning, interview). Ultimately, the ISF became more an effort aimed at articulating urban principles than one of proposing immediate actions to solving crisis conditions. When public participation was incorporated into the process after ISF 2, several criticisms focused on its lack of a short-term strategy or prioritization of needs (CWMC 1993). In the end, ISF delivered a vision of urban form rather than a set of concrete actions.

Absent the adoption of an overall ISF plan for the Johannesburg region, politicians and policy bureaucrats have had to address the difficult balancing act between short-term crisis response and strategic plan-making in a policy environment where there is neither an effective instrument for short-term actions nor a long-term policy framework. M. Gilbert (interview) describes how the Johannesburg city planning department is attempting to initiate local actions and develop broader frameworks concurrently: "We try to contextualize one with the other—creating longer term development frameworks while at the same time responding to short term crises. We are trying not to be saddled with the long term impacts of responding to crises only." In the Baralink project that will functionally and spatially link Soweto and Johannesburg, "we try to develop mechanisms that are appropriate to that specific area; in developing these, we are also reviewing planning mechanisms that will be appropriate to other previous black communities generally." In a sense, there is an attempt here to construct broader policy based on the concrete experiences of more place-specific public actions.

The urbanization department within metropolitan government, established to directly connect community-identified needs to government resources, also faces this tension between specific actions and broader policymaking. Its intended role is twofold—to develop policy and to manage crises related to housing and shelter, informal trading, and social services. In actuality, the department has evolved into a crisis response unit dealing with informal settlements, homelessness, and land invasions (E. Ebdon, Urbanization Department, interview). This emphasis is traceable to an earlier phase of the ISF process. When it became apparent that the ISF was not satisfying the need to stimulate and guide short-term actions, a Project Facilitation Group was set up within the Chamber to stimulate project actions, particularly in black areas. As local governance was transformed with the establishment of the Transitional Metropolitan Council in late 1994, this project-specific function was then transferred into the Urbanization Department.[45] What this means is that the department's mission today has become intimately connected to crisis control and management. E. Ebdon (interview) recalls the reorientation of the department in late 1994: "Our department's policy orientation has almost been put aside since December 1994. Our work is now more operations than policy—solving immediate problem areas that are coming onto my desk all the time." Problematic to urbanization department employees is how to effectively respond to these short-term demands without support from a broader policy framework. T. Mashinini (Urbanization Department, interview) reflects that, "while certain principles—integration and accessibility—exist as building blocks, there is no effective medium or long-term vision regarding such issues as informal settlements." With no clear policy parameters coming from the metropolitan council, "policy is being developed ad-hoc as we go along" (E. Ebdon, interview). As the department endeavors to develop policy at the same time it is responding to myriad crises (foremost among them, land invasions), "one feels often that things are going too fast, and that ordered policy development work is suffering" (E. Ebdon, interview). Mashinini echoes this concern in stating that "we must avoid the temptation to 'deliver, deliver, deliver' without managing the process of reconstruction."

The delicate balance between action-taking and framework-development is also evident in public discussions regarding development in the greater Soweto area (H. Sekoto, city planning department; I. Kadungure, RDP support unit, metropolitan Johannesburg, interviews). Regarding development plans in the Kliptown area, Sekoto argues the need for a broader framework that would move governmental involvement beyond project-specific and ad-hoc actions. In a circumstance where developers are calling the shots along with their consultants, there needs to be a balanced approach by the TMC that would coordinate individual initiatives and competing interests. The temporal dilemma caused by the dual imperatives of policy—one short-term and demand-dictated; the other long-term and plan-oriented—is also recognized by metropolitan politicians (interviews: L. Bremner and P. Flusk, TMC councilpersons). Bremner is chair of the TMC Urbanization and Housing Committee and is in the unenviable position of responding to the tremendous number of land invasions in the urban region. She reflects that during her first six months we "were just putting out fires" outside of a planning framework. Within this crisis condition, "we try to do things now in responding to land invasions that won't jeopardize the long term process of housing provision."

Time and Space

Mekhukhu: temporary dwellings

—Sotho language

Those shacks are part of the solution, as long as they are supported. Left alone, they will become islands of poverty.

—Ish Mkhabela, Chair, National Housing Board (interview)

If peripheral growth is the route that development takes, we're going to continue to have dysfunctional cities in the future.

—Graeme Reid, Lawyer—Planact (former) (interview)

Integration of short-term actions and longer-term vision-building puts significant burdens on the policy development process, but is essential because short-term crisis response may conflict with longer-term spatial normalization goals. A critical case involves policy aimed at improving the dire conditions of those occupying Johannesburg's mekhukhu. Due to land market dynamics and community resistance, certain policy responses to the region's severe housing needs may produce outcomes antithetical to the goal of creating a compact and integrated post-apartheid city. At that point, policymakers must choose between a temporal imperative related to crisis control and a spatial one demanding the restructuring of metropolitan form. This essay first examines two significant manifestations of the black housing shortage in the Johannesburg region—informal settlements and land invasions. These phenomena create substantial strains on the urban system and its inhabitants and pose a complex challenge to urban policymakers. Second, I evaluate efforts to subsidize new shelter arrangements for these homeless,[46] including the government's first foray in land development. Can urban policy regarding shack settlements respond to their crisis and emergency conditions within a framework of overall metropolitan development consistent with post-apartheid urban goals?

Informal Settlements and Land Invasions. Shacks—makeshift structures made of plastic, wood, corrugated iron, blocks, or brick—are a consequence of decades of national policy restrictive of urban black population overlaid upon the demographic realities of increased migration of blacks from rural to urban areas in search of employment. The prevalence of shacks is both a sign of apartheid's short-term success in delimiting "formal" housing opportunities and its longer-term failure in constraining black urban growth. Shack settlements that are free-standing from formal communities and services are the largest growth component of informal dwellings, mushrooming in the Johannesburg region over the last five years.[47] This growth is due to at least two reasons. First, shacks increased tremendously with the loosening up and eventual abandonment of influx control by government in the 1980s and 1990s. Second, and more recently, during the transition period there has been a tremendous growth in land invasions and shack construction as many homeless sought to stake their claim through squatting (L. Bremner, TMC councillor, interview). Within the Central Witwatersrand area, it was estimated that in 1995 there were between 60,000 and 100,000 free-standing informal dwellings in 78 identified shack settlement communities that shelter be-tween 340,000 and 500,000 people (interviews; T. Mashinini and E. Ebdon, Ur-banization Department, Johannesburg TMC).

Although backyard shacks and outbuildings in townships are more common types of informal dwellings, it is these free-standing shack settlements that are the ma-jor concern of urban policymakers. This is due to inadequate urban services, pub-lic health dangers, their location within the urban system, and their propensity to incite often class-based land-use conflict. Unlike backyard shacks and outbuild-ings, shack communities' "free-standingness" means they are often disconnected from even the rudimentary services and facilities found in townships.[48] In addi-tion, they are often erected in areas of geotechnical instability (such as floodplain or dolomite areas) or are susceptible to political tension (T. Mashinini, inter-view). Shack settlements are also commonly located in peripheral locations in the metropolitan system, directly at odds with the compact city goals of post-apartheid policymakers. Finally, the recent geographic spread of new and expand-ing shack settlements is encroaching upon established middle-income residential space (both white and black), creating class-based struggles over land. The spread of new shack settlements into "white" Johannesburg has particularly heightened demands that post-apartheid urban policymakers address land invasions. "What used to be 'their' problem in Soweto is now in everybody's backyard," says I. Kadungure (RDP support unit, TMC, interview).

    Shack settlements are the "flotsam and jetsam of urban African society" (Masha-bela 1990). They face harassment in the form of shack demolitions, and the threats of removals are constant sources of conflict and concern. At times, land invasions and shack construction arise from a genuine community effort to deal with ex-treme need[49] (E. Ebdon, Urbanization Department, TMC, interview). However, in part because the "wider community tends to ignore them" (H. Mashabela, South African Institute of Race Relations, interview), shack settlements are also an organizational instrument that can be used by political or criminal interests (L. Bremner, TMC councillor, interview; and E. Ebdon, interview). In these cases, political parties such as the ANC or IFP will help move their supporters onto a piece of land, possibly displacing those of other parties (H. Mashabela and E. Ebdon, interviews). In other cases, a grassroots leader will exploit the homeless by organizing them to move onto land in return for an often lofty payment (E. Ebdon, interview).

No matter the motivations behind shack settlements and land invasions, they present a major policy challenge, both because of the sheer size of shelter needs and the difficult policy choices involved. The explosion of land invasions and the prevalence of shack settlements in contemporary metropolitan Johannesburg mean that urban policymakers must learn how to appropriately respond to these dynamics. The TMC (1995b) is aware of this, stating that "the manifestation of housing demand through land invasions and the growth of informal settlements is already occurring within the short term, requiring guidance and necessitating some form of planning response." In particular, policymakers, says T. Mashinini (Urbanization Department, TMC, interview), must coordinate actions so they respond to these crises in ways that are compatible with medium- and long-term metropolitan developmental goals.

Land invasions put urban policymakers in the most reactive and defensive position, obstructing the process of formulating responsible and sustainable housing and shelter policy. Rapid and illegal occupations of public or private vacant land for the purpose of establishing an informal settlement are the most visible and immediate manifestation of the housing shortage problem in greater Johannesburg.[50] One estimate for Johannesburg/Soweto counted about 4000 shacks (containing 16,000 people) erected as a result of land invasions during 1994 alone, with the bulk on public open space (Johannesburg TMC 1995b). The Urbanization Department of the TMC is charged with dealing with invasions and informal settlements, and "develops policy ad-hoc as we go along because there are no clear policy parameters from the metropolitan council" (E. Ebdon, interview). Lacking a well-administered system of formally housing people, it becomes hard to discourage land invasions as a way to gain a foothold toward shelter and services. Local and provincial governments acknowledge that land invasions are an indicator of the larger housing backlog problem (Gauteng Provincial Government 1995a; T. Mashinini, TMC Urbanization Department, interview). At the same time, though, they realize that they must prevent further land invasions to stabilize the situation in order to allow more normal processes of housing delivery to take place (T. Mashinini, interview). Thus, a moratorium on land invasions was initiated in June 1994 at the same time that government began to formulate policies to facilitate the delivery of

housing and more suitable land. This puts new government officials in the difficult situation of evicting ANC constituents, as was done in December 1995 in
the forceful eviction of Moffat Park shack settlers.

Even if land invasions can be successfully curtailed, urban policymaking must
then find ways to improve the living conditions of those inhabitants in the large established set of shack settlements around greater Johannesburg. One policy option is to upgrade or normalize the living conditions in-situ. Upgrading usually
takes the form of "site and services": the provision of land and supporting bulk
services such as water, sanitation, and electricity. Site and service schemes as the
main form of upgrading in the past have faced criticism that contemporary policymakers must address. They have been built in an ad-hoc way, far remote from
metropolitan centers of activity, provided no tenure rights, included few social
and community goals, and have provided submarginal services based on initial
capital expense, not life-cycle costs (Viljoen and Adler 1993).[51] The biggest problem is that once site and services were provided, inhabitants have then been abandoned and left to their own devices to build housing. In essence, government said
to shack settlers, "you're going to have a house now; you just need to make
arrangements with Standard Bank or United Bank" (H. Mashabela, SAIRR, interview). With a vast majority of blacks too poor to fit financial institutions' profiles
for borrowing, this has meant that many site and service schemes resulted in, or
re-created, the informal settlements they were aimed at eradicating (A. Motsa,
Planact, interview). In addition, government intent to upgrade an informal settlement, in effect, acts as a magnet for the homeless. In the case of a shack settlement in an inappropriate location but where eviction is not practical, the provision of basic services to prevent the outbreak of communicable diseases can be
seen as a statement of acknowledgement by government (T. Mashinini, interview). Where site and service schemes are used, they are commonly oversub-
scribed, tense, and vulnerable to exploitation by unscrupulous dealers (T. Hart,
SRK Engineers, interview). Government thus seeks to have the informal settlement targeted for upgrading monitor its own growth so the number of toilets and
water outlets provided does not quickly become overrun by demand.

What is needed in today's site and service schemes is to use them as launching
points for further development that is supported by multiple sectors—financial
institutions, government, and community. Government must support communities with services, proximate economic development activities, common spaces,
and community facilities such as schools (I. Mkhabela, National Housing Board,
interview). Provision of these urban resources might increase average income by
inhabitants and help them gain access to loans for formal housing construction.
Yet, this would be a long-term program unable to alleviate the need for shack
construction in the near term. A shorter-term approach would include the provision of property rights to shack settlers as a form of equity that would facilitate

bank loans needed to construct a formal unit.[52] Unfortunately, however, traditional banks have been reluctant to recognize this form of equity alone as sufficient for borrowing (T. Hart, SRK Engineers, interview). In addition, the granting of tenure rights must be done in a way not to encourage land invasions as a viable form of gaining land rights.

On a metropolitan scale, upgrading of commonly remote shack settlements will improve living conditions but reinforce the apartheid geography of dispersion that inhibits accessibility to diverse opportunities. In other cases, upgrading is clearly not appropriate given the geologically unsuitable locations of some settlements. Accordingly, relocation of shack settlements to more suitable locations must be a major part of creating a post-apartheid metropolis. However, relocation in the past has provided only partial and inadequate solutions to the homelessness problem. It has tended to place shack settlers in locations even more remote than their original locations, the primary example being the development in the 1980s of Orange Farm which is some 20 miles south of Johannesburg. Relocation strategies have numerous limitations. First, relocation will tend to be more expensive than upgrading in-situ, especially when the new location is privately owned and must be acquired by government and/or if it is on more expensive inner-city land. Second, relocation often relies on site and service schemes in the new location, entailing problems similar to upgrading in-situ. Third, relocation uproots existing community networks, inhabitants' sense of security, and their links to often informal economic opportunities (J. Erasmus, metropolitan planning; T. Hart, interviews). Fourth, relocation efforts that use government subsidies (which is the common pattern) can expose illegal immigrant inhabitants who are not eligible for subsidies and exacerbate tension and violence (L. Bremner, TMC, interview). Finally, government must be sure of their criteria for relocation (and upgrading, for that matter) so that nonrecipient individuals or communities do not feel aggrieved (L. Bremner, interview).

In the end, informal settlement policy should accommodate as many options for shelter improvement as possible (T. Hart, interview). Stabilization and comprehensive upgrading of certain informal settlements would occur together with relocation of others that are in unsafe, already use-designated, or spatially disconnected locations.[53] Site and services would likely be a necessary component of this approach, but would need to be supplemented by efforts to open up subsidy and end-financing markets. The goal in the long term would be some normalization of the housing market so that it would provide choice to the majority poor, moving them away from the current situation where they feel "I better grab this now because I don't know where the next opportunity will come around." Despite its inherent problems, relocation of shack settlements through government subsidies holds the key to reshaping apartheid space and increasing inhabitants' access to urban opportunities. Most significant to the overall effectiveness of future

relocation strategies will be whether they increase urban compaction and integration or continue to spatially marginalize the poor black population. Policy must
swim here against a powerful current, as I now consider.

Housing Provision and the Compact City.   Nowhere is the tradeoff between
the temporal demand of crisis control and the spatial imperative to reorder urban
form as clear as in emerging government housing policy and subsidization. On the
one hand, policy must respond to the pent-up demands and high expectations for
shelter improvement for the urban majority. On the other hand, policymakers
rightfully seek to transform the distortions of the apartheid metropolis to open up
longer-term opportunities for this majority. Time and space are uneasy bedfellows, however, in an urban system of private land markets and community dynamics that resist basic transmutation. In this essay, I first explore two government housing programs that have the possibility for significantly reshaping
metropolitan space. It is the interplay of these locational programs, together with
government financial subsidies, that will determine whether housing policy can
address both time and space effectively. A detailed examination of the mechanisms
and likely outcomes of the democratic government's first housing program provides important warnings to policymakers seeking to meet both temporal and
spatial demands of post-apartheid urbanization.

Relocation efforts aimed at spatially restructuring metropolitan space must target appropriate land in suitable locations, and provide financial mechanisms to develop shelter in those locations. Spatial targeting is to occur through two programs—the provincial Rapid Land Development Programme (RLDP) and
Metropolitan Johannesburg's "potential development areas" program. These are to
be linked to a project-based housing subsidy to help the urban poor improve their
shelter arrangements. Relocation over the short term is to occur through the Gauteng Province's RLDP. This program seeks to "deal with land pressure and homelessness in specific local areas, and to limit land invasions, through the rapid release
of serviced sites for development" (Gauteng Provincial Government 1995a). The
program seeks to rapidly release publicly owned land for development in suitable
locations. This is to be a fast-track effort targeted, foremost, at the relocation of
those shack communities that are located on geologically unsafe land.[54] A second
program aimed at targeting new housing development areas is the TMC's "potential
development area" (PDA) program, which is to identify public or private land
within the urban fabric and close to employment nodes which would be appropriate receiving zones for relocated settlements. Whereas the RLDP concentrates in
the short term on shantytowns in greatest crisis, the PDA is a medium-range program aimed at a fuller restructuring of a post-apartheid compact and integrated
city. The main financial mechanism for housing introduced by the new government
is the project-based individual subsidy. This government subsidy is available for per-

sons earning less than R3,500/month, with the fullest subsidy of R15,000 (U.S.$4,250) available to those making less than R800/month. The subsidy can be used to pay for a site, bulk services (water and sewer infrastructure), and/or construction of the housing unit (superstructure). The National Housing Board sets eligibility criteria and other conditions for subsidy money. Provincial Housing Boards can then put in place supplemental criteria such as location of subsidized housing, nature of projects, or mandates regarding the use of emerging black contractors (M. Nel, vice-chairman, National Housing Board, interview).

Together, these programs have the potential to link the identification of suitable sites within the existing urban fabric to the use of government subsidies which put people on adequately serviced land. However, there are certain realities—finite budgetary resources, land and housing market forces, and socio-spatial conflict—that create deterrents to the creation of a compact and spatially integrated city. These obstacles and tradeoffs are best illustrated through a close look at the anatomy and mechanisms of the Rapid Land Development Programme. The first obstacle facing the RLDP is limited budget resources. The province in the program's first year allocated only enough money to service about 4,000 sites. This falls far short of the 20,000 shacks estimated by the TMC to be in immediate need of relocation due to geotechnical or political stress, and the overall number of about 65,000 free-standing shacks in greater Johannesburg (E. Ebdon and T. Mashinini, Urbanization Department, TMC, interviews). A second major problem is that RLDP implementation has tended to facilitate peripheral development antithetical to the vision of a compact post-apartheid city (P. Waanders, Chief Director, Planning Services, Gauteng Province, interview; M. Nel, interview). This is because the lion's share of publicly owned land eligible for resettlement is in remote areas contiguous to formal townships.[55] Also, there are established middle-class communities and vested financial interests that strongly resist attempts to channel housing subsidies inward toward the existing urban fabric.

Locating low-income communities within the urban fabric—a key element of a compact city strategy—creates contestation: between communities, between sectors of society, and between government departments. The "not-in-my-backyard" (NIMBY) syndrome common in the USA is unsurprisingly part of the Johannesburg development landscape. Worries over property value depreciation combine with near-paranoia concerning exorbitant criminality to produce fierce opposition from middle-class communities, both white and black.[56] Such NIMBYism stands in the way of integration attempts. An effort by the metropolitan government, for example, to buy land near existing towns for low-cost housing for Alexandra inhabitants met with vociferous objections by Sandton and other formerly white authorities (T. Mashinini, interview). A second form of contestation over the location of low-cost housing takes place between financial and government sectors. The Gauteng Provincial Housing Board (PHB), which decides on

the locational attributes of subsidized housing, is composed of multiple stakeholders of banking, government, and community interests. Yet, it is the banks and
other financial interests that have been able to carry the argument concerning the
negative effects of integrated low-cost development (M. Swilling, University of
the Witwatersrand; M. Narsoo, housing director, Gauteng Province, interviews).
Banking and developer interests make the claim that low-cost housing will de-
value area property values and, over time, put the entire asset base of the banking
industry at risk. Such weakening of the property asset base is then linked in this
argument to lower municipal revenue and municipalities' constrained ability to
borrow money (M. Swilling, interview). This financial argument is not without
merit, admits M. Narsoo (interview), "but it means the apartheid city—the divided city—remains." This financial logic has thus far defined the basic parameters
of the Gauteng Housing Board's approach to low-cost housing location, dampen-
ing its ability to channel subsidies consistent with compact city goals.[57]

Tensions also result within government from the different imperatives associated with the provision of low-cost housing, in particular between housing departments concerned with supply enhancement and land planning departments
concerned with the spatial location of such housing. Whereas the Gauteng
Province Department of Local Government and Housing emphasizes housing
supply enhancement as its key goal, the province's Department of Development
Planning, Environment, and Works (DDPEW) seeks to locationally channel low-
cost housing to further densification and integration goals (L. Boya, Chief Director, Development Planning, DDPEW, interview; Gauteng Provincial Government
1995a). For the RLDP and future housing initiatives, it will be necessary for these
two departments (and their local government counterparts) to fashion a development vision able to accommodate both short-term housing needs and longer-
term spatial imperatives.

The Rapid Land Development Programme is the first land program in the
country shaped by the democratically elected government (M. Swilling, interview). A prototype program in many respects, it exhibits the tradeoffs involved
between rapidity of policy implementation and compact city goals. The RLDP is
not of such size as to seriously compromise long-term spatial goals. At the same
time, it indicates the formidable obstacles that any ongoing medium- and long-
term policies must overcome if they too are not to reinforce the apartheid geography of the past. And, because these longer-term programs, like the potential development area program of the TMC, will target publicly *and* privately owned
land as potential receiving zones, they will face the additional centrifugal force of
prohibitively expensive land values in inner areas. Because inner-city land costs
would consume a sizable amount of subsidy, making shelter construction unlikely,
it is likely that housing subsidies will be applied to peripheral locations in order to
stretch limited public resources.

Compact city goals, when applied to integrating poor blacks into an existing urban system, place enormous demands for a complex interrelated sequence of actions to occur. One advantage of longer-term policies in terms of their being able to facilitate city integration and compaction is they have time on their side. This might allow the state to develop more progressive and proactive policies to overcome the pervasive economic and community obstacles to integration. These approaches would necessitate a greater state role and risk-taking in inner-city low-income residential ventures. For instance, special development zones could be identified within the urban fabric where higher government subsidies and cross-department holistic efforts would be concentrated.[58] At the same time, resistance from established middle-class communities will need to be overcome. Low-income units could be incorporated into larger mixed-income developments to dampen some of this resistance. Increased security measures would need to be part of densification efforts to assuage NIMBY-related fear of crime. Social compacts and cross-community organizational networks could be established to open up communication between new and established communities. In the end, however, continued community resistance might need to be overcome through low-income inclusionary zoning requirements mandated upon local governments by the metropolitan council.[59]

Land market, economic, and class-based interests now shape urban geography, not the old centralized apartheid state. However, the spatial results and outcomes can look similar. Apartheid geographies will not be overcome simply through the absence of racial zoning. The removal of apartheid is necessary, but not sufficient, to the post-apartheid integration of the urban majority. Upon the repeal of an apartheid that was ruthless and active in its quest, Lemon (1991) doubts that policymakers should allow in a passive way for the market to embark on a gradual correction of previous distortions. Without some greater state role, the deracialized urbanization of the future may lead to some integration, but it will likely not be of the poorest of the poor. To emphasize density in the city center will be like "tweaking at the mustache" in terms of affecting the problems of poverty-stricken squatters and shack settlers (S. Goldblatt, consultant for Land and Agricultural Policy Centre, interview). The removal of old apartheid barriers is a great breakthrough. Yet, for the marginalized black majority to be brought into the existing urban system of opportunities, there must be strong counterstrategies that anticipate the economic and community obstacles to urban integration goals. Without such a state role, the fact that financial and class-based interests that spatially marginalize blacks today are devoid of racial content will provide little solace to those left outside of post-apartheid urban opportunities.

This exposition on temporality and urban policy choices has located the delicate balancing of time as the essential challenge facing post-apartheid urban policymaking. First, I focused on the phased reconstituting of basic structures of local

and metropolitan governance and its disruptive effects on the coherency of policymaking. Policies must withstand, and evolve during, changing stakeholder
membership and shifting governance structures. Second, I examined how post-
apartheid policy choices must be prioritized and sequenced relative to two different temporal imperatives—one dealing with short-term, crisis-related needs; the
second with the development of a longer-term framework conducive to metropolitan sustainability. Third, I outlined the specific programmatic and implementation tensions between housing crisis response and spatial reconstruction.
Choices by urban policymakers concerning the timing and sequencing of policy
initiatives responsive to urban needs will have significant effects on whether urban
policy transforms or reinforces racial geography. Crisis-related actions that are
appropriately taking priority will tend to compromise longer-term spatial normalization goals. At the same time, these initial post-apartheid policy interventions provide important lessons and warning indicators to those policymakers
who wish to ensure that human upliftment occurs within a sustainable and equitable framework of metropolitan development.

Notes

1. Demographic statistics are notoriously unreliable due to apartheid planners' willing
inattention, and likely undercounting, of black urban population.

2. Nationally, the approximate 40.3 million population in 1994 (including formerly
"independent" homelands) was estimated as 76 percent black; 13 percent white; 8.5 percent "coloured"/mixed race; and 2.5 percent Indian (Bureau for Market Research 1994).
There are nine major black ethnic groups, the largest four of which are the Zulus, Xhosas,
North Sothos, and Tswanas. The white population is about 60 percent Afrikaner (Dutch
ancestry); 35 percent British ancestry.

3. Apartheid policies occurred at three levels. State apartheid involved the designation of
native reserves and homelands in remote areas of the country where blacks would be relocated. Urban apartheid involved city- and neighborhood-level segregation. Personal apartheid
affected the use of amenities and other forms of interpersonal contact and relations.

4. Race was rigidly defined, and statutorily enforced, by the 1950 *Population Registration
Act*. Three basic groups were identified: white, black, and coloured, the latter with multiple subcategories including Indian.

5. Freehold means these were areas that under previous laws allowed black ownership
of houses.

6. Note that informal shacks are almost the same magnitude as formal "bricks and mortar" houses in the township areas.

7. R=South African Rand, which at time of writing (October 1995) was worth about
.28 U.S. dollar or 3.6R=1 U.S. dollar. The Rand weakened considerably over the subsequent nine months, with an exchange rate of 4.4R=1 U.S. dollar recorded in July 1996.

8. Nationally, the official unemployment rate in 1995 was 33 percent, according to
Central Statistical Services (Gumede 1996).

9. As far back as 1913, the Natives Land Act prohibited the purchase of land by black Africans outside of designated rural Native Reserves constituting 13 percent of the country's area.

10. Only 5,300 formal housing units in all of South Africa in 1992 were built for black Africans.

11. About $11,500 U.S.

12. Formal housing constitutes only slightly above 50 percent of shelter arrangements in Soweto.

13. The same report reported that 7 million people countrywide were living in informal circumstances. This would mean that the PWV complex was home to 35 percent of the country's informal resident population.

14. "Unreticulated" refers to the lack of a formal distribution system.

15. Apartheid planners restricted commercial and industrial development in black townships, in part, because such areas were viewed as providing only "temporary" residence for urban black Africans (Mandy 1984; I. Kadungure, town planner, Soweto Administration, interview).

16. Political deaths in these two years were occurring at a rate of about 10 per day nationwide (SAIRR 1994). Loss of life in the early 1990s period was substantially higher than the second most deadly period of recent violence. In the four years 1984–1987, approximately 2,500 deaths occurred total. Unreporting of violence data is characteristic of all periods.

17. Some of the increase in reported crime may be also attributable to greater confidence of the citizenry in the police, especially by black complainants (Smit 1995).

18. Mainstream here refers to the philosophy of the African National Congress, which received 63 percent of the vote in the 1994 national elections. It should be noted, however, that ANC nationalism was not always inclusive; nonblacks could not become members until the early 1960s (Neuberger 1990).

19. Significant national-level negotiating forums included CODESA (The Convention for a Democratic South Africa) I and II, and the Multiparty Negotiating Council.

20. The National Party controls Western Cape Province (whose main city is Cape Town); the Inkatha Freedom Party kwaZulu/Natal (whose main city is Durban). In one additional province, there is no majority party. Gauteng Province was the new name given in December 1994 to what was the PWV Province.

21. The "non-statutory" sector included those political parties banned under apartheid, civic organizations, women's groups, trade unions, and others who had no official role in the old local authorities.

22. At that time, called the Transvaal Provincial Administration. It has since been broken into four new provincial governments, of which Gauteng is one.

23. Statutory representatives did concede a strong metropolitan government, however, to redistribute wealth. In addition, the proposal sought a separate MSS for the Johannesburg central business district (CBD) in the belief that urban management issues would be different there.

24. Demarcation and powers/functions disputes postponed elections in Cape Town, Durban, and most of Natal Province until mid-1996.

25. Due to this guarantee of white minority representation, local and metropolitan councils elected in Johannesburg and elsewhere are still technically *transitional* councils. The interim stage of local government restructuring will not end until fully democratic local elections pursuant to new constitutional principles are conducted before the year 2000.

26. The ANC majority on the metropolitan council could be as high as 85 percent. The ANC captured 12 of the 20 directly elected seats on the metropolitan council. The other 40 seats were to be chosen by the ANC-majority MSSs.

27. The Central Witwatersrand Metropolitan Chamber, Metropolitan Negotiating Forum, Transitional Metropolitan Council (appointed), and TMC (elected).

28. I date the transition period in Johannesburg this way because the CWMC was established in early 1991, and local and metropolitan elections took place in late 1995.

29. Other counter-apartheid recommendations included the building of low-income housing on mining land close to central city employment areas, and an increase in formal employment in low-income areas (JOMET 1992).

30. These include L. Boya (provincial government), and I. Kadungure, T. Mashinini, and L. Royston (metropolitan government). In addition, M. Swilling is director, Graduate School of Public and Development Management, University of the Witwatersrand, Johannesburg.

31. Although significant resistance from white suburban authorities existed to some of the ISF recommendations.

32. Other forums included the National Economic Forum (now the National Economic, Development and Labour Council), Local Government Negotiating Forum, National Education and Training Forum, and the National Rural Development Forum.

33. Calculation of the ratio between low-income-type employment opportunities and low-income population for different subareas of the urban region showed distorted distributions of 1:6 in the southwest (Soweto) and 1:9 in the northeast (Sandton/Alexandra) (CWMC 1992a).

34. Land that is vacant, underdeveloped, or with minor geological constraints was considered "available." Land that is public open space, a site of major mining residuals, or having major geological constraints was considered "unavailable."

35. A further possible limiting factor is the presence of subsurface dolomite, a mineral found in limestone and associated with geological instability. The land availability study states that about 2,000 hectares of the high-priority land may be affected by dolomite.

36. This is based on the study's estimated potential densities of between 20 units and 50 units per hectare.

37. The population projections come from the Urban Foundation (1990a) and Naude, Muller, and de Beer (1988), respectively.

38. So named because it seeks to link the area near Baragwanath Hospital, the biggest employer in Soweto, to the surrounding areas, and to the inner city and southern parts of Johannesburg city.

39. In similar spirit, section 2.5 (Housing) of the RDP states its commitment "to establishing viable communities in areas close to employment opportunities and to health, educational, social amenities and transport infrastructure."

40. The five spatial patterns endorsed are: invest in inner city, urban infill, filling in of buffer zones, township upgrading, and along activity corridors focused on transportation routes (C. Olver, interview).

41. On the white stakeholder side, membership and participation were also unstable. Not until formal participation channels were opened after ISF 2 publication did recalcitrant white ratepayers' groups and old municipality representatives come forth with wholesale criticisms of the ISF process "that took us back to the very purpose of the ISF 1 document" (J. Erasmus, interview).

42. J. Robinson, in an unpublished 1995 paper, argues that the incremental phases of local government reform required by national legislation prevented the domination of a singular vision of the future in metropolitan negotiations.

43. Identity of interview source withheld upon request.

44. This original short-term frame of the ISF was debated internally. Some planners argued that there be three time phases to policy—short, medium, and long—so that crisis management would not occur outside a strategic framework (J. van de Merwe, Metropolitan Planning, interview).

45. The head of the former Project Facilitation Group, Tshipso Mashinini, is now deputy director of the Urbanization Department.

46. "Homeless" is here defined to include all those living in forms of shelter other than "formal" bricks and mortar structures and where security of tenure is lacking. This is consistent with the definition used by M. Narsoo, Housing Director, Gauteng Province (interview).

47. Other types of informal dwellings include backyard shacks and outbuildings within black townships.

48. "Free-standing" shack settlements can be located within or outside black townships— it is their disconnection to community networks that defines them, not their location.

49. A good example here is the development of Wattville in the East Rand.

50. All land invasions are formally "illegal." It becomes more a question of practicality than legality whether to try to evict invaders. Evictions by the democratic government become more likely if invasions occur on designated park land or would likely cause social strife (T. Mashinini, TMC Urbanization Department, interview).

51. Site and services schemes commonly provided low-flush on-site latrines, one water standpipe per 20 households, small site sizes (200 square meters and smaller), and no tenure rights (Viljoen and Adler 1993).

52. The national Reconstruction and Development Programme (African National Congress 1994, 20) has the following objective: "strengthen the property rights of communities already occupying land."

53. In certain locations, upgrading would be accompanied by de-densification that would require relocation of some of the community's inhabitants.

54. "Free-standing" shack settlements thus have priority over informal dwellers within otherwise formal townships (T. Mashinini, interview). A second priority of RLDP is to relocate communities that are socially stressed. These include both densely occupied shack communities and backyard dwellers.

55. This is a legacy of the old government buying up remote land for black township extensions in order to assure future metropolitan racial segregation (M. Nel, interview).

56. One must keep in mind, however, that these property values "were artificially maintained by the old system" (J. van de Merwe, metropolitan planning, interview).

57. One exception to this is the Gauteng PHB's commitment to allocate subsidies for a total of 5000 units located within the Johannesburg inner city over a three-year period (Gauteng Provincial Government 1995b).

58. The TMC in early 1995 considered the establishment of "RDP zones" that would facilitate low-income residences within the urban fabric. Gauteng Province has also considered a pilot program that would seek to create inner-city sustainable development (L. Boya, Gauteng Province, interview).

59. Such requirements are part of the local government landscape in the United States, most notably in New Jersey and California. These requirements in greater Johannesburg could be part of land development objectives developed under the Development Facilitation Act (discussed in the next chapter).

8

Rebuilding
Government Legitimacy

The Dual Faces of Post-Apartheid Planning

Paul Waanders. Town planner. Formerly—Community Development Branch, Transvaal Provincial Administration. Currently—Chief Director: Planning Services, Department of Development Planning, Environment and Works, Gauteng Provincial Government.

Themba Maluleke. Member—African National Congress. 1995 Master's degree in Development Planning from University of the Witwatersrand. Currently, Project Manager for the Katorus Special Integrated Project, consultant to Department of Local Government and Housing, Gauteng Provincial Government.

Urban policy amidst societal transformation not only requires that policy choices be made amid significant uncertainty, but also demands a critical self-evaluation of the paradigms and basic assumptions of urban policy practice and administration. In this section, I contrast two distinctive paradigms of growth policies—one connected to town planning's historic proclivities toward regulatory control; the other rooted in anti-apartheid community mobilization and linked to a more expansive definition of development. The overhauling of fundamental urban policy assumptions challenges both formally trained and community-rooted "planners" to engage in a joint process of transformative social learning through which a new form of African planning may emerge.

Controlling Space, Managing Development

Planners have grown up providing services for a well-understood and familiar client—white and affluent.

—Tim Hart, SRK Engineers, Johannesburg (interview)

We need a planning system that can deal with the dual faces of Johannesburg.

—Lauren Royston, J'burg Metropolitan Planning (interview)

There is a battle between development planners and control administrators going on in all parts of the public sector.

—Lawrence Schlemmer, Independent consultant (interview)

During a time of fundamental institutional transformation, a "blueprint" and control approach to planning and development appears ill-suited. Acting within conditions of uncertainty, it appears more appropriate for there to be an iterative development of policies aimed not at a preferred end-state, but at facilitating and managing the growth process. This contrast in policy approaches permeates the current debate among urban policymakers about how best to engage in Johannesburg reconstruction. The debate highlights two paradigms having different historic bases, proponents of strikingly dissimilar personal histories, and contrasting views of the goals, requisite skills, and canons of city-building.

The traditional model of town planning in South Africa has been focused on regulatory control and spatial allocation, administered in a centralized and hierarchical fashion, oriented toward the specification of "blueprint" end-states, and lacking in community consultation. The spatial and regulatory emphasis is derived from the application of common British and European methods of planning to South Africa in the early years of this century.[1] This focus was then particularly useful to the apartheid government in its implementation since mid-century of strict urban racial blueprints. Town planning had an intimate, compatible connection to apartheid policy. Requiring a highly centralized, hierarchical governmental system for its execution, apartheid was implemented through demarcation of group areas by a central government Land Tenure Advisory Board (renamed the Group Areas Board in 1955). Regional plans and town planning schemes were then expected to guide development within the parameters set by the larger racial zoning of the central government. Guide plans were long-range regional land use plans which served as a legally binding framework for local, provincial, and central government planning. Through their general allocation of residential and industrial activities, guide plans "ensured that planning and land allocation take place within a framework of continued segregation" (Festenstein and Pickard-Cambridge 1987). Guide plans were produced by committees of national government officials, ministerial appointees, and local authority representatives and were commonly rigid blueprints of the urban future with no mechanism for revision (J. Muller, University of the Witwatersrand, interview). These regional land use plans supported the goals of racial segregation through their manipulation of employment opportunities, residential facilities, and land availability. For example, the 1986 draft Central Witwatersrand Guide Plan says the "provision of land should be used to limit development in the region" in order to support governmental policy regarding deconcentration of the black population (Claassen 1993).

On the local level, town planning schemes developed by municipalities were then to allocate land uses on a parcel-specific basis in a way that was consistent with guide plans. Frequently, town planning schemes were prepared only for white areas of the Johannesburg urban region. As of 1995, there were twelve different town planning schemes for white parts of Johannesburg. In black areas, land use development was controlled more directly, and restricted, by one central government department empowered by the so-called Bantu Administration Act. As of 1995, no town planning schemes existed to guide and provide a vision for urban growth in greater Soweto (P. Flusk, Transitional Metropolitan Council member, interview).

In formal terms, there existed some duality of planning processes—one based on group areas racial delineations; the other on land use allocation. And, as Mabin (1992) points out, "the Group Areas Act did not directly provide for planners to add racial criteria, restrictions and uses to their armory." Yet, in practice, there was much compatibility between racial zoning and land use planning. The latter, in effect, provided race-blind professional devices and rationales that consolidated and implemented the goals of apartheid racial segregation.[2] Town planning's traditional emphases on efficiency, order, and control were not at odds with notions of ethnic segregation and ordering. As such, the Group Areas Act "both derived from established planning practices, and enticed town planners into the implementation of racial segregation" (Mabin 1992). "The construction of racial categories," assert Parnell and Mabin (1995), "has been intimately interwoven with the broader questions of urban regulation." In the end, "apartheid proved to be a seductive way of seeing the city for many practitioners and planners who were deeply involved in its implementation" (Parnell and Mabin 1995). Chipkin (1993) describes the relationship between apartheid regulation and town planning more in terms of confiscation than collaboration. He asserts that "ideas inherent in the planning culture of the 1940s would be misused and misappropriated in the 1950s by political ideologues: neighborhood concepts misused for ethnic division. . . . urban renewal misapplied as mass removals." Still, basic compatibility between apartheid and town planning was evident in the "smooth transition" that occurred from the pre-1948 technical planning principles and reform ideas to the coherent apartheid policies of the 1950s. The apartheid regime, for instance, was able to locate its slum clearance and removal program in the larger context of post–World War II urban renewal (Chipkin 1993). Government could thus describe South African removal schemes and township development as "areas laid out amid clean surroundings, planned from the start like modern towns in any Western country" (South African Information Service 1961).

The local and metropolitan planners I interviewed reflected on their roles in apartheid city-building with mixed, but always introspective and private, emotions. Some displayed an operationally detached view of the past. J. Erasmus (Johannesburg metropolitan planner) states that "planners then were bound by legislation and you worked within a specific reference. We now have a new set of parameters and interests." J. van der Merwe (metropolitan planner) attests that "almost every planner one talks to today will say that they were or are against apartheid" and asserts that town planners today are overly defensive in their reaction to assumptions that they were the chief implementers of apartheid. A planner interviewed who supported apartheid goals and ideology states that a large majority of professionals played their role within the system, with only a few challenging basic assumptions (D. Viljoen, interview). Other planners express a longing not for the ideology of apartheid, but for the more straightforward methods and greater independence of planning in the past. B. van der Walt (Gauteng provincial planner) advances that "we accept that we can't do top-down planning anymore. In the past, it was very easy to do planning—it was just sit down and do a plan." Other views expressed a certain combativeness regarding the past. "Yes, planning was done within a political framework," claims P. Waanders (provincial planner), "but I will never say it was servant to the master. Planning can survive and adapt." Planning educator J. Muller (interview) asserts, however, that the town planning profession is guilty of "going down the long road of coercion and domination" (J. Muller, interview). Ironically, though, town planning erected urban and regional conditions that over time contributed to the downfall of the apartheid system that it worked so hard to support. "Apartheid planning was terribly effective in achieving its goals";[3] yet, its success created unsustainable urban conditions of segregation that co-contributed to the stress and breakdown of the larger political system, illuminating the inherent fallacy of partisan planning.

In the post-apartheid reconstruction of the Johannesburg region today, the regulatory and control system of town planning used primarily for healthy white cities in South Africa seems to have little utility for reconstructing ailing and wounded black urban areas. Not only is the blueprint paradigm discredited because of its alignment with apartheid, but there is a disconnection between the black majority and this traditional model of development control. Where black needs are socio-economic, the town planning model focuses on physical space. Where black needs concern empowerment and participation, the South Africa town planning model is nonconsultative and hierarchical. Where black needs center on upliftment, town planning offers control and compartmentalization. And, where black needs seek transformation of basic conditions of livelihood, the traditional planning model offers reform-minded, yet ultimately conservative, prescriptions.

In response to such discrepancies, a new paradigm of *development planning* has emerged since the downfall of apartheid. It poses a different set of city-building techniques and, indeed, a fundamental reconceptualization of, and thus challenge to, traditional town planning. Development planning is defined by three main characteristics:[4]

- It integrates traditional spatial planning with social and economic planning. Development planning is "a process and methodology of coordinating different types of planning" (L. Boya, Chief Director: Development Planning, Gauteng Provincial Government, interview). It views societal processes to be "human-centered, complex and holistic in character" (van Zyl 1993).
- It attempts to restructure the general budget to coordinate development policy objectives that cut across governments, sectors, and departments; it does this by linking the planning process to budgetary processes (L. Boya, interview).
- It includes a participatory process aimed at empowering the poor and marginalized. Development planning extends beyond physical reconstruction in its concern with "the psychological, emotional and spiritual well-being of citizens so they can feel they are part of a town and have a role to play" (L. Boya, interview).

Development planning is a broadening of substantive scope, objectives, and clientele. In its social-economic-physical integration goals, it challenges the narrow parameters of the town planning profession. The move from town planning to development planning represents a shift from maintenance of urban space to creation of new socioeconomic opportunities, and a refocusing of primary attention from place to human development. In its link to budgetary processes, it intends to significantly reorient the behavior of other departments and government at-large toward developmental and upliftment objectives. And, its role in empowering communities aims to make new connections in South Africa between government and community. Each of these roles of development planning constitutes major challenges which will encounter either bureaucratic or community-based obstacles to their effective realization.

In addition to the broadening of scope, goals, and clientele, development planners have distinctly different personal histories than traditional town planners. Most are black Africans with life experience not in traditional planning, but in nongovernmental organizations (NGOs). There, they developed a broad set of skills related to community development, social mobilization, and negotiation which were directed at anti-apartheid resistance and the improvement of basic living conditions for marginalized communities and people (L. Boya, interview).[5] This is in contrast to traditional town planning, the domain of white South Africans trained and educated in the technical, legal, and regulatory foundations of physical development control and whose skills were applied to assuring orderly and high-quality development of white communities. Most assuredly, these rival paradigms are the dual faces of post-apartheid planning.

A critical difference between planning's two faces involves their engagement with the community. Development planning, in South African usage, connotes strongly the empowerment of the deprived majority, according to J. Muller (interview). Planning has a role to play in supporting those principles and activities that promote democracy. Traditionally trained town planners fall short here. The lack of community consultation in the town planning model meant that such planners worked in closed rooms in developing spatial frameworks. "You did 'what was best for society' and society had to accept whatever you did," recalls Paul Waanders (Chief Director: Planning Services, Gauteng Province, interview). Traditional town planners developed spatial and physical master plans which allocated future land uses and provided the rationale for strict regulation of growth. They worked with civil engineers and other technical professionals and engaged in practices such as quantitative analysis, surveying, and mapping. The range of interests drawn into the town planning process was limited to white residential and commercial clients (T. Hart, interview), and, in reality, "whites did not even consult whites" (D. Viljoen, interview). The absence of a consultative legacy in South African town planning creates ill-fitting community participation attempts by traditional planners under the new regime today.

In contrast, a role within the domain of development planning is that of mediator or coordinator in the development process between community needs and government resources (interviews: T. Maluleke, KATORUS project, Gauteng Provincial Government; and T. Mashinini, Urbanization Department, Metropolitan Johannesburg). Those interviewed see their key characteristic as an ability to speak two languages—that of the community in helping them identify their needs, and that of the bureaucrat having knowledge of governmental processes and realities. T. Mashinini helps the community identify those needs to which government can realistically respond. He seeks to tell communities what government programs and resources are available, and to advise the community on options and realistic possibilities. Thus, community decisions are informed ones, not the pie-in-the-sky demands that result when government goes into a community with a blank slate. He then takes those community needs and converts them into more technical terms operational to government engineers and others. In his technical representation of community needs, his actions are analogous to the technical assistance function of a nongovernmental organization, except now these functions are occurring in-house.[6] The result of governmental deliberations might often be achievable proposals that can be taken back to the community for their support. Because the proposal is achievable, subsequent delivery is likely which can both empower communities and legitimize urban governance.

Development planners, experienced as community organizers during the struggle, combine knowledge of the everyday with some insight into government realities and constraints. Inside knowledge of governmental processes was gained initially as the communities for which they worked used various tools to engage the state and its transformation; subsequently, it has been developed during their tenure as public administrators. Development planning, however, remains embryonic in South Africa and its methods appear only broadly articulated. "Nobody has been trained in doing the work that we do," says T. Mashinini (interview), adding that an individual who combines community and public administrative background "is a rare species around here." At the same time, the community mediator's emphasis on participation, not blueprint specification, may be susceptible to a certain degree of "incrementalism" detached from larger goals. T. Maluleke (interview) concedes that "sometimes you don't even know where you are"; thus, he asserts the importance of having his own identified goals to guide the participation process when it is in danger of unraveling.[7] Development planning also is in danger of losing a core identity as it encompasses increasingly broader scope and tasks. Descriptive terms such as "umbrella" and "catch-all" (J. Muller and A. Motsa, interviews), and the mixed skills and backgrounds of development planners,[8] foreshadow a potential stretching of its core tasks to the point of ineffectiveness.

The shift in planning approach from controlling spatial outcomes to managing development processes comes to the fore in debates concerning how planning and land use control should be applied across the Johannesburg landscape. The urban system itself represents dual faces—one first-world, modern and orderly; the other third-world, poverty-stricken, and marginalized—that present contrasting challenges to policymakers. In formerly "white" areas of good urban services, social and commercial opportunities, and high-quality residential stock, the challenge is to maintain a certain quality of life to discourage out-migration from the urban system entirely. Town planning schemes which specifically control development, density, height, and land use locations are the controlling documents in these areas. These schemes are exacting in their explication of five residential and four business categories of land use, and in their emphasis on orderly and controlled development so that communities, and their property values, are maintained. In formerly black areas that are peripheral and face multiple community-wide and household-specific deprivations, the challenge is to significantly improve residents' quality of life by connecting them to urban opportunities. Ironically perhaps, town planning, which was so instrumental on a regional level in creating black locations and marginalizing township residents, is almost completely lacking on a community level within formerly black areas. Once the state fulfilled its goals regarding black peripheralization and containment, it lost interest regarding development control on the more specific community level. The 1986 Town Planning and Townships Ordinance, although formally color-blind, was in practice a "white ordinance" never used in black areas (P. Waanders, Gauteng planning services, interview).

Accordingly, there are no town planning schemes in black areas aimed at creating orderly and well-functioning environments. In addition, there are only six formally established townships (out of 29) in greater Soweto, a necessary precondition for property registration and transfer (J. McCrystal, Johannesburg city planning, interview). In the absence of town planning ordinances, land use conditions in black townships are attached to each and every stand's[9] title deed or "conditions of establishment" (P. Waanders, interview). Sole reliance on stand-specific regulations means there are no coherent community-wide plans that seek to incorporate areawide social or economic objectives. Title deed conditions, at the same time, provide some flexibility of land use that would not be legally possible in formerly "white" areas. For example, a home-based *spaza* (shop) is possible if it does not create a nuisance or health hazard to adjoining properties or the community (P. Waanders, interview).

In seeking the reconstruction of Johannesburg, how should planners reconcile these two separate systems of land use allocation and regulation across the two faces of the urban system? A single uniform system having common standards across both stressed and healthy faces would be consistent with the spirit of equality in the new South Africa. On the other hand, two separate systems of land use planning—with higher development standards in formerly "white" areas and greater flexibility in formerly "black" areas—would more realistically acknowledge starkly differential objective conditions and ways of life. Most significantly, which land use regulatory approach—uniform or differential—is more capable of counteracting the place-based inequalities of apartheid?

In the short term (0–2 years), it is likely that objective conditions in transitional and nonwhite parts of Johannesburg will dictate that planning and regulatory ordinances there be different from the detailed schemes applied in white areas. For example, in transition zones around the inner city or in more distant areas whose development would fill in apartheid discontinuities,[10] nonstatutory development frameworks are being prepared rather than rigid structure plans. These development frameworks are not blueprints for development, but put forth a set of guiding principles, images, and policy suggestions and are viewed as possible prototypes for planning in formerly black areas generally (M. Gilbert, interview). Principles contained in the Baralink framework connecting Soweto and south Johannesburg include the creation of a democratic spatial system through grid layouts that increase choice of movement, development structured around "local districts" or neighborhoods, and diverse, mixed, and integrated development (Thorne 1995).

Planning regulation, in the form of town planning schemes, will likely be extended to black townships. In the short term, though, these schemes will likely be broader and more flexible than found in traditionally white areas (interviews: B. van der Walt and P. Waanders, Gauteng Planning Services). The extension of "first world" planning standards to black areas would likely be ill-fitting where the goal there is not orderly development per se, but human upliftment and basic growth generally. The implantation of "white" zoning schemes to black areas could cause more harm than good by imposing rigidity and specificity upon communities of deprivation. One interviewee[11] candidly assessed that "it will take awhile for places like Soweto to act as a white city; until then, flexibility is needed." In black townships, the policy focus instead shifts from exacting specification of lot sizes, uses, heights, and densities to the identification of key initiatives and mechanisms that would increase investment in peripheral areas. Land use standards and principles would still be applied to guide township development so as to assure urban functioning and public health, but they would allow certain mixing of activities not thought of as appropriate in formerly white areas (B. van der Walt, interview). More specifically, land use categories would be simplified,[12] and home-based businesses would continue to be allowed as long as they pass nuisance and public health tests.

This broadening and flexibility of land use standards in black township areas, even though intended toward facilitating human upliftment and growth there, is susceptible to criticism that it is condoning physical inequalities. Differential land use standards run counter to the basic ethic of equality in the new South Africa. The social-psychological message put out by differential zoning must not be underestimated. Statements by planners that flexible land use standards are needed to "accommodate their style of living" or are "aligned with their traditional way of doing business and how they live" do bear similarity to the patriarchical and racist rationales of apartheid.[13] More concretely, some in the townships argue that the weakening of land use standards endangers their private investments and puts the black middle class there at a risk not encountered by the white middle class (A. Kotzee, Gauteng Planning Service, interview).

This debate about different "black" and "white" land use standards may eventually become obsolete. Short-term differentiation of planning and land use standards may in the medium term (2–5 years) evolve into, and be usurped by, a new type of land use control system applied uniformly across the urban system. This system would bear resemblance to neither "black" nor "white" planning control of today, but would be a radical departure and redefinition of planning goals and mechanisms. The initial restructuring of the land use regulatory system occurred in late 1995 with the passage of the national Development Facilitation Act (DFA). The immediate purpose of the DFA is to expedite land development projects, and to bypass bottlenecks in existing regulations, especially those impeding the delivery of serviced land for low-cost housing. In addition to this objective of responding to short-term needs, however, it fundamentally changes the way land and development are regulated. Growth and development are to be governed by land development objectives (LDOs) rather than by detailed property-specific spatial parameters and regulations (such as height or property setbacks). These LDOs include specification of levels of public services and facilities, desired qualities of urban growth and form (including integration of low-income communities into existing areas), identification of developmental strategies and delivery mechanisms, and quantifiable goals (regarding the number, provision method, and rate of new housing units and sites) (Development Facilitation Bill 1994). Land development objectives are to be developed by local government, but must be approved by the appropriate provincial minister as being consistent with provincial and national development principles. National principles include goals pertaining to integration, jobs-housing proximity, compaction, and the distortion of historically distorted spatial patterns of development (Development Facilitation Bill 1994). There is also to be the setting by national and provincial governments of performance criteria and targets related particularly to land development for low-income communities. These criteria, in effect, will be the means by which provinces evaluate local government's land development objectives and actions.

The development facilitation strategy represents a fundamental shift toward a system that monitors areawide outputs and outcomes of development rather than regulating property-specific attributes such as use, height, or site layout.[14] According to C. Olver (RDP Development Branch, Office of the President, interview), it is a powerful facilitative instrument in its prescribing of timeframes and its ability to override restrictive regulations; at the same time, it seeks to force development to comply with community guidelines dealing with low-cost housing, urban form, and levels of public service. The DFA moves Johannesburg away from its past of blueprint planning and iron-clad zoning and establishes a strategic approach to development based on equity objectives and performance criteria. Significant questions and issues remain, nonetheless. Foremost among these is the intergovernmental allocation of planning and standard-setting powers across provincial, metropolitan, and local governments; and the relationship between the existing and new planning systems during the transition from traditional town planning schemes to DFA principle–led planning.

The Development Facilitation Act is a major piece of legislation that provides the stage upon which the shifting paradigms and restructuring of South Africa planning practice will play out. It seeks to change a rigid town planning approach aimed at maintenance and orderly development into one that employs urban space as a launching pad for the pursuit of development planning's socioeconomic and reconstruction objectives. Its goal is to create some equality of treatment— some regulatory uniformity—across both well-functioning and marginalized parts of the urban system, while at the same time recognizing the special circum- stances and unique histories of different communities.

Adapting to Change

With rigidity, the profession and future of the planner is protected. With flexibility, anybody can do planning.

—Ivan Kadungure, Soweto Town Planner (interview)

I've heard that I am now to be a teacher, facilitator, mediator, psychologist, social worker; please be anything but don't be a planner because then I am elitist and reactionary.

—Jane Eagle, Johannesburg City Planning (interview)

Town planning and development planning are uneasy bedfellows in their common pursuit of a more humane Johannesburg. Town planning must contend with its im- age as "old guard," its past links to apartheid implementation, and its lack of soul or connectiveness to community. However, it provides a methodology and techni- cal capacities essential to city-building. Development planning, meanwhile, is as- cendent from community-based struggle and newly knighted as the way forward for urban South Africa. Yet, it is a young practice whose techniques are not clearly developed, and one that is burdened by demands for it to be all things to all peo- ple. The two faces of post-apartheid planning come in contact at both provincial and metropolitan levels. At both levels, one detects a clash of personalities and comfort zones—town planners rooted to existing systems, rules, and regulations; development planners more proactive and sympathetic to lateral thinking (P. Waanders, Gauteng planning services, interview). Each tends to view the devel- opment process and policy's appropriate role through different lenses.[15] And, town planners tend to be white and from within the system; development plan- ners tend to be more racially diverse and from the outside.

In the face of a clearly ascendent development planning function, traditional town planners are reacting in ways ranging from defensive rigidity, to counterattack, to uncertainty, to productive acceptance of the need to change assumptions and tech- niques. L. Boya (chief director: development planning, Gauteng province, inter- view) detects "subtle rigidities" on the part of traditionally trained town planners. He notes a certain willingness of town planners to adapt, but he is also cognizant that it is early in the transformation process: "At the moment, there are two systems in place—planning services and development planning. In the future, though, when we more radically change planning, we will be saying in a sense that 'there is no future in the town planning profession as it is currently structured.' How will they respond?" P. Waanders (chief director: planning services, Gauteng province) concedes that town planning, to survive, will need to move away from its professional moorings. He points to a thick statute book specifying the contents of rigid town planning and zoning schemes, and states that "many planners cannot cross the river of change because of this little bible that they have." Professional biases toward spatial control are impediments to change: "it is very difficult for many planners to get out of the groove of doing up nice maps and pictures on the wall. It is part of the education system they carry with them" (Waanders, interview). Other town planners, however, defend traditional planning's value and criticize any wholesale move toward development planning. J. Eagle (City Planning, interview) asserts that criticism of traditional planning too simplistically positions planners as technicians worthy of marginalization in the face of emergent community mediators. Further, she redirects criticism back at development planning, asserting that "because development planners know about daily life, they feel they can deal with planning issues and problems. They know about certain aspects of development and that is important. But, we can't just hand all of planning over to them because they don't always have the bigger picture."

Traditional planning's defense of its contribution to city-building is brought out in other observations. I. Kadungure, TMC black planner (interview), states that "community specialists and social workers in the Urbanization department are needed for communication purposes, but at the end of the day someone else must come in to deal with technical issues such as water provision and engineering capacity." Similarly, J. Muller (interview) states that the urbanization department's community work is essential to uplifting deprived places, but it is not fundamentally a consciousness of the future, the forte of the planning profession. A. Kotzee (Gauteng planning services, interview) puts forth an additional contribution of town planning—an ability to maintain property values and municipal tax bases, and to assure protection of property rights and investment. Some town planners surveyed expressed great job insecurity and professional uncertainty amidst institutional transformation.[16] Faced with the feeling that one has to accept change or move on, many town planners have chosen the exit door.[17] The TMC city planning department, for instance, has experienced a crippling loss of experience with fifteen resignations over a two-year period (H. Sekoto, interview). At the same time, though, some traditionally trained planners are rising to the challenges thrust upon them by adopting a learning approach. For these planners, it is an invigorating time to develop new techniques of community consultation (M. Gilbert, City Planning, interview), or to question assumptions and theories of the past (J. Erasmus, Metropolitan Planning, interview). For these practitioners, post-apartheid planning is exciting because they are getting feedback on what they do, no longer comfortably isolated by the closed channels of apartheid policymaking.

Does traditional town planning have the capacity to effectively engage in the post-apartheid reconstruction of metropolitan Johannesburg? The answer is negative, if we refer to a town planning profession as it has been constituted and practiced in Johannesburg. Ironically, however, the community facilitation function of the new development planning paradigm "is giving a certain credibility to what has been a discredited profession in this country"[18] (J. Muller, interview). This provides town planning with an opportunity to resurrect itself by employing new techniques that support the ascending paradigm. Town planning, if it adapts and evolves, could have a significant role to play in the future because only town planning is capable of embedding the community facilitation practices of development planning within longer-term and more systematic analyses of urban interrelationships. The two sides of post-apartheid planning could be positioned in a side-by-side working posture, rather than in a face-to-face confrontational pose.

In order for the town planning profession to be relevant and valuable in the new South Africa, it must consciously transform itself. First, town planning must shift away from its control mode into a practice which enables empowerment and capacity building in the interests of social justice (J. Muller, interview). It should embrace the new ideas and viewpoints advocated in the development planning paradigm by incorporating community participation and integration into city-building principles. At the same time, reactionary and rigid elements within the profession need to understand the need for change or be overcome. Planning education at the graduate level (at Witwatersrand, Natal, and Cape Town universities) must shift from control to lateral planning orientations, and fight the urge to teach only the more easily communicated and comfortable technical planning matters. Second, town planning should redirect its energies from strict spatial zoning to performance and output-based measures that will support the new development planning paradigm's facilitative approach to land management. Town planning should play a central role in the calculation and monitoring of desired areawide outputs, and in assuring that objectives are appropriate and realistic. Third, town planning must continue to bring in diverse personal histories into its educational and professional tracks; in particular, black Africans whose local experience comes from community activism and facilitation. This fresh channel of experiential and inductive knowledge built from the experiences of nonwhite community mobilization will enliven and bring soul to the formal changes in professional methods and emphases.

Black entry into town planning educational and professional tracks is gradually increasing but it will take time for the profession to reach representativeness. At the University of the Witwatersrand, the undergraduate town and regional planning degree program is now about 34 percent black and 38 percent white (J. Muller, department chair, interview). In the graduate development planning degree program, a strong majority of students is black. In Gauteng Province, the

Planning Services division remains primarily white, and there was not yet in mid-1995 racial representativeness in the Development Planning division, although there was progress at management level (L. Boya, interview). In the City Planning department of the TMC, less than 10 percent of its 60 employees were black in 1995 (M. Gilbert, interview). Significant change in the racial composition of planners will take time. First, there is the "problem of the pool" (H. Sekoto, interview), wherein the size of the black professional class and those coming through planning education or training is still relatively small. Second, blacks in this group tend to be very marketable, leading many potential black administrators and planners to turn toward more lucrative private sector opportunities (M. Gilbert, interview).[19] Because it will take a considerable time to increase black representation in the planning profession, it is critical that the attitudes of traditional, primarily white, planners change. Here is probably the most critical component of town planning change in the future—the advent of a learning and adaptational mode of professional practice. Such a learning approach to town planning practice will mean that tomorrow's planners and planning organizations will be "not valued for their ability to adhere to detailed prepared plans, but for having a well developed capacity for responsive and anticipatory adaptation" (Korten 1980, 1990).

For planners with traditional training, adaptation and learning will encompass getting away from the perceptions of the past, and committing oneself personally to community consultation, equity, and working with disadvantaged communities. This is not easy, because even those white planners with good intentions often view themselves as "potential enemies" when they go into black areas (H. Sekoto, interview). Such psychological distance increases the likelihood that planners will view themselves as working *for* the community, and not *with* it. Dealing within governmental bureaucracies with the planning problems in places like Soweto then can become peripheralized. Technically sophisticated town planning must adapt to, and come to terms with, the "African-ness" of South Africa. This may mean, according to J. Muller (interview), a phenomenologically based[20] practice connected to black African notions of community and human nature. The communitarian black African philosophy best expressed in the proverb *umuntu ngumuntu ngabantu* ("a person depends on persons to be a person") and in the concept of *ubuntu* (group solidarity in the face of adversity) represents a path that morally based planning can follow (Shutte 1993). It asserts a set of goals pertaining to communalism, egalitarianism, and human freedom that are connected to local development visions, but achievable through planning techniques based on an Anglo-American analytical tradition. This black African communitarian ethos provides an entry point for traditional planners to engage in self-transformative learning, whereby planners become more human and holistic through the communities for which they plan.[21]

The new paradigm of development planning described in this section represents an historic attempt to create a system of social guidance that utilizes the legacy and lessons of social mobilization. Town planning practice has a vital role to play in supporting this movement from mobilization to management because development planning, alone, does not yet have the methodologies or systematic knowledge bases to fully engage in city-building. But, town planning can only contribute if it significantly changes its basic assumptions, techniques, and orientation. It must be enabling rather than controlling in its objectives, performance-based in its regulatory emphasis, engaged in by professionals with diverse personal histories, and directed at adaptive learning rather than rigid adherence.

To respond creatively to the enormous challenges of reconstruction, there must be both development planning and town planning. If these two faces of post-apartheid planning are effectively combined, the result would likely not be the simple sum of its parts, but an altered and evolved process of community-based urban planning encompassing both social mobilization and rational governance. Systematic urban analysis and formal, deductive knowledge would become deepened and enlivened (and altered) by experiential, inductive understanding gained through community action. At the same time, new types of inputs from community-based planners would be enhanced by town planners able to contextualize them within strategic and systems-based thinking. These attributes, together, would constitute a new structure of societal planning and guidance not led by blueprints, but premised on future learning and openness. It is only this new and evolved type of African planning that can meaningfully contribute to a remaking of metropolitan Johannesburg that is both socially just and functionally efficient. Such would be a true gift to future generations.

Organizing for Peace-Building

Herman Sekoto. Born and raised in Naledi, Soweto. Former public school teacher. Master's degree in town and regional planning, University of the Natal. Currently: town planner, strategic issues division, City Planning Department, Johannesburg Transitional Metropolitan Council.

Angela Motsa. Born in Johannesburg. Raised in Swaziland. Master's degree in Town and Regional Planning, University of the Witwatersrand. Currently: town planner, PLANACT (nongovernmental provider of technical assistance to poor communities). "In a way, I feel guilty not being here during the struggles; on the other hand, it allows me to bring in a certain amount of objectivity."

Government's ability to effectively organize itself and its relation to the public will measure the advance of South African governance from its embryonic and transitional form in the mid-1990s to a more stable government regime capable of building and reinforcing peace and democracy. Appearing on the surface less extraordinary than the negotiated transformative processes discussed earlier, these governing tactics are nonetheless critical to the future performance of democratic public authority in Johannesburg and South Africa (Urban Foundation 1990e). As A. Bernstein (executive director, Center for Development and Enterprise) stated,[22] "putting politics first was probably necessary, but now there is the need to move on and ask, 'how can these political arrangements implement programs and produce outcomes?'" These outcomes will affect not only the urban residents of Johannesburg, but will determine the quality and sustainability of the country's new democracy. I focus here on the critical issues of peace-building in post-apartheid Johannesburg involving local governmental capacity and the role of citizen participation.

Local Governance Capacity

Masakhane: Let us build each other.

—*Zulu language*

This government, especially at local level, has the unenviable challenge of restoring government in communities that in many cases have been without it for over 10 years.
—**Paul Pereira, South African Institute of Race Relations (interview)**

Nowhere are issues of governance and implementation as critical as at the local government level, the most visible and immediate form of governance in South Africa. Mass-based mobilization against urban governance during the apartheid regime took many forms—rent and service charge boycotts, nonparticipation in local authority elections, disobeying of racial restrictions on access to health and recreation facilities, struggles against state-imposed educational requirements, and consumer boycotts, mass marches, land invasions, and strikes (Planact 1992). Many of these "tactics of ungovernability" were utilized during the 1980s to resist efforts by the apartheid government to establish rump township governments (called black local authorities or BLAs).

In 1982, the Black Local Authorities Act provided for locally elected BLAs with most of the same powers as white local authorities. In reality, fiscal weakness produced by decades of apartheid restrictions on township industrial and commercial development, and on homeownership, made the BLAs chronically unviable. When these financially hamstrung local authorities sought to increase service charge payments to pay for local services, popular resistance and hostility ensued. The most sustained and visible form of resistance to apartheid township government was the refusal by residents to pay rent and service charges. Nonpayment protests began in the Vaal area south of Johannesburg in 1984 and spread to

Soweto and other areas, triggering violent unrest in much of the country that was not suppressed by police and army action until 1986. The first major boycott of payments in Soweto was in 1986. Since then various accords have been struck to write off rent and service charge arrears or set a lower tariff.[23] Still, payment levels in Soweto since 1986 have seldom been above 30 percent of the amount charged[24] (Development Bank of Southern Africa 1994). Such low payment levels mean that about R3.9 million per month in assessed fees are not paid (Shaw 1994). For all BLAs in the province in 1992–93, local residents contributed only R6 million (or 0.4 percent) to the total budgeted expenditure of R1.5 billion.

The local anti-apartheid struggle, according to Christianson (1994), succeeded brilliantly in rendering townships ungovernable. Indeed, by January 1991, more than 100 of the country's 272 BLAs had collapsed (Planact 1992). At the same time, however, the struggle's very success has undermined cultures of localism and governance in townships. Thus, even with the political roots of nonpayment behavior removed with the demise of apartheid and the BLAs, rent and service payment levels remain low in Soweto (24%) and Alexandra (18%) townships (Drogin 1996). The anti-apartheid struggle has created heritages of detachment and resistance, such as the "culture of non-payment," that challenge the local democratic governments of today.[25]

In post-apartheid South Africa, local government is to play a vital role in the national Reconstruction and Development Programme (RDP) through its direct provision of basic services, its engagement in economic development, its redistribution of public resources, and its ability to empower local residents to assure that the RDP is a "people-driven process" (South Africa 1994; ANC 1994). In order for this to happen, however, local governance must gain credibility amidst a legacy of local ungovernability and resistance. Whereas most black Africans have experiences in various forms of anti-apartheid resistance and social mobilization against government, now they are being asked to accept, or even participate in, government and its formulation and implementation of public policy. A major part of achieving local government credibility was the transformation and democratization of local and metropolitan government in the mid-1990s. Political leaders for each of the four local governments ("metropolitan sub-structures"), and the over-layer metropolitan government, are now chosen based on a combination of ward and proportional electoral methods. As of November 1995, each of these governments has absolute ANC majorities in control. Patrick Flusk, former civic activist and now metropolitan councillor, exemplifies what this transformation means in terms of increased government credibility and accountability: "I use myself as an example. I tell the community, 'I'm here, you know my circumstances, my history, my hardships; now go out and get what you think is yours. You have no excuse now. You have access.'" He also recalls the culture of illegitimacy from which local government today is emerging: "Do not call me 'councillor' because that distances me from the people. I always had an attitude toward that term because they never changed. That's the activist part of me."

Supporting this essential organizational restructuring, however, both government and community must contribute two symbiotic elements to effective governance—a visible and reliable delivery of basic services on the part of government must be returned in kind by an increased willingness of residents to pay for them. It is this dual set of responsibilities that is at the heart of the national *Masakhane* campaign. Launched in 1995, the "let us build each other" campaign seeks to increase and normalize local government's ability to provide basic services, and to persuade residents to pay their fair share of rent and service charges. To facilitate improvement of municipal services, and thus increase local government credibility, in the short term, the national government has funded an R850 million, two-year Rehabilitation and Extension of Municipal Services Programme. Described by RDP development planning director C. Olver as "our end of the deal on the rent and services boycott," the program will repair and expand infrastructure such as water, electricity, roads, sewerage, and community facilities. In return, payments for services are expected to increase. "The principle of payment for services," the Office of the President states in its RDP White Paper (South Africa 1994), "is fundamental to the implementation of the RDP."[26]

Whereas the Masakhane and municipal services programs are aimed at the transitional and urgent needs of local governments, communities, and residents, a longer-term national support mechanism for local government is envisioned in the draft national urban strategy (Ministry in the Office of the President 1995). This would entail a central government 10-year, R60–70 billion urban infrastructure investment program to support the transformation of the country's cities toward urban equity and effectiveness goals. About 40 percent of capital funding will come through central government grants. The remainder will come from local sources, including redirection of capital budgets, borrowing, equity raised through privatization, and higher levies assessed against high-income households. Operating funding is expected to increasingly be generated at the local level through an increased willingness to pay for services and increasing tariffs and taxes. As the draft strategy asserts, "the principle that people should pay for the services to which they have access is central to this strategy" (p. 34).

In terms of local resident service payments, the basic principle in this long-term program is that "services and infrastructure will be introduced in line with the affordability levels of communities affected" (Ministry in the Office of the President 1995, 34). Thus, poorer communities will have lesser levels of services offered to them than healthier areas, although all communities will be provided with at least basic levels. At the end of this program, it is expected that 55 percent of communities would have "full" services, 25 percent "intermediate" level services, and 20 percent "basic" services.[27] The alignment in this long-term investment program of service provision with ability to pay represents an acute awareness that the nonpayment legacy in South Africa is due at least in part to the economic distress of the nonpayers. Levels of unemployment in townships are extremely high, and for many residents service charges represent a very high proportion of total household revenue. The investment program seeks through differentiated service delivery to provide services that are financially sustainable (from both national budgetary and local cost-recovery perspectives) while offering to all the benefits of at least basic services. In aligning service provision and resident costs to household income level, government is attempting to set charges at levels high enough to sustain a selected level of local services, but low enough to not overburden community residents and perpetuate the problem of nonpayment. At the same time, this service provision approach tied to ability to pay represents a "bounded" equity strategy whose goals are to lessen, but not eliminate, community service differentials.[28] Its use of household income as a trigger for service quality can also be questioned on the grounds that household incomes have been severely depressed through the years by omnipresent apartheid restrictions and humiliations.

In addition to service provision, the role of local governments in furthering economic development in the new South Africa is crucial. Economic development has been called the *sine qua non* for the effectiveness of the new government (Meyer 1995). Government's ability to stimulate economic growth, employment creation, and tax base enlargement will play a decisive role in whether the basic living conditions of the black majority will improve over the next twenty years. Economic growth at the local level, for example, would translate directly into property tax base enhancements which can fund equity-based extensions of community facilities and physical services. To promote such economic development, post-apartheid public policy will need to capacitate and energize local governments to engage more actively in economic policies. Yet, apartheid in many ways killed such local government initiative. Policies aimed at the promotion of local economic development (LED), employment creation, and tax base enhancement that had been employed by local governments in the 1920s through the 1940s effectively perished when local government was subsumed in the 1940s and 1950s within the strong central state-led spatial planning of apartheid (C. Rogerson, University of the Witwatersrand, interview). During the apartheid years, local functions increasingly took on the characteristics of developmental control pursuant to directives of the central state, rather than promotion of development. However, with the decline of the apartheid state, local government's role in economic development policy has emerged as critical to South Africa's future. It promises greater local government and community initiative and involvement in programs aimed at economic development and human upliftment and empowerment (R. Hunter, interview). This represents a radical redirection of local government efforts and requires organizational capacity and technical expertise that are undeveloped and unevenly distributed across local units (interviews: R. Hunter; C. Rogerson).

The practice of local economic development in South Africa will likely utilize a set of local government tools. These include local regulatory, taxation, and service delivery powers to promote development;[29] conditions attached to local government contracts specifying, for instance, the use of black contractors or small and emergent businesses; the establishment of local government labor relations standards related to wage and benefit levels; and local technical assistance. Local government can act as facilitator of economic activities through joint funding or the partial underwriting of a developer's financial risk; and can access development funds through borrowing or the creation of local capital banks. Public sector tendering procedures could favor large companies that link into the informal sector. Local service centers, meanwhile, can support emerging black entrepreneurs through technical and human skills assistance, networking, and marketing. A particular area of interest will likely be technical support by local government of small, medium, and micro-enterprises headed by black entrepreneurs, a major potential source of economic growth (C. Rogerson, interview).

We must not perpetuate the separation of our society into a "first world" and a "third world"—another disguised way of preserving apartheid.

—Reconstruction and Development Programme,
African National Congress 1994 (p. 5)

Another key issue of local governance capacity in the new South Africa involves its ability to effectively redistribute urban resources to overcome the individual and communal scars of urban apartheid. In a period of tight budgetary constraints and limited new spending, it is through the difficult redirection of government budgets and the reconfiguration of governance structures that marginalized individuals and communities are to be disproportionately benefitted. On the local level, two fundamental questions come to the fore regarding this redistributive imperative: (1) how to best configure post-apartheid local government boundaries to financially integrate marginalized communities into preexisting systems of governance? and (2) how to design the distribution of governmental powers between local and metropolitan levels to best effect such redistribution?

Boundary-drawing in ethnically contested urban environments is contentious because it directly affects power. It becomes "much more than debates about lines on a map, but connected to issues of political and financial power" (L. Bremner, TMC councillor, interview). In apartheid Johannesburg, the white local authorities of Johannesburg city, Sandton, Randburg, and Roodepoort contained substantial commercial and industrial tax bases that enabled good municipal services at moderate tax rates. In contrast, black local authorities in Soweto and Alexandra, and other nonwhite areas such as Lenasia (Asian) and Riverlea/Eldorado Park ("coloured"), were fiscally depleted owing to restrictions on nonresidential uses and the illegality of homeownership. Open-field informal settlements outside of black townships, meanwhile, faced marginalization and even exclusion from the local governance system entirely. The limited subsidization of black township budgets practiced by "host" white authorities stopped in 1973 with the reallocation of black township control to central administrative boards. From 1973 through 1988, there had been no fiscal connection between white and black authorities wherein redistribution could occur. The Central Witwatersrand Regional Services Council, created in 1988, did increase spending for infrastructure in black townships based on a levy assessed against businesses in the region (Moolman 1990). The RSC did this, however, using a structure in which white local authorities stayed separate, and indeed, in control.[30]

As the transition period began in Johannesburg in 1990 with the deliberations of the Central Witwatersrand Metropolitan Chamber, negotiators sought unsuccessfully to amalgamate the region's segregated local authorities into new local authorities with nonracial boundaries. Resistance came from white local authorities protective of the advantageous territorial status quo. The issue of internal boundaries for greater Johannesburg was ultimately referred to an arbitrator, who decided in favor of a model having seven local governments (called *metropolitan sub-structures*, MSSs). This 7-MSS scheme, shown on the left in Figure 8.1, continued the fiscal and political isolation of much of Greater Soweto by creating a new Western MSS for the area, and kept the well-off and white northern suburbs detached from nonwhite and poorer communities of the south and southwest. It also created a Central Business District (CBD) MSS that would be separated from the other six MSSs and under the direct control of metropolitan government. A Local Government Demarcation Board for Gauteng Province was then appointed to review local and metropolitan government boundaries pursuant to the Local Government Transition Act of 1993.

The Board reviewed the arbitrator's decision in April 1995 and found it "seriously flawed" for establishing MSSs that would be of questionable vitality and for segregating the Central Business District MSS. By this time, local government elections scheduled for late 1995 brought increased attention to local boundaries, not only in terms of their salience to redistribution goals, but also in terms of the relative powers of the ANC, National Party, and Democratic Party in each of the MSSs. The issue of local government boundaries ultimately ended up in a Special Electoral Court, which approved only three months before scheduled elections a 4-MSS model (see Figure 8.1). It was upon these boundaries that local elections on November 1, 1995, were held, resulting in absolute majorities for the ANC in each of the four MSSs and the overarching Greater Johannesburg Transitional Metropolitan Council.

The enacted 4-MSS configuration seeks to balance the richer north and the poorer south by, first, putting the CBD within the southern MSS; and secondly, by

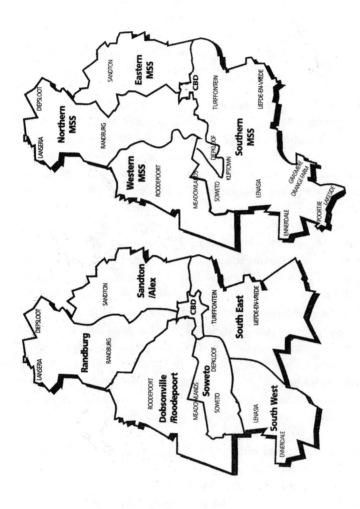

FIGURE 8.1   Redrawing Political Boundaries in Metropolitan Johannesburg

Source: The Star (Johannesburg, May 16, 1995), p. 2. Reprinted by permission.

Note: This figure depicts two competing models of local government in metropolitan Johannesburg—the 7-MSS model that continued the isolation of Soweto and separated the tax base of the CBD from other MSSs and the 4-MSS model ultimately enacted that integrated former white and black authorities and linked central Johannesburg with much of Greater Soweto.

integrating parts of Greater Soweto with three different MSSs—Johannesburg/CBD, Randburg, and Roodepoort.[31] It also seeks to evenly distribute votes, commercial and industrial activities, and tax bases across the four MSSs while taking advantage of the preexisting administrative capacities of formerly white authorities.[32] The chairman of the Special Court stated that this local governance model would be most effective in eliminating the vestiges of old group areas (Lund 1995). A key point of contention, and one that illustrates the fundamental unease among whites and business leaders over how to operationalize redistribution in the new Johannesburg, concerned the jurisdictional location of the CBD in the new structure of local governance. The 7-MSS model politically separated the CBD from the remainder of the region. Its main proponents—the liberal Democratic Party (DP) and business interests—argued that it needed to be protected and controlled by the TMC as a metropolitan-wide tax resource. Only with this setup could economic development be stimulated in the inner city which would create a bigger revenue pool to partially fund redistribution. The enacted ANC government 4-MSS model did not trust such inter-MSS redistribution and, instead, addresses redistribution more directly through boundary-drawing that politically integrated the CBD with the poorest southern MSS. This argument concerned a fundamental tension between economic development and equity goals in government, with the DP and business community arguing that allocating the CBD to the poorest MSS would overly burden it and dampen its economic potential.

Without strong metropolitan governments, our redistributive aims will be compromised.
—Crispian Olver, Office of the President (interview)

The ANC favors strong locally based government, but the timing is such that we need strong metropolitan government for redistribution. It's where we are in history.
—Lindsay Bremner, Councillor–Metropolitan Johannesburg (interview)

In addition to local boundaries, a second issue involving local redistribution is how to effectively allocate financial powers such as taxation and revenue-raising between local and metropolitan levels. In greater Johannesburg, the Transitional Metropolitan Council is a 50-member body composed of 20 members directly elected by the voters based upon a proportional representation system, and 30 members appointed by the four MSSs. Combined with boundary-drawing that connects rich to marginalized communities, the creation of a strong metropolitan government with the ability to redirect budgetary resources across MSS boundaries would provide an added assurance to equity advocates. Compared to local boundary demarcation, the debate over relative metropolitan and MSS powers was not near resolution as of early 1996. The negotiating framework established by the national Department of Constitutional Affairs allowed a variety of regional governance structures to evolve. The general rule in Gauteng Province so far has not been strong metropolitan rule.[33] In greater Johannesburg, the TMC in the immediate term was given clear and powerful roles in governance (L. Boya, Gauteng development planning branch, interview). Yet, the long-term metropolitan-local relationship has yet to be clearly defined, with the expectation that some number of government functions will be handed down (or "devolved") to MSSs in the future.

In terms of budgetary power, a system consisting of a weak TMC and strong local MSSs, even if each is now more racially integrated, may not be capable of the intergovernmental transfers needed to target assistance toward black townships and marginalized communities. Economic competition between MSSs with little coordination from the TMC could erode particular local authorities' ability to address their disadvantaged areas. For these reasons, strong metropolitan government has been viewed by the ANC as necessary to more effectively target resources to marginalized areas (ANC 1994, 129).[34] Two potential means of budgetary redistribution could be the pooling of some part of local revenue streams to create a metropolitan account, and/or the introduction of a new metropolitan tax. In either case, monies would be allocated back to MSSs based on a yet-to-be-determined formula. The claim that a strong metropolitan government role in regional budgets is needed to help repair the scars of apartheid was endorsed by most surveyed individuals. C. Olver (Office of the President, interview) foresees failure in achieving equity objectives and the exacerbation of problems such as inner-city decline and township isolation without strong metropolitan bodies. G. Reid (Planact, interview) questioned whether equity could be left up to MSSs that would be in competition with one another. P. Waanders (Gauteng province, interview) claimed that a strong TMC was necessary for reconstructive efforts, while L. Boya (Gauteng province, interview) stated that strong metropolitan councils were needed to coordinate budgeting and planning powers across MSSs.

A "People's Democracy"?

Monty Narsoo. Grassroots experience with the Seven Buildings Project, an affordable and social housing effort in inner-city Johannesburg. Currently, director of housing, department of local government and housing, Gauteng Provincial Government.

"Development is not about the delivery of goods to a passive citizenry," states the Reconstruction and Development Programme (ANC 1994, 5); rather it is "about active involvement and growing empowerment." Critical to the flourishing of democracy is the active involvement of "civil society" and citizens in the formulation and implementation of urban public policy. However, major challenges exist in the new Johannesburg regarding an appropriate and effective relationship between government, community, and citizen.

Civil society includes community-based organizations (CBOs or "civics"), trade unions, social movements, technical assistance providers, "think-tanks," and mass-based organizations that were essential instigators of change, and which together constitute an important layer of advocacy and representation between citizen and state. In South Africa, a vibrant and resilient civil society during the apartheid struggle has been weakened by its very successes and many nongovernmental organizations have had to search for a proper niche in a democratic South Africa or face extinction. Nongovernmental oppositional bodies played pivotal roles in articulating the problems created by apartheid and in advocating forcefully for change. Yet, as the country's political transition advanced on two levels, it ironically eroded the capacity of civic organizations. First, in April 1994, provincial and national elections legislatively solidified the new period, and much of the local leadership was absorbed into the ANC and into political and administrative positions at these extralocal levels. Second, the Johannesburg metropolitan negotiating forum evolved in composition, effectively pushing out civic groups with the incorporation of organized ANC political interests. L. Boya (interview), then with Civic Associations of Johannesburg (CAJ), reflects back on this period with mixed feelings, happy about the impact of community groups on the negotiations but sad that the community perspective was overshadowed by larger political networks near the end of the process. Internal squabbles within the CBO movement, in particular between CAJ and the South African National Civic Organization (SANCO), further weakened this sector by fragmenting local energies (L. Royston, interview). In effect, the growing success of the political transition—newly elected extralocal governments and a clearer articulation of post-apartheid Johannesburg governance—meant that the civics were losing their reason for being. Foreign money that had reached the CBOs during the anti-apartheid struggle was increasingly being directed through normal government-to-government channels (Paul Pereira, SAIRR, interview). Together with a depletion of their experienced leadership absorbed into government positions,[35] civics by 1995 were in a state of exhausted crisis and their future utility was being questioned.

The question facing post-transition urban policymakers and community activists involves the utility of CBOs in an age of legitimate government. One opinion holds that it is now elected local officials who are the proper conduits for community needs; thus, a more limited CBO sector is preferable in which those remaining groups would be more focused and effective. The other view upholds the vitality and flourishing of CBOs as critical to the nurturing of a culture of post-apartheid democracy. Without a strong civil society, there is no intermediary between the state and community and a strong democratic culture will not be sustained (E. Molobi, Kagiso Trust, interview). The question of the value of CBOs and NGOs in the new South Africa is itself dependent on a second question, "what role would they play?" The ANC (1994, 131) suggests that NGOs are faced "with the challenge of transforming their activities from a largely oppositional mode into a more developmental one." This means that civics must change from opposition to constructive engagement, from resistance to partnerships and proactive roles, in the rebuilding of urban society. However, it will be difficult for a majority of community-based organizations to embrace these new reconstructive and developmental roles because of limited levels of skills, experience, and resources (Tomlinson 1994; Seekings 1992). Rather, a more realistic and important niche for most post-struggle civics may be as advocates and articulators of community needs and aspirations. Their roles would be to push their local needs onto local political agendas for consideration, with the local political body then responsible for prioritizing competing claims. Without this community-based advocacy layer in the new South Africa, democracy would lack depth and responsiveness. Civics who can shout are a valuable part of the democratic equation and should be nurtured and sustained.

There is an issue, however, of whether the typical CBO is truly representative of the community or whether it is led by strong-willed and self-interested individuals. This concern in the 1980s was overshadowed by the need to put forth a united front in the anti-apartheid struggle. Now, however, as CBOs fight for a legitimate role in the reconstruction of South Africa, this representativeness question becomes more germane. To some, it would be ludicrous for hard-fought elected democratic government to now be held ransom by unrepresentative and unaccountable CBOs (P. Pereira, SAIRR, interview). The inadequate representativeness of some civics, and intracommunity divisions, present a problem to those seeking to help poor communities. Ironically, it is the availability of financial and technical assistance to communities that can highlight and even exacerbate existing divisions within communities (L. Royston, interview). Antagonistic sides in the community seek to gain control of these resources as a means to gain or maintain power. When a technical assistance organization deals with communities, it frequently learns that the organization they were working with was not fully representative of local residents. Within this context, "we had to work with the organized structure that was there, but we also had to get beyond that to the lower parts of the community" (L. Royston, interview). An associated problem with post-apartheid civics is their relative weakness. This puts nonprofit service providers into tight spots where they are acting in the absence of a strong civic voice. A. Motsa (Planact, interview) recalls that "it is almost as if we are convincing the civics of something and then pulling them along."

These problematic features of CBOs can be used as a pretense by government in the future to curtail community participation. This, however, would be dismissing a valuable layer of community activism. Community accountability and capacity-building of CBOs are needed in the future, not their abandonment. Funds to support organizational development can require that recipients institutionalize community-based voting, hold open and frequent public meetings, and create street or block committees (interviews: G. Reid, Planact; P. Pereira, SAIRR). Project-based funding can be provided only to those CBOs with these community-based democratic structures. Assessment of a CBO's representativeness, or "community-proofing," should be a regular part of grant proposal review. The nongovernmental Kagiso Trust, in deciding on grant applications, goes beyond simple paper review and "sends our eyes and ears out there to find out if there is somebody lurking behind the CBO using the community to raise money" (E. Molobi, interview). As part of this check, the program officer also works to create a management committee of local people to administer and oversee a funded project. Through these methods of community-proofing and capacity-building, both the local organizations and the projects funded have a greater chance at long-term sustainability.

People feeling that they must be consulted is a need itself that must be addressed. It is part of confronting our past legacy.
> **—Eric Molobi, Executive Director, Kagiso Trust (interview)**

It is hard to maintain grassroots and people's power at the same time as governing.
> **—Lindsay Bremner, Councillor-Johannesburg TMC, Member-ANC (interview)**

It is a mistake to over-romanticize community consultation. At the same time, we must not forego it entirely.
> **—Tim Hart, SRK Engineers (interview)**

The debate over post-apartheid civil society is embedded within the broader question of the appropriate relationship between government implementation and citizen participation in the new South Africa. In the span of only five years, there has been a metamorphosis from a top-down, nonconsultative state apparatus to an intensely consultative environment wherein public programs are now to "be implemented through the widest possible consultation and participation of the citizenry of South Africa" (South Africa 1994). A pervasive ANC philosophy and ideology of "people's government," "people-driven" development, openness, and transparency took root in government. Negotiating forums of key stakeholders from as wide an array of interest groups as possible have been instrumental to the formulation of public policy during the transition, developing a highly participatory approach to public policy. Consultation and inclusiveness are anticipated to continue in the future through "social compacts," "community development forums," and "local development forums" that will seek to assure that community needs and concerns are properly included in government programs and policies. Responding to the legacy of apartheid, there is a general belief among public officials that "if people aren't with you all the way, you are somehow autocratic" (P. Pereira, SAIRR, interview). Town planners feel today that they must consult with as many interests as possible before they act (J. van der Merwe, interview). And, community consultation is employed to check the fit between government programs and local needs (E. Molobi, interview).

However commendable this philosophy of wide citizen consultation, it can be at odds with government's desire to move rapidly and forcefully to address the abundant unmet basic needs of its citizens. Broadly inclusive community consultation highlights competing agendas that can delay or hijack government programs. Where successful introduction of new resources into deprived communities occurs, new faultlines among community interests can be created as preexisting community power relationships are shifted. Community consultation can also create platforms for "not-in-my-backyard" resistance on the part of established residents to new low-cost housing and other unwanted development nearby. Taken to its extreme, an overreliance on citizen consultation and consensus is contrary to the notion of representative government, wherein elected officials are delegated the tasks of policymaking and implementation by the citizenry. Indeed, community groups captured by strong and unrepresentative local interests may even sever their links with legitimate government structures.

As of late 1995, amidst growing frustration with the slow pace of housing and service delivery, there was an emerging perception among public officials that community consultation requirements were a primary factor delaying development and service delivery[36] (E. Molobi, Kagiso Trust, interview). Consensus over the value of extensive community consultation was fragmenting as policy implementation and delivery were not forthcoming. In Gauteng Province, the economic affairs and housing ministers—both ANC members—were expressing frustration with the delivery logjam and pointing fingers at participation principles (D. Christianson, DBSA, interview). Johannesburg metropolitan councillor P. Flusk (ANC member and former community activist, interview) worries that government "must not become democrazy" and that there must be some "cut-off point to consultation." In some respects, the participatory philosophy has taken on a life of its own, with limited articulation of the goals toward which such empowerment is directed (L. Royston, Johannesburg metropolitan planning, interview). Or, as stated by G. Reid (Planact, interview), "everyone is saying 'participation,' but I'm not sure they are clear by what they mean by that."

It is foreseeable that public objectives pertaining to citizen participation will be revised for the sake of effecting meaningful change on the ground. How this modification is undertaken, however, has implications that extend well beyond issues of service delivery to the core characteristics of public authority in the new South Africa. Two potential paths of change have radically different consequences for the quality of the post-apartheid relationship between government and community. The first path is a reactionary and adverse one. Unfettered community consultation mandates run the risk of taking public officials to a breaking point where more authoritarian mechanisms are substituted for discredited consultative processes. P. Pereira (SAIRR, interview) explains that "restoring a sense of proper government can not be done through this type of 'stadium democracy'; indeed, it carries the risk of something less than democracy." Politicians, pressured by the imperative to develop, may become susceptible to foregoing participatory processes entirely, especially in the context of a weakened and less financially independent CBO sector. In such an overreaction brought on by frustration, genuine democratic principles pertaining to citizen involvement may get thrown out along with the overreaching ideology of "people's government" and consensus.

The second path is anticipatory and seeks to manage or shape participatory processes so that genuine community consultation can be accommodated in policy processes in ways that avoid delivery paralysis. One effort in this spirit is government's intent to coordinate civil society through the establishment and accreditation of a network of broadly inclusive community development forums (CDFs) and local development forums (LDFs) that would empower people and facilitate interaction with government (Vista 2 1995a and 1995b). There are valid concerns about this approach to managing community participation. It appears that it may be establishing a parallel system of governance whose relationship to elected bodies is potentially counterproductive. When local authorities were illegitimate, local CBOs were established as parallel entities and were genuine expressions of public opinion. Attempts today, however, to create parallel local entities in a time of democratic local government appear misplaced. Built upon an apartheid-era lack of faith in municipal and metropolitan government, creation of post-apartheid CDFs and LDFs runs the risk of nonelected community forums undermining the efforts of elected local government officials.[37] There is also concern that such local forums cannot effectively be "created" per se, but rather must grow organically from the community itself (E. Ebdon, Johannesburg urbanization department, interview). Even further, "creation of these forums could lead to the undermining of what is beneath them," in particular the already weakened civics (L. Royston, interview).[38]

The structural and organizational approach toward managing community consultation, as exemplified by government-encouraged CDFs, is not the only way to shape participation. A second way relies on the interpersonal mediation skills of key people in government and nongovernmental organizations to shape the contours of community consultation. Here, the problem as diagnosed is not the lack of government-community interaction, but the unfocused and conflictual character of it when it occurs. T. Maluleke (project manager of Katorus, interview) explains that "the mistake government departments often make about community participation is that they make it too open-ended." This approach opens the floodgates at public meetings because "public participation is a new experience in South Africa which is coupled with significant expectations" (T. Maluleke, interview). This view is echoed by another community mediator (T. Mashinini, interview), who asserts that "when departments come into communities with blankslates, they miss out on the opportunity for genuine community empowerment." At other times, intracommunity political, ethnic, and age-based divisions can terminate even the most well-intentioned efforts at community engagement (I. Mkhabela, Interfaith Community Development Association, interview).

Efforts at community facilitation and mediation commonly rely on interpersonal skills and strategies and are thus diverse. Katorus mediator Maluleke, for example, adopts a "diplomatic, sometimes militaristic, strategy" in dealing with local residents. He "manipulates the community in terms of pragmatic guidance" in order to steer the community toward what government is capable of doing, to maintain sufficient agreement during the process, and to create visible results on the ground. At some point, he states, "you have to make a pragmatic decision that will benefit the community, even if it is unpopular." This steering of the process is necessary because "breakaway groups" claiming exclusion will usually form after visible benefits start to flow into a community. Without strong guidance and visible results, projects and programs will be hijacked by intracommunity fragmentation and breakaway interests. Johannesburg mediator T. Mashinini seeks to inform communities of what government can realistically deliver to them. By changing initial community expectations to a more achievable level, he is then better able to connect public programs with community needs. Empowerment, wherein residents are able to effect change in their communities, is then possible. In dealing with politically and ethnically based community conflict, I. Mkhabela focuses on common issues (such as road safety, crime, employment generation, the built environment, crime, and drugs) that span ideological divides and disrupt the normal tendencies for warring sides to remain isolated from one another. Stereotyping of the other becomes more difficult because "when you move closer, you find commonalities." He brings together the local religious congregations around common community issues because religious work "can transcend the political divide to a certain extent." There is the need, he suggests, for new mediating institutions and community facilitators "who go beyond the political organizations and challenge ourselves to accommodate diversity."

This approach to the management of community consultation relies today on the interpersonal skills of public servants like Maluleke, Mashinini, and Mkhabela. Each of these men's personal histories and struggles, rather than formal training, have been the primary influence on their community practice. Thus, this approach to managing community consultation appears more idiosyncratic than the effort to rationally create a set of community-based organizations such as CDFs. Yet, it is this interpersonal approach which holds the greater promise and should be supported and enhanced in the future. The great challenge facing education and training programs in town planning, development planning, and public administration is to develop curricula that inculcate these personal talents and basic methodologies of community consultation to the next generation of public servants. Community mediation techniques are central to the emerging practice of development planning. Indeed, development planners' most important role in post-apartheid South Africa may be their ability to guide community engagement in a way that avoids both reactionary authoritarianism and an unfettered "people's democracy."

Notes

1. We saw earlier how these features were predominant in the case study of British planning in Belfast, Northern Ireland.

2. Whereas municipal planners unevenly implemented pre-apartheid segregation goals (Christopher 1994), highly centralized and rigid apartheid structures took away local discretion. When Johannesburg planners were seen as too lax in restricting Soweto growth, a centralized West Rand Administrative Board preempting local government was created in 1973 (Mandy 1984).

3. Identity of interviewee withheld upon request.

4. I distill these essential components from interviews and from discussions of the national Forum for Effective Planning and Development (1995).

5. Some development planners have formal higher education in either town planning or development planning. The University of the Witwatersrand offers a two-year graduate program in development planning.

6. It is no coincidence that T. Mashinini gained formative experience working with the nongovernmental organization of Planact in Johannesburg, which supplies technical assistance for communities.

7. T. Maluleke labels this approach as "mixed-scanning," which Etzioni (1968) describes as the articulation of fundamental decisions or goals that set the context and guide more incremental bit decisions.

8. Staff of the development planning directorate in the Department of Development Planning, Environment, and Works in Gauteng Provincial Government includes town planners, development planners, economists, political scientists, and community workers and organizers (L. Boya, Chief Director, interview.)

9. "Stand" in USA parlance would be a legal lot or parcel.

10. Development frameworks ongoing for inner-city transition zones include eastern suburbs (Bertrams, Troyeville, Jeppestown), Pageview/Vrededorp, western sector of inner city, and eastern sector of CBD (Johannesburg TMC 1995a, d). Baralink is the most significant development framework for an area of discontinuity.

11. Anonymity requested by interviewee.

12. As in Schedule F of the 1991 Less Formal Township Establishment Act.

13. Interviewees' identities withheld upon request.

14. In USA planning parlance, this type of land use regulation is referred to as *performance* or *output* zoning. Not in widespread use, it is used most often to regulate pollution or traffic outputs from development proposals.

15. These different lenses are illustrated in the collaboration between TMC Urbanization and Planning departments in defining criteria for the Rapid Land Development Programme. Urbanization spoke of "beneficiary communities"; Planning of "land selection."

16. Names of interviewees withheld upon request.

17. Some of these have established private planning practices that employ both traditional planning and community facilitation tenets, or as one source said, "they do both first and third world planning."

18. It should also be noted that the new government, and its RDP, are planning-oriented in their requirements dealing with business plans and performance criteria.

19. Most marketable are those black exiles who received professional training or education outside the country.

20. Phenomenology rejects empirical explanations of social phenomena, emphasizing interpretation of human intent and purpose to be at the core of social science and action (Paris and Reynolds 1983). Empirically based practice can be especially problematic in cases like South Africa, where planners' training in western-world behavioralism and economic modelling often clashes with black African community representations of reality.

21. See Mbigi and Maree (1995) for how traditional black African values can be harnessed in the transformation of South African institutions.

22. Presentation at the launch of CDE, September 8, 1995.

23. The major agreement being the Greater Soweto Accord of 1990, which also established the Central Witwatersrand Metropolitan Chamber as a negotiating forum.

24. Service charges assessed are inadequate to cover the costs of services. Thus, even 100 percent payment would require external subsidization. During metropolitan negotiations, service levies for Soweto were first set at R23 per month plus metered electricity in an effort to break the "culture of non-payment," then set by negotiators in August 1994 at R45 per month (Shaw 1994).

25. Another legacy of resistance and detachment is the presence of a large number of disaffected and militant youths, called *tsotsi* (comrades or gangsters), who have turned toward criminal behavior in post-apartheid South Africa (Seekings 1992; Hewitt 1993).

26. The need for local payments becomes even greater because it is expected that direct transfers from central government to township areas will likely decrease in the future (D. Christianson, Development Bank of Southern Africa, interview). The 1995 shortfall of Durban City Council of R90 million is traceable to their absorption of black townships that formerly were funded through the central fiscus.

27. "Full" means connected water supplies, full waterborne sanitation, paved roads, and 60 amps electricity with prepaid meters for households. "Intermediate" entails water provision through yard taps, simple waterborne sanitation, narrow paved roads, and 30 amps electricity per household. "Basic" means communal standpipes, on-site sanitation, gravel roads, and streetlight electricity only (Ministry in the Office of the President 1995, 38–39).

28. The equating of service delivery and "ability to pay" bears a likeness to local education funding in the USA until the early 1970s. In a system where local property taxes were the major source of funding for public education, wide interlocal disparities in educational quality were accepted.

29. The Development Facilitation Act is an example of restructuring local regulatory regimes for developmental purposes.

30. The RSCs in Central Witwatersrand and elsewhere brought together local authorities of all four races and were, thus, the first constitutional structures on which black Africans were represented (Moolman 1990). At the same time, though, councillors' voting powers were based on the "service consumption levels" of their constituencies, thus cementing white local authorities' power (McCarthy 1992).

31. The other MSS—the Eastern—politically integrated white Sandton and black Alexandra.

32. Information from T. Mamonyane, Communications Directorate, Office of the Premier, Gauteng Provincial Government. Facsimile dated July 3, 1995.

33. The Pretoria TMC has only a bulk service role; West Rand and East Rand areas have loose regional service councils and no TMCs; MSSs are preeminent in the Northwest TMC, and regional-local powers were not yet decided for the Vaal Triangle TMC (P. Waanders, Gauteng planning services, interview).

34. It is also consistent with its "one municipality—one tax base" campaign platform.

35. This also meant in many cases the residential out-migration of civic activists from the communities they formerly served.

36. There is limited empirical support that participatory requirements are a culprit. Rather, delays could well be caused by the time needed to reorganize and restructure delivery mechanisms constructed to carry out apartheid.

37. In the USA, for the purposes of political empowerment, the federal Community Action Program of the 1960s bypassed local government and directly funded community groups so that they could exert pressure on local authorities to effect change (Matusow 1984).

38. Community forums are intended to be composed of multiple groups, of which civics would be one (L. Royston, interview).

9

Johannesburg and Peace

Key Interventions in Peace-Building

Business cannot and should not operate in its own "special universe" and think that their deci-sions have business-only effects.
—*Saki Macozoma, Member of National Parliament, Member ANC National Executive*[1]

The 1994 elections brought the nation together on agreement on a few fundamental facts. There are differences, however, about how to achieve these goals.
—*N. F. Oppenheimer, Deputy Chairman, Anglo-American Corporation and DeBeers*[2]

The capacity of local and metropolitan governance, and the role of government vis-à-vis citizens, are significant organizational issues pertaining to the future gover-nance of South Africa. Also critical, and the subject here, are questions involving government's appropriate role vis-à-vis economic markets and private sector processes in its pursuit of the reconstruction of the Johannesburg region. The quality and degree of government interventions at key points in economic and developmen-tal processes will substantially determine the relative effectiveness of post-apartheid urban policy in achieving the goals of compactness, integration, equity, and poverty alleviation. I identify three targets of key state intervention—violence-torn commu-nities, low-cost housing provision, and land development at strategic locations. For each, I describe the importance of state intervention and explain the policy choices and difficulties facing policymakers in their efforts to affect private sector processes and outcomes to achieve public ends.

Torn Communities

Most immediate among government interventions into development processes are curative actions aimed at reconstructing those places and individuals severely crip-pled by racial hatred and war. Without the physical and social reconstruction of these highly volatile areas, violence and social instability will likely threaten rehabilitation efforts across the metropolitan landscape. A strong role of government in the rebuilding of these crisis-ridden communities is necessary because private housing and development markets are nonexistent in such areas of instability.

Special Integrated Presidential Projects (SIPS), such as the Katorus project seeking the reconstruction of the *Ka*tlehong, *To*koza, and Vosloo*rus* townships southeast of Johannesburg, constitute the government's main foray into place-based resuscitation. The role of government is to provide a stimulus for community recovery that would not occur otherwise due to the breakdown of normal development processes. These are central government efforts to "kick-start" development through a multifaceted approach related to security, housing, engineering services, and social services. Katorus and other SIPS[3] are intended as "pilot" interventions that will hopefully reveal existing blockages in the urban development delivery system (Ministry in the Office of the President 1995). Normalization of the Katorus area is anticipated to proceed along a continuum from initial efforts to stabilize health and security, to the repair and upgrading of the physical environment, to the eventual development of new facilities and services (Katorus 1995a, b). Recovery efforts pertaining to torn communities, however, are problematic and may unwittingly precipitate or accentuate intracommunal conflict. As Hindson, Swilling, and Appleton (1994) note, material differences *within* black peripheral communities can be significant as squatter communities, hostel dwellers, and inhabitants of formal housing coexist alongside one another. Political differences are then frequently overlaid upon, and indeed exploit, these disparities in physical circumstances to produce situations ripe for internecine violence. Introducing development into these deprived and internally tense communities can increase antagonisms as the new resources become subject to preexisting power struggles. A case study of an earlier unsuccessful effort in the Tokoza area of Katorus from 1990 to 1992 points to urban policymakers' "inadequate conceptualization of development within the highly volatile political context surrounding Phola Park and its complex internal social and economic dynamics" (Bremner 1994, 23).[4] The development approach was appropriately integrated and multifaceted, yet an overly technical one that "failed to recognize real political, social and economic conflict, or the divisions that the prospect of development would foment" (Bremner 1994, 41).

The current SIPS strategy in Katorus appears cognizant that new development resources can inflame existing community tensions and of the need to incorporate power structures into the redevelopment process. Physical reconstruction is only one part of the equation. Repair of housing damaged due to social and political violence in 1994, for example, must address the tense issue of what to do with Inkatha Freedom Party (IFP)–aligned squatters who moved into these dysfunctional units after the tenants left out of fear. Twenty-eight Action Area Committees have been established in an effort to transcend political party groupings. These local groups are to identify and negotiate needs among themselves as a prerequisite to formally requesting funding from government. Project director T. Maluleke (interview) explains that these groups are intended "to bring enemies together and into the process so that they can speak to each other and fight, but not physically." Particularly problematic here are efforts to bring the disaffected youth into the process of rebuilding. T. Maluleke (interview) describes the 4000 youths of the area as "dogs of war" who now feel abandoned after apartheid and remain outside the reconstruction process. The Katorus project seeks as part of community reconstruction to incorporate these youths of the ANC's "special defense units" and the IFP's "special protection units" into the reservist component of a newly legitimized South African Police Service. Without such integration into new societal structures, many of these militant youths (*tsotsi* or gangsters) would be left with criminal behavior as their only viable livelihood.

Progress through 1995 in the reconstruction of Katorus has been mixed in its efforts to repair between 1000 and 1500 violence-damaged houses, upgrade significant collections of hostels and informal settlements, and provide new and additional housing and services. Upgrading of about 1000 hostel beds has occurred in the Vosloorus area. In Tokoza, the relationship between hostel residents and township residents is "still problematic" (Katorus 1995c). Due to continuing violence in Katlehong, local negotiations pertaining to hostel upgrading had not yet commenced seven months after program commencement (Gauteng Provincial Government 1995c). In contrast, the upgrading of informal settlements in Phola Park had resulted in over 1600 serviced sites by August 1995 with about 300 persons taking occupation of newly serviced sites. However, a progress report warns that "redevelopment of this community has reached a critical stage and community leadership is fragmenting badly" (Katorus 1995c, 4). The report noted that IFP-aligned gangs (so-called *Amakosi*) had forced the closure of the project site office through the use of intimidatory tactics and were threatening to force removal of persons occupying newly serviced sites.

The Katorus project and other place-based reconstructive efforts point to the critical and complex role of government in attempting to rehabilitate the torn physical and social structures of apartheid's peripheral settlements. Government is seeking to stimulate physical rebuilding in areas where private development processes never have existed and to create social structures needed to stabilize hemorrhaging communities. Government's role in physically rebuilding these communities will likely be extensive for some time, given the poor perception of these areas by private sector institutions. Social stability is also not likely to occur in the short term because community power cleavages have solidified over the many decades of material deprivation. Primary among the lessons of place-based reconstruction is that the two aspects of addressing torn communities—physical reconstruction and conflict resolution—must be addressed simultaneously. One without the other would result, in the first case, in development-initiated fanning of internecine fires, and in the second case, in a tenuous peace unsupported by material upliftment.

Low-Cost Housing Provision

At minimum, one million low-cost houses should be constructed over five years.
—**Reconstruction and Development Programme, African National Congress, 1994, p. 22**

The government housing policy, as is, is not viable.
—**Lawrence Schlemmer, Independent Consultant (interview)**

Twenty years from now we will come to the conclusion that shantytowns are not homeless.
—**Matthew Nel, Vice-chair, National Housing Board (interview)**

We need consensus regarding the role of the state. Housing policy now views the private sector
as playing a lead role in supply, but you don't have normalized markets here.
—**Monty Narsoo, Director of Housing, Gauteng Provincial Government (interview)**

A second key area of state intervention involves low-cost housing provision for black Africans. Here, the state role is not to act as in Katorus as a substitute for an absent private sector, but to supplement or otherwise modify private development processes to achieve public goals. The challenges are enormous, with an estimated 500,000 housing unit backlog in Gauteng Province alone (M. Narsoo, interview). Recent private sector activity, meanwhile, shows that an average of less than 50,000 units had been built annually *in all of South Africa*, of which in 1992 only 5,300 formal housing units were constructed for black Africans (SAIRR 1994). Affordability of new formal housing units to black Africans is a major obstacle. The grinding poverty and survival existence of substantial parts of the black population put even government-subsidized housing beyond their reach. It is estimated that 50 percent or more of the black population in the Johannesburg urban region cannot afford the lowest-priced formal housing unit of 40,000 Rand,[5] even with a 15,000 Rand subsidy going toward land purchase and shelter (J. McCrystal, Johannesburg city planning department, interview). Nationally, of 580,000 households looking for alternative housing arrangements, it is estimated that only about 100,000 of these households could afford a 45,000 Rand housing unit, given a 15,000 government subsidy and current bank practices (L. Schlemmer, interview).

Housing policy through 1995 has positioned the state as a facilitator of private housing development processes rather than as a direct deliverer. The main efforts have included the project-based housing subsidy, the Rapid Land Development

Programme, and government assumption of private investment risk. The project-based individual subsidy is available for persons earning less than R3,500/month, with the fullest subsidy of R15,000 (U.S. $4,250) available to those making less than R800/month. The subsidy can be used to pay for a site, bulk services (water and sewer infrastructure), and/or construction of the housing unit (superstructure). The Rapid Land Development Programme (RLDP) of Gauteng Province seeks to release and use government-owned land to accommodate those living currently in informal settlements under crisis conditions. The Mortgage Indemnity Scheme (MIS) insures private investment in communities against loss due to political unrest and instability, and the Builders Warranty Scheme insures developers against faulty construction.

Progress in housing delivery through 1995 was slow and the target of substantial frustration on the part of the general public and policymakers. The project-based subsidy has been insufficient to build formal low-cost housing units (M. Nel, vice-chair; and I. Mkhabela, chair, National Housing Board, interviews). According to a Gauteng provincial report (1995c) developers estimate that the development costs for a site are about R12,000 and that local governments charge about R500 for rates and taxes. This leaves less than R3000 (about U.S. $800) of the government subsidy for the actual housing structure. Private sector investment by banks then becomes crucial to the process. However, because financial and community risks are perceived by the private sector as too high, housing construction loans have not been forthcoming. Large numbers of people lacking formal housing operate close to the breadline and without any type of equity that would facilitate bank lending. According to the Development Bank of Southern Africa, two-thirds of the adult (largely black) population in Gauteng Province earned less than R883 per month. This income level is far from what is needed to activate private investment and lending. Thus, government subsidies for these poor individuals can help supply a site and services, but "at an income level of less than R1,500 per month, banks are not budging"[6] (M. Narsoo, interview). Another obstacle to the process is that developers are reluctant to become involved because of resistance by established communities to the building of low-cost housing.

These private sector hesitancies to participate in low-income housing have meant that government policy in the first year amounted more to a site and service scheme than the construction of formal units. More than one year after the new government's establishment, housing delivery at low-income levels was poor. By July 1995, only 1,200 housing units had been delivered under the subsidy scheme in Gauteng Province (compared to the estimated 100,000 units needed annually to address the Gauteng housing backlog).[7] On the other hand, the subsidy scheme was able to provide services and tenure for 19,000 sites in the province (Gauteng Provincial Government 1995c). This was mainly in collaboration with the short-term Rapid Land Development Programme, which utilizes government-owned land and thus lessens costs to developers (Gauteng Provincial Government 1995a). The private sector during this time was not entirely dormant. At the commercial level (above R65,000) of housing, which excludes about 75 percent of the province's black population, a housing boom responding to the long-suppressed demand of the emerging nonwhite middle class had forced the industry to work almost at capacity (M. Narsoo, interview).

Prescriptions for government's role in improving low-cost housing delivery in the face of such enormous unmet needs differ between those who favor a direct role in delivery and those who want government to play a facilitative, but subordinate, role in promoting private sector activity. Gauteng director of housing M. Narsoo (interview) asserts that a more assertive state role is needed. The government, for example, might play a proactive role in initiating large residential developments, releasing public land, or in assuming greater amounts of risk for private developers involved with actual low-cost delivery. Because of low effective demand for homeownership possibilities, government-assisted rental housing development would appear logical. In many ways, it seems to be a missing ingredient in South African housing policy (Newhco Group 1995). The city of Johannesburg decided that government's role should be promoter, not direct deliverer, of rental housing. Nonetheless, it does not preclude a direct public role in delivery, if government is unable to achieve its housing vision in any other way (Johannesburg TMC 1995c, d). There are major concerns about the fiscal sustainability of government-owned rental stock (E. Ebdon, Urbanization Department, Metropolitan Johannesburg, interview). Indeed, government is going the opposite direction in its effort to privatize some 64,000 public rental units in Soweto (E. Ebdon; L. Bremner, Metropolitan Council; interviews).[8]

Public underwriting of private financial risk appears to be needed for government to effectively pursue its compact city goals. A proposed Jeppestown Oval residential project—combining affordable and commercial rate housing—in the eastern inner city of Johannesburg is the first large affordable housing scheme in the inner city in the last twenty years. Key to the private project's feasibility, J. McCrystal (city planning department, interview) attests, is that it would occur on council-owned land and the Johannesburg Metropolitan Council would cover some financial risks to the developer. Even with this public assistance, the lowest subsidized price of Jeppestown Oval units (R40,000 for 1 and 2 bedroom units) would remain out of the reach of over 50 percent of the area's black population (J. McCrystal, interview). This experience suggests that publicly supported private housing in the inner city can reach an important black household base and may play a key role in stabilizing inner-city neighborhoods. Yet, it also indicates that densification of urban form achieved solely through subsidized private projects like Jeppestown Oval will exclude the majority black poor in the name of economic feasibility.

A contrasting view of government's role in low-cost housing is that it should be facilitative of private sector activity, not interventionary. The chair of the statutory National Housing Board (I. Mkhabela, interview) advances that it is probably not wise for government to prescribe how housing is to take place, but rather it should promote and accommodate diverse types of housing projects and initiatives.[9] The proper policy stance is to assist the housing process, rather than delivering houses directly; thus, says I. Mkhabela, "I don't think the 15,000R subsidy can build houses, but it can assist the housing process." Advocates of this policy approach argue that the development market will produce certain outcomes that will normalize Johannesburg housing *if* it is provided with certain incentives (M. Nel, vice-chair, National Housing Board, interview). The main role of government is facilitation of private sector involvement and stabilization of the housing policy environment to reduce developer and bank uncertainty. Facilitation could occur through tax or regulatory incentives, direct subsidies, cooperative public-private ventures, public underwriting of risk, and the encouragement of cooperative or collective housing (M. Nel, interview). A provincial community bank could provide credit at the lower ends of the market through nontraditional lending institutions, housing associations, or cooperatives (M. Narsoo and M. Swilling, interviews). Government's facilitative role would also include the stabilization of the investment environment through the underwriting of risk,[10] direct public investment,[11] and regulation and enforcement of rates payments and landlord-renter relations (M. Narsoo, interview).

One model of low-cost housing provision being explored by Gauteng Province would position government's role as greater than private sector facilitation but less than direct delivery and full ownership. "Social housing" is where a nonprofit institution maintains long-term control over a property through ownership to ensure that the housing is and remains affordable. Government might co-invest in the development costs or purchase of existing property by contributing a stated proportion of the purchase price in order to encourage private investment. The government may retain equity in the development, or upon resale, share proportionately in the proceeds, which could then be used for further equity-sharing projects. Examples of social housing efforts in Johannesburg include those of the Newhco Group and the Inner City Housing Upgrading Trust (ICHUT). The nonprofit Newhco Group has built housing schemes in collaboration with Johannesburg City Council, while the city-supported ICHUT underwrites the risk associated with the rehabilitation and conversion of existing inner-city buildings for residential purposes.

In summary, the housing challenge represents probably the most difficult one facing urban policymakers. Private development capital on its own will not invest in certain places or in ways that meet the needs of the lower income groups. Government facilitation through financial incentives and risk alleviation is thus most assuredly needed to stimulate involvement by private capital and developers. But, housing needs in the Johannesburg urban region are so extreme, and effective demand by the black majority is so low, that even an energized private market will be incapable of meeting public goals pertaining to housing opportunities. No matter the combination of governmental facilitative and stabilization efforts, the fact is that a gap will remain between the lowest-cost formal housing unit and the affordability level of the black majority. Low-cost housing provision in the inner city is an integral part of efforts to spatially connect the torn urban landscape and provide proximate opportunities to the black majority, yet at the same time high inner-city land costs translate into subsidized private housing that is well out of the reach of the black majority. The residential densification that would occur in post-apartheid Johannesburg would thus exclude the poor and marginalized. To combat these market effects, government would need to act more aggressively than private sector facilitation by, for instance, purchasing inner-city land, putting in infrastructure, and building high-density affordable housing. However, such direct government participation heightens fiscal vulnerability and public debt and runs counter to central government's fiscal stabilization goals.[12]

Housing policy also presents policymakers with emotional issues over the type and definition of "housing" that government should pursue. Given fiscal realities and the dire state of housing needs, the government is faced with an ongoing choice in housing policy between depth and width of benefits. A housing policy that aims at a "formal" bricks-and-mortar product would provide comprehensive benefits to recipients, but the reach of this approach would be narrower and gradual. In contrast, a housing policy that is based on incremental housing approaches (such as "site and services") would provide the barest of shelter benefits, but the reach of this approach would be wider and faster. This important housing policy choice regarding housing quality will determine the timing of policy benefits to the country's black population. Based on estimated budget allocations, government subsidization of formal housing would mean that it would take about 40 years— more than one generation—to address Gauteng Province's 500,000 housing unit backlog (M. Narsoo, director of housing, Gauteng Province, interview). Housing benefits would be comprehensive but would affect only a limited pool of recipients each year. With the provision of a high standard housing product, there would also likely be "islands of privilege surrounded by seas of ghettoes and informal housing" (M. Narsoo, interview). In contrast, a policy emphasizing "site and services" would more widely distribute benefits and affect a larger pool of recipients each year. Such a policy approach would cover the Gauteng backlog in about eight years (M. Narsoo, interview). However, the shelter benefits provided would be a bare minimum and, indeed, would often not include the built structure itself among its direct benefits. The expectation here is that, with the provision of land tenure supported by adequate urban services and amenities, "viable communities can develop in informal settlements" (Ministry in the Office of the President 1995, 47).

The debate over the definition of, and proper governmental approach toward, low-cost housing has created tension both within central government, and between central and Gauteng provincial leaders. For example, the ANC has consistently supported formal housing provision; yet, the late Joe Slovo, as national housing minister, was a primary advocate of incremental approaches to low-cost housing provision. Despite philosophical differences with incremental housing, the central government in its draft national urban strategy (1995) admits that "the housing backlog will simply be beyond the reach if fully serviced, formal housing is the norm." Incremental approaches address both the fiscal constraint and affordability problems facing housing policymakers. At the same time, however, it is susceptible to a "toilet in the veld" syndrome that perpetuates a dual class-based housing market and peripheralization of growth. For incremental programs to produce decent housing and communities in the end, they must be accompanied by assistance in the form of small loans and credit, access to material supplies, technical assistance, and serious government investments in community facilities and schools.

Fundamental choices grip post-apartheid housing policymakers. Greater governmental involvement and expenditures in housing provision appear essential to address equity and urban integration objectives, yet runs counter to central government's goals pertaining to fiscal stabilization and debt reduction. At the same time, the choice between "bricks and mortar" and incremental "site and services" objectives requires a moral judgment on the part of policymakers. Future directions in housing policy may likely include greater consideration of social housing strategies that incorporate joint equity-sharing arrangements between government and nonprofit or private development entities. In addition, the draft 1995 national urban strategy proposed a separate national infrastructure subsidy scheme (Ministry in the Office of the President 1995, 39). If enacted, it would significantly lessen the burden of the project-based housing subsidy scheme which today must cover both services and shelter. Housing policy must in the future also be appropriately integrated with other public goals targeting the inequalities of the past and present. Housing policy should not stand alone, but rather be linked to community development and job creation strategies that can change the equations regarding housing affordability. In national debates prior to the 1994 election, housing policy discussions frequently ran ahead of economic growth deliberations because housing was "more visible and deliverable to politicians" (M. Narsoo, director of housing, Gauteng Province, interview). Now, as urban public policymakers engage more creatively in urban economic development strategies, they have the opportunity to exploit the synergetic benefits of housing and economic policy in order to temper market mechanisms that would otherwise sustain the inequalities of the old apartheid urban order.

Strategic Locations

A third critical point of public intervention into economic markets and processes involves government in the development of those vacant and underutilized areas which are keys to spatially connecting the dysfunctional fabric of apartheid Johannesburg. Three major strategic locations are identifiable—a wide swath of underutilized mining land close to the inner city; a vacant former apartheid buffer zone area between Soweto and Johannesburg; and vacant inner-city "infill" land close to inner-city opportunities. The utilization of inner-city "infill" sites, discussed earlier, will play an instrumental role in achieving compact city principles. In this essay, I focus on the mining land and buffer zone areas and examine those public policies and interventions that may be required to stitch these strategic locations into the larger post-apartheid quilt of Johannesburg.

In 1992, an audit of vacant land and its potential for development in the metropolitan Johannesburg area was conducted amidst continued pressure to develop peripheral sites (CWMC 1992b). The study sought to determine the amount and location of vacant land that, if developed, would further the creation of a post-apartheid compact city. Arguably the most strategic location identified in the vacant land audit was the wide swath of underutilized mining land that stretches along the main reef from Randfontein in the west to Boksburg in the east. This land is characterized most visibly by mine dumps and slimes dams. Many of these vacant or underutilized sites occur in the center of the Central Witwatersrand and are proximate to both inner-city opportunities and an east-west industrial belt to the north. In addition, they are served well by highway arterials and rail connections (CWMC 1992b). The land audit evaluated for future residential development vacant land that was unconstrained by the presence of mining residuals such as dolomite or shallow undermining. Of the top 18 sites across the entire metropolitan area, nine of these were in the mining swath subarea. Seven central sites to the south of the inner city and in the general vicinity of Soweto were assessed as high priority (CWMC 1992b). The approximately 750 hectares in these areas that are unconstrained by geotechnical limits could hold between 15,000 and 37,500 dwelling units (based on an assumed density of between 20 and 50 units per hectare).[13] There are considerations beyond geology, however; foremost among these is that the land is proclaimed mining land and owned mostly by large firms and mining houses.

This mining land represents a tremendous asset and opportunity to policymakers in their efforts to create a spatially and functionally integrated compact city where residence and employment opportunities are proximate. Johannesburg is geographically unique in the world, with this swath of underutilized land running east-west close to the central business district and central city (T. Hart, SRK Engineers). An urban region of such extreme basic needs appears to have been given a gift from

God. But, the mining land also represents a challenge to policymakers because much of it, and the site-specific technical data concerning potential developability, is privately held by economically powerful mining and industrial concerns. The mining land question is a clear illustration of the need for public and private sectors to work together to create a post-apartheid Johannesburg. If such public-private cooperation was to occur, both sides would have to compromise. From the private sector side, the government debate in the initial phase was too unidimensional in its attention to low-cost housing (M. Nel, interview). This assuredly jeopardizes economic return on the land and dissuades landowners from actively participating in public discussions. On the other hand, mining interests are obdurate in holding onto their land over the long term in case the currently depressed gold market makes the land economically viable to mine again.[14] As G. Reid (Planact, interview) explains, "nobody is willing to make the decision to establish a village there and face the consequences twenty years off if it turns out mining is viable due to the market."

The outlines of a public-private agreement concerning high-priority mining land would likely include strong government intervention to increase the developability of specific mining land, and allowance by government for mixed uses to assure profitability to current owners. The approach to developing mining land, suggests H. Pienaar (Midrand town planner, interview), should be driven by goals, not constraints. Government would strategically intervene to decommission and remove slimes dams, to overcome any undermining problems, and to build highways to further open up mining lands. The costs of these efforts would be justified on the basis of the benefits that would flow to future generations; accordingly, rent and tax payments over the next twenty years could be used to pay for government growth-facilitative actions today.[15] The development to occur on mining lands would not be all low-cost housing since this retards private sector interest in mining land reclamation. Rather, local government would allow mining companies to build intense commercial and industrial development on part of the mining land in exchange for low-cost housing on other parts. Private sector interests in this case may endure assertive facilitative actions by government if they are assured of reasonable economic return. Under this scenario, private sector and market processes that would otherwise be blocked are stimulated through facilitative government actions that allow both profit-related private and equity-based governmental objectives to be addressed.

It is the responsibility of all designers and planners to demonstrate to Sowetans that design can make the future better than the past.
—*Stephen Thorne, Architect, 1995,* **Baralink Development Framework** *(p. 102)*

A second strategic location in Johannesburg's metropolitan landscape is the southwestern apartheid buffer zone that has for the past four decades spatially separated black Soweto from white Johannesburg. This area is about 1,500 hectares, approximately the size of Johannesburg's central business district; and much of it was owned in mid-1995 by public authorities. Appropriate development of this spatial discontinuity would create a development bridge from Soweto to the southern suburbs of the former Johannesburg city. Development of this former no-man's land is consistent with compact city objectives in that it directs growth *inward* from Soweto, not outward toward the metropolitan periphery. It would increase accessibility of residents to urban opportunities through two means. First, residential development in this area would bring residents closer to central city Johannesburg economic activities. Second, nonresidential development between Johannesburg and Soweto would bring jobs closer to the existing residents of Soweto townships. A strategy of building in the southwestern buffer zone exists in the middle ground between "jobs-to-people" and "people-to-jobs" approaches.[16] Jobs-to-people efforts, in their well-intentioned efforts to bring economic activities out to the unemployed residents of Soweto, would face criticism for effectively reinforcing apartheid's geography of separateness. In contrast, "people-to-jobs" efforts to facilitate the movement of people to where jobs are would face criticism for effectively emptying out Soweto over time. Filling in the southwestern gap between Soweto and Johannesburg—the synthesis of these two approaches—is buffered from the criticisms of each. It seeks to both provide opportunities for current Soweto residents *and* transform the apartheid geographies of remoteness and discontinuity.

The *Baralink*[17] Development Framework (Thorne 1995) prepared for the old southwestern buffer area recommends a set of guiding principles aimed at mixed-use integration, accessibility and facilitation of movement, the building of residences around walkable "local districts" or neighborhoods, and the integration of commercial and residential activities to increase security. Urban form is positioned as capable of democratizing and empowering society, and thus is seen as playing a key role in societal transformation. As Thorne (1995, 59) states, "more democratic and sustainable spatial patterns and urban systems need to be developed in order to balance opportunity and reduce prejudice." Under these development principles, it is expected that about 35,000 homes could be built in the area, housing between approximately 150,000 and 200,000 people. There is no presumption that this would be a mixed-race area; all residents are expected to be black. At the same time, there was no explicit effort as of late 1995 to develop part of the formal housing stock for low-income households, although upgrading of informal settlements in the area would provide some relief (J. McCrystal, interview). It is expected that about 900,000 square meters of industrial space could be accommodated along with 700,000 square meters of commercial development. Both high-intensity uses would occur along existing major transportation links, many of which would be improved as part of Baralink. Commercial activities are anticipated to be retail originally; over time, however, the nonresidential part of Baralink is seen as finding a niche in the metropolitan economic system (J. McCrystal, interview). One possibility here is that Baralink will become a center for distribution and outlet type economic activities, such as building supply and fruit markets. This would establish Baralink's niche in a regional economic system composed of banks, services, and institutions in the central business district, manufacturing and industry to the east, and office and commercial to the north.

Baralink constitutes an extraordinary opportunity for post-apartheid planners in their efforts to normalize the divided cityscape through the correction of distorted spatial patterns. However, such a democratic and empowering spatial system will likely not come of its own accord; rather, government has a critical guiding role to play in assuring that Baralink reaches its potential. These roles include subregional coordination, public investment, and project facilitation and oversight. The Transitional Metropolitan Council (TMC) of greater Johannesburg must first assure that the larger subregional development picture is taken into account. This oversight role is necessarily the TMC's because Soweto townships have politically been broken up into three different local governments.[18] The TMC should assure that interlocal competition does not unnecessarily erode economic development efforts in the Soweto area, and that the benefits of growth are fiscally shared among the three local governments. Baralink is the largest effort southwest of Johannesburg, yet it is not the only one. A potential commercial complex to the west of Baralink could adversely compete with Baralink proposals (I. Kadungure, Soweto planner, interview). To the east, meanwhile, the existing and successful Southgate shopping area has already captured a significant share of the market. These projects point to the need to integrate Baralink into the larger subregional system to assure that overcommercialization of the area does not occur. It is important economically and symbolically that Baralink and other projects in the Soweto area succeed in a sustainable way.

Government must also take the lead in rebuilding Soweto through targeted public investment (Thorne 1995; J. McCrystal, interview). Particularly salient here are road- and bridge-building and upgrading that will both internally link the Soweto area and connect it to Johannesburg. Expansion of Old Potchefstroom Road, along which the major Soweto kombi-taxi rank is located, will enhance this critical arterial connector in the area. Further, government should function as project facilitator and overseer. Of currently developable land in the Baralink site, over 80 percent is owned by a diverse array of public authorities (Thorne 1995). Government is thus capable of playing a leading role in facilitating privately sponsored projects that fit into its democratizing development vision. The Development Framework is aware of this opportunity in recommending that government control the release of its land to avoid "winner takes all" development where broader social issues, such as affordable housing and urban quality, are largely ignored. Public land, the report states, should only be released once all performance criteria have been met in development proposals. In addition, government in joint actions with the private sector can be instrumental in developing catalytic or prototype projects that set important precedents for subsequent development. These key projects (such as a sports complex, retail outlet, taxi rank, and produce and craft markets) would have the "function of setting the standard and tone of development, as well as begin to structure the spatial legibility of the area" (Thorne 1995, 75).

Baralink, the mining swath, and inner-city infill sites are strategic locations for planners and policymakers in their efforts to stitch together the ruptured urban system of Johannesburg. The extent, quality, and accessibility of development in these locations hold important keys to the future of post-apartheid Johannesburg. It is ironic that these strategic locations are available today because of the actions of governmental and economic forces which subordinated the black majority and tore apart the urban system. The apartheid system of land use separation, through its creation of buffer zones and a "white" inner city of overserviced and low-density development, unintentionally created today's zones of spatial opportunity. At the same time, the mining economic sector which has so long exploited black labor has today left an underutilized swath of opportunity for the blacks of the Johannesburg region. There is no better use of these spatial legacies of urban and economic apartheid than their employment in the restructuring and eradication of Johannesburg's landscape of racial hate.

*   *   *

I have examined government's appropriate role vis-à-vis the private sector in three policy areas critical to Johannesburg's reconstruction—rebuilding of violence-torn communities, providing low-cost housing to the black majority, and developing strategically located land. The interplay of government and business actions will help produce post-apartheid Johannesburg and determine the degree to which it fulfills the objectives of equity, opportunity, and democracy. The private sector brings significant capabilities and resources to the process of urban reconstruction, but it cannot be relied upon solely to achieve a more equitable Johannesburg. Left to its own signals, the private sector will likely not invest in strife-torn communities, be able to produce inner-city housing that is affordable to the peripheralized poor, or develop a Baralink that is democratizing. Local and extralocal governments must be prepared to assume facilitative, substitutive, and oversight roles to achieve the post-apartheid goals of compactness, integration, equity, and poverty alleviation.

In some cases, government must *facilitate* the engagement by the development community in projects it would otherwise forego. This is exemplified by the possible public underwriting of private risk in the Jeppestown Oval project, the stabilization through targeted public investment in communities, and creative ventures with the private sector, as may be needed to break the logjam over privately held mining land. In other cases, such as in the reconstruction of crisis-ridden Katorus, government must *substitute* for private sector mechanisms where they are reluctant to engage. Direct government provision of inner-city low-cost housing may be required because private housing, even when publicly subsidized, will not incorporate the peripheralized poor into the urban system. Finally, in an *oversight* role, the state creates development frameworks which will ensure that broader social issues, such as affordable housing and urban accessibility, are part of future built landscapes. Such management of urban development is exemplified by government's attachment of performance criteria to public land in Baralink released to the private sector.

Race, Class, and Sustainability

Circuits of capital have replaced the dictatorship of the administrative state.
—**Mark Swilling, University of the Witwatersrand (interview)**

We cannot compete with the Koreas and Malaysias out there, but it's not because we can't match their productivity. It's because we achieved political democracy before economic growth.
—**Monty Narsoo, Director of Housing, Gauteng Provincial Government (interview)**

How do we divest completely from the old order?
—**Ish Mkhabela, Chair, National Housing Board (interview)**

Johannesburg's is an unfolding story of transformation away from one society toward an uncertain new one. Resolution of the root causes of city-based ethnic conflict, further advanced here than in Belfast, promises fundamental change in urban policymaking. Options for future public policy directions are both more developed and salient than in Belfast, where urban alternatives remain politically constrained (as of mid-1998). Yet, Johannesburg's political "peace" is associated with distressing conditions of unmet basic needs. The reality weighing down today's transformative South African spirit is that the successful resolution of the root political and ideological causes of racial conflict is not sufficient to affect significant upliftment in human conditions for the deprived majority. Removal of apartheid and its barriers is necessary but not sufficient to truly reconstructing the urban region of Johannesburg. Other obstacles exist that have the advantages of legitimacy, color-blindness, and international condonation or even encouragement.

In this concluding section, I first examine the challenges of normalizing Johannesburg in a deracialized society. Urban "normalization" has contrasting meanings—one emphasizing reparative social justice, the other market-based predominance—that may conflict in the creation of post-apartheid Johannesburg. I then look at the challenging combination of public goals—fiscal discipline, economic growth, and redistribution—being pursued simultaneously in the new South Africa.

Nonracial Urbanization

The driving ideology behind post-apartheid city-building is reconciliation and normalization through the creation of a compact, functionally integrated city. Through significant changes in the environmental design of the metropolis, the black majority is to be brought closer to urban opportunities and neighborhoods that offer better and wider services. Overall, land needed for this spatial reconstruction appears available. Thus, with the repeal of apartheid, there is the expectation by some that government can allow in a passive way for the market to embark on a gradual correction of previous distortions (Lemon 1991). Government might help subsidize and encourage certain types of development, but it is the energy of the private sector that is to respond to the massive needs of the black majority. Decisions by financial capital and businesses are to guide the pace and nature of Johannesburg's reconstruction process. Government's role is to be facilitator of such development processes and hospice-keeper for the many who are marginalized and excluded from the processes. In this scenario, the centralized state apartheid apparatus is not to give way to a centralized African socialism that scares away white and foreign investors and antagonizes world financial institutions. However, the market, like apartheid, is not neutral but produces spatial and economic injustices (D. M. Smith 1994). Reliance on market-based mechanisms of "normalization" as the primary allocators of services and opportunities in the new Johannesburg will produce only marginal progress toward the goals of post-apartheid urban compactness and integration. Beyond this, economic and development markets will likely create new forms of class-based spatial inequalities that would far overshadow progress toward reparative social justice. As Morris and Hindson (1992, 167) state, "a path of reconstruction which accentuates class distinctions, ie. the neo-liberal path currently dominant, cannot form an acceptable or viable point of departure for a process of stable social reconstruction."

Spatially, market-based "normalization" of the Johannesburg urban region will likely produce intraregional disparities that eclipse urban compaction efforts. Banking and financial capital and developers have little interest in a compact urban system (M. Swilling, University of the Witwatersrand, interview). Mabin (1995) anticipates some compactness of urban form but also "new and extended fragmentation producing new disabilities for oppressed groups in the city." These new forms of economic segregation are the multiple northern suburban subcenters of office, specialty retail, high-technology, and information-based industries that exist in Rosebank, Sandton, and Midrand (see Figure 9.1). Such spatial economic fragmentation not only stratifies investment patterns within the Johannesburg urban region, but can remove economic activities and jobs out of the Johannesburg metropolitan revenue stream. The town of Midrand is approximately 30 kilometers from Johannesburg. New government boundaries politically separated the town from the Johannesburg metropolis, despite its immediate functional connections with it (H. Pien-aar, Midrand town planner, interview). Growth in Midrand along a major highway has been phenomenal, with 30 percent growth in office, commercial, and industrial floor space *each year* for the past five years. Midrand's central business district is expected to be the size of Johannesburg's (Midrand 1991). By 2010, promises town planner Pienaar, "one will not recognize this place." Such a regional pattern of investment promises to loosen the glue that would otherwise help hold the new Johannesburg together. Firms and businesses in these decentralized areas have abandoned Johannesburg central city as a possible location and migrated to these northern subcenters based on rational market signals—to be close to their middle- and upper-class labor force and customer base. Selective abandonment by corporate and financial interests of Johannesburg's inner city and the development of these suburban subcenters are viewed as necessary components in the enlarging of new Johannesburg's regional economic pie. M. Nel (development consultant, interview) condones this functionalism of economic activity, asking "why from a policy view would it not be desirable to allow these market processes to happen?"

Moving from the apartheid city to a "normal" system of urbanization presents planners and policymakers with an array of emergent obstacles tied to economic forces rather than to formal racially based laws. Market-based processes have their

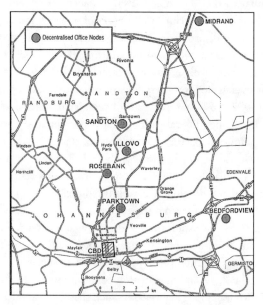

FIGURE 9.1   Decentralization of Office Employment
Source: Rogerson, C. M. "Dispersion Within Concentration: The Location of Corporate Headquarter Offices in South Africa." *Development Southern Africa* (13, 4: 1996), p. 573. Reprinted by permission.

own set of signals that guide the actions of businesses and financial interests. And, we have seen several illustrations of how reliance on these private sector land and development markets and processes will likely reinforce peripheralized apartheid geography. As long as the private land market remains the main allocator of land uses, in the absence of strong public planning or a greater state role in provision, much housing development will be built on the cheaper urban fringe. This is because only the immediate and minimal costs to the private sector are factored into the locational decision, not the longer-term public costs of transport subsidies and bulk services. A development market may likely emerge to facilitate such peripheral growth, with semiformal landlords purchasing farmland and renting it to informal settlers in a circumstance where "it's more profitable to farm people than it is to farm crops" (Tim Hart, SRK Engineers, interview). In other cases, established ownership patterns can impede spatial reconstruction, exemplified by the privatized, underutilized mining swath that could put thousands of blacks closer to central city opportunities. In certain inner-city neighborhoods, disinvestment by capital interests will occur in anticipation of, or in response to, black ghettoization and degradation of the urban fabric. This economic logic can destroy public efforts aimed at inner-city residential stability. Finally, reliance on the formal economic sector to uplift the conditions of the black majority appears misplaced. The absorptive capacity of that formal economy has declined dramatically over the last 20 years, from about 50 percent of school-leavers to today's 15 percent (C. Rogerson, University of the Witwatersrand, interview).

The problem is not that the private sector utilizes their internal signals pertaining to investment, efficiency, and locational advantage. Rather, it is that government is relying strongly on this system to produce an urban spatial structure of opportunities for the formerly disempowered black minority. The primary effects of such private sector–led reconstruction appear to be anathema to the new democratic spirit of the country. These include:

- increasing geographic disconnection regionally between major sources of job opportunities in northern suburban subcenters and the labor pools of Soweto and Alexandra.
- reinforcement of the apartheid geography of peripheral housing due to land value and ownership impediments to city compaction.
- creation of new forms of class-based metropolitan disparity, with enhancement and self-containment of middle-class northern suburbs and decline of inner-city neighborhoods.
- maintenance of broadly homogeneous neighborhoods and residential insularity based on class which will solidify an inward, group-oriented consciousness obstructive of intergroup reconciliation.

- continued exclusion of major segments of the black majority from formal economic opportunities.

Upon repeal of an apartheid that was active and ruthless in its segregative goals, it does not appear to be morally just for urban policymakers to allow the private development market to be the primary influence on the post-apartheid urban region. Rather, an alternative agenda of reconstruction is called for that acknowledges market-based "normalization" mechanisms as incapable, on their own accord, to produce measurable gains in post-apartheid urban equity. This approach, in the words of Morris and Hindson (1992), seeks to "contain the excesses of the market/private property system rather than trying to eliminate them." An alternative strategy seeks to supplement traditional production-centered development with a people-centered approach based on inclusive participation supported by a strong but responsive state, and aimed at appropriate economic growth that is equitable and sustainable (Friedmann 1992). Such a growth path includes economic efficiency as one objective, but also considers how growth meets the needs and rights of citizens, especially the disempowered. Likewise, Swilling's (1990) democratic urban policy does not shut down the profit-seeking development sector, but establishes a nonprofit channel of development alongside it to deliver land, services, and housing to the poor. This nonprofit circuit would utilize subsidized development capital; community-controlled development organizations; nonprofit loan finance capitalized by state, corporate, and international aid; and collective tenure arrangements that remove housing from economic pressures (Swilling 1990).

An alternative spatial approach to development must be capable of constructively engaging with the increasing economic functionalism and fragmentation of the region. Policymakers must either strengthen their ability to shape regional growth patterns to support Johannesburg city as the central node, or seek to incorporate social and equity objectives within the emerging realities of a metro-province having dispersed and multiple activity nodes. In the first case, policymakers would need to enact on a regional basis an "urban growth boundary" that would discourage growth outside the regulatory line.[19] Absent this, densification of Johannesburg that does occur will be overshadowed by larger-scale decentralization and subcentering. In the second case, urban policy would anticipate a multiple-center urban region and seek to create compact nodes integrative of low-income housing. Anticipatory public land banking could take advantage of relatively lower land costs prior to the onset of economic competition and attendant land value appreciation. Such multinodal development patterns are capable of providing greater pockets of space near employment where nonprofit and state entities could constructively engage. Johannesburg metropolitan and Gauteng provincial policymakers must decide which regional model of growth—monocentric or multinodal—will guide their social and investment policies. Strategies such as those in the Integrated Strategic Framework which seek to densify a dominant Johannesburg center will fail in the absence of a regional system of growth management because an affluent and "un-African" northern corridor of residents and economic activities will psychologically secede from an unstable Africanized center. At the same time, policies that would condone, and build upon, a multicentered metropolitan system must be based upon a better understanding of regional economic dynamics than currently exists. Metropolitan and provincial policymakers must create a regional development framework for future economic growth and equity.

In the end, Johannesburg and Gauteng policymakers must be careful of their aspirations when they speak of "normal" urbanization. Two standards of urban normalcy exist—the colonial African city consisting of inner zones of privilege surrounded by peripheral shantytowns, and the American city of affluent suburbs circumscribing an impoverished center. Absent aggressive state counterstrategies, these models may combine in the Johannesburg urban region to create a metropolitan mosaic of inequality and disadvantage comparable in effect to the dark years of apartheid.

Inequality and Democracy

Much of the stability of the new Johannesburg and South Africa depends upon a sustained level of economic and job growth to facilitate a fairer distribution of material benefits. The ability of government in the new South Africa to stimulate economic growth, employment creation, and increases in tax bases will play a decisive role in whether the basic living conditions of the black majority improve over the next twenty years. Without significant economic and human development, equity objectives will be bounded by the government's commitment to fiscal discipline—its funding of programs through the redirecting of existing budgets rather than increases in spending and debt. Economic growth and development can change the equations facing policymakers in many areas; for example, employment gains can alleviate the housing affordability problem by moving some housing demand from subsidy schemes to commercial rate housing. At the local level, economic growth translates into local property tax base enhancements which can fund new and expanded community and physical services.

The simultaneous pursuit by government of these three objectives—economic growth, fiscal discipline, and redistribution—puts government in the position of a swimmer who has been underwater for fifty years, comes to the surface, and is told to swim the backstroke at Olympian level. Achieving less than all three of these objectives would likely lead to a lethargic and handicapped urban democracy in Johannesburg. With existing budgetary resources tight, the amount of spending in existing budgets able to be redirected is limited. Redistribution through the income and property tax systems past a tipping point runs the risk of diminished services in white areas, and attendant political backlashes and out-migration or evasive action on the part of whites.[20] At the same time, increasing spending and/or public debt as a way to finance programs to alleviate poverty is constrained by concerns over inflation, overtaxation, and reactions by interna-tional financial overseers.[21] Given these conditions, the attraction of foreign in-vestment and external capital flows is viewed as the most effective method of stimulating the economy while holding down government debt. This emphasis on direct foreign investment reinforces fiscal conservatism on the part of govern-ment and inhibits redistributive possibilities in the immediate term. Such fiscal discipline by the government is applauded as setting the proper long-term frame-work to attract foreign investment (L. Schlemmer, business consultant, inter-view). At the same time, in the nearer term, it constrains government's ability to meet more than a minimal amount of the country's extreme basic needs. In addi-tion, it limits government's capacity to restructure its delivery mechanisms in fields such as health, training, and education because such restructuring often re-quires investment of new money up-front[22] (interviews: R. Hunter and L. Schlemmer). In this way, outside investment may be achieved in the short term at the expense of public sector efficiencies and effectiveness in addressing the needs of its deprived residents (R. Hunter, interview).

The economic growth challenge facing South Africa is daunting. By most esti-mates, the economy must grow about 4.8 percent per year to absorb labor force expansion brought on by forecasted increases in the working-age population and to compensate for labor rationalization (L. Schlemmer, business consultant, in-terview). Adding increased wages likely under new collective bargaining agree-ments, approximately 6 percent growth per year is needed (L. Schlemmer, inter-view).[23] Recent economic growth has been nowhere near this mark due to weak world prices for gold and commodities, the cost of enforcing apartheid, and an accompanying evaporation of business confidence. Growth in the country's gross domestic product from 1981 to 1990 was 1.5 percent per year; from 1991 to 1993, the economy contracted an average 0.7 percent per year (South African Reserve Bank 1994). The formal economic system was stingy in its opportuni-ties, with only one-half of the extended labor force by 1991 working in the for-mal sector (compared to two-thirds in 1980)[24] (Development Bank of Southern Africa [DBSA] 1995b). Between 1980 and 1991, the formal economy created a net total of 350,000 jobs, whereas the labor force grew by 4.5 million people. Today, only 15 of 100 school-leavers will find employment in the formal sector; in the 1960s, in contrast, the labor absorption capacity was around 50 percent (C. Rogerson, interview; Ligthelm and Kritzinger–Van Niekerk 1990). The six percent annual economic growth rate needed to make a dent in the mid-1990s' official unemployment rate of 33 percent would put South Africa on equal foot-ing with Malaysia, Indonesia, or South Korea, each of which has high levels of craft skills and / or high investments in education. Lacking these characteristics at least in the medium term, the best South Africa might expect is about 3.5 percent annual growth (L. Schlemmer, interview). Continuation at this level of economic growth over the medium term would likely increase unemployment levels among the economically active black population from approximately 41 percent in 1995 to close to 53 percent (L. Schlemmer, interview). In 1995, national economic growth reached 3.3 percent for the year. However, only 40,000 new jobs in the private sector had been created nationally from mid-1994 through the end of 1995 (South African Reserve Bank 1996).

Even if market-based "corrections" of the apartheid legacy are capable of improving aggregate economic indicators, however, they would still produce a society deeply cleaved by class. A World Bank report (Fallon and Pereira de Silva 1994) asserts that "sustained growth . . . in itself is not enough. Growth without redistribution would almost certainly falter as social tensions rose." Growth of the formal economy will not be capable in the short and medium term of securing the equitable reconstruction of society. Indeed, once the explicit racial and ethnic layer is rubbed off, one finds a layer of class division characteristic of advanced capitalism. "We are essentially talking about class," states M. Nel (interview), "and we always have been in this country, although with a racial overtone."

Equitable reconstruction and societal reparation require more than reliance on post-apartheid capitalism. The extreme level of inequality cries for an assertive, responsible state role that can address more widely than capitalism the basic needs of apartheid's victims. It demands a stronger set of government and nonprofit actions that redress the disparities and equalize the competitive positions of black Africans. It shouts for increased state expenditures on black primary health care, job training and education, housing and related urban services;[25] spending that both increases redistribution and assists economic recovery. It calls for public programs that are consistent with, and build upon, the communitarian ethic of black African culture. It warrants actions that assist and empower the informal sectors of the economy and connect them to channels of capital. It calls for strong place-based counterstrategies in areas like Soweto to combat future class-based inequalities and to increase equality of urban opportunity. The democratic capitalism of post-apartheid South Africa and Johannesburg must address both collective gain and distributive equity. State power must not be privately appropriated for particularistic ends; indeed, in stark contrast, business and the private sector must contribute to the larger public goals of deracialization and equity and not see their actions as having "business-only" effects. At the same time, a "corporatist" structure of governance composed of the state, business, and labor unions, but excluding the small business sector and the 80 percent of workers who are nonunionized, should be avoided (Adam and Moodley 1993). Any privatization of the large "parastatal" economic sector should take into account its effect on equity objec-

tives as well as economic efficiency and competition.[26] Private domestic investment must be raised from its currently depressed levels.

South Africa can take pride in its successful transition from apartheid to democracy. The result of the complicated and drawn-out transformation process has been a
"rambling and shambling democracy that will get its act together sometime down
the line" (M. Narsoo, Director of Housing, Gauteng Provincial Government, interview). An intricate organizational fabric has been created that is probably capable of
managing democratic processes, yet may not be able to develop coherent policies or
avoid crisis-driven actions. One future scenario is that South Africa will incremen-
tally muddle through because it "has neither the work ethic to be a Taiwan nor the
overwhelming zealousness to be a Bosnia" (P. Pereira, SAIRR, interview). Or, as L.
Schlemmer (interview) predicts, "we will flow along in a kind of sea of mediocrity
with decreasing racial inequality and increasing class inequality."

The vitality and sustainability of a post-apartheid democracy are not guaranteed.
An effective and active government sector must be able to ameliorate the class-
based inequalities which would be inevitable in a society dominated by private enterprise. Otherwise, mass poverty and these seemingly "new" forms of deracialized
inequality will frustrate those who are marginalized and threaten political stability.[27]
There would be a growing echo of the frustration expressed in 1995 by H. Mashabela (SAIRR, interview): "I don't understand. I had looked forward to the day when
we would be in the position that we are in. Yet, we seem to be condoning the further
degradation of the black person." With major portions of its population abandoned
to the margins of social life, Johannesburg and other urban areas might become
"warlord" cities containing major centers of criminality and alienation disconnected
from democratic structures (M. Swilling, interview). Amidst such class and social
divisions in the "new" South Africa, an increased statism and authoritarianism would
likely emerge in an effort to stabilize and hold together the fractured society. In this
future, point out Morris and Hindson (1992), "we will have shaken off apartheid
only to find ourselves in a new form of authoritarianism."

The new democracies of Johannesburg and South Africa are sustainable, but
only if a collective freedom associated with social justice takes precedence over
the freedom of individual economic choice.

Notes

1. Presentation. Center for Development and Enterprise. Carlton Centre, Johannesburg. August 8, 1995.

2. Ibid.

3. Other SIPS include Cato Manor in Durban, Ibhayi in Port Elizabeth, and Duncan Village in East London.

4. Tensions in the area include those between Inkatha-aligned hostel dwellers and Phola
Park residents; and, within Phola Park, between relocated backyard tenants from Tokosa,

migrants from the Transkei region of the country, and illegal immigrants from Mozambique (Bremner 1994).

5. About $11,500 U.S. at time of writing.

6. This is true even with governmental guarantees against financial loss due to community instability.

7. Whereas government had budgeted for almost 80,000 subsidies worth R369 million, only 676 had been used by developers worth R6.1 million.

8. Privatization of council housing stock has its own set of attendant problems, including conflicting claims of tenancy amidst poor records, and displacement of those not able to afford privatized stock (G. Reid, Planact, interview).

9. There are concerns within government, however, that such flexibility may in the end cater to privileged groups and not produce low-cost housing (I. Mkhabela, interview).

10. The public underwriting of risk spans the boundaries between direct and facilitative roles of government. It constitutes lesser government involvement than a direct provision role, yet tends to obligate government resources more than a strictly facilitative role.

11. For example, Gauteng government's 1995 decision to relocate from Pretoria to Johannesburg may help stabilize inner-city Johannesburg and attract private sector investment.

12. Note that government would save on infrastructure and transportation costs compared to the alternative of having new housing built on the periphery.

13. For the region as a whole, about 9000 hectares were identified as available and unconstrained. This land could house between 180,000 and 450,000 units.

14. Much of the central mining land has been "mined out" at current gold prices. Further mining is possible, but would be at deeper and more expensive levels not economically feasible at current world gold prices.

15. This process in the USA, where new development pays over the long term for today's government borrowing, is used to redevelop downtowns. The financial mechanism is called "tax increment financing."

16. The choice involves whether government should target resources to places or to people. One of the first elucidations of this choice in government reports in the USA can be found in the *Kerner Report: The 1968 Report of the National Advisory Commission on Civil Disorders*. There, the choice is between *enrichment* of black ghettoes and *integration* of blacks into the white residential fabric. Much of U.S. urban policy has had a place-oriented, jobs-to-people orientation, although that has changed since the early 1980s; see *A National Agenda for the Eighties* (President's Commission for a National Agenda for the Eighties, Washington D.C., 1980, 165–169).

17. The name comes from the area's proximity to Baragwanath Hospital and its overriding theme of linking together what apartheid tore apart.

18. This was done in order to distribute across formerly white local authorities responsibility for assisting poorer and fiscally weaker black townships.

19. In the USA, the state of Oregon plus several cities have enacted urban growth boundaries, which include incentives for growth within the boundary. See Knaap and Nelson (1992) and Nelson and Duncan (1995).

20. *De facto* redistribution from white to black areas is occurring through the privatization of police and education in white areas, removing these burdens on the public fisc (Paul Pereira, SAIRR, interview). In 1995, there were 100,000 policemen in South Africa, compared to 400,000 registered private security guards.

21. The overall tax burden of 25 percent of gross domestic product is high and unlikely to be increased to fund new programs. The public deficit in 1995 of 6.2 percent of Gross Domestic Product is very high by international standards; service costs on this debt were running at 18 percent of national budget (L. Schlemmer, interview).

22. An example is the need to invest new money in the health system to change it from a tertiary to a primary care emphasis which will save money in the longer term.

23. The University of South Africa's Bureau of Market Research estimated a needed economic growth rate of between 8 and 9 percent per year, given existing labor-capital ratios.

24. The "extended" labor force consists of people in formal employment, the unemployed, those in informal sectors, and those in marginal (i.e. subsistence agriculture) activities. It grew between 1980 and 1991 at 3.2 percent per year, and totaled 15.8 million people in 1991 (DBSA 1995b, 34).

25. These are what J. O'Connor (1973) calls "social capital expenditures."

26. Parastatals, or companies wholly owned by government, have assets worth more than R100 billion and employ about 210,000. They include telecommunications (Telkom), electricity supply (Eskom), airways (Sun Air), and weapons (Denel, formerly Armscor). Eskom is playing a major role in the extension of electricity to poor areas.

27. This would entail a likely splintering of the African National Congress into two political parties—a mainstream party accommodative of private enterprise, and a party advocating stronger state control.

PART FOUR

Conclusions

10

Urban Peace-Building

Contested cities do not change into post-conflict cities any more than socialist societies transform themselves readily into capitalist ones or the Cold War world changes into one of peace and reconciliation. Rather, the pathways of change appear indeterminate and variable. The processes of stabilization and reconstruction of contested cities, like the other processes, must be managed continuously and effectively by political and community leaders. Without progressive urban management, strife-torn environments may not be reconstituted or transformed, but rather reinforced by seemingly benign policy choices. Ethnic tribal needs for separation must not dictate city peace-building. Neither should the power and desires of economic actors to "normalize" the urban fabric be the primary guide for reconstruction. Policymakers should not have recourse to simply replacing an old ethnic state with a new neutral one.

The case studies of Belfast and Johannesburg have illustrated how urban policymakers acting amid uncertain and shifting political circumstances cope with the legacies and current manifestations of rival urban communities. In cities such as these two, urban policymakers endeavor to translate larger goals related to peacemaking and interethnic group stability into on-the-ground outcomes in urban arenas. Yet, a city introduces a set of characteristics—proximate ethnic neighborhoods, territoriality, economic interdependency, symbolism, and centrality—that can obstruct or promote peace-building at city and neighborhood levels. The urban arena is a complex and volatile system which can resist peace-building goals. City policies have made a difference in effecting change in ethnic relations in Northern Ireland and South Africa, but it is a mixed record. In Belfast, they have stabilized territoriality but hardened ethnic compartmentalization and urban sclerosis. In Johannesburg, they unwittingly played an instrumental role in creating the metropolitan conditions for apartheid's unsustainability and downfall. Today, however, urban policies threaten to obstruct urban reconstruction due to their reliance on private sector economic processes and imperatives.

Policy, Polarization, and Peace

The Belfast encapsulation of nationalistic conflict demonstrates the insufficiency of neutral policy intervention in a city of strict territoriality and shifting demographics. Antagonistic groups are both proximate and separate, creating a set of physical ethnic interfaces with both psychological and tangible benefits and costs to city residents and policymakers. An inordinately large public sector has been needed in response to a fraying society. Policy neutrality amidst ethnic strife, or "greyness where color matters," may be successful in not adding new sources of ethnic tension. Management of ethnic space in this way is viewed by the government as reacting to, and reflecting, residents' wishes, and as the best way to avoid exacerbation of sectarian tension. Yet, it appears incapable of creating coexistent viability of antagonistic communities because these two communities experience different needs and face contrasting future trajectories. Neutrality is associated with unequal outcomes, poor public perception, and ineffective upliftment of Belfast's economically deprived. In addition, when development agencies necessarily engage in tactics of engagement that deviate from color-neutral principles, these interventions occur on an ad-hoc and project-specific basis in the absence of a strategic framework of progressive ethnic management that could guide them. Because the urban arena is intimately connected to the prospective larger peace, the urban policy framework used for over 25 years aimed at maintenance and stability may no longer be appropriate. Urban policy should meet the demands of peace by redirecting its energies toward the vitality of people and community, not the protection of a lifeless and dysfunctional geography of hate.

The Johannesburg case shows not just the damage inflicted by partisan planning, but the tremendous obstacles that policymakers face in seeking to overcome its legacies. Even if societies are able to transcend partisanship and neutrality in their urban policymaking, it will likely require generations to effectively untie the knots of previous policies of domination and subjugation. Johannesburg faces many practical difficulties along the path of urban and societal transformation. Foremost is the need for there to be a delicate balancing of time. First, the phased reconstitution of basic structures of local and metropolitan governance was essential to societal transformation, but disruptive to the coherency of post-apartheid policymaking. In a transforming environment, policies must withstand, and evolve during, changing stakeholder membership and shifting structures. Second, post-apartheid city-building policies aspiring to stitch together apartheid's urban discontinuities and integrate the torn parts and peoples of Johannesburg must be prioritized and sequenced relative to two different, often conflicting, temporal imperatives. One deals with short-term, crisis-related needs; the other with the development of a longer-term framework conducive to metropolitan sustainability.

Apartheid planning in Johannesburg through the early 1990s substantiates the fallacy of partisan planning. The apartheid regime created an urban system fundamentally at odds with the majority of people using it. The narrow ground of apartheid Johannesburg was dissimilar to Belfast's in that there was no proximate and contentious residential territoriality of antagonistic groups. Rather, it was the functional and economic requirements of the city for cross-racial propinquity and interaction that complicated ethnonationalist governmental goals. Urban proximity was more a functional than spatial concept in apartheid Johannesburg. While urban policy and planning had an intimate and compatible connection with urban apartheid policy, its exercise in operationalizing apartheid ideology also highlighted the inevitable tensions and difficulties resulting from efforts to spatially segment functionally complex and interdependent components of the urban system. In the end, operationalization of apartheid exposed its serious faultlines and facilitated its seemingly abrupt transmutation. Today, urban policy amidst societal transformation demands critical self-reflection of the paradigms and assumptions of urban policy practice. Two distinctive planning paradigms now exist—one connected to town planning's historic affinity toward regulatory control; the other rooted in anti-apartheid community mobilization and linked to a more expansive definition of development. "Peace" in Johannesburg coexists alongside distressing conditions of unmet basic needs. Spatially, market-based "normalization" of Johannesburg will likely produce intraregional disparities that eclipse urban equity and spatial compaction efforts. Economically, market "corrections" to apartheid will produce a society deeply cleaved by class. The vitality and sustainability of a post-apartheid democracy are threatened by mass poverty and new forms of inequality. South African democracy is sustainable only if a collective sense of social justice is the primary criterion underlying public policy.

The two cities investigated share a common sorrow, but they also provide insight into the role and effects of government intervention in societies that are at different points along a continuum from disruptive strife to sustainable peace. The professional demeanor and neutral intentions associated with Belfast urban policy-making seek to suspend war and take some hesitant steps toward peace. The resolver and equity planning of Johannesburg is further toward peace, having begun the processes of transformation after addressing the root causes of conflict. Yet, this South African peace exposes a set of damaging and dehumanizing urban effects of ethnic warfare, problems that are still submerged in Belfast by the relative neutrality of policymaking. Similar to alcoholic drinkers who differ widely in the extent to which they confront their basic problems and defects, these two cities show disparate approaches to the root issues underlying urban ethnic conflict and tension. The Belfast policymaker is an abstainer who has stopped drinking for now but is doing little to change basic behaviors associated with imbibing, while the Johannesburg policymaker constitutes a recovering alcoholic who is addressing the basic underlying causes of urban conflict. As a requisite along this path of recovery, though, Johannesburg policymakers must deal with the gross and inhuman inequalities that led to interracial strife and state terrorism in the first place, and the severe psychological pains and scars that permeate black African society today. The pain felt by South Africans today is still to come in the future of Northern Ireland.

Three different tables of comparative information are presented to highlight differences and similarities across the case study cities.[1] Table 10.1 describes the differing contexts of conflict found in the contested cities. Table 10.2 emphasizes the diverging urban policy goals and strategies. And, Table 10.3 highlights the public sector and community participants and relationships involved in the implementation of each city's urban policies.

The cultural, psychological, and political aspects of ethnic conflict, as well as the spatial and economic characteristics of the urban arena, establish contexts which inform the more specific explorations of urban policy. In terms of the cultural nature of the conflict (Table 10.1, number 1), the South African conflict encompasses a clash between fundamental values and cultural meanings between an "advanced" north and a more "primitive," communitarian south. In contrast, both sides of the Protestant-Catholic clash in Northern Ireland use European terms of reference and encompass more an intracultural split. Paradoxically, the psychology of the conflict (2) in contemporary South Africa displays considerable intergroup reconciliation, pragmatism, and forgiveness. In contrast, the Northern Ireland conflict is as between ignorant strangers with a considerable degree of callousness. Conflict is experienced differently in the cities (3). The Northern Ireland conflict is experienced as parochial and peripheral, while the South African conflict in many ways is felt as one of several primary examples in the world of disconnection between the developed and developing world.

In terms of political power in the societies (4), power in Belfast has been held over the past 25 years by a third party from the outside—the British government—although argument over this characterization is part of the conflict itself. In democratic Johannesburg, the formerly excluded are now in formal control of the government, yet de facto control over the city's future is likely exercised by a combination of governmental, domestic private, and international investors and funders. The nature of security in the urban arenas, as well as the means toward achieving this sense of safety, bears differences and similarities (5). In Belfast, interpersonal security from political and targeted violence is emphasized that encourages segregation and physical partition of competing ethnic groups. Ethnic groups have retreated—under governmental oversight—into their respective territories amidst the hell of urban civil war. Contemporary Johannesburg's security emphasizes criminal and random violence more than the politically targeted or in-

TABLE 10.1   Contexts of Conflict

1. Cultural Nature of Conflict

Belfast	Intraculture split. No abyss of cultures. North-south/east-west components but both within European context.
Johannesburg	Clash between cultures. European versus African. North versus south. "Modern" versus "primitive." Individualism versus communitarianism (*ubuntu*).

2. Psychology of Conflict

Belfast	Conflict out of ignorance; learning about/through stereotypes. "Strangers."
Johannesburg	Apartheid: Afrikaners threatened without a home, black Africans dominated in their home. Post-apartheid: Pragmatic white minority, forgiving black majority.

3. Felt Significance of Conflict

Belfast	Parochial, peripheral.
Johannesburg	Developed world/developing world.

4. Power

Belfast	A third party from outside.
Johannesburg	The formerly excluded in formal control of government, but de facto control over future exercised also by domestic private sector and international overseers.

5. Security and Threat

Belfast	Interpersonal security through segregation and partition of ethnic groups.
Johannesburg	Interpersonal security from criminal and random violence more than group-based safety from political and targeted violence. Defense of white residential territoriality from invasion by black poor.

6. Urban Scale

Belfast	Proximity and tight quarters.
Johannesburg	Distorted and sprawled. Geography of racism.

7. Urban Segregation

Belfast	Segregation/ethnic geography strict.
Johannesburg	Ethnic geography fluid; desegregation started during last years of apartheid. Maintenance of segregation post-apartheid will be based on class more than race.

8. Use and Meaning of Land

Belfast	Different demands on land due to Protestant-Catholic divergent demographic profiles.
Johannesburg	White-black divergent views concerning landownership and planning.

9. Urban Growth Prospects

Belfast	Stagnancy and limited growth. A city of the economic past.
Johannesburg	Uneven and uncertain. Includes a modern, advanced economy.

spired violence of the apartheid years. Whereas during apartheid the major means of creating white security was through state terrorism and crude racial separation, today it involves increasing the defensibility of individual residential areas and actions. Retreat, defense, and fortification of whites in Johannesburg today reinforce racial compartmentalization in the face of political and economic processes that threaten to infiltrate it. The geographic scale of an urban arena of conflict (6) presents different sets of obstacles and opportunities to policymakers interested in peaceful urban coexistence. Belfast's scale is one of tight quarters and proximity, with limited opportunities for spatial distance between antagonistic sides. Middle-class migration to suburbs outside the city does enlarge the scale of the urban system, but not necessarily the scale of conflict because greater interethnic accommodation more commonly occurs in Belfast's suburbs. Johannesburg's scale is dispersed and distorted, characterized by extreme sprawl and racial and functional separation. Spatial distance was used directly and aggressively as a means of achieving the political goals of apartheid, creating a disfigured and dysfunctional geography of racism.

Related to geographic scale is the degree of segregation between ethnic groups (7). Belfast has strict ethnic segregation in the sense that warring sides do not live next to each other on the same street. Ethnic segregation in Johannesburg, meanwhile, is experiencing greater flux, with residential "greying" initiated well before the formal end of apartheid. Nevertheless, a probable future is a resegregation based on class occurring within the larger desegregative trends in the Johannesburg urban region. The use and meaning of the land resource in contested cities commonly have underlying political and cultural meanings (8). In Belfast, different demands put upon the land resource are caused by contrasting demographic trajectories. A faster growing Catholic population puts pressure on government to find underutilized "orange" land for housing and community purposes. The declining Protestant population, meanwhile, fights adamantly to maintain existing ethnic territoriality, pushing for government programs that might bring suburbanized Protestants back into the city. In contrast, in Johannesburg the use and meaning of land have culturally based dissimilarities between white and black Africans. The commodification of land by the white society is distinguishable from a communitarian ethnic of land use and ownership among black Africans. These cultural differences are today being translated into post-apartheid urban policy, where the old planning of the white regime emphasizing control and regulation is being usurped by a development planning model emphasizing community empowerment as the core part of its identity. Finally, the prospects for urban economic growth (9) provide a context that can either disrupt or stabilize ethnic conditions in a city. Belfast has been in the unfortunate position over the last three decades of dealing with sectarian strife amidst a context of economic stagnancy and socioeconomic deprivation. The "zero-sum" character of ethnic conflict becomes highlighted in such a circumstance of scarce economic resources. The growth prospects of Johannesburg are more uncertain, and are also more determinative of that city's future. A modern, advanced economy exists alongside widespread poverty and an informal, survivalist economy, while international capital remains hesitant despite a fiscal conservatism adopted by the government consistent with the wishes of international financial overseers.

I compare in Table 10.2, and subsequently discuss, the specific urban policy goals, strategies, and techniques used in the two cities. These contrasts constitute the core part of the research project, investigating the characteristics of urban policymaking amidst city polarization and peace-building. Government goals (1) assert the ends toward which public actions are to be guided in a society of conflicting ethnic groups. In both Northern Ireland and contemporary South Africa, government goals transcend group-based loyalties. In the Northern Ireland case, this is because public authority has been held by a third-party overseer; in the case of contemporary South Africa, it is because public goals stress civic, not ethnic, nationalism. The British government, in its urban policymaking in Belfast, emphasizes violence prevention and urban ethnic stability as its overriding goal. The primary policy goal in contemporary Johannesburg pertains to urban-based reconciliation and normalization.

Urban operationalization (2) in a contested city seeks to derive from often abstract political goals—be they security and control, stability, or reconciliation—a set of practical objectives that direct day-to-day urban policy decisions. In Belfast, violence prevention and urban stability are to be achieved through a neutral stance by government that seeks noninflammatory treatment of each ethnic group but otherwise suffers from a limited strategic view toward solving practical urban problems. In Johannesburg, reconciling past urban divisions requires transformation in both decisionmaking structures and policy techniques. On the ground, reconciliation is to occur spatially through urban integration, compaction, and the stitching together of the torn and disfigured metropolitan fabric. Fundamental disagreements over the policy strategies and techniques that would secure urban reconciliation and normalization, however, indicate that implementation of even harmonious goals or ideologies may be difficult in urban systems containing complex influences and relationships. It is interesting to observe that both Belfast and Johannesburg political leaders speak a similar language of stability and security, yet the urban forms policymakers are seeking to create to obtain these goals are extraordinarily different. In pursuit of urban stability, the British government in Belfast condones strict ethnic territoriality reinforced by physical partitions. The British government's focus on security at the individual level lends itself to urban segregation and containment strategies. In contrast, security and stability in democratic Johannesburg are to come through a greater diversity of urban fabric that undermines racial compartmentalization and exclusion. What is thought in the

TABLE 10.2   Urban Peace-Building Goals, Strategies, and Techniques

1. Governmental Goal (Ideology)
Belfast   Violence prevention and stability.
Johannesburg   Reconciliation and normalization.

2. Urban Operationalization
Belfast   *Neutralize*—manage ethnic territoriality in a way that accepts physical barri-
               ers, but otherwise sacrifices strategic policymaking.
Johannesburg   *Transform*—restructure urban decisionmaking and policy techniques toward
               urban integration, compaction, and connecting torn fabric.

3. Urban Policy Strategy
Belfast   Neutral.
Johannesburg   Resolver; equity ("bounded").

4. Policy and Ethnic Identification
Belfast   "Color-neutrality" in order not to disturb volatile territoriality.
Johannesburg   Nonracialism.

5. Spatial Techniques
Belfast   City divisions as increasing manageability; viewed as necessary. Environmen-
               tal methods of diffusing interface tensions.
Johannesburg   Integration, compaction, densification, upgrading.

6. Policy "Lens"
Belfast   Territoriality (fine-grained). Micro-scale (neighborhoods, housing estates).
Johannesburg   Temporality. Short-term stabilization and longer-term management.

7. Spending Allocation
Belfast   Spending allocation influenced by combination of objective needs and politi-
               cal demands.
Johannesburg   Equity spending to poor and marginalized communities, but "bounded" by
               ability to pay criterion, budget limits.

8. Planning Potency
Belfast   Planning passive, reacting to perceived demands (for separation and secu-
               rity). Hesitant to facilitate change toward a different urban future. Shy away
               from moral responsibility.
Johannesburg   Planning potentially active. Facilitate reconstruction. Moral obligation to re-
               dress past wrongs. Unsure state roles and fiscal discipline may constrain
               planning role.

9. Planning and Bias
Belfast   Perception of bias; presence of conspiracy theories. Alternative explanations
               subordinate to perceptions. Perceptions of policy tied to larger feelings of
               isolation and community threat.
Johannesburg   Historical legacy necessitates a new orientation and vocabulary of planning.
               Development planning may help legitimate discredited town planning pro-
               fession.

Belfast case to suspend conflict is viewed in the Johannesburg case as instrumental in intensifying intergroup disparities and conflict.

Each of the urban policy strategies (3) elucidated in chapter 2 is represented in the case study cities. In the histories of both cities, conflict was created and intensified by *partisan* policymaking which built unequal opportunities, marginalization, and exclusion into the metropolitan fabric. Both cities have had to deal with the human and urban legacies of partisan government (in Northern Ireland, by Protestant rule 1920–1972; in South Africa, by white governing regimes in the twentieth century). In Belfast since 1972, the British government's strategy to deal pragmatically on an impartial, professionalized basis with the day-to-day, local-level symptoms of sovereignty conflict constitutes the *neutral* approach. Removal of the urban policymaking function to an extralocal level sought to remove territorial questions from the local level and to depoliticize planning. Belfast metropolitan plans commonly downplayed or disregarded the role played by ethnic conflict in fundamentally shaping the city's social geography. Intergroup equity issues are excluded from metropolitan plans, public housing allotment formulae utilize color-blind procedures, and town planning marginalizes itself by separating its spatial planning concerns from the broader social concerns of housing, social services, and ethnic relations.

Post-apartheid Johannesburg illustrates two roles that urban policymakers have played during the demise of apartheid. From 1991 to 1995, urban officials engaged as *resolvers* of core issues during the transformation of local and metropolitan governance in the urban region. Officials of the old regime, nongovernmental representatives, and those from the formerly excluded black communities collaborated in a self-transformative process that changed the basic parameters of representation, decisionmaking, participation, organizational structure, and urban goals. Local leaders recognized that black political empowerment and restructuring of local governance were necessary prerequisites to effective post-apartheid city-building. Thus, metropolitan negotiators transcended a sole emphasis on urban symptoms of racial polarization and targeted the need to radically transform the basic parameters of apartheid-based urban governance. City-building issues dealing with day-to-day consumption problems and the black boycotting of service charges were successfully connected by nongovernmental and opposition organizations to root political empowerment issues. Since local and metropolitan elections in late 1995, the urban policy strategy in Johannesburg has been more focused on *equity* objectives. This strategy seeks to address the horrendous urban symptoms of past racial conflict by lessening the gross disparities in urban opportunities and outcomes across races. Mechanisms and goals of urban policymaking were restructured toward city-building which would facilitate empowerment and peaceful urban coexistence. The effectiveness of such an equity approach in Johannesburg, however, is constrained, or "bounded," by multiple realities—the sheer magnitude of urban black needs, land- and market-based obstacles to spatially re-structuring housing and economic opportunities within the metropolitan region, restricted "ability to pay" for basic services on the part of black customers, a cul-ture of government illegitimacy, and budgetary restraints owing to fiscal conser-vatism and international financial requirements.

The identification and treatment of ethnicity by urban policymaking (4) is de-rived from government goals and strategies. In Belfast, one of the primary aims of government policy has been to establish and maintain itself as a color-neutral par-ticipant not biased toward either "orange" (Protestant) or "green" (Catholic). In Johannesburg, nonracialism in governmental policy is an understandable response to apartheid's hyperactive era of racial identification. Urban services and benefits are to be delivered based on individual needs, not channeled to areas solely based on their ethnic compositions. In addition, legal and institutional barriers are to be removed that discriminated against blacks and other ethnic groups. The appropri-ateness of nonracial policies can be contested, however. First, the principle can obstruct equity policies that target racial groups for remedial, or affirmative, ac-tion. Second, nonracialism overlooks other forms of class-based inequality that re-main active in Johannesburg. It is provocative to note that governments in both Belfast and Johannesburg seek to downplay the ethnic/racial dimension in future policymaking; yet, Johannesburg's nonracialism allows for greater equity-based targeting of resources to blacks than Belfast's neutral policy stance allows in terms of redistributing resources to Catholics. That urban policymakers may adopt dif-ferent means toward achieving the same general goal of diminishing group affilia-tions illuminates the nondeterministic nature of city-building amidst broader im-peratives.

In order for urban policy strategies to physically shape the city, specific spatial techniques (5) must be applied to the urban arena. These techniques are viewed through a policy "lens" (6) based on larger spatial or societal contexts. Belfast ur-ban policy attempts to diffuse intergroup tensions along interfaces by sustaining each group's territoriality. The "lens" is a fine-grained territorial one, with segre-gation occurring at a micro-scale between proximate neighborhoods and even sin-gle housing estates. The tight territoriality of Belfast increases the likelihood that relatively minor government actions involving development or service provision will set off local unrest, and can explain much of the hesitancy of government planners to engage in actions that might be construed as disruptive of the territo-rial status quo. The spatial techniques of contemporary Johannesburg emphasize restructuring the urban system to increase urban compaction (densification) and integration and the upgrading of marginalized peripheral black settlement areas. The territorial legacies of apartheid's coarse-grained, macro-scale racial separa-tion create a fundamental matrix of inequality in today's Johannesburg. Yet, the more significant policy "lens" for contemporary policymakers is one of temporality rather than territoriality. Two imperatives consistently confront post-apartheid policymakers in seeking the transformation of the urban system—the demands for the short-term stabilization of a dysfunctional metropolis, and the need for the creation of a policy framework for longer-term regional development. Specific choices by urban policymakers concerning the prioritization of these two temporal imperatives will have significant effects on whether urban policy spatially transforms or reinforces the urban region's racial geography.

In addition to policies that affect the spatial distribution of growth in the urban region, city governments also allocate urban services and spending across ethnic neighborhoods (7). Objective needs and political demands in Belfast have commonly become entangled in determining urban spending decisions. This is so because strictly needs-based allocations (such as public housing construction) that commonly favor Catholics are seen as threats by Protestants to their community viability and may thus stimulate intergroup tension. In areas such as employment, major questions remain regarding whether equality of opportunity requires removal of discriminatory barriers only, or affirmative action that compensates for past disparity in treatment or current structural obstacles. Johannesburg's urban spending is equity-focused and based on objective needs, providing land, shelter, and/or bulk public services (water, sewer, and electricity) to the residents of poor and marginalized black communities. However, this equity spending is handicapped by tight budgetary constraints and the limited ability of poverty-ridden residents to pay for the ongoing costs of urban services.

The strength of the planning and policymaking function (8) contrasts sharply in the two cities. In apartheid South Africa, partisan policies required forceful regulation and development actions to create and maintain white advantage and to reinforce domination. In contemporary Johannesburg, policymaking will likely need to be active and strong to redress past wrongs, facilitate reconstruction, and overcome market-based reinforcement of apartheid geography. However, the potency of the policy function in the future is still unclear and potentially inhibited by fiscal conservatism and the weak capacity of African public administration. In contrast, Belfast policymaking has been passive, seeking to suspend sectarian tensions by managing ethnic space in a way that reacts to, and reflects, residents' wishes. In both cities, urban policymaking has been or currently is associated with bias (9). The bias in contemporary Belfast's policymaking is more perceived than actual. Conspiracy theories by both communities claim that urban policy has sought ends that intentionally harm one ethnic group or the other. Whether it is claims of "de-Protestantizing" neighborhoods, or the punishment of republican Catholic ones, feelings of community isolation and threat drive perceptions more than actual policy outcomes. The bias of past Johannesburg's urban policymaking—aligned with hierarchy, racism, and regulatory control—has discredited the town planning profession today. In the emerging development planning paradigm, planning is being redirected toward the enabling of empowerment and capacity building in the name of social justice. The new form of planning in Johannesburg is seeking to build a new orientation and vocabulary that is participatory, facilitative, and empowering.

The contextual qualities of city conflict and the urban-specific characteristics of policy goals, strategies, and techniques have now been discussed. Table 10.3 next explores the significant policymaking participants and relationships in both cities. The formulation and implementation of urban policy amidst ethnic polarization and peace-building can generate internal tension within the implementing government. This includes conflicts in purpose between agencies at a common level of government, or between two or more levels of government. Policy implementation can also substantially influence a sense of community on the part of an ethnic group and the development of a viable set of nongovernmental institutions.

Two different foci of urban policymaking exist—a regulatory capacity that seeks to manage future development through plan-making and ordinances; and a developmental capacity that seeks to promote and otherwise facilitate urban growth (1). Whereas the former creates a framework for city growth, the latter is more involved in project-specific changes to the urban landscape. In an ethnically polarized city undergoing peace-building efforts, these policy foci should be integrated to support a post-conflict vision. In Belfast, the regulatory part of town planning in Belfast has absolved itself from issues of ethnic tension and management, forfeiting its potential role in outlining urban principles of ethnic coexistence. Absent this ethnic planning framework, development agencies have stepped into the void and, out of necessity, undertaken project-specific actions that explicitly recognize the city's ethnic divide. The result is that ethnic planning is reduced to a set of ad-hoc and tactical responses to ethnicity, rather than seeking its proactive and strategic management. In apartheid Johannesburg, much compatibility existed between apartheid's racial dictates regarding development and local land use regulation. The post-apartheid transformation of urban policymaking includes its restructuring away from solely spatial and regulatory emphases to include grassroots-oriented development and capacity building. The emergent development planning function may use the constructive aspects of "old" regulatory planning, or decide to abandon them entirely.

In addition to the intralevel relations above, there exist important interlevel (central-regional-local) aspects of urban policy formulation and implementation (2). The local planning function in both cities is, or has been, shaped or preempted by national planning objectives. It is provocative to consider that urban policy has required centralization in order both to embed government policy within the ethnic arena (apartheid Johannesburg) and seek to remove it neutrally above the partisan fray (Belfast). The question in contemporary South Africa is whether central-

TABLE 10.3   Participants and Relationships

1. Planning: Developmental Versus Regulatory

Belfast	Development part of planning dominates regulatory. Regulatory planning limited role and power. Development agencies more explicitly recognize ethnic issues. Relationship between regulatory and development arms not constructive.
Johannesburg	Planning being redefined to broaden scope beyond regulatory and spatial foci. Tension between development planning and town planning. Potential for significant split between "old" and "new" planning. Regulatory/control planning must adapt to survive.

2. Local and Central Relations

Belfast	Local government impotent amidst central policies of neutrality and inattention.
Johannesburg	Local/central government relations being defined. Legacy of local government illegitimacy. Local capacity seen as key to implementation of central policies. Provincial government may intervene if/when local capacity insufficient.

3. Local Politics

Belfast	Unionist councilors reinforce divisions amidst demographic decline of constituents. No Catholic boycott. Sinn Fein part of local politics since 1981.
Johannesburg	Need to legitimize local government and deliver urban services to the marginalized. Capacity question. Local government transformation one year after national/provincial. Boundary-drawing to cope with apartheid geography.

4. Community

Belfast	Goal of community identity and self-sufficiency for each side.
Johannesburg	Torn and crippled black communities. Greying process in inner city presents possibility of integrated stable communities.

5. Civil Society

Belfast	Two civil societies or one? Problematic relationship between community development (single-identity work) and cross-community efforts.
Johannesburg	Role in new South Africa unclear. Limited due to end of struggle, government legitimacy, and transfer of community leadership.

ization may also be needed to reconstruct and equalize a torn society, and how this fits or contradicts post-apartheid imperatives regarding local empowerment. The Belfast case represents an extreme intergovernmental case, with direct rule having removed decisionmaking authority from local policymaking bodies. Because it emphasizes vertical and tactical policy rather than comprehensive, or lateral, planning, this centralization of urban policymaking in Northern Ireland fragmented government initiatives among numerous extralocal bodies. Thus, land use/spatial concerns become detrimentally separated (as in the 1987 Belfast Urban Area Plan) from related issues of housing, social services, and ethnic relations. Lacking an effective local political forum capable of making "trade-off" decisions across policy areas, urban policy becomes the net outcome of a set of uncoordinated, single-function centralized interventions. In apartheid Johannesburg, local initiative regarding land use regulation was subsumed within the strong central state-led spatial planning of apartheid. Today, the legacies of local government weakness and illegitimacy present major roadblocks to the implementation of central government reconstruction policies. In designing intergovernmental relations in the new Johannesburg, two imperatives are at odds—integrated control of government spending to effect meaningful urban change; and distribution of resources to allow for dispersed power and community consultation.

The handicapped and distorted nature of local governance is evident in both cities (3). The local political level in Belfast, partly owing to its impotent character, has been a platform for derisive nationalistic fervor. The inclusion of the republican wing of Catholic politics—Sinn Fein—in local politics since 1981 fueled the confrontational and divisive quality of local politics. Faced with Sinn Fein's presence, and the erosion of its constituent base through demographic decline, Unionist local politicians have felt cornered and commonly reinforce and intensify city divisions through their rhetoric. The transformation of local government in Johannesburg came over a year later than national and provincial restructuring. Nonetheless, drawing of new municipal and ward-electoral boundaries appears successful in eradicating former white-black political separation, and in empowering blacks at city and metropolitan government levels. Challenges remain, however. After decades of minority-controlled local government, post-apartheid democratically elected local politicians in Johannesburg must now redirect budgetary values toward the marginalized amidst a legacy of local government illegitimacy, black nonpayment boycotts, and undeveloped local administrative capacity.

The sense of local community amidst ethnic polarization and contested government can take a beating (4). In Belfast, community is intimately connected to territoriality. The symbols of identity—religious institutions, schools, language, murals—are of paramount importance to the maintenance of ethnic territoriality. A minority but demographically ascending Catholic population, together with a majority but declining Protestant population, creates a difficult condition whereby both communities feel under threat. In Johannesburg, a great number of black communities have been either torn by violence or crippled by apartheid limitations on housing, services, and commercial development. A key question in contemporary Johannesburg involves whether the desegregation ("greying") of inner-city neighborhoods will result in resegregated black ghettos or socioeconomically stabilized neighborhoods with some integration of races and incomes. The welfare of existing black communities and their local organizations will be partly dependent upon whether government actions disperse or consolidate black neighborhoods. Internal and natural divisions within Catholic and black South African populations have enabled urban governing regimes to manipulate political resistance through the intentional exploitation and intensification of these cleavages. In Belfast, political vetting of funds for community development sought to enhance a split between nationalists and republicans that is in part driven by differing economic circumstances and an inherent disagreement over appropriate political strategy. In apartheid Johannesburg, government actions intensified differences between African National Congress and Inkatha Freedom Party supporters and those between ethnic Xhosas and Zulus.

Civil society is that layer of nongovernmental organizations (NGOs) and community-based organizations that exists between community and government (5). In antagonistic settings, where normal channels of political expression are blocked by government, NGOs can play key roles in expressing opposition to government policy and legitimacy, enabling political opportunities at the urban level for an aggrieved party, and nurturing local organizing capacity on the part of an out-group. In the absence of effective local government in Belfast, local NGOs have been critical in bringing community needs and demands to the British government. It is a city, however, characterized by dual civil societies. This presents a dilemma to government as to whether it should assist the development of each community separately or work to bridge NGO work through cross-community efforts. The role of NGOs in the new Johannesburg is unclear. A vibrant and resilient civil society during the "struggle" has been paradoxically weakened by the success of the political transformation for which it was working. NGOs must find their appropriate niche in a democratic South Africa, amid government legitimacy and transfer of community leadership to public positions.

Stabilizing and Reconstructing Contested Cities

Contested cities such as Johannesburg and Belfast are urban organisms transformed into symbols of wider group-based territorial and political claims. Confronted with this difficult mixture of ethnic and nationalist issues and local service disputes, urban policymakers in the two cities studied have used different approaches—partisan (apartheid Johannesburg), neutral (contemporary Belfast), resolver (transition-period Johannesburg), and equity (contemporary Johannesburg). Urban policymaking assumes a critical role in efforts to operationalize broader ideologies and political goals related to peace-building. In Belfast, urban policy is directed at stabilizing urban ethnic relations amid potential hostilities and uncertain political advances. In post-apartheid Johannesburg, it is connected to urban restructuring and ethnic reconciliation subsequent to the country's historic negotiated political settlement. Whereas Belfast seeks to preserve existing urban territoriality, Johannesburg seeks to transform and democratize metropolitan geography. In both cases, urban policymakers seek to give concrete meaning to peace-building goals such as stability, reconciliation, reconstruction, security, and fairness. Yet, urban operationalization of peace-building imperatives is neither mundane nor straightforward, but rather capable of producing contradictions, internal tensions, and adverse consequences.

In Belfast, the containment and abeyance of conflict have been primary motivations behind the urban policy of the British government. The main means toward conflict containment—the condoning and formalization of ethnic separation through housing, planning, community development, and "peaceline" policies—will likely provide short-term stability at the expense of longer-term opportunities for intergroup negotiation and reconciliation. A centralized technocratic approach that separates development goals from ethnic realities might suspend community power struggles, but it will contribute little toward solving them. Intergroup conflict may be contained in the short term, at the same time that Protestant-Catholic divisions are perpetuated by a hardening of territorial identities that may paralyze the city long after any political restructuring of Northern Ireland. The limitations of a distant, professional planning approach in polarized cities are exposed in Belfast. Because urban institutions in a polarized city are often rejected by the minority group, such government intervention will, at worst, exacerbate conflict or, at best, be unsuccessful in ameliorating macro-conflict. This is so because municipal planning concerned with how material resources are distributed sidesteps the root causes of sovereignty conflict. During the past three decades, while the Belfast Protestant majority might view British rule as bearable, the Catholic minority has viewed it as a top-down reinforcement, if not imposition, of the Protestant majority's ideology. Despite hard-earned praise in specific policy areas (such as public housing allocation), it is ironic that a policy approach which seeks neutrality creates a gap in community connectiveness that is filled in by conspiratorial theories on both sides of the ethnic divide. Protestants focus on policymakers' apparent efforts to displace "orange" neighborhoods to make room for Catholics, while Catholics equate policymakers' inability to meet objective urban needs with their political allegiance to a United Kingdom inclusive of Northern Ireland.

Centralized policymaking as practiced in Belfast has created a local political atmosphere of reaction and dependency, one that obstructs the emergence of cross-community forums that might mediate ethnic tensions. Lacking local political forums, urban policy commonly puts local community groups in defensive postures which tend to solidify intergroup antagonisms. Similarly, community development efforts within an ethnic neighborhood aimed at supplying needed self-confidence and capacity to a threatened area also lead more often to ghettoization and interneighborhood competition than to Catholic-Protestant bridge-building and cooperation. The legacies of community activism in the absence of local democracy, and in rejecting or criticizing urban authority, have created a multilayered terrain upon which constructive government-community partnerships must be built.

The neutral policymaking of Belfast will lessen relative group deprivation between Protestants and Catholics. Intergroup material conditions will not intensify differential political claims, as occurs when partisan planning is exercised. However, the inability of urban policy to significantly affect the deep extent of socioeconomic deprivation across *both* Protestant and Catholic populations maintains an environment that punishes community confidence and debilitates efforts to improve sectarian relations. In addition, a symptomatic approach to the polarized city focused on material conditions is inherently incapable of effectively dealing with the political roots of urban ethnic territoriality and dysfunctionality. Postponement of political instability may have been achieved, but with tremendous opportunity costs incurred along the way. The reactive protection of the status quo by a policy aimed at neutrality, maintenance, and stability defends a dysfunctional and sterile territoriality, and reinforces the physical and psychological correlates of urban civil war. If urban policy is to shift direction so that it is part of the change process toward peace, and not a burden to it, it must direct its energies toward the vitality of people and community, not the protection of a petrified territoriality that reifies mutually exclusive political positions. It must shift part of its stabilization energies toward the restructuring and reconstituting of Belfast's sectarian landscape.

In South Africa, it was within urban arenas such as Johannesburg that apartheid's most serious faultlines and contradictions were exposed. The horrendous conditions of societal instability were suppressible only through attempts to "purify" urban apartheid of its inevitable tensions and operational difficulties and through state-sponsored terrorism. Major apartheid conflicts disproportionately occurred in and around the Johannesburg area and had spreading effects to the rest of the country. The boycotting of school classes to protest the introduction of Afrikaans in Soweto stimulated the riots of 1976 and 1977. The Witwatersrand region was the major center of unrest in the 1984 and 1985 violence—accounting for 39 percent of all political deaths nationwide (Hewitt 1993). In 1993, violence in the East Rand townships of Katlehong, Tokoza, and Vosloorus was instigated in part by the circumstances of the physical environment—proximity of hostel, shack settlers and township formal tenants amidst scarce resources. The Reef violence spread to other areas of the country in 1993, constituting South Africa's most fatal period of violence in its modern history. Apartheid Johannesburg was a center of hope as well as despair. It became the focal point of local reconciliation efforts in South Africa. The signing of the Soweto Accord between white and black authorities, and the subsequent creation of the Metropolitan Chamber, predated other local and metropolitan transformations in South Africa and established important models of governmental restructuring that informed other metropolitan efforts and national legislation pertaining to post-apartheid local government.

Today, resolution of the root political causes of city-based conflict coexists with distressing conditions of unmet basic needs. There is a palpable sense of forgiveness on the part of the black population, and a certain pragmatism and acceptance on the part of whites. Yet, the absolutely essential and remarkable resolution of root political issues in South Africa will not, by itself, better interracial relations. Amidst a legacy of race hatred that permeated the urban landscape and created intense structural inequalities, there must be workable and equitable tactics of governability. Whether a young democracy that faces international fiscal constraints and internal capacity limitations will be capable of such effective equity policymaking is an open question. It is likely that urban policymaking will be partially successful in lessening black-white relative group deprivation. However, the urban spatial and functional legacies of apartheid's distortions will be long-lasting and will apply major structural "brakes" to Johannesburg's movement toward equity. Spatially, market-based "normalization" of Johannesburg will likely produce intraregional disparities that eclipse urban equity and spatial compaction efforts. Economically, market "corrections" to apartheid will produce a society deeply cleaved by class. Nonethnic, class-based factors will increasingly replace ethnic engineering as allocators of goods and resources in the new South Africa.

The vitality and sustainability of a post-apartheid democracy are threatened by mass poverty and new forms of inequality. Gaps between black aspirations and improvements to their quality of existence may lead to growing unease among the populace. Frustration by government with the pace and extent of service delivery could lead to the rejection of legitimate community consultation as part of policy-making. With major portions of its population abandoned to the margins of social life, Johannesburg and other urban areas would contain major centers of criminality and alienation disconnected from democratic structures. Having one of the highest criminally motivated violence rates in the world, violence in Johannesburg has been democratized as property-related crime increasingly targets white South Africans that were immune from earlier periods of violence. A resulting culture of paranoia on the part of the middle and upper classes would reinforce and strengthen social, spatial, and economic partitions between the have's and the have-not's. Amidst post-apartheid class and social divisions, an increasing statism and authoritarianism would likely emerge in an effort to stabilize and hold together the fractured society. Politically, this would entail a splintering of the umbrella African National Congress into two political parties—a mainstream party accommodative of private enterprise, and a party advocating stronger state control. The vitality of the new democratic system will be threatened by the tremendous demands put upon it.

*   *   *

Processes of stabilization, recovery, and reconstruction differ from normal city-building and planning, and urban operationalization of peace-building goals stresses and challenges basic assumptions and practices of policymaking. Beneath the surface of urban strategies lie the motivations and rationales of urban policymakers and planners who operate daily in ethnically polarized cities. In Belfast, policymakers' public stance of "color-neutrality" has separated urban planning from ethnic realities. The overly technocratic and compartmentalized character of town planning, specifically, is symptomatic of a profession which has retreated from contributing on a strategic or comprehensive basis to ethnic management. Despite the land use and territorially based implications of much of sectarianism, town planning, whose professional foundation is land use, has played a minor role in addressing ethnicity. In contrast to government's public stance, ethnic sensitivity on the part of policymakers and bureaucrats in internal discussions is acute and figures prominently in decisionmaking. There are also emerging urban policy approaches that consider more progressively the city's sectarian realities. Yet, policymakers remain hesitant to speak explicitly in public forums about ethnicity and urban policy, and the emerging strands of innovative ethnic policy remain isolated and disconnected from a broader vision of progressive ethnic management.

The psychology of urban policymaking in Johannesburg—in both apartheid and contemporary periods—is provocative. Compatibility between centralized dictates regarding apartheid racial sorting and urban land use regulation existed, with planners providing race-blind professional devices and rationales that implemented and consolidated the goals of apartheid racial segregation. Those local and metropolitan planners interviewed reflected on their roles in apartheid city-building with mixed emotions which were always introspective and difficult. These included operational detachment from apartheid ideology, defensiveness, denial, and nostalgia for the clearer planning methodology of the past. Urban policymakers from that era confront today in their minds and actions their past alignment with coercive and dominating forces. Contemporary urban policymaking in Johannesburg is undergoing a critical self-evaluation of the paradigms and assumptions of its practice. Two distinctive psychologies of planning exist alongside each other: (1) town planning with its historic affinity toward regulatory control; and (2) development planning rooted in anti-apartheid mobilization and linked to a more facilitative and empowering model of development. Development planning seeks to create a system of social guidance that utilizes the legacy and lessons of social mobilization and community activism. Those within this embryonic field whom I interviewed stressed the practice-based and crisis-linked learning process they are involved in, and highlighted their ability to speak two languages—that of the community and that of government. In the face of this clearly ascendent development planning function, traditional town planners are reacting in ways ranging from defensive rigidity, to counterattack, to uncertainty, to productive acceptance of the need to change assumptions and techniques.

* * *

Cities independently affect the relationship between the goals of a civic, ethnic accommodating ideology and peace-building outcomes, but in ways that are complex and not easily predicted. This is not to suggest that political and ideological
imperatives do not significantly shape contested cities. Indeed, competing ethnic
tribes in Belfast have spawned aberrant peacelines throughout the urban tissue and
a government ideology of "color-neutrality" since direct rule has produced an
equally anomalous dichotomized urban policy. And in South Africa, the apartheid
policy of separateness had tremendous impacts in producing the inhumane and
gross urban landscape of the Johannesburg region. Nevertheless, cities introduce
a set of characteristics—proximate ethnic neighborhoods, territoriality, economic interdependency, symbolism, centrality—not present to such an extent on
wider geographic scales. And, these urban features can bend or distort—for better or worse—the relationship between political goals (be they peace-building or
partisan) and their urban manifestations. Policy and planning decisions regarding
land use, housing, economic development, and service delivery can independently
moderate or harden intergroup cleavages. Because urban policymakers and planners affect through their daily decisions important spatial and psychological elements of the politicized urban geography, they are not impotent in the face of
strong political winds, but rather important mediating agents. In operationalizing
peace at the city scale, urban policymakers can be either facilitative or obstructive
agents.

    The urban system appears too complex and multidimensional to be fully
molded by civic ideologies of peace-building. This is due, in part, to the inherent
difficulties of defining on a concrete level the operative forms of often abstract
ideology. In Belfast, the government goal of violence prevention and stability has
been operationalized as a policy strategy that condones separation and containment of ethnic groups. Yet, this reactive local policy approach accepting of community divisions is not the single self-evident operationalization of the government's goal of urban stability. In contemporary Johannesburg, the government
goal of urban normalization does not self-evidently connote a particular urban
spatial arrangement nor the appropriate roles for government and private interests in such a reconstruction process. It is frequently not possible to express fundamental ideologies in terms of clear-cut urban methods and techniques. Such
ambiguity provides urban policymaking with its semi-autonomous space.

    Urban operationalization thus becomes capable of generating unforeseen con-
sequences and contradictions that endanger peace-building goals themselves. In
Belfast, significant practical problems are associated with a color-neutral policy
approach amidst differing objective and perceptual community needs. And, significantly, such a "hands-off" approach toward ethnicity aimed at the containment of

violence and the achievement of an urban equilibrium likely strengthens in the long term the urban conditions of sectarian compartmentalization conducive to intergroup instability. Seemingly successful in operationalizing fundamental ideology, British urban policymakers may find themselves paradoxically sustaining the very conditions of urban volatility that government goals were formulated to avoid. In South Africa, the formal ideology of apartheid, when squeezed through the tight urban web of Johannesburg, became distorted, modified, and finally abandoned. The social and economic interdependencies inherent in the urban system both reflected and precipitated the unworkability of urban apartheid. Now, in democratic Johannesburg, new ideologies associated with democracy, equal opportunity, and nonracialism must be operationalized and imprinted onto the urban system. Again, larger political goals are endangered in the process of their urban operationalization, this time by market-based barriers that could produce an economic apartheid similar in effect to administrative apartheid.

The nexus between urban policy and ethnic territoriality highlights the internal tensions created when broad ideologies or goals are operationalized in the urban arena. Territorial control sought by partisan policymaking can be elusive. One of the central means of operationalizing apartheid ideology in South Africa involved the dispersal of the black population in order to diminish its group coherence and ability to coalesce politically. Yet, this effort at territorial control created conditions of interpersonal insecurity, vulnerability, and urban imbalance. Strict separateness of races achieved at the level of the urban arena was found to be insufficient in the face of the city's economic magnet effect. The solution proposed by apartheid engineers was to activate "grand" apartheid policy operative at the countrywide scale. Failure to de facto control territorially the urban system, apartheid planners attempted the even more futile vision of controlling the entire national landscape. In this evasive and economically irrational scheme to separate races, territoriality engendered territoriality (Sack 1986).

Territoriality also intervenes in the urban implementation of peace-building goals. Belfast's color-neutral approach to policymaking does not excuse planners from addressing sectarian territoriality. Indeed, neutrality obligates policymakers to monitor the distribution of policy benefits and costs across ethnic territory. Whereas in other cases the disruption of ethnic territories in an effort to dominate the landscape would destabilize intergroup relations, the Belfast case shows that abundant respect for territoriality also has ill effects. Policymakers, in their acquiescence of strict territoriality, put themselves in the position of institutionalizing what are in reality artificial boundaries, protecting a lifeless and dysfunctional geography of hatred rather than directing their energies toward the vitality of people and community. As ethnic territories are solidified, the dynamic channels and flows of interaction needed for healthy urban functioning become sclerotic and degenerative. It appears that territoriality in a polarized city should not be disrupted to the point of threat and intergroup instability, but at the same time it must not be allowed to solidify and harden to the point of urban system dysfunctionality. The contemporary Johannesburg case represents a distinctly different type of territoriality, one likely in the future to be more aligned with class than race. The effective stitching together of the torn fabric of *Egoli* will necessitate breaking down this class-based territoriality (both middle-class white and nonwhite areas) and the "not in my backyard" neighborhood opposition associated with it. If the process of urban "normalization" is hitched to market mechanisms, the resulting class-based territoriality will likely create a metropolitan landscape every bit as unequal as the imposed racial compartmentalization of Johannesburg's apartheid nightmare. The case illuminates the mutative quality of territoriality in cities that successfully shift from a polarized environment to one of negotiated peace. A peaceful city divided by class may not be sustainable over the long term.

*   *   *

Peace-building efforts must be conscious not only of the complex dimensions of urban systems, but also of the differences between stabilization and reconstruction objectives. The Belfast and Johannesburg cases illustrate that difficult choices often have to be made between these two purposes. Building peace in contested cities involves both enhancement of urban stability in terms of supporting ethnic group identity and distressed habitation zones and urban reconstruction in terms of reconstituting built landscapes and intergroup relations distorted by decades of violence. In the first case, policymakers must often react to concerns over the maintenance of ethnic group identity or the meeting of basic human needs. In the second case, they seek to reconfigure the urban system to transcend the ethnic geography and inequalities of civil strife. Whereas stabilization is critical to meeting the immediate needs of people and ethnic groups, reconstruction is more complex and vital and seeks to promote spatial, social, and economic conditions for long-term metropolitan sustainability.

In Belfast, stabilization of sectarian territoriality may attenuate the continuation of violence at the same time that it impedes an evolution or normalization of the urban landscape. In Johannesburg, responses to the crisis conditions created by land invasions and shantytowns address immediate public health and safety concerns, but restrict a restructuring of the urban system that would open more urban opportunities to the black majority. Policymakers must decide how much stabilization can occur before long-range damage to the urban system irrevocably occurs—in Belfast, through the institutionalization of sectarian barriers, in Johannesburg through the solidification of apartheid geography. Concurrently, policy officials involved in the planned restructuring of metropolitan space must be concerned with the potential destabilizing effects of such endeavors—in Belfast, exemplified by Protestant anger over peaceline shifting; in Johannesburg, by middle-class opposition to the incorporation of the poor into the existing urban fabric. Policymakers must be cognizant of these tensions between stabilization and reconstruction in making choices about the appropriate blend of peace-building techniques at any one time and over an extended period.

*   *   *

In the future, current urban governing strategies in Johannesburg and Belfast, although neither is partisan, will likely enable vicious patterns and processes to occur which are obstructive of urban ethnic coexistence. The insufficiency of policy- neutrality in Belfast solidifies ethnic mental and physical maps, making color-neutral policy both increasingly difficult to implement and irrelevant, if not damaging, to larger peacemaking. The transformation and normalization of Johannesburg run the risk—owing to fiscal constraints and market reliance—of falling short of urban and social equity goals, and ultimately, of contributing to the breakdown of its new democratic system.

Actions taken in these cities by national and local policymakers will play critical roles in whether these somber trajectories are fulfilled, or whether alternative futures of sustainable mutual coexistence are pursued. Despite the dissimilar urban environments and histories of Belfast and Johannesburg, they share common ground. In both regions, future urban policymaking will need to be cognizant of group-based differences, vigilant of how group identities and strife can be hardened through even well-intentioned policy, and active in implementing innovative policies which deliver benefits across urban groups. These urban arenas hold key positions in operationalizing "ideologies of co-existence" as a means toward contributing to larger peace processes among peoples and nations. In Belfast, future policy strategies can potentially constitute a progressive approach to sectarian relations that can both respond to the differential objective needs of the two traditions in an urban setting, and establish an urban laboratory of mutual coexistence which can anchor that society's move toward peace. In Johannesburg, urban policy strategies can define the appropriate roles of governmental, private, and nongovernmental sectors in the reconstruction of the metropolitan region, and thus clarify and operationalize the sustainability requirements of the emergent democracy in the new South Africa. These urban arenas may provide the sense of shared crisis necessary for peace to be constructed out of their daily conflicts and challenges. There will be no Northern Irish peace absent Belfast, and no racial reconciliation in South Africa separate from Johannesburg.

In Belfast, urban policymaking would need to be reconceptualized so that it is part of the change process toward peace, not a burden to it. Government should facilitate those spatial forms and living patterns that are most conducive to community viability and identity for *both* ethnic groups. Equity does not imply replication of policy for the two groups, nor numerical balance in government outputs. Rather, it means that policy should be sensitive to the unique needs of each community while keeping in mind the overall good of the city. Both Protestant and Catholic communities have significant objective and psychological needs related to social and economic deprivation and group identity. In terms of urban policy formulation, however, there are different primary community imperatives that effective governance must address: (1) objective needs of the Catholic population for new housing and community services; and (2) social-psychological needs of the Protestant population for community viability and identity. Decline in the Protestant population must be more strategically managed in order to produce a vital but geographically consolidated Protestant population. The goal would not be the maintenance of Protestant territories, but the viability of Protestant communities. A consolidated, more viable Belfast Protestant community would over time feel less threat, and a greater willingness to allow some normalization of Belfast's geography to meet some of the Catholic objective needs. Town planning has a moral and professional responsibility to shift out of its technical and land use blinders to incorporate consideration of the social, economic, and psychological dynamics and requisites for coexistent viability of Protestant and Catholic groups.

The Johannesburg case illustrates the significant role to be played by urban policymaking in the post-resolution, reconstructive phase of a city and society. Resolution of ethnic conflict is not actualized solely through changes in political power or institutions—however momentous these may be—but must be nurtured by progressive on-the-ground policies that deepen and sustain political change. The chances will increase that democracy in Johannesburg (and South Africa) will be sustainable if a collective sense of social justice is the primary criterion underlying public policy, and if there exists a productive relationship between government initiative and community participation. Urban policy intervention will be required in market processes that, alone, would attenuate or obstruct equity outcomes that morally must be part of post-apartheid urban life. Actions in key areas of potential state intervention—violence-torn communities, low-cost housing provision, inner-city neighborhood stability, central city economic development, and strategic urban locations—will have significant effects on whether urban policy transforms or reinforces the racial geography from the past. The timing and sequencing of these and other urban policy initiatives responsive to intense unmet needs should assure that human upliftment occurs within a sustainable and equitable framework of metropolitan development. Urban policymakers must also be able to engage with communities in a way that avoids both reactionary authoritarianism and an unfettered "people's democracy." The emerging model of more Africanized community-based urban planning may be capable of reaching such a middle ground—facilitating, but also managing, community participation. In the end, the degree of progress cities such as Johannesburg make regarding their physical, social, and economic reconstruction will either enhance or hinder future interracial reconciliation and political stability in the "new" South Africa. Not only do cities such as Johannesburg hold spatial and economic "keys" to the reconciliation puzzle, but they constitute important arenas where a participatory and functional post-apartheid relationship between government and community can be nurtured and sustained.

The Challenge of Urban Peace

This study has illuminated the inherent complexities of urban policymaking aimed at stabilizing and reconstructing strife-torn urban regions. Neutral planning suspends more than increases antagonisms in the short term, but buys such abstinence from violence at the expense of reconciling competing visions of nationalism and sovereignty. Equity planning and redistributive decisionmaking that would favor members of the materially disadvantaged ethnic groups—Belfast Catholics and apartheid Johannesburg blacks—are improbable where interethnic relations are seen as a zero-sum game and basic political parameters remain contested. For urban policy strategies to introduce, strengthen, and solidify peace, they must seek coexistent viability of antagonistic groups in the urban setting, moderate processes of "normalization" that would reinforce urban inequalities, and connect these efforts to larger peace and reconstruction efforts. Urban strategies cannot address directly the root ideologically based causes of urban polarization. That is the domain of diplomatic national-level negotiations. But, "resolver" urban policymakers can contribute practical principles which foster the coexistent viability of antagonistic sides in terms of territorial claims, public service availability, and preservation of ethnic identity. They can connect daily issues of urban living and conflict to underlying issues of political disempowerment and unfair governance structures. They can increase the understanding by political negotiators and international organizations of how root causes of urban ethnic polarization can be addressed and reconciled on the city scale.

The goal of a "resolver" urban strategy is to accommodate competing ethnic needs without sacrificing the soul of urban life and the city itself and to contribute urban peace-building principles to national-level negotiations dealing with overarching political claims, basic social structures, and power relationships. The narrow ground of urban life does not need to be one of boundedness and coercion, but can provide the opportunity for policymakers in these settings to be more creative in designing urban arenas of coexistent viability.

For urban policy to perform resolver and peace-advancing roles, the process and practice of city-building will need to be reconceptualized in order that it may inspire or support larger political agreements over the form and substance of ethnically accommodative urban democracies. An urban strategy of "co-existent viability" is indicated for cities that are susceptible to, immersed in, or emerging from conditions of intense intercommunal conflict and violence. Urban policy will need to acknowledge and honor the centrifugal tendencies of ethnicity while maintaining the integrative institutions and processes of city-building and administration. Specifically, urban policymaking must, in its methods of analysis and decisionmaking, explicitly account for the importance of ethnic community identity, territoriality, and symbolism embedded in the urban landscape. At the same time, it must be able to address constructively the city's ethnicity when it is obstructing the functionality of the urban region and the meeting of basic needs regarding public health, shelter, public services, and economic opportunities. In other words, city planners must both respect ethnic territoriality where it constitutes a healthy source of community cohesiveness, and break ethnic territorial boundaries where they impose chains that enervate and distort urban functionality and vitality. Often, territoriality is linked to political claims for sovereignty and control. Here, urban policymakers can contribute their expertise and analyses to political deliberations regarding the land and resource needs that would be required for the self-sustainability of possible new semi-autonomous political units in the urban region. In other cases, territoriality is linked to fear and threat of community decline on the part of a majority and/or empowered ethnic group. Urban planners can be instrumental in these cases in dealing with the social-psychological needs for community identity, viability, or security.

A key challenge in reconstructing contested cities is to address the real concerns of communities and individuals and to delink these concerns from the maintenance of a static or counterproductive territoriality. An accommodative urban strategy will likely require an engagement in equity policy that disproportionately targets territorial and material benefits to the objectively disadvantaged ethnic group (in the case study cities, Belfast Catholics and Johannesburg blacks) while tending to the psychological needs and well-being of the materially advantaged, in terms of their security, ethnic identity, and neighborhood vitality. Just as the territorial protectionism of Belfast's Protestants obstructs normal evolution of the city's neighborhoods, so do white South Africans' fears of economic loss limit redistributive spending, and their fears of property value decline and violence obstruct racial and spatial integration. The solution to urban policymakers is not to run roughshod over these concerns, but to acknowledge and address them as valid social-psychological attributes of threatened populations living under uncertain and shifting political circumstances.

At the same time as acknowledging the complex social-psychological attributes of ethnic groups in contested cities, urban policymakers must not fall back upon seemingly impartial and benign processes as the most appropriate paths toward city reconstruction. Private sector processes of land development and housing provision can bring much energy and many resources to reconstruction, especially after many years of pent-up activity due to ethnic conflict. The same can be

said for international aid organizations. Yet, in the absence of effective and assertive government policies that facilitate, moderate, or even substitute for private or foreign investment, profitability criteria and donor requirements run the
risk of reinforcing or extending the unequal legacies of ethnic wartime. The logic
of economic functionalism and suburbanization can remove resources from the
political jurisdictions of contested cities, obstructing their ability to redirect
spending to combat disparities and neighborhood deprivation. Meanwhile, international aid organizations' relative inexperience with local, community-based
peace-building means that reconstruction efforts can turn into a patchwork of un-
related projects that might even consolidate ethnic divisions.

An urban policy strategy that seeks the building and advancement of urban
peace must re-create the contested city as part of reconstituting society, economy,
and polity. It is a much more vital, complex, and transformative task than the rebuilding of physical structures and infrastructure. It should adhere to an overriding ethic of peace-building that eschews both reactive, protective neutrality and
subordination to economic market imperatives. It should plan for coexistent viability of ethnicities, conscious of the differential needs of these groups within an
ethnically saturated urban system and able to respond to these needs while maintaining a coherent metropolitan logic. At the same time, it must anticipate and
counteract those nonethnic forces of urban change which would solidify current
disparities and seek actively to transform the spatial matrices of opportunity and
disadvantage created before and during urban ethnic entrenchment and conflict.

*   *   *

What is the relationship of urban and community peace-building to broader
processes of negotiated peacemaking? Must cities await larger peace advancement
for there to be improvement of urban life, or can actions within cities assist and even
precede larger peacemaking? Some would argue, on the one hand, that city peace
will need to await larger advances in peacemaking. In this scenario, the city retards
the advancement of peace. Urban living is stimulative of conflict due to the proximity and economic interactions that are a necessary part of a functioning urban system. If intergroup status levels are unequal (or are perceived to be), increased contact increases interpersonal tension. Amid subcultural diversity and political
conflict, "to know one another better is often to hate one another more violently"
(Wirth 1931). Proximity can intensity feelings of group-based relative deprivation
and threats to collective identity. Urban policies that have direct effects on territoriality, material well-being, and cultural expression can help mobilize an urban-based
political opposition which can energize or solidify national-level resistance. Such urban conditions and actions may provide the spark that disrupts and impedes national
diplomatic efforts. In addition, an urban governing regime's efforts to suppress and
fragment political protest and resistance can ignite in-migration of more radicalized

political interests into the urban political void. Where partisan planning has created an urban framework of subordination and inequality, ethnic mistrust and conflict are fomented. Past manipulation of potent ethnic territoriality can create intergroup geographic interfaces vulnerable to localized explosions of violence and more sustained threats to the regime that disrupt vital urban economic processes and psychological well-being. Urban problems can be used by an ethnic group in ways that obstruct international and national peace negotiations. Under this scenario of a peace-retarding city, the best that urban policymakers can do is to avoid escalation in order to buy time for larger peacemaking achievements to occur.

Yet, cities are not necessarily regressive agents within political transitions. Rather, they may be important laboratories in which the addressing of urban ethnicity assists, and may even be formative of, larger advancements in peace. To the extent that the city's daily interconnectedness and forced coexistence thrust upon intimate urban enemies some modicum of mutual tolerance, cities are buffers or mitigators of intergroup conflict. The extension of material benefits—urban services, social security or unemployment insurance, urban employment—may moderate a relative deprivation effect that is one cause of political mobilization. A co-optative relationship between city government and out-group community elites may act as a wall preventing broader hostilities from entering the urban arena. Further, a territorial separation of opposing ethnic groups in an urban system may be less difficult than at national scales, providing some political stability and facilitating federalism or two-tier governance as a solution to the broader sovereignty conflict. The benefits of urban peace and coexistence can be a spark to larger political negotiations, with concrete principles of daily life supplementing and reinforcing the more abstract principles of internationally negotiated settlements. Because cities are important microcosms of regional and international conflict, they can provide useful models of ethnic relations to national negotiators and diplomats. The 1996 United Nations Conference on Human Settlements (Habitat II) was an indication of the growing recognition by international institutions of the significant roles of urban policymakers and local nongovernmental organizations in the modern world. A set of international-national-urban linkages is emerging which may grow in the future as the nation-state is decreasingly seen as the territorial answer to the problems of human political, economic, and social organization. Such relationships would likely increase the use by the international community of urban systems as intervention points in efforts to catalyze larger peace.

I argue here that urban policymaking should not await larger peace processes, but in and of itself can play key formative and facilitative roles in larger peacemaking. The Johannesburg case bears witness to this potential, as city-building problems in the early 1990s were connected to root empowerment issues and were facilitative of larger political deals. Assuredly, peace-building at the local level should be part of political agreements and will play a crucial role in bringing the tangible benefits of peace to torn places and torn residents. But, urban policymaking that advances mutual tolerance on the streets and in the neighborhoods may also precede, and create the terms of deliberation for, larger political negotiations. Properly designed urban development and policy can create the preconditions for a larger peace by producing confidence-building outcomes and by articulating the key components of viable ethnic coexistence generalizable to regional and national levels. Urban policymaking cannot only consolidate peaceful relations, but may be able to help create them in the first place.

Yet, even if cities are important potential positive forces during political change, the accommodation of ethnic coexistence at a city scale, by itself, would most assuredly not pull the rest of the country or region into a similar state of ethnic peace. Thus, the proper role of urban policymaking would likely be as essential *companion* of, not replacement for, larger peacemaking endeavors. Policies and principles of urban coexistence are not to be a substitute for larger political negotiations and would indeed fail outside a framework of national peace and reconciliation. At the same time, though, urban strategies of accommodation will likely be an indispensable part of overaching political deals. Urban-based strategies that incorporate ethnic management criteria can supply useful lessons for broader interethnic negotiations and policymaking, and can furnish models for the distribution of international financial aid by governments and private organizations meant to solidify and deepen a negotiated peace. Tangible urban-level efforts and diplomatic national-level negotiations must constitute an inseparable peacemaking amalgamation. Urban accommodation without a national peace would leave the city vulnerable and unstable, while a national peace without urban accommodation would be one unrooted in the practical and explosive issues of intergroup and territorial relations.

Progressive and ethnically sensitive urban peace-building can facilitate and anchor negotiated agreements concerning local political power. There are three main political options concerning the structuring of local governance in contested cities—physical separation, two-tier federated governance, and consociational city government. These run the gamut from least to most interethnic cooperation.

In a physically partitioned city, sovereignty is divided and ethnic groups are isolated from one another.[2] Physical segmentation of a contested urban setting expresses a symmetry of territorial claims. With the penetration of daily urban policy decisions by territorial conflict lessened, the potential for constructive local leadership to address urban frictions on a cooperative basis could increase. In Belfast, amid de facto partitioning by peacelines and continued fracturing of peacemaking efforts, a community separation option cannot be dismissed. However, physical segmentation presents numerous logistical problems, especially where competing ethnic groups, although segregated from each other, are not concentrated in particular sectors or directions. Belfast's sectarian geography of eastern Protestants and western Catholics is complicated by the Protestant heartland to the west and a segregated mosaic pattern to the north. A primary argument against physical partition is its effect on city diversity and functionality. When contemplating this urban future, one must then consider whether the cost of physical separatism—the death of the old city—is a worthy sacrifice.

The creation of a two-tier system of local government shares the sovereignty of the urban areas between two ethnic-specific local authorities. There is unity or co-operation at the higher level of government (metropolitan or city) but functional and political division at the lower level (city or borough). Two-tier governance structures include the creation of a metropolitan government that manages the entire urban region, with ethnically homogeneous local governments expressing their own interests and needs.[3] Or, there might be a single city government supported by autonomous cantons or boroughs of ethnic homogeneity. In contested Jerusalem, a Borough Plan was debated from 1968 to 1977, envisioning a single municipal government under dual sovereignty, the representation of Palestinians in the running of the city, and the creation of separate boroughs such as existed in the Greater London Council.[4] However, where urban ethnic geographies are intertwined, the creation of ethnic local governments (or boroughs) becomes logistically problematic. Either drastic relocation must occur to ethnically sort the urban region, or local boundaries must be drawn in disfigured, noncontiguous ways that dampen ethnic community cohesiveness. Two-tier governance utilizing metropolitan and local levels can be particularly useful during political transitions. Johannesburg (and other South African cities) emphasized the metropolitan level of politics both as the focal point for local government transition negotiations and as a necessary element of post-apartheid redistributive and reconstruction policies. The South African approach used metropolitanism as a means to integrate and transcend old local authority boundaries in order to eliminate their mono-racial basis. This metropolitan strategy is in contrast to one which would retain, even create, single ethnic-dominant local governments as essential to the territorial and political expression of each side.

A third approach to the political restructuring of contested cities is to create a local "consociational" democracy. Here, there is accommodation or agreement between political elites over a governance arrangement capable of managing ethnic differences. A consociational or power-sharing government is one of joint sovereignty wherein two nations or peoples exercise sovereignty. A local conflict-accommodative government can be established that utilizes power-sharing, ethnic proportionality within the public sector, community autonomy, and minority vetoes. Transition-period Johannesburg was characterized by a local consociational form of power-sharing between officials of the old regime, black political leaders, and nongovernmental organizations.[5] If such a local authority was to be established in Belfast, it would mimic the power-sharing Northern Ireland Assembly created in 1998.

Restructuring of political power through any of the means above is likely required for resolution of urban tensions that exist in places such as Belfast, Johannesburg, Jerusalem, Brussels, and Beirut. However, these formal solutions to political contestation may provide autonomy or political control at the expense of ethnic separation and isolation and, ultimately, urban and regional dysfunctionality. Physical separation tears at the heart and soul of the urban region, hermetically sealing antagonistic sides behind walls of hatred. Political separation through a two-tier structuring of local government is more moderate; yet, without urban strategies aimed at coexistent viability of both sides, it also can lead to a functionally disconnected and economically stagnant urban area for one or both groups. Even joint, power-sharing political control of the city, without on-the-ground urban strategies that reify mutual tolerance and coexistence, can disintegrate into a condition of urban paralysis amidst policy vetoes.

Negotiated agreements over the restructuring of political power and control are essential, but not sufficient, for peace to advance. It is, instead, urban policy-making that is uniquely positioned to operationalize an ideology of ethnic coexistence amid historical contentiousness. Urban policy strategies that improve inter-ethnic coexistence are a critical part in the advancement of peace, and should be part of, and contribute to, regional and international peace and reconstruction efforts. Methods of ethnic conflict alleviation at the local level, more than buying time for diplomatic peacemaking, can illuminate essential elements of a larger negotiated peace settlement. Urban ethnic accommodation can facilitate a formal restructuring of political power that incorporates a greater level of intergroup cooperation, and help avoid more drastic and debilitating segregationist partitioning of the urban system. After formal political changes are enacted, local policies aimed at the basic needs and coexistent viability of competing ethnic groups likely constitute the sole authentic source of ethnic centripetalism and tolerance amid local and national political agreements that would otherwise be susceptible to ethnic hardening and fraying.

National and international agreements over political power and control, while absolutely essential, impose abstract and remote sets of rules and institutions upon the urban landscape. Political arrangements such as consociational democracy that might emerge from such national peace accords respond to the basic dual needs for sovereignty and political control, but represent agreements at the political level, not those of daily interaction between ethnic groups and individuals. By contrast, urban strategies are capable of addressing the complex spatial, social-psychological, and organizational attributes of historically antagonistic urban communities and of bringing the material and emotional benefits of formal peace to streets and neighborhoods. In the case of two-tier governance, they can foster interaction between semi-autonomous local ethnic governments and hinder a de facto separation that might otherwise develop with political separation. In the case of consociational democracy, properly designed urban strategies can provide a policy space of positive-sum outcomes that can obstruct the development of a mentality of policy gridlock and obstructive ethnic vetoes.

Urban peace-building plays a primary role in solidifying and extending peace after a negotiated resolution of political conflict. Yet, the ultimate value of urban policymaking may lie further upstream, in its potential capacity to facilitate national peacemaking by connecting the principles and practices of urban coexistence to the restructuring of a country's basic political parameters. City policymaking can help create, as well as reinforce, these basic parameters of negotiated settlements. Contested urban arenas—such as Johannesburg and Belfast—are spatial, economic, and emotional keys to the challenges of national ethnic stability and reconciliation.

Notes

1. Unless noted in the tables, assessments of Johannesburg are based on contemporary, post-apartheid conditions and prospects.

2. In Nicosia (Cyprus), a "green line" physically separates the city into Greek (south) and Turkish (north) municipalities. This has created separate and self-contained municipalities of contested yet equal standing on either side of the barrier, and has resulted in each of the two urban regimes having a solid territorial base that has set the foundation for some bridge-building. As a result, the Greater Nicosia Master Plan 1981–2001 planned for two scenarios (with and without partition), incorporated elements of flexibility and openness, and has resulted in functional integration across the urban partition (Wolfe 1988).

3. Examples of two-tier systems of metropolitan (county)-local governance in North America include Toronto, Dade County/Miami, and Minneapolis–St. Paul. In Europe, examples include Rijnmond and The Hague (Netherlands), Copenhagen (Denmark), Stockholm (Sweden), Frankfurt (Germany), Barcelona and Madrid (Spain), and Paris (Norton 1983).

4. The Greater London Council was created as a central authority which worked with 52 separately elected borough governments from throughout the urban region. The boroughs had primary authority over local services, the GLC authority over regional issues, with some powers concurrent or shared.

5. In Johannesburg, less collaborative political arrangements that would have partitioned the urban region physically or politically likely did not transpire because the demographic ratio between blacks and nonblacks was lopsided.

Appendix 1: Research Issues
Expanded Outline

Contextual Factors

Ethnicity and legal frameworks	To what extent are deep ethnic cleavages acknowledged within the legal frameworks of urban policy and planning? Is differential treatment by ethnic group directly legislated? indirectly facilitated?
Urban institutional differentiation	Is there ethnic-based differentiation of city and neighborhood institutions and organizations, or efforts to institutionally integrate competing ethnic groups?
Basic values	Within each ethnic group, to what extent are there shared (or conflicting) values concerning ethnic issues across the participants in the planning process (politicians, administrators, planners, residents)?

Policy Issues and Goals

Urban ethnic issues	What are the major urban manifestations of ethnic conflict? Is it possible to classify different types of urban symptoms based on their degree of conflict and/or potential for resolution?
Treatment of ethnic conflict	Is amelioration of ethnic conflict acknowledged explicitly as an appropriate role for urban planning policy? If so, through what means is this amelioration to occur? Are issues of ethnicity depoliticized at the city level and through what means?
The city's interest: policy goals and objectives	How is the public interest defined—overarching or differentiated by ethnicity? To what degree do development goals and objectives differ between ethnic/racial communities?
Citizen participation— processes	What is the quality of citizen participation in the formulation of policy? Are intergroup collaborative policy processes used? What are the characteristics of community organizations within contested urban environments?

Urban Decisionmaking

Agenda-setting | How inclusive is the identification of alternative urban policies that might further city goals and objectives? In what ways do ethnic or ideological factors limit local policy and planning alternatives?

Decisionmaking rules | What decisionmaking criteria are used to allocate urban services and policy benefits? (1) functional-technical? (2) proportionate-equity? How do these two criteria relate to one another? Do these criteria differ by type of urban issue?

Planning/policymaking roles | What is the practicality and effectiveness of the planning models—neutral, equity, and resolver—in a polarized city? What combinations of strategies are used, and why? Are there alternative models of urban planning? How does policymaking deal with historic link to partisan policy?

Territoriality and policy | Do planners deal with ethnic or racial territoriality? If so, through what means do they seek to acknowledge or transform it? Is there the identification of *neutral*, or bicommunal, geographic areas? If so, for what purposes?

Policy Outcomes

Implementation | Are policies modified during implementation to accommodate or combat conflicting ethnic needs? What discretion do administering entities have to modify policy to address ethnic realities?

Results | What is the geographic distribution of urban spending and services across ethnic subareas of the city? *

National-local intergovernmental relations | Degree of national-local intergovernmental friction. Are there compromises available to integrate national and municipal perspectives?

Conflict Outcomes and Mechanisms

Patterns of conflict amelioration (intensification) | To what extent do local policies lessen or intensify ethnic conflict? In what circumstances does urban policy lessen ethnic conflict? When does it intensify ethnic conflict or produce a breakdown in planning policy process?

---

*For overall urban spending patterns and within specific service categories—land use/plan designations; building permit approvals; housing construction; economic activities; transportation projects; other infrastructure; noxious facilities.

Formal mechanisms for reducing conflict	What formal governmental mechanisms are present to mediate interethnic differences over urban policy issues? Use of concessions or interethnic negotiated agreements?
Informal mechanisms for reducing conflict	What informal channels/modes of political contact exist to deal with grievances on practical urban matters? Role of community leaders and institutions representing the historic out-group?
Intra-ethnic effects, cross-cutting cleavage patterns	What are the effects of urban policy decisions on *intra*-ethnic relations? Mass versus elite differences? Differences between classes of like ethnicity? Between neighborhoods of like ethnicity? On what issues does support (or opposition) for urban policy cut across ethnic lines (Catholic-Protestant; black-white South African)?

Community Dynamics and Organization

Intersection of national and local interests	Within a single ethnic group, in what ways do national issues and political leaders influence the organization and potential effectiveness of urban interests and initiatives? Conversely, is community activism in urban settings capable of influencing national-level policy and political discussions?
Community organization in a controlled environment	What survival techniques are available to community groups suppressed by a controlling government? What are the more effective means of expression under conditions of subordination?
Restructuring community	In times when greater autonomy is granted and/or a controlling regime is ended, how can communities and their leadership transform themselves from protest organs into productive copartners?

Change and Evolution

| Changes in urban policy amid transition | How do urban policymakers perceive the role of local policy amid larger political processes and transitions? Should urban policy lead or lag advances in peacemaking at broader political levels? |
| Changes in planning strategies | In advance of, or correlated with, changes in intergroup relations, what changes, if any, have occurred in how ethnic factors are addressed in the urban aspects above: (1) city planning goals; (2) legal and institutional relationships; (3) urban decisionmaking rules; (4) planning roles and strategies; (5) conflict management strategies? |

| Change—underlying factors | Are changes in planning strategies due to economic, political, or ideological imperatives? Have changes been locally inspired or imposed on city from external governmental levels? |
| Change—effect on ethnic conflict | How have changes in planning strategies, if any, affected the level and nature of ethnic conflict in the urban region? In the country at-large? |

Appendix 2:
Interviews Conducted

Belfast (34)

January 13–March 30, 1995

Frederick Boal	Professor of Geography, School of Geosciences. Queen's University of Belfast.
John Hendry	Professor of Town and Regional Planning. Department of Environmental Planning. Queen's University of Belfast.
Ken Sterrett	Town and Country Planning Services. Department of the Environment for Northern Ireland.
Gerry Mulligan	Central Statistics and Research Branch. Department of the Environment for Northern Ireland.
Mari Fitzduff	Director. Northern Ireland Community Relations Council.
John McPeake	Assistant Director for Strategy, Planning and Research. Northern Ireland Housing Executive.
Brendan Murtagh	University of Ulster, Magee College. London/Derry.
George Worthington	Head. Belfast Divisional Office. Town and Country Planning Service. Department of the Environment for Northern Ireland.
Dennis McCoy	Central Community Relations Unit. Central Secretariat. Northern Ireland Office.
Sam Corbett	Central Community Relations Unit. Central Secretariat. Northern Ireland Office.
Will Glendinning	Development Staff—Work and Community. Northern Ireland Community Relations Council.
Tom Lovett	Community Education, Research and Development Centre. University of Ulster, Jordanstown.
Frank Gaffikin	Lecturer. University of Ulster, Jordanstown.

Mike Morrissey	Lecturer. University of Ulster, Jordanstown.
Paul Sweeney	Advisor. Department of the Environment for Northern Ireland.
Michael Graham	Northern Ireland Housing Executive. Belfast Regional Office. Information Officer.
David Murphy	Northern Ireland Housing Executive. Belfast Regional Office. Client Technical Services.
Bill Morrison	Superintending Planning Officer. Belfast Divisional Office. Town and Country Planning Service. Department of the Environment for Northern Ireland.
Julie Harrison	Research Officer. Making Belfast Work. Department of the Environment for Northern Ireland.
Victor Allister	Springvale Development Team. Belfast Development Office. Department of the Environment.
Rowan Davison	Team Leader. Upper Shankill Action Team. Department of the Environment.
Jackie Redpath	Greater Shankill Development Agency/Greater Shankill Regeneration Strategy.
Nelson McCausland	Councillor. Belfast District Council. Castle Electoral Area. Ulster Unionist Party.
Bill Neill	Professor of Town Planning. Department of Environmental Planning. Queen's University. Head of Royal Town Planning Institute—Northern Ireland.
Vincent McKevitt	Team Leader. Ardoyne/Oldpark Action Team. Department of the Environment.
Deirdre MacBride	Housing and Projects Officer. Community Development Centre, North Belfast.
Colm Bradley	Northern Ireland Council for Voluntary Action (NICVA). Belfast.
Robert Strang	Independent Consultant. Formerly Assistant Director of Development and Planning. Northern Ireland Housing Executive.
Andreas Cebulla	Northern Ireland Economic Research Centre. Belfast.
Ronnie Spence	Permanent Secretary. Department of the Environment for Northern Ireland.
William McGivern	Regional Director–Belfast. Northern Ireland Housing Executive.
Billy Hutchinson	Project Director. Springfield Inter-Community Development Project. Belfast.
Joe Austin	Councillor. Belfast District Council. Oldpark Electoral Area. Member: Sinn Fein.
Brian Murphy	Making Belfast Work—Central Office. Formerly Team Leader—Springfield Action Team. Department of the Environment.

Johannesburg (37)

July 8–September 29, 1995

Steven Goldblatt	Lawyer/consultant. Land and Agricultural Policy Centre. Johannesburg.
Johan van der Merwe	Acting Director. Metropolitan Planning. Johannesburg Administration. Greater Johannesburg Transitional Metropolitan Council.
Jan Erasmus	Acting Deputy Director. Regional Land Use. Johannesburg Administration. Greater Johannesburg Transitional Metropolitan Council.
Tshipso Mashinini	Deputy Director. Urbanization Department. Johannesburg Administration. Greater Johannesburg Transitional Metropolitan Council.
Paul Pereira	Senior Public Affairs and Policy Manager. South African Institute of Race Relations. Johannesburg.
Lindsay Bremner	Councillor and Chair. Urbanization and Housing Committee. Greater Johannesburg Transitional Metropolitan Council. Member: African National Congress.
Lauren Royston	Metropolitan Planning. Johannesburg Administration. Greater Johannesburg Transitional Metropolitan Council. Formerly—Planner, Planact.
Graeme Reid	General Manager/Lawyer. Planact.
Paul Waanders	Chief Director: Planning Services. Department of Development Planning, Environment and Works. Gauteng Provincial Government.
Matthew Nel	Development Consultant. Vice-Chairman, National Housing Board. Formerly Executive Director, Housing—The Urban Foundation.
Herman Pienaar	Chief Planner—Midrand Town Council. Formerly: Planner, City Strategies Division, City Planning Department, Johannesburg.
Morag Gilbert	Deputy Director. Strategic Issues Division. City Planning Department. Johannesburg Administration.
Harry Mashabela	Senior Research Officer. South African Institute of Race Relations. Johannesburg.
Lawrence Boya	Chief Director: Development Planning. Department of Development Planning, Environment, and Works. Gauteng Provincial Government.
Ben van der Walt	Town and Regional Planner. Planning Services Directorate. Department of Development Planning, Environment, and Works. Gauteng Provincial Government.
Alida Kotzee	Town and Regional Planner. Planning Services Directorate. Department of Development Planning, Environment, and Works. Gauteng Provincial Government.

John Muller	Professor and Head. Department of Town and Regional Planning. University of the Witwatersrand, Johannesburg.
Mark Swilling	Director and Professor. Graduate School of Public and Development Management. University of the Witwatersrand, Johannesburg.
Tim Hart	Urban Geographer. SRK Engineers. Johannesburg.
Graeme Hart	Professor. Department of Geography and Environmental Studies. University of the Witwatersrand, Johannesburg.
Ivan Kadungure	Reconstruction and Development Programme (RDP) Support Unit, Office of the Chief Executive; and Town Planner, Soweto Administration. Johannesburg Transitional Metropolitan Council.
Erica Ebdon	Deputy Director: Policy and Operations. Urbanization Department. Johannesburg Transitional Metropolitan Council.
Herman Sekoto	Planner. Strategic Issues Division. City Planning Department. Greater Johannesburg Transitional Metropolitan Council.
Roland Hunter	Director-General: Finance. Department of Economic Affairs and Finance. Gauteng Provincial Government.
Themba Maluleke	Project Manager: KATORUS. Department of Local Government and Housing. Gauteng Provincial Government.
Monty Narsoo	Director of Housing. Department of Local Government and Housing. Gauteng Provincial Government.
Jane Eagle	Planner. Strategic Issues Division. City Planning Department. Greater Johannesburg Transitional Metropolitan Council.
Patrick Flusk	Councillor and Chair, Human Services Committee. Greater Johannesburg Transitional Metropolitan Council. Member: African National Congress.
Lawrence Schlemmer	Independent Consultant. Instructor, Graduate School of Business Administration, University of the Witwatersrand.
Ishmael Mkhabela	Chair, National Housing Board. Executive Director, Interfaith Community Development Association.
Jo McCrystal	Planner. Strategic Issues Division. City Planning Department. Greater Johannesburg Transitional Metropolitan Council.
Chris Rogerson	Professor. Department of Geography. University of the Witwatersrand. Johannesburg.
Angela Motsa	Town and Regional Planner. Planact.
Dik Viljoen	Planning Consultant. Plan Associates. Pretoria.
Crispian (Chippy) Olver	Director: RDP Development Planning. Ministry in the Office of the President. Pretoria.

David Christianson   Institutional Specialist. Development Bank of Southern Africa.

Eric Molobi   Executive Director. Kagiso Trust. Johannesburg.

Other Individuals Consulted

Nelson Mandla   Research—KwaMashu township (Durban).

Thabo Makgoba   Reverend, St. Mary's Cathedral, Johannesburg.

Malcolm Lupton   Lecturer, Department of Geography and Environmental Studies, University of the Witwatersrand, Johannesburg.

Peter Weir   Research—Greater Soweto, Johannesburg.

Cosmos Moyo   Research—Johannesburg.

Anthony Lemon   Professor of Geography, Mansfield College, Oxford, U.K. (visitor to University of Witwatersrand, August 1995).

David Goldblatt   Photographer.

Robin Bloch   Centre for Industrial and Metropolitan Research, Johannesburg.

References

Articles and Books

Adam, Heribert and Kogila Moodley. 1993. "South Africa: The Opening of the Apartheid Mind." In McGarry, John and Brendan O'Leary (eds.) *The Politics of Ethnic Conflict Resolution: Case Studies of Protracted Ethnic Conflicts.* London: Routledge.

African National Congress (ANC). 1994. *The Reconstruction and Development Programme: A Policy Framework.* Johannesburg: Umanyano.

Agnew, John, John Mercer, and David Sopher (eds.) 1984. *The City in Cultural Context.* Winchester, MA: Allen & Unwin.

Akenson, Donald Harman. 1992. *God's Peoples: Convenant and Land in South Africa, Israel, and Ulster.* Ithaca, NY: Cornell.

Allport, G. W. 1954. *The Nature of Prejudice.* Cambridge, MA: Addison-Wesley.

Alterman, Rachelle. 1992. "A Transatlantic View of Planning Education and Professional Practice." *Journal of Planning Education and Research* 12, 1: 39–54.

Andrusz, Gregory. 1996. "Structural Change and Boundary Instablility." Pp. 30–69 in Andrusz, Gregory, Michael Harloe, and Ivan Szelenyi. *Cities and Socialism: Urban and Regional Change and Conflict in Post-Socialist Societies.* Oxford, U.K.: Blackwell.

Ardoyne/Oldpark Belfast Action Team. 1994. *Strategy Document 1994–97.* Belfast: MBW/BAT.

Arnstein, Sherry R. 1969. "A Ladder of Citizen Participation." Journal of the American Institute of Planners. 35 (July): 216–224

Ashkenasi, Abraham. 1988. "Commuanl Policy, Conflict Management, and International Relations." *Jerusalem Journal of International Relations* 10, 2: 109–127.

Azar, Edward E. 1991. "The Analysis and Management of Protracted Conflict." Pp. 93–120 in Volkan, Vamik D., Joseph V. Montville, and Demetrios A. Julius (eds.) *The Psychodynamics of International Relationships. Volume II: Unofficial Diplomacy at Work.* Lexington, MA: Lexington Books.

Bailey, F. G. 1969. *Stratagems and Spoils: A Social Anthropology of Politics.* New York: Schocken Books.

Baldassare, Mark (ed.) 1994. *The Los Angeles Riots—Lessons for the Urban Future.* Boulder, CO: Westview.

Barry, Brian. 1989. *Theories of Justice.* London: Harvester-Wheatsheaf.

Beavon, K. S. 1995. "Johannesburg: Getting to Grips with Globalization from an Abnormal Base." Paper presented at the Pre-Habitat II Conference on The World Cities and the Urban Future. Tokyo. August 23–25, 1995.

Beavon, K. S. 1992. "The Post-Apartheid City: Hopes, Possibilities, and Harsh Realities." In Smith, David M. (ed.) 1992. *The Apartheid City and Beyond: Urbanization and Social Change in South Africa*. London: Routledge.

Beavon, K.S. 1982. "Black Townships in South Africa: Terra Incognita for Urban Geographers." *South African Geographical Journal* 64: 3–20.

Beirne, Maggie. 1993. "Out of the Bearpit." *Fortnight* 317.

Belfast Areas of Special Social Need. 1977. Belfast: HMSO.

Belfast Areas of Special Social Need. 1977. Belfast: HMSO.

Benvenisti, Meron S. 1995. *Intimate Enemies: Jews and Arabs in a Shared Land*. Berkeley: University of California Press.

Benvenisti, Meron S. 1987. Presentation at Salzburg Seminar #257. "Divided Cities." February 11. Salzburg, Austria.

Benvenisti, Meron S. 1986. *Conflicts and Contradictions*. New York: Villard Books.

Bilski, Raphaella and Itzhak Galnoor. 1980. "Ideologies and Values in National Planning." Pp. 77–98 in Bilski, Raphaella, Itzhak Galnoor, Dan Inbar, Yohahan Manor, and Gabriel Sheffer. 1980. *Can Planning Replace Politics? The Israeli Experience*. The Hague: Martinus Nijhoff.

Birrell, Derek and Carol Wilson. 1993. "'Making Belfast Work': An Evaluation of an Urban Strategy." *Administration* 41, 1: 40–56.

Blackman, Tim. 1991. *Planning Belfast: A Case Study of Public Policy and Community Action*. Aldershot, U.K.: Avebury.

Boal, Frederick. 1996. "Exclusion and Inclusion: Segregation and Deprivation in Belfast." In Musterd, Sako and Herman van der Wusten (eds.) *Segregation and Exclusion in Western Metropolitan Areas*. London: Routledge.

Boal, Frederick. 1995. *Shaping a City: Belfast in the Late Twentieth Century*. Belfast: Queen's University, Institute of Irish Studies.

Boal, Frederick. 1994. "Belfast: A City on Edge." In Clout, Hugh (ed.) *Europe's Cities in the Late Twentieth Century*. Amsterdam: Royal Dutch Geographical Society.

Boal, Frederick W. 1990. "Belfast: Hindsight on Foresight-Planning in an Unstable Environment." Pp. 4–14 in Doherty, P. (ed.). *Geographical Perspectives on the Belfast Region*. Newtownabbey, NI: Geographical Society of Ireland.

Boal, Frederick W. 1982. "Segregating and Mixing: Space and Residence in Belfast." Pp. 249–280 in Boal, Frederick W. and J. Neville Douglas (eds.). *Integration and Division: Geographical Perspectives on the Northern Ireland Problem*. London: Academic Press.

Boal, Fred. 1971. "Territoriality and Class: A Study of Two Residential Areas in Belfast." *Irish Geography* 6, 3: 229–48.

Boal, Fred. 1969. "Territoriality on the Shankill-Falls Divide, Belfast." *Irish Geography* 6, 1: 30–50.

Boal, Frederick W. and J. Neville Douglas (eds.) 1982. *Integration and Division: Geographical Perspectives on the Northern Ireland Problem*. London: Academic Press.

Boal, Frederick W., P. Doherty, and D. G. Pringle. 1974. *The Spatial Distribution of Some Social Problems in the Belfast Urban Area*. Belfast: Northern Ireland Community Relations Commission.

Bollens, Scott. 1998. "Urban Planning Amidst Ethnic Conflict: Jerusalem and Johannesburg." *Urban Studies* 35, 4: 729–750.

Bollens, Scott. 1996. "On Narrow Ground: Planning in Ethnically Polarized Cities." *Journal of Architectural and Planning Research* 13, 2: 120–139.

Boutros-Ghali, Boutros. 1992. *An Agenda for Peace: Preventive Diplomacy, Peacemaking, and Peacekeeping.* New York: United Nations.

Boyle, Kevin and Tom Hadden. 1994. *Northern Ireland: The Choice.* London: Penguin Books.

Bradley, Colm. 1993. *Resourcing Local Community Development.* Belfast: NICVA, NIVT, and Resource Centres.

Breen, R. and B. Miller. 1993. "A Socio-Economic Profile of the Making Belfast Work Area." Belfast: MBW.

Bremner, Lindsay. 1994. "Development and Resistance: The Lessons for the Planners of Phola Park." *Urban Forum* 5, 1: 23–44.

Brogan, P. 1990. *The Fighting Never Stopped: A Comprehensive Guide to World Conflict Since 1945.* New York: Vintage.

Brogden, Mike and Clifford Shearing. 1993. *Policing for a New South Africa.* New York: Routledge.

Brown, Michael E. 1993. "Causes and Implications of Ethnic Conflict." Pp. 3–26 in Brown, Michael E. (ed.) *Ethnic Conflict and International Security.* Princeton, NJ: Princeton University Press.

Brown, Michael E. (ed.) 1996. *The International Dimensions of Internal Conflict.* Cambridge: Massachusetts Institute of Technology Press.

Brown, S. 1985. "City Centre Commercial Revitalization: The Belfast Experience." *Planner.* June: 9–12.

Buckley, Anthony D. and Rhonda Paisley. 1994. *Symbols.* Belfast: Community Relations Council, Cultural Traditions Group.

Budge, Ian and Cornelius O'Leary. 1973. *Belfast: Approach to Crisis, A Study of Belfast Politics 1613–1970.* London: Macmillan.

Building Design Partnership. 1969. *Belfast Urban Area Plan.* Belfast: BDP.

Bureau for Market Research. 1994. *Socio-Economic Profile of the Nine Provinces.* Research report no. 207. By Martin, J. H., A. A. Ligthelm, M. Loubser, and H. de J. van Wyk. Pretoria: University of South Africa.

Burton, John W. 1991. "Conflict Resolution as a Political System." Pp. 71–92 in Volkan, Vamik D., Joseph V. Montville, and Demetrios A. Julius. *The Psychodynamics of International Relationships.* Volume II. Lexington, MA: D.C. Heath.

Burton, John W. (ed.) 1990. *Conflict: Human Needs Theory.* New York: St. Martin's.

[Cameron]. 1969. *Disturbances in Northern Ireland: Report of the Commission Appointed by the Governor of Northern Ireland* (the Cameron Report). Belfast: HMSO, Cmd. 532.

Carmichael, Stokely and Calvin V. Hamilton. 1967. *Black Power: The Politics of Liberation in America.* New York: Random House.

Cawthra, Gavin. 1993. *Policing South Africa.* Atlantic Highlands, New Zealand: Zed Books.

Cebulla, Andreas. 1994. *Urban Policy in Belfast: An Evaluation of Department of Environment's Physical Regeneration Initiatives.* Belfast: Department of the Environment for Northern Ireland, Central Statistics and Research Branch.

Celik, Zeynep. 1997. *Urban Forms and Colonial Confrontations: Algiers Under French Rule.* Berkeley: University of California Press.

Central Community Relations Unit, Northern Ireland Office. 1995. *Community Relations Research Strategy 1995–1997*. 2nd edition. Belfast: CCRU.

Central Witwatersrand Metropolitan Chamber (CWMC). 1993. *An Interim Strategic Framework for the Central Witwatersrand. Document 2: Policy Approaches*. ISF Working Group, Planning Framework Task Team, Physical Development Working Group. Prepared by GAPS: Architects and Urban Designers. June.

CWMC. 1992a. *Interim Strategic Framework: Policy Guidelines.*

CWMC. 1992b. *Report A: Land Availability Study*. Prepared by Rosmarin and Associations, Civic Associations of Johannesburg.

Chipkin, Clive. 1993. *Johannesburg Style: Architecture and Society 1880s–1960s*. Cape Town: David Philip Publishers.

Christianson, David. 1994. "Local Government the Loser." *Indicator SA* 11, 4: 27–32.

Christopher, A. J. 1994. *The Atlas of Apartheid*. London: Routledge.

Claassen, Pieter E. 1993. "The Changing Role of City Planning in the 'New' South Africa." Paper read at the 35th Association of Collegiate Schools of Planning (USA) Conference. Philadelphia. October.

Clarke, R. V. 1992. *Statistical Crime Prevention: Successful Case Studies*. New York: Harrow and Heston.

Coakley, John. 1993. "Introduction: The Territorial Management of Ethnic Conflict." Pp. 1–22 in Coakley, John (ed.) *The Territorial Management of Ethnic Conflict*. London: Frank Cass.

Coakley, John. 1992. "The Resolution of Ethnic Conflict: Towards a Typology." *International Political Science Review* 13, 4: 343–58.

Cohen, Ronald. 1978. "Ethnicity: Problem and Focus in Anthropology." *Annual Review of Anthropology* 7: 379–405.

Community Development Centre, North Belfast. 1994. *Annual Report 1993–94*. Belfast: CDCNB.

Community Planning Weekend. Shankill, Belfast. February 3–6, 1995. Shankill Leisure Centre.

Compton, Paul and John F. Power. 1986. "Estimates of the Religious Composition of Northern Ireland Local Government Districts in 1981 and Change in the Geographical Pattern of Religious Composition Between 1971 and 1981." *Economic and Social Review* 17, 2: 87–105.

Cowan, C. 1982. "Belfast's Hidden Planners." *Town and Country Planning* 51, 6: 163–67.

Crankshaw, O. and C. R. White. 1992. "Results of the Johannesburg Inner City Survey." Group for Human Resources, Human Sciences Research Council. Johannesburg.

Cropper, Stephen A. 1982. "Theory and Strategy in the Study of Planning Processes—The Uses of the Case Study." *Environment and Planning B* 9: 341–57.

Cullen, Kevin. 1991. "Democracy Undone at Belfast City Council," *The Boston Globe*. May 4.

Darby, John. 1986. *Intimidation and Control of Conflict in Northern Ireland*. Dublin: Gill and Macmillan.

Davidoff, Paul. 1965. "Advocacy and Pluralism in Planning." *Journal of the American Institute of Planners* 31: 596–615.

Davies, R. J. 1981. "The Spatial Formation of the South African City." *GeoJournal*. Supplementary Issue 2: 59–72.

Davies, R. J. 1976. "Of Cities and Societies: A Geographer's Viewpoint." New Series No. 38. Inaugural Lecture. University of Cape Town. May 20.

Davis, Mike. 1990. *City of Quartz: Excavating the Future in Los Angeles*. New York: Vintage.

Dawson, G. M. 1984. "Planning in Belfast." *Irish Geography* 17: 27–41.

Dear, Michael and Allen J. Scott (eds.) 1981. *Urbanization and Urban Planning in Capitalist Society*. London: Methuen.

Deloitte & Touche. 1993. *Problem Statement*. Report produced for the Central Witwatersrand Metropolitan Chamber, Water and Sanitation Task Team. Johannesburg.

Department of Economic Development (Northern Ireland). 1989. *Fair Employment in Northern Ireland: Code of Practice*. Belfast: DED.

Department of the Environment for Northern Ireland (DOENI). 1995. *Making Belfast Work: Strategy Statement*. March. Belfast: MBW.

DOENI. 1994a. *Belfast Residents Survey*. Belfast: DOENI.

DOENI. 1994b. *Planning Bulletin*. DOENI: Town and Country Planning Service. Issue 4.

DOENI. 1994c. *Making Belfast Work: Strategy Proposals*. April. Belfast: MBW.

DOENI. 1993a. *Integrated Regeneration Strategy for Belfast*. Belfast: DoE. (AU: Ester Christie and Bill Morrison.)

DOENI. Department of Education. 1993b. *Springvale: Development of a Campus for the University of Ulster, Belfast*. Preliminary Evaluation. Private/confidential. April.

DOENI. 1992a. *North Belfast Strategic Review*. Belfast: DOENI. Unpublished and confidential.

DOENI. 1992b. *Development Scheme C.D.A. 110: Springvale*. Belfast: DOENI.

DOENI. 1990a. *Belfast Urban Area Plan 2001*. Belfast: Her Majesty's Stationery Office (HMSO).

DOENI. 1990b. Belfast Development Office. *Northgate Enterprise Park: A Development Concept for Inner Noth Belfast*. Interim Report. Unpublished. Internal circulation only.

DOENI. 1989. *Belfast Urban Area Plan 2001: Adoption Statement*. Belfast: HMSO.

DOENI. 1988. "Pre-Inquiry Response to CTA's Objections to the Draft BUAP." Pp. 187–221 in Blackman, Tim. 1991. *Planning Belfast: A Case Study of Public Policy and Community Action*. Aldershot, U.K.: Avebury.

DOENI. 1987. *Belfast Urban Area Plan 2001*. Draft. Belfast: HMSO.

DOENI. 1977. *Northern Ireland: Regional Physical Development Strategy 1975–95*. Belfast: HMSO.

Development Bank of Southern Africa (DBSA). 1995a. *South Africa's Nine Provinces: A Human Development Profile*. Development Information Paper 28. Halfway House: DBSA.

DBSA. 1995b. *Addendum to the 1995 Annual Report*. Halfway House: DBSA.

DBSA. 1994. "The State of Local Government Finance." Discussion Document, version 1, September 16.

Development Facilitation Bill. 1994. Second Redraft After Publication. April. Pretoria, South Africa.

Diefendorf, Jeffrey M. 1993. *In the Wake of War: The Reconstruction of German Cities After World War II*. New York: Oxford University Press.

Douglas, J. Neville. 1982. "Northern Ireland: Spatial Frameworks and Community Relations." Pp. 105–135 in Boal, Frederick W. and J. Neville Douglas (eds.). *Integration and Division: Geographical Perspectives on the Northern Ireland Problem*. London: Academic Press.

Douglas, J. Neville and Frederick W. Boal. 1982. "The Northern Ireland Problem." Pp. 1–18 in Boal, Frederick W. and J. Neville Douglas (eds.). *Integration and Division: Geographical Perspectives on the Northern Ireland Problem.* London: Academic Press.

Drogin, Bob. 1996. "Lingering South African Habit of Nonpayment Has High Costs." *Los Angeles Times.* January 7, A1, A4.

du Toit, Pierre. 1995. *State Building and Democracy in Southern Africa: Botswana, Zimbabwe, and South Africa.* Washington, D.C.: U.S. Institute of Peace.

Elazar, Daniel J. 1980. "Local Government for Heterogeneous Populations: Some Options for Jerusalem." Pp. 208–228 in Kraemer, Joel L. (ed.). *Jerusalem: Problems and Prospects.* New York: Praeger.

Environmental Design Consultants. 1991. *Belfast Peacelines Study.* Prepared for the Belfast Development Office. In conjunction with the Northern Ireland Housing Executive.

Eriksen, Thomas H. 1993. *Ethnicity and Nationalism.* London: Pluto Press.

Erwin, Alec. 1992. "Economic Reconstruction." *African Communist* 129.

Esman, M. J. 1985. "Two Dimensions of Ethnic Politics: Defence of Homeland and Immigrant Rights." *Ethnic and Racial Studies* 8: 438–441.

Esman, M. J. 1973. "The Management of Communal Conflict." *Public Policy* 21, 1: 49–78.

Etzioni, Amitai. 1968. *The Active Society: A Theory of Societal and Political Processes.* New York: Free Press.

Eversley, David. 1989. *Religion and Employment in Northern Ireland.* London: Sage.

Eversley, David and Valerie Herr. 1985. *The Roman Catholic Population of Northern Ireland in 1981: A Revised Estimate.* Belfast: Fair Employment Agency.

Ewing, Deborah. 1995. *Guide to Local Government Elections.* Durban, South Africa: Y Press.

Fair, T.J.D. 1986. "Johannesburg and the Central Witwatersrand: Concentration at the Center." Johannesburg: Urban Foundation.

Fair Employment Commission (Northern Ireland). 1993. *Summary of the 1992 Monitoring Returns.* Commission.

Fallon, Ivan. 1996. "At Last South Africa Has an Official Economic Strategy." *The Star and SA Times International.* June 26, p. 8.

Fallon, Peter and Luiz A. Pereira de Silva. 1994. *South Africa: Economic Performance and Policies.* Discussion Paper No. 7 (Informal Series). Southern Africa Department, Africa Region, World Bank.

Feldman, Allen. 1991. *Formations of Violence: The Narrative of the Body and Political Terror in Northern Ireland.* Chicago: University of Chicago Press.

Festenstein, Melville and Claire Pickard-Cambridge. 1987. *Land and Race: South Africa's Group Areas and Land Acts.* Johannesburg: South African Institute of Race Relations.

Fick, Johan, Christo de Coning and Nellie Olivier. 1988. "Ethnicity and Residential Patterning in a Divided Society: A Case Study of Mayfair in Johannesburg." Department of Development Studies. Rand Afrikaans University. Johannesburg.

Fisher, Ronald J. 1990. *The Social Psychology of Intergroup and International Conflict Management.* New York: Springer-Verlag.

Fitzduff, Mari. 1993. *Approaches to Community Relations Work.* 3rd edition. Belfast: NI Community Relations Council.

Flammang, Robert A. 1979. "Economic Growth and Economic Development: Counterparts or Competitors?" *Economic Development and Cultural Change* 28, 3: 47–61.

Forester, John. 1993. *Critical Theory, Public Policy and Planning Practice: Toward a Critical Prag-matism*. Albany: SUNY Press.

Forester, John. 1989. *Planning in the Face of Power*. Berkeley: University of California Press.

Forum (National) for Effective Planning and Development. South Africa. 1995. "Guide-lines for the Development Planning Process in Government." July.

Fray, Paula. 1995. "Getting the Province's Housing Backlog Unplugged." *The Star* (Johan-nesburg). July 25, p. 19.

Frazer, Hugh and Mari Fitzduff. 1994. *Improving Community Relations*. 3rd edition. Belfast: NI Community Relations Council.

Friedmann, John. 1992. *Empowerment: The Politics of Alternative Development*. Cambridge, MA: Blackwell.

Friedmann, John. 1987. *Planning in the Public Domain*. Princeton, N.J.: Princeton Univer-sity Press.

Friedman, Steven. 1991. "An Unlikely Utopia: State and Civil Society in South Africa." *Politikon: South African Journal of Political Studies* 19, 1: 5–19.

Friend, John and Allen Hickling. 1987. *Planning Under Pressure: The Strategic Choice Approach*. Oxford: Pergamon.

Gaffikin, F., S. Mooney, and M. Morrissey. 1991. "Planning for a Change in Belfast: The Urban Economy, Urban Regeneration and the Belfast Urban Area Plan 1988." *Town Planning Review* 62, 4: 415–430.

Gaffikin, Frank and Mike Morrissey. 1990. "Dependency, Decline and Development: The Case of West Belfast." *Policy and Politics* 18, 2: 105–117.

Gans, Herbert J. 1962. *The Urban Villagers: Group and Class in the Life of Italian-Americans*. New York: The Free Press.

Gant, George. 1979. *Development Administration: Concepts, Goals, Methods*. Madison: Univer-sity of Wisconsin Press.

Gauteng Forum for Effective Planning and Development. Undated. "Constitution and Terms of Reference."

Gauteng Provincial Government. Departments of Development Planning, Environment and Works; and Local Government and Housing. 1995a. "Towards a Strategy for the Rapid Development of Land and Housing in Gauteng Province."

Gauteng Provincial Government. 1995b. Department of Development Planning, Environ-ment and Works. *Inner City Ivukile*. Delegate Notes for Summit held at Johannesburg City Hall. May 12.

Gauteng Provincial Government. 1995c. *Progress Report: Implementation of Housing Invest-ment Plan, Hostels Redevelopment Programme, Flashpoints and RDP*. July 27.

Gauteng Provincial Government. Department of Development Planning, Environment and Works. Undated. "Towards a Development Planning and Environmental Policy for the PWV." Draft 3 and charts.

Gibbs, J. 1989. "Conceptualization of Terrorism." *American Sociological Review* 54: 329–40.

Gilbert, Paul. 1994. *Terrorism, Security and Nationality: An Introductory Study in Applied Politi-cal Philosophy*. London: Routledge.

Giliomee, Hermann and Lawrence Schlemmer. 1989. *From Apartheid to Nation-Building*. Cape Town: Oxford University Press.

Gladdish, K. R. 1979. "The Political Dynamics of Cultural Minorities." In Alcock, Antony E., Brian K. Taylor, and John M. Welton (eds.) *The Future of Cultural Minorities*. London: MacMillan Press.

Godschalk, David R. (ed.) 1974. *Planning in America: Learning from Turbulence*. Washington, D.C.: American Institute of Planners.

Goldsmith, William W. and Edward J. Blakely. 1992. *Separate Societies: Poverty and Inequality in U.S. Cities*. Philadelphia: Temple University Press.

Goldstein, Arnold P. 1994. *The Ecology of Aggression*. New York: Plenum Press.

Gorecki, Paul K. 1995. "Economic Implications of Peace." Paper presented at INCORE seminar, Belfast, February.

Grant, Joanne (ed.) 1968. *Black Protest*. New York: Fawcett World Library.

Greenberg, Stanley B. 1980. *Race and State in Capitalist Development: South Africa in Comparative Perspective*. Johannesburg: Raven Press.

The Guardian (London: newspaper). February 28, 1995.

The Guardian (London: newspaper). February 13, 1995.

The Guardian (London: newspaper). September 1, 1994.

Guinier, Lani. 1994. *The Tyranny of the Majority: Fundamental Fairness in Representative Democracy*. New York: The Free Press.

Gumede, William M. 1996. "Unemployment Resists Feeble Assaults." *The Star and SA Times International*. June 19.

Gurr, Ted R. 1993. "Why Minorities Rebel: A Global Analysis of Communal Mobilization and Conflict Since 1945." *International Political Science Review* 14, 1: 161–201.

Gurr, Ted R. 1970. *Why Men Rebel*. Princeton, NJ: Princeton University Press.

Gurr, Ted R. 1968. "A Causal Model of Civil Strife: A Comparative Analysis Using New Indices." *American Political Science Review* 62: 1104–24.

Gurr, Ted R. and Barbara Harff. 1994. *Ethnic Conflict in World Politics*. Boulder, CO: Westview.

Gurr, Ted R. and M. Lichbach. 1986. "Forecasting Internal Conflict." *Comparative Political Studies* 9: 3–38.

Gutmann, Emanuel and Claude Klein. 1980. "The Institutional Structure of Heterogeneous Cities: Brussels, Montreal, and Belfast." Pp. 178–207 in Kraemer, Joel L. (ed.). *Jerusalem: Problems and Prospects*. New York: Praeger.

Hadfield, Brigid. 1992. "The Northern Ireland Constitution." Pp. 1–12 in Hadfield, Brigid (ed.). *Northern Ireland: Politics and Constitution*. Buckingham: Open University Press.

Harber, Anton and Barbara Ludman (eds.) 1995. *A–Z of South African Politics*. London: Penguin.

Harloe, Michael. 1996. "Cities in the Transition." Pp. 1–29 in Andrusz, Gregory, Michael Harloe, and Ivan Szelenyi. *Cities and Socialism: Urban and Regional Change and Conflict in Post-Socialist Societies*. Oxford, U.K.: Blackwell.

Hart, Graeme H.T. Undated. "Resegregation Within a Process of Desegregation: A Precursor to Social Polarization in the South African City." Unpublished manuscript. University of the Witwatersrand, Johannesburg.

Harvey, David. 1973. *Social Justice and the City*. London: Edward Arnold.

Heady, Ferrel. 1996. *Public Administration: A Comparative Perspective*. Fifth edition. New York: Marcel Dekker.

Hendry, John. 1989. "The Control of Development and the Origins of Planning in Northern Ireland." In Bannon, Michael J. (ed.). *Planning: The Irish Experience 1920–1988*. Dublin: Wolfhound Press.

Hettne, Bjorn. 1983a. "Peace and Development: Contradictions and Compatibilities." *Journal of Peace Research* 20, 4: 329–342.

Hettne, Bjorn. 1983b. "Peace and Development: What Is the Relationship?" *Development and Peace* 4, 2: 149–163.

Hewitt, Christopher. 1993. "A Growing Crisis: Changing Patterns of South African Violence." Pp. 139–156 in Kriesberg, Louis, Michael Dobkowski, and Isidor Wallimann (eds.). *Research in Social Movements, Conflicts and Change*. Volume 15. Greenwich, CT: JAI Press.

Hillyard, P. 1983. "Law and Order." In J. Darby. *Northern Ireland: The Background to the Conflict*. Belfast: Appletree.

Hindson, Doug, Mark Swilling, and Colin Appleton. 1994. "Peace, Reconstruction and the Project Cycle in Urban Development Projects." *Urban Forum* 5, 1: 93–101.

Hinojosa, Rene C., Thomas S. Lyons, and Frank D. Zinn. 1992. "The Relevancy of North American Planning Education for Overseas Practice: A Survey of Graduates." *Journal of Planning Education and Research* 12, 1: 39–54.

Hoffman, B. 1992. "Current Research on Terrorism and Low-Intensity Conflict." *Studies in Conflict and Terrorism* 15: 25–37.

Horn, Andre, Phillip Hattingh, and Jan Vermaak. 1992. "Winterveld: An Urban Interface Settlement on the Pretoria Metropolitan Fringe." In Smith, David M. (ed.) *The Apartheid City and Beyond: Urbanization and Social Change in South Africa*. London: Routledge.

Horowitz, Donald L. 1985. *Ethnic Groups in Conflict*. Berkeley: University of California Press.

Hugue, Admed Shafiqul. 1990. *Paradoxes of Public Administration: Dimensions of Development*. Dhaka, Bangladesh: University Press Limited.

Human Rights Watch. 1993. *World Report*.

Hunter, Roland. 1994. "Local Economic Development Strategies for PWV." Pp. 215–230 in Tomlinson, Richard. *Urban Development Planning: Lessons for the Economic Reconstruction of South Africa's Cities*. Johannesburg: Witwatersrand University Press.

INCORE (Initiative on Conflict Resolution and Ethnicity). 1994. *Program Information*. University of Ulster at Coleraine (Northern Ireland) and The United Nations University.

The Independent on Sunday (London: newspaper). March 21, 1993.

International Labour Office. 1977. *Meeting Basic Needs: Strategies for Eradicating Mass Poverty and Unemployment*. Geneva: ILO.

Isaac, Stephen. 1971. *Handbook in Research and Evaluation*. San Diego: EdITS Publishers.

Isaacson, Rupert. 1995. *South Africa*. London: Cadogan.

Jochelson, Karen. 1990. "Reform, Repression and Resistance in South Africa: A Case Study of Alexandra Township, 1979–1989." *Journal of Southern African Studies* 16, 1: 1–32.

Johannesburg, City of. 1993. "Towards a Development Framework for the Inner City." Unpublished paper. Johannesburg: City Council.

Johannesburg, City of. 1986. *Guide (General) Plan*. Draft.

Johannesburg (Greater) Transitional Metropolitan Council. 1995a. "Integrated Framework: Medium Term Approach." Report to the TMC by the Planning and Development Line Function Team.

Johannesburg (Greater) Transitional Metropolitan Council. 1995b. "Report on Land Invasion, Squatting and Homelessness." Report to the TMC by the Johannesburg Administration—Health, Housing and Urbanization.

Johannesburg (Greater) Transitional Metropolitan Council. 1995c. "Housing Strategic Project: Vision, Strategy and Proposed Methodology." Report to the TMC by the Johannesburg Administration (Health, Housing and Urbanization; and Planning).

Johannesburg (Greater) Transitional Metropolitan Council. 1995d. "Inner City Planning Initiatives." Report to the TMC by the Johannesburg Administration, City Planning Department.

Johannesburg Metropolitan Planning Department. ISF Working Group. 1995. "Issues Identified by Stakeholders." Comments to ISF 2. Braamfontein: Greater Johannesburg Transitional Metropolitan Council.

JOMET (Johannesburg Metropolitan Transport Area). 1994. *Fourteenth Interim Transport Plan, 1994–1995.* Unpublished. Johannesburg: JOMET.

JOMET (Johannesburg Metropolitan Transport Area). 1992. *JOMET Strategy and Lutsplans.* Compiled by Metropolitan Planning Department.

Kagiso Trust. 1995. *Kagiso Trust Review 1994/5.* Johannesburg.

Katorus Special Presidential Project. 1995a. Action Plans for Stability, Reconstruction and Development of the Katorus Special Integrated Presidential Project.

Katorus Special Presidential Project. 1995b. *Supplementary Business Plan for 1995/96.* June.

Katorus Special Presidential Project. 1995c. *Progress and Problems Report.* Prepared for the Standing Committee on Housing and Local Government. August 30.

Keane, Margaret C. 1990. "Segregation Processes in Public Sector Housing." Pp. 88–108 in Doherty, P. (ed.). *Geographical Perspectives on the Belfast Region.* Newtownabbey, NI: Geographical Society of Ireland.

Keating, M. 1988. *State and Regional Nationalism.* New York: Harvester and Wheatsheaf.

Kelman, Herbert C. 1990. "Applying a Human Needs Perspective to the Practice of Conflict Resolution: The Israeli-Palestinian Case." Pp. 283–297 in Burton, John W. (ed.) *Conflict: Human Needs Theory.* New York: St. Martin's.

Kelman, Herbert C. and Stephen P. Cohen. 1976. "The Problem-Solving Workshop: A Social Psychological Contribution to the Resolution of International Conflicts." *Journal of Peace Research* 13, 2: 79–90.

Kiernan, M. J. 1983. "Ideology, Politics, and Planning: Reflections on Theory and Practice of Urban Planning." *Environment and Planning B: Planning and Design* 10: 71–87.

Knaap, Gerrit and Arthur C. Nelson. 1992. *The Regulated Landscape.* Cambridge, MA: Lincoln Institute of Land Policy.

Knox, Colin and Joanne Hughes. 1994. "Equality and Equity: An Emerging Government Policy in Northern Ireland." *New Community* 20, 2: 207–225.

Korten, David C. 1990. *Getting to the 21st Century: Voluntary Action and the Global Agenda.* West Hartford, CT: Kumarian.

Korten, David C. 1980. "Community Organization and Rural Development: A Learning Process Approach." *Public Administration Review* 40, 5: 480–511.

Krishnarayan, V. and H. Thomas. 1993. *Ethnic Minorities and the Planning System*. London: Royal Town Planning Institute.

Krumholz, Norman and Pierre Clavel. 1994. *Reinventing Cities: Equity Planners Tell Their Stories*. Philadelphia: Temple University Press.

Krumholz, Norman and John Forester. 1990. *Making Equity Planning Work: Leadership in the Public Sector*. Philadelphia: Temple University Press.

Lake, David and Donald Rothchild. 1996. *Ethnic Fears and Global Engagement: The International Spread and Management of Ethnic Conflict*. Policy Paper No. 20. University of California, San Diego: Institute of Global Conflict and Cooperation.

Lake, Robert. 1987. *Resolving Locational Conflict*. New Brunswick, NJ: Center for Urban Policy Research.

Lemon, Anthony (ed.) 1991. *Homes Apart: South Africa's Segregated Cities*. Cape Town: David Philip.

Levine, Marc V. 1990. *The Reconquest of Montreal: Language Policy and Social Change in a Bilingual City*. Philadelphia: Temple University Press.

Levine, Robert A. and Barbara R. Williams. 1992. "Public Policy and the Inner City: Across Three Decades." Pp. 17–51 in Steinberg, James B., David W. Lyon, and Mary E. Vaiana (eds.) *Urban America: Policy Choices for Los Angeles and the Nation*. Santa Monica, CA: RAND.

Ligthelm, A. A. and L. Kritzinger–Van Niekerk. 1990. "Unemployment: The Role of the Public Sector in Increasing the Labour Absorption Capacity of the South African Economy." *Development South Africa* 7, 4: 629–41.

Lijphart, Arend. 1977. *Democracy in Plural Societies: A Comparative Exploration*. New Haven: Yale University Press.

Lijphart, Arend. 1968. *The Politics of Accommodation: Pluralism and Democracy in the Netherlands*. Berkeley: University of California Press.

Lindblom, Charles E. 1977. *Politics and Markets: The World's Political-Economic Systems*. New York: Basic Books.

Lindblom, Charles E. 1959. "The Science of Muddling Through." *Public Administration Review* 19: 79–88.

Lineberry, Robert L. 1977. *Equality and Urban Policy: The Distribution of Municipal Public Services*. Newbury Park, CA: Sage.

Livingstone, Stephen and John Morison. 1995. "An Audit of Democracy in Northern Ireland." *Fortnight* 337 (supplement).

Local Government Demarcation Board for the Province of Gauteng. 1995. *Minutes and Records of Proceedings*. April–November.

Longland, Tony. 1994. "Development in Conflict Situations: The Occupied Territories." *Community Development Journal* 29, 2: 132–140.

Loughlin, John. 1992. "Administering Policy in Northern Ireland." Pp. 60–75 in Hadfield, Brigid (ed.). *Northern Ireland: Politics and Constitution*. Buckingham: Open University Press.

Lovett, Tom, Deirdre Gunn, and Terry Robson. 1994. "Education, Conflict and Community Development in Northern Ireland." *Community Development Journal* 29, 2: 177–186.

Lund, Troye. 1995. "Tokyo Wins Battle for New Borders." *The Star* (Johannesburg). August 5, p. 1.

Lustick, I. 1979. "Stability in Deeply Divided Societies: Consociationalisation vs. Control." *World Politics* 31: 325–344.

Mabin, Alan. 1995. "On the Problems and Prospects of Overcoming Segregation and Fragmentation in Southern Africa's Cities in the Postmodern Era." Pp. 187–198 in Watson, Sophie and Katherine Gibson (eds.) *Postmodern Cities and Spaces*. Oxford: Blackwell.

Mabin, Alan. 1992. "Comprehensive Segregation: The Origins of the Group Areas Act and Its Planning Apparatus." *Journal of Southern African Studies* 18, 2: 405–429.

Mabin, Alan and Roland Hunter. 1993. "Report of the Review of Conditions and Trends Affecting Development in the PWV." Final draft prepared for the PWV Forum.

Mallaby, Sebastian. 1992. *After Apartheid*. London: Faber and Faber.

Mandela, Nelson. 1994. *Long Walk to Freedom*. Boston: Little, Brown.

Mandy, Nigel. 1988. "Central Witwatersrand Case Study." Johannesburg: Urban Foundation.

Mandy, Nigel. 1984. *A City Divided: Johannesburg and Soweto*. New York: St. Martin's.

March, James G. and Herbert A. Simon. 1958. *Organizations*. New York: John Wiley and Sons.

Mashabela, Harry. 1990. *Mekhukhu: Urban African Cities of the Future*. Johannesburg: South African Institute of Race Relations.

Mashabela, Harry. 1988. *Townships of the PWV*. Johannesburg: South African Institute of Race Relations.

Mashile, G. G. and G. H. Pirie. 1977. "Aspects of Housing Allocation in Soweto." *South African Geographical Journal* 59, 2: 139–49.

Masser, Ian. 1986. "Some Methodological Considerations." In Masser, Ian and Richard Williams (eds.) *Learning from Other Countries: The Cross-National Dimension in Urban Policy-Making*. Norwich, U.K.: Geo.

Matthew, Sir R. H. 1964. *Belfast Regional Survey and Plan 1962*. Belfast: HMSO.

Matusow, Allen J. 1984. *The Unraveling of America: A History of Liberalism in the 1960s*. New York: Harper and Row.

Mayer, Robert R. and Ernest Greenwood. 1980. *The Design of Social Policy Research*. Englewood Cliffs, NJ: Prentice-Hall.

Mbigi, Lovemore and Jenny Maree. 1995. *Ubuntu: The Spirit of African Transformation Management*. Randburg: Knowledge Resources.

McAdam, Doug, John D. McCarthy, and Mayer N. Zald. 1996. "Opportunities, Mobilizing Structures, and Framing Processes—Toward a Synthetic, Comparative Perspective on Social Movements." Pp. 1–20 in McAdam, Doug, John D. McCarthy, and Mayer N. Zald (ed.) *Comparative Perspectives on Social Movements*. Cambridge: Cambridge University Press.

McCarthy, Jeff. 1992. "Local and Regional Government: From Rigidity to Crisis to Flux." In Smith, David M. (ed.) 1992. *The Apartheid City and Beyond: Urbanization and Social Change in South Africa*. London: Routledge.

McGarry, John and Brendan O'Leary (eds.) 1993. *The Politics of Ethnic Conflict Regulation: Case Studies of Protracted Ethnic Conflicts*. London: Routledge.

McGivern, William. 1983. "Housing Development and Sectarian Interface Areas." In Murtagh, Brendan (ed.). *Planning and Ethnic Space in Belfast*. Occasional Paper No. 5. Centre for Policy Research. University of Ulster.

Meyer, Roelf. 1995. "Provincial and Local Government in the Reconstruction and Development Programme." Pp. 65–74 in RDP Office, South Africa, *Human Resource Development in the RDP*. Randburg: Ravan.

Midrand (Town of). 1991. *Midrand Structure Plan—Revision 1991*. Prepared by Van der Schyff, Baylis, Gericke, and Druce—Town and Regional Planners.

Mier, Robert. 1993. *Social Justice and Local Development Policy*. Newbury Park, CA: Sage.

Mills, Glen. 1989. "The Shape of Housing in South Africa." *Open House International* 14.

Milnor, Andrew J. 1969. *Elections and Political Stability*. Boston: Little, Brown.

Ministry in the Office of the President. South Africa. 1995. *Remaking South Africa's Cities and Towns: The Government of National Unity's Urban Strategy*. September 7 draft. Pretoria: Ministry.

Molobi, Eric. 1995. "Decision Making in Implementation of the Reconstruction and Development Programme." Pp. 75–86 in RDP Office, South Africa, *Human Resource Development in the RDP*. Randburg: Ravan.

Moolman, Mauritz. 1990. *From Town to Township: Regional Service Councils Assessed*. Johannesburg: South African Institute of Race Relations.

Mooney, S. and F. Gaffikin. 1987. *Belfast Urban Area Plan 1987: Reshaping Space and Society*. Belfast: Centre for the Unemployed.

Morley, David and Arie Shachar. 1986. "Epilogue: Reflections by Planners on Planning." In Morley, David and Arie Shachar (eds.) *Planning in Turbulence*. Jerusalem: Magnes Press, Hebrew University.

Morris, Mike and Doug Hindson. 1992. "The Disintegration of Apartheid: From Violence to Reconstruction." Pp. 152–170 in Moss, Glenn and Ingrid Obery (eds.) *South African Review 6: From "Red Friday" to Codesa*. Johannesburg: Ravan.

Muller, John. 1994. "Community Development and Decision-Making." *Urban Forum* 5, 1: 11–22.

Murphy, A. B. 1989. "Territorial Policies in Multiethnic States." *Geographical Review* 79: 410–421.

Murray, Michael. 1991. *The Politics and Pragmatism of Urban Containment: Belfast Since 1940*. Aldershot, U.K.: Avebury.

Murtagh, Brendan. 1994a. *Ethnic Space and the Challenge to Land Use Planning: A Study of Belfast's Peace Lines*. University of Ulster, Jordanstown. Centre for Policy Research.

Murtagh, Brendan. 1994b. *Land Use Planning and Community Relations*. A report to the Northern Ireland Community Relations Council. University of Ulster.

Murtagh, Brendan. 1993. "The Role of the Security Forces and Peace Line Planning." In Murtagh, Brendan (ed.). *Planning and Ethnic Space in Belfast*. Occasional Paper No. 5. Centre for Policy Research. University of Ulster.

National Advisory Commission on Civil Disorders. United States. 1968. *The Kerner Report*. New York: Bantam Books.

Naude, A., E. Muller, and E. P. de Beer. 1988. "Black Urbanization and Land Requirements in the PWV Complex."

Nelson, Arthur C. and James B. Duncan. 1995. *Growth Management Principles and Practices*. Chicago, IL: American Planning Association.

Neuberger, Benyamin. 1990. "Nationalisms Compared: ANC, IRA, and PLO." Pp. 54–77 in Giliomee, Hermann and Jannie Gagiano (eds.) *The Elusive Search for Peace: South Africa, Israel and Northern Ireland*. Cape Town: Oxford University Press and IDASA.

Newhco (Group). 1995. *Securing Delivery: Towards One Million Homes*. Annual Report 1994. Johannesburg: Newhco.

Newman, O. 1975. *Design Guidelines for Creating Defensible Space*. Washington, D.C.: U.S. Government Printing Office.

Nordlinger, Eric A. 1972. *Conflict Regulation in Divided Societies*. Boston: Center for International Affairs, Harvard University.

Northern Ireland Census 1991: Belfast Urban Area Report. Belfast: HMSO.

Northern Ireland Community Relations Council. 1994a. *Fourth Report*. Belfast: NICRC.

Northern Ireland Community Relations Council. 1994b. *Symbols*. Belfast: NICRC, Cultural Traditions Group.

Northern Ireland Council for Voluntary Action (NICVA). 1994. *The Implementation of Targeting Social Need*. Belfast: NICVA (Public Affairs Project).

NICVA. 1993. *Twenty Years of Deprivation: A Comparative Analysis of Deprivation in the Belfast Urban Area Using Census Findings Published in 1991, 1981, and 1971*. Belfast: NICVA (Public Affairs Project).

Northern Ireland Housing Executive (NIHE). Belfast Division. 1995. *Belfast Housing Strategy Review*. Belfast: NIHE.

NIHE. 1994a. *Integration/Segregation: Preliminary Views and Approach*. Housing Policy Review Paper. Belfast: Integration/Segregation Group (NIHE).

NIHE. 1994b. *Annual Report*. April 1993–March 1994. Belfast: NIHE.

NIHE. 1991. *Building a Better Belfast*. Belfast: NIHE.

NIHE. 1990a. *The Housing Selection Scheme: Applying for a Housing Executive Home*. Belfast: NIHE.

NIHE. 1990b. *Alliance North Belfast: A Case for Action*. Belfast: NIHE.

NIHE. 1988. *Coping with Conflict: Violence and Urban Renewal in Belfast*. Belfast: NIHE.

Norton, Alan. 1983. "The Government and Administration of Metropolitan Areas in Western Democracies: A Survey of Approaches to the Administrative Problems of Major Conurbations in Europe and Canada." Birmingham, England: Institute of Government Studies, University of Birmingham.

O'Connor, James. 1973. *The Fiscal Crisis of the State*. New York: St. Martin's.

O'Connor, Robert. 1988. "Dateline Belfast: Government Officials Are Hoping That a New Plan Will Help Heal the City's Wounds." *Planning* 54, 10: 27–32.

O'Leary, Brendan and John McGarry. 1995. "Regulating Nations and Ethnic Communities." Pp. 245–289 in Breton, A., G. Galeotti, P. Salmon, and R. Wintrobe (eds.) *Nationalism and Rationality*. Cambridge: Cambridge University Press.

Osborne, Robert D. and Dale Singleton. 1982. "Political Processes and Behavior." Pp. 167–194 in Boal, Frederick W. and J. Neville Douglas (eds.). *Integration and Division: Geographical Perspectives on the Northern Ireland Problem*. London: Academic Press.

Palley, Claire. 1979. *Constitutional Law and Minorities*. London: Minority Rights Group.

Paris, David C. and James F. Reynolds. 1983. *The Logic of Policy Inquiry*. New York: Longman.

Parnell, Susan and Alan Mabin. 1995. "Rethinking Urban South Africa." *Journal of Southern African Studies* 21, 1: 39–61.

Parnell, S. M. and G. H. Pirie. 1991. "Johannesburg." In Anthony Lemon (ed.) *Homes Apart: South Africa's Segregated Cities*. London: Paul Chapman Publishing.

Partrick, Neil. 1994. "Democracy Under Limited Autonomy." *News from Within* 10, 9: 21–24. Jerusalem: Alternative Information Center (newsletter).

Pesic, Vesna. 1996. *Serbian Nationalism and the Origins of the Yugoslav Crisis*. Peaceworks Paper no. 8. Washington, D.C.: United States Institute of Peace.

Piven, Francis and R. Cloward. 1971. *Regulating the Poor: The Functions of Social Welfare*. New York: Pantheon.

Planact. 1993. *Planact Annual Report 1992/93*. Yeoville.

Planact. 1992. *Resource Document: The Reorganization of Local Government in South Africa*. Yeoville: Planact.

Platzky, L. and C. Walker. 1985. *The Surplus People: Forced Removals in South Africa*. Johannesburg: Ravan.

Polikoff, Alexander. 1986. "Sustainable Integration or Inevitable Resegregation: The Troubling Questions." In Goering, John M. (ed.) *Housing Desegregation and Federal Policy*. Chapel Hill: University of North Carolina Press.

Poole, Michael. 1990. "The Geographical Location of Political Violence in Northern Ireland." Pp. 64–82 in Darby, John, Nicholas Dodge, and A. C. Hepburn (eds.) *Political Violence: Ireland in a Comparative Perspective*. Ottawa, Ontario: University of Ottawa Press.

Poulsen, Lone. "Inner City Communities and Urban Environments: The Role of the Physical Planning Professions." *Urban Forum* 5, 1: 45–60.

President's Commission for a National Agenda for the Eighties. United States. 1980. *A National Agenda for the Eighties*. Washington, D.C.: United States Government Printing Office.

Przeworski, Adam and Henry Teune. 1970. *The Logic of Comparative Social Inquiry*. New York: Wiley.

Putnam, R. D. 1993. *Making Democracy Work: Civic Traditions in Modern Italy*. Princeton, NJ: Princeton University Press.

Rawls, John. 1971. *A Theory of Justice*. Cambridge, MA: Harvard University Press.

Redpath, Jackie. 1991. "Power and the Protestant Community." In *Community Development in Protestant Areas: A Report on Two Seminars*. Belfast: Northern Ireland Community Relations Council.

Reintges, Claudia. 1992. "Urban (Mis)management? A Case Study of the Effects of Orderly Urbanization on Duncan Village." In Smith, David M. (ed.) 1992. *The Apartheid City and Beyond: Urbanization and Social Change in South Africa*. London: Routledge.

Robinson, Jennifer. 1996. *The Power of Apartheid: State, Power, and Space in South African Cities*. Oxford, U.K.: Butterworth Heinemann.

Robson, Brian, Michael Bradford, and Iain Deas. 1994. *Relative Deprivation in Northern Ireland*. Policy, Planning and Research Unit. Department of Finance and Personnel. NIO. PPRU Occasional Paper #28.

Robson, Brian, et al. 1994. *Assessing the Impact of Urban Policy*. Department of the Environment. Inner Cities Research Programme. London: HMSO.

Rodney, Derek. 1996. "No Respite in Battle Against Rising Crime." *The Star and SA Times International*. June 5.

Rogerson, C. M. 1996. "Dispersion Within Concentration: The Changing Location of Corporate Headquarter Offices in South Africa." *Development South Africa* 13, 4: 567–579.

Rogerson, C. M. and J. Rogerson. 1995. "Central Witwatersrand: A Metropolitan Region in Distress?" Report prepared for Centre for Development and Enterprise, Johannesburg.

Rolston, Bill. 1992. *Drawing Support: Murals in the North of Ireland*. Belfast: Beyond the Pale.

Romann, Michael. 1995. *Managing Conflict: Some Lessons from Israeli Rule in East Jerusalem*. Jerusalem: Mekhon Yerushalayim Ie-heker Yisra'el.

Romann, Michael and Alex Weingrod. 1991. *Living Together Separately: Arabs and Jews in Contemporary Jerusalem*. Princeton, NJ: Princeton University Press.

Rose, Richard. 1976. *Northern Ireland: A Time of Choice*. New York: Macmillan.

Roseman, Curtis C., Hans Dieter Laux, and Gunter Thieme. 1996. "Modern EthniCities." Pp. xvii–xxvii in Roseman, Curtis C., Hans Dieter Laux, and Gunter Thieme (eds.) *EthniCity: Geographic Perspectives on Ethnic Change in Modern Cities*. Lanham, MD: Rowman and Littlefield.

Rothman, Jay. 1992. *From Confrontation to Cooperation: Resolving Ethnic and Regional Conflict*. Newbury Park, CA: Sage.

Rowthorn, Bob and Naomi Wayne. 1985. *Northern Ireland: The Political Economy of Conflict*. Cambridge: Polity.

Rule, James B. 1988. *Theories of Civil Violence*. Berkeley: University of California Press.

Rule, S. P. 1989. "The Emergence of a Racially Mixed Residential Suburb in Johannesburg: The Demise of the Apartheid City?" *Geographical Journal* 155: 196–203.

Russett, B. and H. Starr. 1989. *World Politics: The Menu for Choice*. 2d ed. New York: Freeman.

Sack, R. 1986. *Human Territoriality: Its Theory and History*. Cambridge: Cambridge University Press.

Sack, R. 1981. "Territorial Bases for Power." In Burnett, A. and P. Taylor (eds.). *Political Studies from Spatial Perspectives*. New York: John Wiley and Sons.

Saff, Grant. 1995. "Residential Segregation in Postapartheid South Africa: What Can Be Learned from the United States Experience." *Urban Affairs Review* 30, 6: 782–808.

Saff, Grant. 1991. "From Race to Space: Reconceptualizing the Post-Apartheid Urban Spatial Environment." *Urban Forum* 2, 1: 59–90.

Saunders, Peter. 1979. *Urban Politics*. Harmondsworth, Middlesex: Penguin.

Schlemmer, L. S. and S. L. Stack. 1989. "Black, White and Shades of Gray: A Study of Responses to Residential Segregation in the Pretoria-Witwatersrand Region." Johannesburg: University of the Witwatersrand, Centre for Policy Studies.

Schmitt, David E. 1988. "Bicommunalism in Northern Ireland." *Publius: The Journal of Federalism* 18, 2: 33–46.

Schultz, R. H. 1991. "The Low-Intensity Conflict Environment of the 1990s." *Annals American Academy of Political and Social Science* 517: 120–34.

Seekings, Jeremy. 1992. "Civic Organizations in South African Townships." Pp. 216–238 in Moss, Glenn and Ingrid Obery (eds.) *South African Review 6: From "Red Friday" to Codesa*. Johannesburg: Ravan.

Seliger, M. 1970. "Fundamental and Operative Ideology: The Two Principal Dimensions of Political Argumentation." *Policy Sciences* 1: 325–338.

Seneque Smit Maughan-Brown and Associates. 1993. "The Jeppestown Oval Precinct." An urban design proposal in response to the Johannesburg City Council's Call for Proposals. November.

Sennett, Richard. 1970. *The Uses of Disorder: Personal Identity and City Life*. New York: Vintage.

Shaw, Mark. 1994. "Transitional Politics in the Central Wits Sub-Region." Centre for Policy Studies. Unpublished report for the Urban Foundation, Johannesburg.

Shutte, Augustine. 1993. *Philosophy for Africa*. Cape Town: University of Cape Town.

Sibley, David. 1995. *Geographies of Exclusion: Society and Difference in the West*. London: Routledge.

Simon, Herbert. 1947. *Administrative Behavior: A Study of Decision-Making Processes in Administrative Organization*. New York: Macmillan.

Singleton, Dale. 1986. "Housing Allocation Policy and Practice in Northern Ireland." In Singleton, D. (ed.) *Aspects of Housing Policy and Practice in Northern Ireland 1984–1986*. Belfast: Queen's University.

Singleton, Dale. 1983. "Belfast Housing Renewal Strategy: A Comment." In Singleton, D. (ed.) *Aspects of Housing Policy and Practice in Northern Ireland*. Belfast: Queen's University.

Sisk, Timothy D. 1995. *Democratization in South Africa: The Elusive Social Contract*. Princeton, NJ: Princeton University Press.

Smit, Dirk van zyl. 1995. "South African Criminal Justice and Criminology in Transition." *The Criminologist* 20, 5: 4, 6, 8–9.

Smith, Anthony D. 1993. "The Ethnic Sources of Nationalism." Pp. 27–42 in Brown, Michael E. (ed.) *Ethnic Conflict and International Security*. Princeton, NJ: Princeton University Press.

Smith, David J. 1987. *Equality and Inequality in Northern Ireland III: Perceptions and Views*. London: Policy Studies Institute.

Smith, David J. and David Chambers. 1991. *Inequality in Northern Ireland*. Oxford: Clarendon.

Smith, David J. and David Chambers. 1989. *Equality and Inequality in Northern Ireland 4: Public Housing*. London: Policy Studies Institute.

Smith, David M. 1994. *Geography and Social Justice*. Oxford: Blackwell.

Smith, David M. (ed.) 1992. *The Apartheid City and Beyond: Urbanization and Social Change in South Africa*. London: Routledge.

Smith, M. G. 1969. "Some Developments in the Analytic Framework of Pluralism." In Kuper, Leo and M. G. Smith (eds.) *Pluralism in Africa*. Berkeley: University of California Press.

Smith, Michael P. 1979. *The City and Social Theory*. New York: St. Martin's.

Smooha, Sammy. 1980. "Control of Minorities in Israel and Northern Ireland." *Comparative Studies in Society and History* 22, 2: 256–280.

Snyder, Jack. 1993. "Nationalism and the Crisis of the Post-Soviet State." Pp. 79–102 in Brown, Michael (ed.) *Ethnic Conflict and International Security*. Princeton, NJ: Princeton University Press.

South Africa (Republic of). 1995. *White Paper on Housing*. Cape Town: Parliament.

South Africa (Republic of). 1994. *White Paper on Reconstruction and Development*. Cape Town: Parliament. November 15.

South African History Archive. 1991. *Images of Defiance: South African Resistance Posters of the 1980s*. Braamfontein: Ravan.

South African Information Service. 1961. *Each a Roof of His Own*. Booklet distributed in the USA. New York: SAIS.

South African Institute of Race Relations. 1994. *Race Relations Survey 1993/94*. Johannesburg: SAIRR.

South African Reserve Bank. 1996. *Quarterly Bulletin*. June.

South African Reserve Bank. 1994. *Quarterly Bulletin*. June.

South African Township Annual. 1993. Rivonia (Johannesburg): IR Information Surveys.

The Star (Johannesburg) newspaper. 1995, August 4.

Sparks, Allister. 1994. *Tomorrow Is Another Country: The Inside Story of South Africa's Negotiated Revolution*. Sandton: Struik.

Sparks, Allister. 1988. *The Mind of South Africa*. London: Heinemann.

Springfield Inter-Community Development Project. 1993. *Life on the Interface*. Belfast: SICDP.

Standing Advisory Commission on Human Rights. 1990. *Second Report on Religious and Political Discrimination and Equality of Opportunity in Northern Ireland*. Belfast: STACHR.

Stanovcic, Vojislav. 1992. "Problems and Options in Institutionalizing Ethnic Relations." *International Political Science Review* 13, 4: 359–79.

Stark, D. 1992. "Path Dependence and Privatization Strategies in East Central Europe." *East European Politics and Societies* 6, 1: 17–54.

Stark, D. 1990. "Privatization in Hungary: From Plan to Market or from Plan to Clan?" *East European Politics and Societies* 4, 3: 351–92.

Stewart, A. T. 1977. *The Narrow Ground*. London: Faber and Faber.

Susskind, Lawrence and J. Cruickshank. 1987. *Breaking the Impasse*. New York: Basic Books.

Sutton, Malcolm. 1994. *An Index of Deaths from the Conflict in Ireland 1969–1993*. Belfast: Beyond the Pale.

Sweeney, Paul. 1991. "From Veto to Achievement." In *Community Development in Protestant Areas: A Report on Two Seminars*. Belfast: Northern Ireland Community Relations Council.

Sweeney, Paul and Frank Gaffikin. 1995. *Listening to People*. A Report on the Making Belfast Work Consultation Process. March. Belfast: Making Belfast Work.

Swilling, Mark. 1990. "Deracialised Urbanization: A Critique of the New Urban Strategies and Some Policy Alternatives from a Democratic Perspective." *Urban Forum* 1, 2: 15–39.

Szelenyi, Ivan. 1996. "Cities Under Socialism—and After." Pp. 286–317 in Andrusz, Gregory, Michael Harloe, and Ivan Szelenyi. *Cities and Socialism: Urban and Regional Change and Conflict in Post-Socialist Societies*. Oxford, UK: Blackwell.

Tarrow, Sidney. 1994. *Power in Movement: Social Movements, Collective Action and Politics*. Cambridge: Cambridge University Press.

Thomas, Huw. (ed.) 1994. *Values and Planning*. Aldershot, UK: Avebury.

Thomas, H. and V. Krishnarayan. 1994. "'Race,' Disadvantage, and Policy Processes in British Planning." *Environment and Planning A* 26, 12: 1891–1910.

Thorne, Stephen. 1995. *Baralink Development Framework*. Johannesburg: Stephen Thorne—Architect and Urban Designer.

Tilly, Charles. 1978. *From Mobilization to Rebellion*. Reading, MA: Addison-Wesley.

Toland, Judith D. 1993. "Dialogue of Self and Other: Ethnicity and the Statehood Building Process." Pp. 1–20 in Toland, Judith (ed.) *Ethnicity and the State. Political and Legal Anthropology* vol. 9. New Brunswick, NJ: Transaction.

Tomlinson, Richard. 1994. *Urban Development Planning: Lessons for the Economic Reconstruction of South Africa's Cities*. Johannesburg: Witwatersrand University Press.

Tomlinson, Richard. 1990. *Urbanization in Post-Apartheid South Africa*. Boston: Unwin Hyman.

Tonge, Jonathon. 1998. *Northern Ireland: Conflict and Change*. London: Prentice Hall Europe.

Torgovnik, Efraim. 1990. *The Politics of Urban Planning Policy*. Lanham, MD: University Press of America.

Touval, Saadia, and I. William Zartman (eds.) 1985. *International Mediation in Theory and Practice*. Boulder, CO: Westview Press.

Tugwell, Rexford G. 1935. *The Battle for Democracy*. New York: Columbia University Press.

Turok, Ben. 1993. "South Africa's Skyscraper Economy: Growth or Development?" Pp. 237–246 in Hallowes, David (ed.) *Hidden Faces—Environment, Development, Justice: South Africa and the Global Context*. Scottsville, South Africa: Earthlife.

Turok, Ivan. 1994a. "Urban Planning in the Transition from Apartheid, Part I: The Legacy of Social Control." *Town Planning Review* 65, 3: 243–259.

Turok, Ivan. 1994b. "Urban Planning in the Transition from Apartheid, Part II: Towards Reconstruction." *Town Planning Review* 65, 4: 355–374.

Ulster Political Research Group. 1987. *Common Sense*. Belfast: Ulster Defense Association.

United Nations. 1996a. *An Inventory of Post-Conflict Peace-Building Activities*. New York: United Nations.

United Nations. 1996b. *The Istanbul Declaration on Human Settlements*. Advance, Unedited Text. June 15. United Nations Conference on Human Settlements (Habitat II). Istanbul. June 3–14.

United Nations. 1996c. Report on world urbanization done for Habitat II conference. Website http:\\www.undp.org\un\habitat. June 15 advance, unedited text.

United Nations. 1993. *Human Development Report*. U.N. Development Program. New York: United Nations.

Upper Shankill Belfast Action Team. 1994. *Strategy Document 1994–97*. Belfast: MBW/BAT.

Urban Foundation. 1991. *Land Reform: An Analysis and a Challenge*. White Paper. Johannesburg: The Urban Foundation.

Urban Foundation. 1990a. *Policies for a New Urban Future, Urban Debate 2010: Population Trends*. Volume 1. Johannesburg: The Urban Foundation.

Urban Foundation. 1990b. *Opening the Cities: Comparative Perspectives on Desegregation*. Johannesburg: The Urban Foundation.

Urban Foundation. 1990c. *Policies for a New Urban Future, Urban Debate 2010: Policy Overview, the Urban Challenge*. Volume 2. Johannesburg: The Urban Foundation.

Urban Foundation. 1990d. *Policies for a New Urban Future, Urban Debate 2010: Tackling Group Areas.* Volume 6. Johannesburg: The Urban Foundation.

Urban Foundation. 1990e. *Policies for a New Urban Future, Urban Debate 2010: Governing Urban South Africa.* Volume 8. Johannesburg: The Urban Foundation.

U.S. Institute of Peace. 1996. "Rebuilding Communities Devastated by War." *Peace Watch* newsletter. Volume II, no. 6, pp. 1, 8–9.

van Zyl, J. C. 1993. *Development and Development Management: A Training Perspective.* Policy Working Papers No. 4. Development Bank of Southern Africa.

Viljoen, Reinhold and Jose Adler. 1993. "Site and Service—Incipient Disaster or Sustainable Development?" Pp. 149–155 in Hallowes, David (ed.) *Hidden Faces—Environment, Development, Justice: South Africa and the Global Context.* Scottsville: Earthlife Africa.

Vista 2. 1995a. "Ready for Delivery with the People." Pre-Conference Information pack. April 8. Gauteng.

Vista 2. 1995b. "Conference Papers." July 29. Gauteng.

Weitzer, Ronald. 1995. *Policing Under Fire: Ethnic Conflict and Police-Community Relations in Northern Ireland.* Albany: State University of New York Press.

Weitzer, Ronald. 1990. *Transforming Settler States: Communal Conflict and Internal Security in Northern Ireland and Zimbabwe.* Berkeley: University of California Press.

Welch, David. 1993. "Domestic Politics and Ethnic Conflict." Pp. 43–60 in Brown, Michael (ed.) *Ethnic Conflict and International Security.* Princeton, NJ: Princeton University Press.

Whyte, John. 1990. *Interpreting Northern Ireland.* Oxford: Clarendon.

Whyte, John H. 1986. "How Is the Boundary Maintained Between the Two Communities in Northern Ireland?" *Ethnic and Racial Studies* 9, 2: 219–234.

Wiener, Ron. 1976. *The Rape and Plunder of the Shankill in Belfast: People and Planning.* Belfast: Nothems.

Wilkinson, P. 1983. "Providing 'Adequate Housing.'" In Hindson, D. C. (ed.) *Working Papers in Southern African Studies.* Johannesburg.

Williams, Robin M., Jr. 1994. "The Sociology of Ethnic Conflicts: Comparative International Perspectives." *Annual Review of Sociology* 20: 49–79.

Wills, T. M. 1988. "The Segregated City." In Laband, J. and R. H. Haswell (eds.) *Pietermaritzburg 1838–1988: A New Portrait of an African City.* University of Natal Press and Shooter and Shuter, Pietermaritzburg.

Winnefeld, James A. et al. 1995. *Intervention in Intrastate Conflict: Implications for the Army in the Post–Cold War Era.* Prepared for the U.S. Army. Santa Monica, CA: RAND.

Wirth, Louis. 1931. "Culture Conflict and Misconduct." *Social Forces* 9 (June).

Wolfe, James H. 1988. "Cyprus: Federation Under International Safeguards." *Publius: The Journal of Federalism* 18, 2: 75–90.

Wood, D. 1991. "In Defense of Indefensible Space." In Brantingham, P. J. and P. L. Brantingham (eds.) *Environmental Criminology.* Prospect Heights, IL: Waveland.

World Bank. 1991. *Urban Policy and Economic Development: An Agenda for the 1990s.* Washington, D.C.: World Bank.

Wright, Robin. 1993. "Ethnic Strife Owes More to Present Than to Past." *The Los Angeles Times.* Special supplement: *The New Tribalism.* June 8.

Yahya, Maha. 1993. "Reconstituting Space: The Aberration of the Urban in Beirut." Pp. 128–166 in Khalaf, Samir and Philip Khoury (eds.) *Recovering Beirut: Urban Design and Post-War Reconstruction*. Leiden, The Netherlands: Brill.

Yiftachel, Oren. 1995. "The Dark Side of Modernism: Planning as Control of an Ethnic Minority." Pp. 216–242 in Watson, Sophie and Katherine Gibson (eds.) *Postmodern Cities and Spaces*. Oxford: Blackwell.

Yiftachel, Oren. 1992. *Planning a Mixed Region in Israel: The Political Geography of Arab-Jewish Relations in the Galilee*. Aldershot, U.K.: Avebury.

Yiftachel, Oren. 1989. "Towards a New Typology of Urban Planning Theories." *Environment and Planning B: Planning and Design* 16, 1: 23–39.

Zartman, I. William (ed.) 1995. *Collapsed States: The Disintegration and Restoration of Legitimate Authority*. Boulder, CO: Lynne Rienner.

Plans and Laws

Belfast

Building Design Partnership. 1969. *Belfast Urban Area Plan*. Belfast: BDP.

Department of the Environment for Northern Ireland. 1990. *Belfast Urban Area Plan 2001*. Belfast: HMSO.

Department of the Environment for Northern Ireland. 1989. *Belfast Urban Area Plan 2001: Adoption Statement*. Belfast: HMSO.

Department of the Environment for Northern Ireland. 1988. "Pre-Inquiry Response to CTA's Objections to the Draft BUAP." Pp. 187–221 in Blackman, Tim. 1991. *Planning Belfast: A Case Study of Public Policy and Community Action*. Aldershot, U.K.: Avebury.

Department of the Environment for Northern Ireland. 1987. *Belfast Urban Area Plan 2001*. Draft. Belfast: Her Majesty's Stationery Office (HMSO).

Department of the Environment for Northern Ireland. 1981. *Belfast Urban Area: Planning Statement and Progress Report*. Belfast: DOENI.

Department of the Environment for Northern Ireland. 1977. *Northern Ireland: Regional Physical Development Strategy 1975–95*. Belfast: HMSO.

Government of Northern Ireland. 1970. *Review Body on Local Government in Northern Ireland* ("The Macrory Report"). CMD 546. Belfast: HMSO.

Matthew, Sir R. H. 1964. *Belfast Regional Survey and Plan 1962*. Belfast: HMSO.

Northern Ireland Housing Executive. 1971–. *Annual Reports*. Belfast: NIHE

Northern Ireland Information Service. 1988. *Making Belfast Work: Belfast Areas for Action*.

The Planning (Northern Ireland) Order 1991. No. 1220 (N.I.). Belfast: HMSO.

Pollak, Andy (ed.) 1993. *A Citizen's Inquiry: The Opsahl Report on Northern Ireland*. Lilliput Press (for Initiative '92).

Shankill Partnership Board. 1995. *Greater Shankill Regeneration Strategy*. As printed in *Shankill People*. February.

Johannesburg

Natives Land Act. 1913.

Natives (Urban Areas) Act. 1923.

Slums Act. 1934.

Native Trust and Land Act. 1936.

Native (Urban Areas) Amendment Act. 1937.

Natives (Urban Areas) Consolidation Act. 1945.

Group Areas Act. 1950. South African Statutes, Act 41.

Population Registration Act. 1950.

Abolition of Passes Act. 1951.

Natives Resettlement Act. 1954.

Group Areas Development Act. 1955.

Bantu Administration Act. 1959.

Community Development Act. 1966.

Physical Planning Act. 1967.

Urban Transportation Act. 1977.

Physical Planning Act. 1991.

Abolition of Racially Based Land Measures Act. 1991.

Less Formal Township Establishment Act. 1991.

Upgrading of Land Tenure Rights Act. 1991.

Local Government Transition Act of 1993. Act No. 209.

Development Facilitation Bill. 1994. Second Redraft After Publication. April.

Ecoplan Consortium. 1979. *Greater Soweto Development Guidance System*. Unpublished. February.

Johannesburg (city of). 1986. *Guide (General) Plan*. Draft.

Johannesburg (city of). 1984. *City Johannesburg: Plan of the Municipal Area*. Town Planning Branch. City Engineer's Department. Johannesburg: The Branch.

Jomet (Metropolitan Transport Board for the Inner Witwatersrand). 1979. *A Summary of the Investigation of Alternative Land Use and Transportation Strategies for 2000 AD*.

President's Council. 1982. *Report on Local and Regional Management Systems in the Republic of South Africa*. Cape Town: Government Printer.

South Africa. 1987. *Present and Future Settlement, Movement and Migration Patterns in Response to Urbanisation Policies* VV1/87. Pretoria: Department of Transport.

South Africa, Republic of. 1986a. *White Paper on Urbanization*. Pretoria: Government Printer.

South Africa, Republic of. 1986b. Department of Constitutional Development and Planning. *Draft Guide Plan for the Central Witwatersrand*. Pretoria: Government Printer.

South Africa, Republic of. 1981. Office of the Prime Minister—Physical Planning Branch. *A Spatial Development Strategy for the PWV Complex*. Pretoria: Government Printer.

South Africa, Republic of. 1961–1986. *Population Census*. Pretoria: Government Printer.

Index

Access to policymaking, and urban planning,
    34–35
ACE. *See* Action for Community Employment
Action Area Committees (Johannesburg),
    241–242
Action for Community Employment (ACE), 82
Action-taking versus framework development,
    192. *See also* Long-range planning versus
    short-term crisis response
African National Congress (ANC), 168, 179,
    230, 242, 284
    assumption of political control, xiii, 40, 171
    and civil society, 231, 232, 233
    victory in local and regional elections, 172,
        223, 227, 229
Afrikaner nationalism, 168, 169
Agreement Reached in the Multi-Party Negotiations,
    39–40, 63, 64
Alexandra, 162
Alliance neighborhood (Belfast), 139–140
Alliance Party, 62
ANC. *See* African National Congress
Apartheid, 29, 41, 202(n3), 203(n15), 210
    change away from, 169, 268
    and deracializing Johannesburg, 254–259
    Group Areas legislation, 157, 163
    and land use separation, 157–162, 208–210,
        253
    repairing and reconstructing after, 172–173,
        180–185, 201
    resistance to, 223, 283
    and town planning, 208–210, 269
    urban, and Johannesburg, 160–162
Appleton, Colin, 241
Ashkenasi, Abraham, 9

Assimilation and city conflict, 11
Austin, Joe, 77, 84, 114, 115

Backyard quarters in Johannesburg, 163
BAN. *See* Belfast Areas of Special Social Needs
Bantu Administration Act, 209
Baralink project, 184, 191, 215, 251–252
Barry, Brian, 15
BAT. *See* Belfast Action Team
BDO. *See* Belfast Development Office
Beirut, 6
Belfast, 5, 6, 34, 39, 40–41, 55
    and changes to urban landscape, 99–106
    and community activism, 81–87
    demographics of, 57–61, 58(figure),
        59(figure), 60(figure), 69, 75, 76,
        80(table), 84, 87(n5), 95
    and direct rule, 61–65
    and economic issues, 77–81
    map of, 56
    place in peace, 144–145
    policymaking and stabilization, 281–291
    See also Belfast and Johannesburg compared;
        Color-blind policymaking in Belfast;
        Housing in Belfast; Segregation, and
        Belfast; Urban policy in Belfast
Belfast Action Team (BAT), 67, 68, 82, 106,
    108, 109, 114–115, 141
    and Northgate, 127, 129
Belfast and Johannesburg compared, 168, 254,
    269–291
    contexts of conflict, 270–272
    policymaking participants and relationships,
        278–281
    stabilization versus reconstruction,
        281–291
    urban policy, 273–278

Belfast Area Plans, 65–66
Belfast Areas of Special Social Needs (BAN),
        135
Belfast City Council, 61, 62–63, 62(table),
        63(table), 66, 86
Belfast Development Office (BDO), 66, 67, 68,
        103–105, 106, 108, 126, 144
    and Northgate development, 127–130,
        146
    and Springvale development, 130–132
Belfast Housing Renewal Strategy, 100
Belfast Housing Strategy Review, 138, 144
Belfast Regional Survey and Plan of 1962, 94,
        107
Belfast Special Action Group (BSAG), 135
Belfast Urban Area (BUA), 57
Belfast Urban Area (BUA) Plan 2001, 95, 96, 97,
        117, 119(n2)
Belfast Urban Motorway, 81
Belfast Urban Strategy, proposed, 143–144
Benvenisti, Meron S., xv, 13
Bernstein, Ann, 222
Black Africans, economic situation of, 162–168
Black Local Authorities Act of 1982, 222–223
Black participation in town planning, 219–220
Black urbanization in Johannesburg, 161
Blease, Victor, 74, 125
Boal, Frederick, 57
Boya, Lawrence, 175, 217–218, 230, 231
Boyle, Kevin, 78
Bradley, Colm, 124
Bremner, Lindsay, 182, 187, 229, 233
British House of Commons, 61
British system of planning, 66, 107, 120(n11),
        177, 208
British Urban Policy, 91–119
BSAG. *See* Belfast Special Action Group
BUA. *See* Belfast Urban Area
Buckley, Anthony D., 91
Builders Warranty Scheme, 244
Burton, John W., 16

CAJ. *See* Civic Associations of Johannesburg
Caledon Affair, 68
Cantonization, and ethnic management, 12, 34
Capital facility planning, 47
Catholic Church, and Troubles in Ireland,
        84–85

Catholics
    demographics in Belfast, 55, 57–61,
        58(figure), 59 (figure), 60 (figure), 69,
        87(n5), 96, 290
    economic disadvantage of, 77–81
CBO. *See* Community-based organizations
CCRU. *See* Central Community Relations Unit
CDS. *See* Comprehensive Development
        Schemes
Cebulla, Andreas, 68, 79, 95, 118
Central Business District in Johannesburg, 227
Central Community Relations Unit (CCRU),
        111, 132–133
Central Witwatersand Metropolitan Chamber
        (CWMC), 170–171, 173, 175–176, 179,
        186–187, 192, 227, 283
Central Witwatersrand Regional Services
        Council, 227
Chambers, David, 111
Change and evolution, as research issue, 45
Chipkin, Clive, 209
Christianson, David, 223
Cities
    characteristics of, xii, 3, 72
    contested, 3–17
    and national peace, 9, 293–295
    sluggishness in, 19–20, 37
Citizen participation in post-apartheid South
        Africa, 231
Civic Associations of Johannesburg (CAJ), 170,
        176, 177, 231
Civic ideologies, 21
Civics. *See* Community-based organizations;
        Johannesburg
Color-blind policymaking in Belfast, 93–94,
        96, 97–98, 107, 110, 124, 149, 276
    limitations of, 111, 123, 142, 285, 287
    See also Neutral urban policies in Belfast
Community activism, in Belfast, 81–87
Community-based organizations (CBO),
        231–233, 235
Community consultation, and local
        governance, 233–237
Community Development Forums, 235
Community dynamics and organization, as
        research issue, 45
Community involvement and development
        planning, 212, 218–219

Community participation and empowerment, 47–48

Community Relations Commission, 81–82

Community Relations Council. *See* Northern Ireland Community Relations Council

Community Technical Aid, 83

Community viability and urban policy, 137–143, 148

Compact city approach, in Johannesburg, 180–182, 184, 201, 251–253, 258, 276

Comprehensive Development Schemes (CDS), 66–67, 103, 104, 138–139

Conceptual framework, of urban peace-building, 20–21, 22

Conflict, contexts of, 271(table)

Conflict outcomes and mechanisms, as research issue, 44–45

Conflicts of ethnonational nature, 3

Consociational local governance, 296–297

Consociation and ethnic management, 12, 28, 34

Conspiratorial perception of public policy, 116–117

Contested cities and political mechanisms, 4–5

Contextual factors, as research issue, 43

Corbett, Sam, 85

Council of the Isles, 63

Cupar Street (Way), 72

CWMC. *See* Central Witwatersand Metropolitan Chamber

Davis, Mike, 17

DDPEW. *See* Gauteng Department of Development Planning Environment and Works

DeKlerk, F. W., 169

Democracy and South Africa, xiii

Democratic Party (South Africa), 229

Democratic Unionist Party, 61–62, 86

Demographics in Belfast, 57–61, 69, 75, 76, 84, 87(n5)

Densification approach in Johannesburg, 180–182, 184, 201, 251–253, 258, 276

Department of the Environment for Northern Ireland (DOENI), 61, 67, 88(n16), 116, 118, 138, 149
  and CDS, 138–139
  and Northgate project, 127–130

and Springvale project, 130–132
  and urban policymaking, 92, 93, 95–96, 126

Development Facilitation Act of 1995 (DFA), 184, 216–217

Development planning in South Africa, 211–221

DFA. *See* Development Facilitation Act of 1995

Direct rule of Northern Ireland, 61–65

Divisional Planning Office. *See* Planning Service Divisional Office

DOENI. *See* Department of the Environment for Northern Ireland

Douglas, J. Neville, 146

Duncairn Gardens (Belfast), 60–61, 104, 108, 127–130

Eagle, Jane, 217, 218

Ebdon, Erica, 192

Economic benefits, and urban planning, 33–34

Economic development policies, 46

Economic issues and Johannesburg, 259, 260–261

Economic situation and Black Africans, 162–168

Education for Mutual Understanding (EMU), 126

EIS. *See* Environmental Improvement Schemes

Employment opportunities in Belfast, 111, 117, 118(table)

Empowerment model of urban planning, 14

EMU. *See* Education for Mutual Understanding

Environment, Department of. *See* Department of the Environment for Northern Ireland

Environmental Improvement Schemes (EIS), 67–77, 103, 104

Equality as outcome of planning strategies, 109–116, 124

Equality of opportunity, 134

Equity urban strategy, xii, 25–27, 275–276, 281, 291

Erasmus, Jan, 183, 188, 210

Ethnic cleansing, 11

Ethnic engagement strategy, in Belfast, 123–127. *See also* Central Community Relations Unit; Making Belfast Work; Northgate development; Springvale development

Ethnicity, 4, 17(n1), 43

Ethnonational conflicts and ideologies, 3, 21
Eversley, David, 79

Fair Employment Act of 1976, 134–135
Fair Employment Act of 1989, 126, 135, 150(n9)
Fair Employment Commission, 79
Falls neighborhood (Belfast), 59, 70
Federalization and ethnic management, 12, 34
Fitzduff, Mari, 86, 122
Flusk, Patrick, 180, 183, 223–224, 234
Forced population transfers, 11
Formal housing in township areas in
    Johannesburg, 162. *See also* Housing in
    Johannesburg
Freedom Charter (of African National
    Congress), 168
Free settlement areas
  in Johannesburg, 162
  See also Housing in Johannesburg
Friedmann, John, 26, 28

Gaffikin, Frank, 78, 81, 133
Gauteng Department of Development Planning
    Environment and Works (DDPEW), 200
Gauteng Provincial Housing Board, 199–200
Geographic models of ethnic environments,
    14–15
Gilbert, Morag, 191
GJTMC. *See* Greater Johannesburg Transitional
    Metropolitan Council
Glendinning, Will, 114, 117, 123, 124
Governance in contested cities. *See* Local
    governance in contested cities, models of
Governance strategies. *See* Urban policy and
    governance strategies
Governing ideologies, 21
Government intervention
  and low-cost housing provision, 243–248
  and strategic land development, 248–253
  and torn communities, 240–243
Government of National Unity, 155, 169
Graham, Michael, 100
Greater Johannesburg Transitional Metropolitan
    Council (GJTMC), 156, 227, 229. *See
    also* Transitional Metropolitan Council
Greater London Council, 296, 298(n4)
Greater Soweto Accord, 170
Greying in Johannesburg, 161, 163, 272

Group Areas Act of 1950, 156–158, 175, 180,
    209
Group Areas Board, 208
Group Areas Development Act, 159
Group identity, maintenance of, and urban
    planning, 35–36
Guide plans and apartheid, 208–209
Gurr, Ted R., 4, 7, 12

Habitat II. *See* United Nations Conference on
    Human Settlements
Hadden, Tom, 78
Harff, Barbara, 7, 12
Hart, Tim, 172, 208, 233
Harvey, David, 15, 26
Hegemonic control as means of ethnic
    management, 11–12, 34
Hendry, John, 66–67, 97, 104, 124
Hettne, Bjorn, 21
Hewitt, Christopher, 167
Hindson, Doug, 241, 255, 258, 262
Horowitz, Donald L., 12
Hostels, around Johannesburg, 162–163. *See
    also* Housing in Johannesburg
Housing in Belfast, 74, 76, 82, 99–106, 110,
    111–115, 138–140, 143
  allocation plan, 97–99, 146
  and color-blind neutrality, 92, 93
  segregation in, 102–103
  See also Northern Ireland Housing
    Executive
Housing in Johannesburg, 161, 182, 184
  and black Africans, 162–163, 165–166,
    193–202, 243
  low-cost and government intervention,
    243–248
  and National Housing Plan (South Africa),
    178–179
  provision and the compact city, 198–202
Housing production and allocation, 47
Hunger strikes of Irish Republican Army, 82
Hutchinson, Billy, 86, 133, 144

ICHUT. *See* Inner City Housing Upgrading
    Trust
IFP. *See* Inkatha Freedom Party
Inequity from neutrality in urban policies,
    109–119, 124

Informal settlements in Johannesburg, 163, 193–198. *See also* Housing in Johannesburg
Inkatha Freedom Party (IFP), 242, 243, 281
Inner City Housing Upgrading Trust (ICHUT), 246
Inner-city infill sites, development of, 251–253
Integration and city conflicts, 11
Integrative analytic approach, xi
Interagency cooperation in Belfast, 127, 129–130
Interim Measures for Local Government Act of 1991, 169
Interim Strategic Framework (ISF), 175–178, 179
  difficulties in implementation, 187–189
  policy approaches, 177, 180–183, 190
  policy guidelines, 176–178
  policy implementation, 178–179, 183, 184
  short- versus long-term actions, 191, 192
International Fund for Ireland, 81–82
Interviews, research, 42, 48–50, 49(table)
Intrastate conflict and cities, 7–9
IRA. *See* Irish Republican Army
Irish Parliament, 63
Irish Republican Army (IRA), xii, 62, 82, 84
ISF. *See* Interim Strategic Framework
Istanbul Declaration on Human Settlements, 8

Jeppestown-Oval development, 184, 245, 253
Jerusalem, 5, 19, 21
Johannesburg, 6, 39, 41
  and democratization, 172–173
  as deracialized society, 254–259, 257(table), 276
  and financial redistribution, 259–260, 261
  its public goals, 259–262
  local and metropolitan governance of, 169, 170–172
  maps of, 156, 158, 159, 160, 228, 257
  planned geography of, 156–162
  private-sector reconstruction, 255, 256–258
  and reconstruction, 281–291
  and segregation, 159–161, 169
  and town planning, 174–175, 208–221
  and urban policy in transition, 173–180
  See also Apartheid; Belfast and Johannesburg compared; Housing in Johannesburg;

Nonstatutory authorities; Statutory authorities
Johannesburg City Council, 170, 246
Johannesburg Metropolitan Council, 186–187, 245. *See also* Transitional Metropolitan Council
Joint Framework Documents, 39

Kadungure, Ivan, 194, 217, 218
Kagiso Trust, 233
Katorus project, 236, 241–243, 244, 254
Khombi taxi system, 167, 252
Kotzee, Alida, 218

Laganside, 66, 67, 97
Land development, and government intervention, 248–253
Land development objectives (LDO), 216
Land invasions in Johannesburg, 193–198
Land Tenure Advisory Board, 208
Land use
  planning, 31–33, 46
  standards, black versus white, 214–216
LDO. *See* Land development objectives
Lemon, Anthony, 201
LGNF. *See* Local Government Negotiating Forum
LGTA. *See* Local Government Transition Act
Lijphart, Arend, 12
Local Development Forums, 235
Local governance capacity in Johannesburg, 222–230
  and boundary issues, 226–229, 228(figure)
  and community consultation, 233–237
  and economic development, 225–227
Local governance in contested cities, models of, 4–5, 295–297
Local Government Negotiating Forum (LGNF), 169–170
Local Government Transition Act (LGTA), 169–170, 186
Local Government Transition Bill, 171
Long-range planning versus short-term crisis response, 185–202
Low-cost housing provision, and government intervention, 243–248

Mabin, Alan, 180, 209, 255
MacBride, Deirdre, 77, 115, 142

Macozoma, Saki, 240
Making Belfast Work (MBW), 69, 70, 83,
    118–119, 126, 149
    and other governmental agencies, 106, 108,
        109
    and targeting social need, 133–137, 141
Maluleke, Themba, 207, 213, 236, 242
Mandela, Nelson, xiii, 40, 168, 169
Manor Street, 103
Market-based means of change in
        Johannesburg, 255, 256
Masakhane, 222, 224
Mashabela, Harry, 162, 166, 262
Mashinini, Tshipso, 173, 186, 190, 192, 195,
        212–213, 236
Matthew plan, 66
MBW. *See* Making Belfast Work
McAdam, Doug, 12
McCarthy, John D., 12
McCausland, Nelson, 85, 114, 115
McCoy, Dennis, 92, 93, 111
McCrystal, Jo, 245
McGarry, John, 11
McGivern, William, 73, 92, 101, 117, 139
McKevitt, Vincent, 84
McPeake, John, 103, 111
Mediators and community consultation,
        235–237
Metropolitan Chamber. *See* Central
        Witwatersand Metropolitan Chamber
Metropolitan Negotiating Forum, 171, 186
Metropolitan Sub-Structures (MSS), 171–172,
        223, 227, 229–230
Midrand, 255–256
Mining land, and government intervention,
        249–250
MIS. *See* Mortgage Indemnity Scheme
Mkhabela, Ish, 189, 193, 236, 246, 254
Mobilization, and progress in peace-building,
        36
Molobi, Eric, 233
Morris, Mike, 255, 258, 262
Morrison, Bill, 94, 102, 107, 111
Morrissey, Mike, 78, 81, 133
Mortgage Indemnity Scheme (MIS), 244
Mostar, 6, 18(n7)
Motsa, Angela, 182, 221
MSS. *See* Metropolitan Sub-Structures

Muller, John, 182, 210, 211, 218
Mulligan, Gerry, 92, 115
Multisector segregation, in Belfast, 70. *See also*
        Segregation, and Belfast
Municipal government organization, 48
Municipal services programs, 213, 215,
        224–225, 226–227
Murphy, David, 93, 97, 100, 103, 125
Murtagh, Brendan, 72, 104, 116, 123, 125,
        143, 144

Narsoo, Monty, 165, 168, 186, 230, 243, 245,
        254
National democratic elections of 1994, 155,
        167, 169
National Housing Board, 179, 199, 246
National Housing Forum (NHF), 178–179
Nationalism, 17(n2)–18(n3), 4
Nationalists, Irish, 84
National Party (South African), 168, 169
National peace and urban accommodation, xiii
National Urban Strategy of 1995, 184, 248
Natives Resettlement Act of 1954, 159
Need, addressing, in urban planning, 138–141
        and Making Belfast Work, 136–137,
        150(n15)
Neighborhoods and neutral policymaking
        orientation, 117–119
Neill, Bill, 114, 120(n11), 125
Nel, Matthew, 243
Neutral urban policies in Belfast, 109–119,
        145–147, 268, 282–283, 285, 291. *See
        also* Color-blind policymaking in Belfast
Neutral urban strategy, xii, 23–25, 275, 281
New Delhi, and Hindu-Muslim tension, 5–6
Newhco Group, 246
New Lodge (Belfast), 61, 104–105, 127, 128
NGOs. *See* Nongovernmental organizations
NHF. *See* National Housing Forum
Nicosia, and Greek and Turkish civil war, 6, 34,
        298(n2)
NIHE. *See* Northern Ireland Housing
        Executive
NIMBY. *See* Not-in-my-backyard syndrome
Nongovernmental organizations (NGOs), 232,
        281. *See also* Nonstatutory authorities
Nonracial urbanization of Johannesburg,
        255–259, 276

Nonstatutory authorities, in Johannesburg, 169, 170, 171, 177, 203(n21), 231–233, 281
Nordlinger, Eric A., 12
Normalizing Johannesburg as deracialized society, 182, 254–259, 284
Northern Ireland: Regional Physical Development Strategy 1975–1995, 95
Northern Ireland, and religion, 55, 56
Northern Ireland Act of 1974, 65
Northern Ireland Assembly, xii–xiii, 63–64, 88(n8), 88(n12), 145
Northern Ireland Community Relations Council, 83, 115
Northern Ireland Housing Executive (NIHE), 57, 67–68, 92, 99–103, 105, 119, 126, 138–141
and housing allocation, 97–98, 110–115
and other agencies, 106, 108, 109
recommended changes for, 144
Northern Ireland Parliament, 61
Northern Ireland Voluntary Trust, 126
Northgate development, 104–105, 127–130, 146
North-South Council, 63
Not-in-my-backyard syndrome (NIMBY), 199, 201, 288

Official Unionists. *See* Ulster Unionist Party
O'Leary, Brendan, 11
Olver, Crispian (Chippy), 179, 216, 229, 230
Operationalizing peace, 21–31, 273, 275
Oppenheimer, N. E., 240
Orange Order lodge, 70
Osborne, Robert D., 82

PAFT. *See* Policy Appraisal and Fair Treatment
Paisley, Rhonda, 91
Parliament, Irish. *See* Irish Parliament
Parnell, Susan, 209
Partisan urban strategy, 29–30, 275, 281
PDA. *See* Potential development area program
Peacelines, 70–72, 71(figure), 72(table), 77, 93, 100, 101
Pereira, Paul, 222, 235
Pesic, Vesna, 10
Physical ecology of aggression, 16–17
Physical partitioning of contested city, 295–296, 297

Pienaar, Herman, 172, 176, 250
Planact, 176–177, 182
Planning, partisan, 30
Planning, town
changes recommended in South Africa, 219–221
in Johannesburg, 174–175, 208–221
in Northern Ireland, 66, 94–97, 98–99, 106–107, 125, 126, 148
See also Densification approach in Johannesburg; Post-apartheid planning
Planning Service Directorate, 66
Planning Service Divisional Office (Belfast), 66, 124, 126
Poleglass estate, 101–102, 116
Policing, urban, 50–51(n4)
Policy Appraisal and Fair Treatment (PAFT), 133
Policy issues and goals as research issue, 43
Policymaking principles in Belfast, 91–94
centralization and fragmentation of, 279–280
Policy outcomes, as research issue, 43–44
Political partitioning, and city conflict, 11
Political science models, and ethnic management, 10–11
Post-apartheid peace-building
and citizen participation, 230–237
and local governance capacity, 222–230
Post-apartheid planning
and development approach, 211–221, 268–269, 285
and spatial and regulatory emphasis, 208–221, 268–269, 285
Post-apartheid public policymaking, 185
Potential development area program (PDA), 198–199
Power sharing, and ethnic management, 12
Pretoria-Witwatersrand-Vereeniging (PWV) complex, 157
Private-sector reconstruction in Johannesburg, 255, 256–258
Progressive ethnic strategy, 123–127. *See also* Central Community Relations Unit; Making Belfast Work; Northgate development; Springvale development
Progressive Unionist Party (PUP), 86
Project Facilitation Group, 192

Proposed Belfast Urban Strategy, 143–144
Protestants
    and demographics in Belfast, 55, 57–61,
        58(figure), 59 (figure), 70, 75–76, 83,
        87(n5), 96–97, 290
    economic advantage of, 77–81
    out-migration, 84, 85, 95, 104
Provincial Housing Boards, 179, 199
Provisional Irish Republican Army (IRA), 39
Public expenditure in Northern Ireland, 65
Public policy and competing time scales,
    185–202
PUP. *See* Progressive Unionist Party
PWV. *See* Pretoria-Witwatersrand-Vereeniging
    complex

Rapid Land Development Program (RLDP),
    198–200, 243–245
RDP. *See* Reconstruction and Development
    Programme
Real estate development promotion, 46
Reconstruction and Development Programme
    (RDP), 179, 184, 223, 224, 230. *See also*
    White Paper on Housing
Reconstruction versus stabilization in peace-
    building, 281–291
Redevelopment projects in Belfast, 99–106
Redpath, Jackie, 85, 114, 116, 137
Regulatory control planning approach,
    208–217
Rehabilitation of housing in Belfast, 99–106.
    See also Housing in Belfast
Reid, Graeme, 193, 230, 234, 250
Religion and conflict in Belfast, 55
Republic of Ireland, xiii, 55
Research issues and methods, 41–50, 44(table),
    299–302
Resettlement of blacks, 159
Resolver policymaking, xii
Resolver urban strategy, 27–29, 275, 281, 291
RLDP. *See* Rapid Land Development
    Program
Robson, Brian, 79
Robson deprivation index, 79
Rose, Richard, 91
Rothman, Jay, 11
Royal Ulster Constabulary (RUC), 50(n4), 72,
    132

Roysten, Lauren, 183, 188, 208
RUC. *See* Royal Ulster Constabulary

Sack, R., 14
SANCO. *See* South African National Civic
    Organization
SANDF. *See* South African National Defense
    Force
SAP. *See* South African Police
Sarajevo, 6, 18(n7)
Schlemmer, Lawrence, 208, 243, 262
SDLP. *See* Social Democratic and Labor Party
Sectarian geographies in Belfast, 69–77
Sectarianism, policymaker response to, in
    Belfast, 91–119
Segregation
    and Belfast, 58–61, 70, 102–103, 112–113
    and Johannesburg, 159–161, 169
Sekoto, Herman, 192, 221
Self-transformative imperatives in urban
    policymaking, 187–189
Shacks in Johannesburg, 163, 193–198. *See also*
    Housing in Johannesburg
Shankill neighborhood (Belfast), 59, 109, 116
Shaw, Mark, 170–171
Short-term crisis response versus long-range
    planning, 185–202
SICDP. *See* Springfield Inter-Community
    Development Project
Singleton, Dale, 82
Sinn Fein, 62, 82, 84, 116, 136, 144, 280
SIPS. *See* Special Integrated Presidential
    Projects
Slovo, Joe, 248
Sluggishness, in cities, 19–20, 37
Smith, David J., 77, 111
Smith, David M., 15, 25
Social Democratic and Labor Party (SDLP), 62,
    84, 136
Social psychology models of urban conflict,
    15–17
Social service delivery, 47
South Africa, economic needs of, 163–168
South African National Civic Organization
    (SANCO), 231
South African National Defense Force
    (SANDF), 50–51(n4)
South African Police (SAP), 50–51(n4)

South Western Townships. *See* Soweto
Soweto, 159–160, 162, 215, 227, 252
   and apartheid, 169, 251
   boycott in, 170, 223, 283
Soweto Accord, 283
Soweto Civic Association, 170
Sparks, Allister, 168, 169
Spatial allocation planning approach, 208–217
Spatial targeting of resources in Belfast, 134–135
Special Integrated Presidential Projects (SIPS), 241–242
Spence, Ronnie, 92–93, 94, 132
Springfield Inter-Community Development Project (SICDP), 86
Springvale development, 130–132
Stabilization versus reconstruction in peace-building, 281–291
STACHR. *See* Standing Advisory Commission on Human Rights
Standing Advisory Commission on Human Rights (STACHR), 79, 110, 111, 112, 120(n12)
Starrett, K., 106
Statutory authorities, in Johannesburg, 169, 170, 171, 203(n23)
Strang, Robert, 67, 76, 114, 140, 141
Strategic investments in Belfast, 141–142
Strategy, lack of, in urban policy in Belfast, 106–109
Subsidy of Northern Ireland, by English, 78
Suffolk (Belfast), 113
Sweeney, Paul, 65, 109, 122, 126, 133
Swilling, Mark, 241, 254, 258

Targeting social need (TSN) in Belfast, 134
Tarrow, Sydney, 12
Temporality and urban policy choices, 185–202, 276–277
Territoriality, 14–15, 31–33, 69–87, 143, 280, 287–288, 291
Third-party intervention and city conflict, 12, 34
Thorne, Stephen, 250, 251
Tiger's Bay (Belfast), 61, 104–105, 113, 127–130
TMC. *See* Transitional Metropolitan Council
Torn communities and government intervention, 240–243

Town and Country Planning Service, 66
Town planning. *See* Planning, town
Town Planning and Townships Ordinance, 214
Town Planning Service (Belfast), 96, 99
Transitional Metropolitan Council (TMC), 171, 186–187, 192, 220, 230, 252
   and potential development area program, 198–199
   and shelter needs, 195
   Urbanization and Housing Committee of, 193
   See also Greater Johannesburg Transitional Metropolitan Council
Transitions, urban, 19–20, 37
Transportation, and South Africa, 166–167
Troubles in Northern Ireland, 55, 58, 69–70, 78, 85
TSN. *See* Targeting social need in Belfast
Tsotsis, 168, 238(n25), 242
Two-tier local governance system, 296, 297, 298(n3)

Ubuntu, 220
UDG. *See* Urban Development Grants
UDP. *See* Ulster Democratic Party
Ulster Democratic Party (UDP), 86
Ulster Unionist Party (UUP), 61–62
Ulster Volunteer Force (UVF), 86
Unemployment
   in Belfast, 78–80
   in South Africa, 165
United Nations, 6, 7–8, 34
United Nations Conference on Human Settlements (Habitat II), 8, 294
University of Ulster, 131–132
Urban decisionmaking, as research issue, 43
Urban Development Grants (UDG), 67, 103, 135
Urban ethnic conditions, and peace-building, 32(figure)
Urban ethnic conditions, and urban policy, xiii, 13–14, 31–36
Urbanization Department, 192, 195
Urban peace-building
   conceptual framework of, 20–21, 22
   goals, strategies, and techniques, 274(table)
   increasing or impeding, 36–38
   participants and relationships, 279(table)
Urban planning, as analytical lens, 45–46

Urban policy and governance strategies,
    23–31, 24(table)
Urban policy and peace-building, 22(figure)
Urban policy in Belfast
    lack of strategy in, 106–109
    policymaking units of, 65–69
    principles of, 91–94
Urban policy in Johannesburg, in transition
    period, 173–180
Urban public policies, 46–48
UUP. *See* Ulster Unionist Party
UVF. *See* Ulster Volunteer Force

Vacant land infilling, 181–182
van de Merwe, Johan, 181, 210
van der Walt, Ben, 210

Violence
    in Belfast, 81–82
    in South Africa, 167–168, 284
Waanders, Paul, 207, 210, 212, 218, 230
Wars, intrastate, 7
Wedge planning, 104
Weitzer, Ronald, 12
Westminster Parliament, 64
White Paper on Housing, 184, 224
Whyte, John, 62, 78
Wills, T. M., 155
Wirth, Louis, 13
Worthington, George, 92, 96, 107, 115

Yugoslavia, 6, 10

Zald, Mayer N., 12